An internal audit textbook comes to life as a must-read tale! Dr. Murdock has masterfully taken essential elements of internal auditing and created an entertaining and compelling story in a book that is hard to put down. He brings us on the journey of how one audit shop, with pressure of dissatisfaction from the Board, adopted progressive techniques to transform their service and, in turn, the organization. The real-life challenges of convincing the team and the company's leadership to incorporate value-added and leading-edge techniques will resonate with auditors of all experience levels. The solutions-focused-approach will encourage every auditor to rethink how they are operating and inspire them to become their own change agents.

Rob Clark, Jr., Chief Audit & Compliance Officer, Howard University

Most books seeking to educate leaders choose one of two recipes, either 1) the instructional "to-do list" of all the things you must do to excel and why, or 2) the case study approach of bombarding readers with examples of what other organizations and leaders have done to make positive change. Dr. Murdock has chosen to deviate from these recipes, and in doing so, creates an internal audit leadership instructional manual that is truly unique. Reading more like a fiction novel, with characters and personalities that develop over time, Dr. Murdock engrosses the reader in a story about how an internal audit leader turned around his department, and significantly increased value to the organization. Most readers will be able to immediately recognize the characters in the story as real-world personalities, with all of the advantages and challenges of those personality types. The drama builds as the main character has to assess his team, re-evaluate his department's value to the organization, and make essential changes to be a sought-after advisor. In reflecting back, I love that I learned some valuable new strategies and ways of thinking, without feeling like I was reading an instruction manual.

Steve Biskie, Principal, National Risk Analytics Leader
& SAP Champion, RSM US

Using a dialogue-based, novel-style of writing, Hernan Murdock weaves a very compelling story of a new Chief Audit Executive needing to make transformational change across all aspects of a fictional company's internal audit function. Many of the challenges are ones faced by all internal audit departments, and ones that will resonate with any internal auditor, audit committee member, or executive leader. Enjoyable and instructive must-read for anyone on the internal audit transformational journey.

Hal Garyn, Managing Director, Audit Executive Advisory Services

The Change Agent: Transforming an Underperforming Internal Audit Department is a must-read for novice and seasoned internal auditors, audit committee members, or business leaders seeking impactful change. The book is an engaging narrative of the impressive overhaul of an internal audit department, cleverly using the metaphor of changing seasons to portray the transformation. The journey begins with the audit committee's 12-month ultimatum to turn around performance or risk being outsourced, to internal audit securing a 'seat at the table,' actively sought for input into future plans and strategies. Addressing professional and personal challenges, it provides an arsenal of best practices and tools to transform the function, delivering substantial value to the organization. This book challenges stereotypes about internal audit while exploring diverse cities, personalities, and cultures, making it an exciting read. It prepares you to grasp how holistic change, collaboration, adaptability, and resilience drive positive organizational transformations.

Mary Ann Khalil, Managing Partner, Knowbility Consultancy

What an amazing book. It fully embraces the challenges of the internal audit's transformational journey. It is fun to read – from cover to cover. The concept of the seasons is fantastic. An internal audit department will go through all the seasons. Dr. Murdock is a great storyteller with great knowledge to share.

Mark Edmead, IT Transformation Consultant
and Trainer, MTE Advisors

The Change Agent was an informative yet very entertaining novel. I was skeptical when I heard about a novel on auditing. How can that be entertaining? And then I read it. And wow, it was just as entertaining as a lot of the novels I read for fun! It can also be a valuable educational tool for those who teach auditing. In fact, I have already recommended it to two fellow instructors. I feel for the characters in this book and wonder what Miriam, Rachel, Tony, and the gang are up to now. To me that is the sign of a great story! The story and roles are so realistic I can assign pieces of my career and co-workers to many of the scenes and situations. Well done.

Denise Cicchella, Executive Director and Trainer, Auspicium

Hernan Murdock has written a clever allegory with believable characters who are dealing with realistic business challenges and situations. Using an easy-to-read writing style, Murdock deftly weaves in sage, time-tested advice and describes useful practices to transform the internal audit from a traditionally financial reporting and compliance-focused activity into a valued business partner. This is a must-read for anyone who wants to create sustainable organizational change.

Ann Butera, Author, Founder and President, The Whole Person Project

I have been fortunate to know Hernan personally and have had the pleasure of watching him develop into a professional training innovator. The concept of a novel about the trials and tribulations of an internal audit and compliance function is a unique approach. This certainly gives leaders in audit, compliance, and governance a new method and potential strategy to introduce continuing education to their teams.

Joel F. Kramer, Managing Director (Retired),
Internal Audit Division, MIS Training Institute (MISTI)

The Change Agent by Hernan Murdock provides a clear and concise roadmap for leading change in an internal audit department, and is full of practical advice and tips. The book is a fictional story about a visionary leader who is hired to transform an underperforming internal audit department. The story is engaging and relatable, and it provides valuable insights into the challenges and opportunities of leading change with real-world examples. I especially appreciated the book's focus on the importance of building a coalition, creating a vision, and communicating effectively. If you are responsible for transforming an underperforming internal audit department, then I highly recommend reading *The Change Agent*. It is a valuable resource that will help you succeed in your mission.

Aliya Noor, Associate Partner, Ahmad Alagbari Chartered Accountants

Throughout his career, Hernan Murdock has been a significant contributor to the education of thousands of internal auditors by emphasizing the importance of internal audit and its positive impact on organizations. In his latest work, *The Change Agent*, Hernan presents an engaging story with relatable characters that successfully illustrates the ups and downs faced by a new CAE and his contemporary internal audit learnings. By reading this book, not only can aspiring internal audit leaders benefit from the insights and experiences shared by the characters, but they can also learn about the change management practices that are implemented in the story. *The Change Agent* is an excellent resource for those who want to improve their understanding of the internal audit function and how it can enable positive change within an organization.

Tom O'Reilly, Area Director, AuditBoard

The Change Agent

John Taylor has been hired to transform the underperforming internal audit unit at InSports. The auditors are not reviewing what the audit committee and executive leadership consider essential for the organization's success, their methodology is subpar, and their relationships with their clients are strained. The audit committee has been patient, but not anymore. Their mandate is clear: make clear improvements in one year or the function will be outsourced.

This is the story of a visionary leader who needs a strategy to transform processes and deliver better results for stakeholders at all levels within the organization. The audit committee, all levels of management, and employees expect more from internal audit. Now, John must lead the group through 12 challenging months as they focus on what matters most when performing audit and advisory services. They must communicate results faster and better, leverage existing quality control and data analytics techniques, and, with every encounter, help the organization address strategic, operational, compliance, and financial risks.

With similarities to "The Goal" and "The Phoenix Project" and leveraging Kotter's 8-Step Process for Leading Change, follow John and the internal audit team from Boston to New York, San Francisco, London, and Buenos Aires, as they address almost insurmountable challenges in their transformation journey.

Security, Audit and Leadership Series

Series Editor: Dan Swanson, Dan Swanson and Associates, Ltd.,
Winnipeg, Manitoba, Canada.

The *Security, Audit and Leadership Series* publishes leading-edge books on critical subjects facing security and audit executives as well as business leaders. Key topics addressed include Leadership, Cybersecurity, Security Leadership, Privacy, Strategic Risk Management, Auditing IT, Audit Management and Leadership

The Change Agent
Transforming an Underperforming Internal Audit Department

Dr. Hernan Murdock, CIA, CRMA

CRC Press
Taylor & Francis Group
Boca Raton London New York

CRC Press is an imprint of the
Taylor & Francis Group, an **informa** business

Designed cover image: Shutterstock

First edition published 2024
by CRC Press
2385 NW Executive Center Drive, Suite 320, Boca Raton FL 33431

and by CRC Press
4 Park Square, Milton Park, Abingdon, Oxon, OX14 4RN

CRC Press is an imprint of Taylor & Francis Group, LLC

Library of Congress Cataloging-in-Publication Data
Names: Murdock, Hernan, author.
Title: The change agent : transforming an underperforming internal audit department / Hernan Murdock.
Description: First edition. | Boca Raton : CRC Press, [2024] |
Series: Security, audit and leadership series | Includes index.
Identifiers: LCCN 2023019966 (print) | LCCN 2023019967 (ebook)
| ISBN 9781032345789 (hardback) | ISBN 9781032345796 (paperback) |
ISBN 9781003322870 (ebook)
Subjects: LCSH: Auditing, Internal. | Organizational change.
Classification: LCC HF5668.25 .M8693 2024 (print) | LCC HF5668.25 (ebook)
| DDC 657/.458--dc23/eng/20230427
LC record available at https://lccn.loc.gov/2023019966
LC ebook record available at https://lccn.loc.gov/2023019967

ISBN: 978-1-032-34578-9 (hbk)
ISBN: 978-1-032-34579-6 (pbk)
ISBN: 978-1-003-32287-0 (ebk)

DOI: 10.1201/9781003322870

Typeset in Times
by SPi Technologies India Pvt Ltd (Straive)

Contents

Winter

Spring

Summer

Fall

About the Author

 **Dr. Hernan Murdock, CIA, CRMA** is vice president – audit content for ACI Learning. He has held positions as director of training for an international audit and consulting firm and various audit positions while leading and performing audit and consulting projects for clients in the manufacturing, transportation, high tech, education, insurance, and power generation industries.

Dr. Murdock was a senior lecturer at Northeastern University where he taught management, leadership, and ethics. He earned a DBA from Argosy University, Sarasota, Florida in 2007; a CSS from Harvard University, Cambridge, Massachusetts, in 1996; and an MBA and BSBA from Suffolk University, Boston, Massachusetts, in 1992 and 1990, respectively. He also holds the following certifications: CRMA Certification in Risk Management Assurance (IIA), 2013; QAR Accreditation in Internal Quality Assessment/Validation (IIA), 2008; AchieveGlobal Leadership and Customer Service: Deliver and Develop Levels, 2007; IDC Certified Instructor (IIA), 2006; and CIA Certified Internal Auditor (IIA), 2001.

He is the author of *Operational Auditing: Principles and Techniques for a Changing World* (2022 and 2017), *Auditor Essentials* (2019), *10 Key Techniques to Improve Team Productivity* (2011), and *Using Surveys in Internal Audits* (2009). He has also written articles and book chapters on internal auditing, whistleblowing programs, international auditing, mentoring programs, fraud, deception, corporate social responsibility, and behavioral profiling.

Dr. Murdock has conducted audits and consulting projects, delivered seminars and invited talks, and made numerous presentations at internal audit, academic, and government functions in North America, Latin America, Europe, and Africa.

Dr. Murdock can be reached at Hernan.Murdock@gmail.com.

Acknowledgments

I want to express my deep gratitude to Hal Garyn, Matt Kelly, Greg Hutchins, Bruce Turner, Dr. Rainer Lenz, Philippe Peret, and Sara James for taking the time to read and provide feedback on my manuscript. Thanks to Robert King, Steven Randall, and Mark Edmead for supporting the idea behind this project before I had written a single word. A special thank-you to Dan Swanson for encouraging and supporting me and other authors that promote our profession and for always helping us become more knowledgeable and effective as internal auditors and risk, compliance, and governance professionals.

Special thanks to Laura and Ryan, who have always been by my side as I've balanced my roles as husband, father, and internal auditor.

Lastly, thanks to all the chief audit executives, board and audit committee members, internal audit professionals in multiple capacities, learning facilitators, and company employees whom I have served, learned from, taught, and in so many ways, interacted with. I learned from your successes, challenges, resourcefulness, and the care you show for your stakeholders.

This novel would not have been possible without your contributions and support.

Disclaimer

The story, all names, characters, and incidents portrayed in this novel are fictitious. No identification with actual persons (living or deceased), places, buildings, and products is intended or should be inferred.

Prologue

The September audit committee meeting finished badly, and worse than several of the recent ones, which were also bad. After a heated discussion about the work of the internal audit department, the chief auditor was terminated. On the spot. It just wasn't working out.

Sanjay, like Jim, had been questioning the value of the information they were receiving for a while and agreed that significant changes were needed in the internal audit department. But Sanjay went further; he was ready to outsource the function to someone else who, in his words "knew what internal audit is all about." They needed to figure things out fast.

The company was under financial hardship. Revenues were down, as was the quality of some of their key products manufactured in Argentina. Several key retail customers and distributors had chosen not to renew their sales contracts, especially in the European and Middle Eastern markets, and the management team didn't want to hear, see, or be anywhere near the company auditors. After several years of getting audited on the same financial topics as the external auditors, and on compliance topics, whose relevance they couldn't understand, they had had enough. "Keep the auditors away from us so we can get some real work done around here. We don't need any more lists of inconsequential findings," said an operations manager last year during a senior management meeting. The CEO, CFO, and Controller shared similarly harsh views of the internal audit function.

When the meeting ended Jim and Sanjay agreed to do three things: Jim would work with HR and contact a recruiter to find a new chief audit executive immediately. Sanjay would focus on finding a new audit committee member, and they both agreed to give themselves a deadline to keep, or outsource, the internal audit function. "If clear improvements are not evident by December next year, out it goes," said Jim.

"Agreed," said Sanjay.

As Jim walked out of the building and onto 5th Avenue, he immediately contrasted the negative energy in the conference room several floors above him, to the positive vibe on the street. It was mild for that time of the year and the diversity of colors, sounds, and smells were invigorating. He passed a halal truck and a line of people ordering food. "These trucks always have customers," he thought to himself. "I like to cook. You have what looks like some fun being in the middle of things. I enjoy socializing around food. So, that could be an interesting thing to do when I retire." He thought as he smiled to himself. Certainly, it looks like a lot less stress than he had been dealing with all year with the internal audit unit.

People walked by him with varied facial expressions, but in general, everyone seemed to be going somewhere, with determination, as was typical of New York City. Move. "If only the internal audit department could move with similar energy and sense of determination. Sprinkle some diversity of thought and then we would be cooking with gas!" he thought to himself.

As he walked past a store, he noticed that among the things on display were items with a nautical theme. He was particularly attracted to the lighthouses of various sizes, shapes, and colors. "It doesn't matter what they look like," he thought, "light-houses protect sailors and aviators, so they know where the shoreline is. Things can be disorienting, and people can lose their way. The shoreline can be perilous due to the rocks, shallow waters, and unpredictable currents. It can be dangerous for pilots and sailors operating in fog and darkness. An apt analogy to the world of risk we live and work in. But the shoreline can also be a safe place where harbors provide protection and a place of enjoyment. Internal audit should be the lighthouse of their organizations. They need to warn of perils, help management understand risk so they can better chart the organization's trajectory. They must provide assurance, or comfort, to leaders and managers. Unfortunately, internal audit's light at InSports has gone dim. We need to restore that light."

He turned and continued his walk at a brisk pace heading North, turned right onto a cross street, and, without looking at the signs overhead, dove into the subway station.

Main Characters

John Taylor: Chief Audit Executive

Tony Barone: Audit Manager

Miriam Abrams: IT Audit Manager

Rachel Williams: Senior Auditor

Carolina Flores: Staff Auditor

Brian Gallagher: Staff IT Auditor

Jim Sinclair: Audit Committee Chair

Sanjay Aggarwal: Audit Committee Member

Jennifer Collins: Audit Committee Member

Frank Benson: Mentor

Ron Watkins: Chief Executive Officer (CEO)

Margaret Prescott: Chief Financial Officer (CFO)

Nihal Patel: Chief Technology Officer (CTO)

Ken Higgins: Chief Operating Officer (COO)

Kathleen Meadows: Chief People Officer (CPO-HR)

Terry Watkins: HR Director

Daniel (Dan) Chavez: Controller

Mary Gallagher: Accounting Staff (Travel and Entertainment – T&E)

Nancy Johnson: Accounting Staff (Accounts Receivable – AR)

Matt Bernard: Accounting Staff (Accounts Payable – AP)

Sam Cheng: IT employee

Nick Angelopoulos: Previous Chief Audit Executive (CAE)

Brenda Levine: Director (Research and Development – R&D)

Pablo Alvarez: Controller (Argentina)

Eduardo Palacios: Loss Prevention Officer (Argentina)

1 Conditions and Urgent Need for Change

Typical winter day in New York City. Busy, energetic, maybe a little crazy, but always a fun place to be.

"I can't get used to the shadows at the street level where the sun only hits the streets intermittently due to the high buildings," thought John. In some areas, only at high Noon, and this being winter it was particularly cold and windy in "the canyon of buildings." Better wait until May for the sun to warm the city in any meaningful way.

He was meeting with his new staff of five: Two managers, a senior auditor, and two staff auditors. Four of them were onsite, while Carolina was joining via Teams from London. Tony had been with the company for nearly 12 years. He was a bit set in his ways. He was a stickler for following procedures and had a wealth of institutional knowledge. Miriam was the IT auditor. Bright, hardworking, and with five years, a relatively new addition to the department. Rachel had been in the department for seven years and clashed with Tony often because she didn't agree with the focus on replicating past audit procedures and using standardized checklists. Carolina lived in London and had been with InSports for one year. Brian was Tony's close friend and was hired nine months ago. He was a confirmed extrovert from California, who moved to New York out of curiosity after receiving an appealing job offer from InSports.

"Good morning, everyone! Happy New Year!" announced John, bringing the meeting to attention.

Miriam replied "Happy New Year" cheerfully. She liked to wear bright-colored outfits because they kept the memory of her upbringing in Florida alive.

"Everyone had a good Holiday break? I live near Boston, so we spent the holidays in a combination of family get-togethers, seeing the street decorations, and a quick trip to New Hampshire to do some skiing. Anyone did anything fun?" asked John encouraging conversation among his team members.

"I visited my family, so I went surfing almost every day," replied Brian.

"You're always in the water, Brian," said Tony.

"If Brian ever spent New Year's Day around here, he would probably be first in line doing the Polar Bear Plunge in Coney Island," said Miriam.

"I probably would," Brian replied.

"Where were you?" asked John.

"I'm from California and my parents still live there," he replied.

"Do you have a Polar Plunge in the UK, Carolina?" asked Miriam.

"Yes, they do it over in Brighton. You won't find me anywhere near there, though. Give me a fireplace, a warm blanket, some red wine and call me in April!" she replied with a big smile on her face.

DOI: 10.1201/9781003322870-1

"Tony," asked Rachel, "how many spreadsheets did you create this time?"

Tony pretended to count with his fingers then said with a smile "a hundred a day, with notes. One for every customer. You have to know your customers! No customers, no business" he said confusing Carolina who couldn't tell if he was serious or joking.

"So," said Carolina replying to Tony, "Excel doesn't get a break during the holidays?"

"Tony's family owns a dry-cleaning business in Queens, and he does the books for them" explained Rachel.

"Oh, Ok. I get it," said Carolina now understanding his meaning.

"Very good," said John as he called everyone to order.

"I like your energy and camaraderie. As you know I'm the new Chief Audit Executive and I have a feeling we're going to get along well. I've been told there is a bit of work to do, and some improvements to be made. A challenge? Yes. Some hard work ahead for us? Yes. But one" he said using his hands as visual markers for his count, "I was told I have a very good team with me, and two, this is a great opportunity! I've spoken with the chair of the audit committee, and Jim explained some of the things we need to focus on. I have meetings scheduled with our key stakeholders, the CEO, CFO, CTO, Controller, and COO. Of course, I'll spend time with each of you as well, so I get to know you better, and you get to know me better too."

"We're going to make some changes around here," said John, taking a short pause for emphasis and to allow his words to sink in. "We are going to make some changes here" he repeated and paused again further highlighting the importance he wanted to convey to his statement. "I use the word 'we' on purpose. This is our department" emphasizing the word "our" for symmetry. "I will naturally lead, but I will engage with all of you, ask for your opinions at multiple levels because we will examine our strategy, our operations, and our delivery. As professionals we are paid to do, but also to think and modern internal auditing is a thinking and doing job. How about that for making your jobs challenging and exciting at the same time?" he said now with a smile accompanied with the strength and confidence of a visionary chief audit executive.

As John confirmed everyone's availability to schedule meetings with them that week, he started to take note of their personality traits as he started noticing them. The surfer, the homebody, the networker, the ambitious worker, and the potential workaholic.

"Hi. How are you doing today?" asked John bringing the meeting with his two managers to order.

"I'm fine. Looking forward to the new year and the audits we are going to complete," said Miriam.

"Good," said Tony shortly after Miriam spoke. "We have several audits lined up for Q1 that we perform every year, so our auditees should be expecting to hear from us soon." He sounded confident and projected a leadership tone befitting the most senior auditor on the team.

"Who has been notified so far?" asked John trying to confirm some of the information he had seen in the shared drives.

"Mary knows we do T&E early in the year, so she won't be surprised to hear from us. I saw her in December and told her we would be visiting for our annual get-together in January or February."

"Good. Anyone else?"

"We're also going to audit Accounts Receivable… again," said Miriam.

"We want to make sure we collect the monies owed to us," said Tony about the second audit for the quarter.

"Yes, I saw those two audits on the planning documents for the quarter. These are typically done in Q1 every year, correct?" asked John seeking confirmation of what he already knew.

"Yes," Tony said right away.

As John thought about the predictable nature of these audits, and the different reactions from Tony and Miriam, he made a mental note about this and turned the conversation to another subject.

"How is the team doing in your opinion?" asked John shifting to personnel management.

"Brian is doing great. He is excited to get going. He should be reviewing the audit programs as we speak," said Tony.

"Reviewing audit programs? Those are done already?" asked John.

"Oh, yes. We have audit programs for all of our recurring audits, so we don't have to spend too much time preparing those. We just have to update administrative details and we're ready to go" replied Tony proud of the system in place.

"Do they get updated before every audit?" asked John.

Miriam answered instead, confirming John's suspicions "Not much gets changed. We often only change the dates because not even the names of the auditors have changed much lately."

"We make changes!" said Tony defending the current process.

"The changes are cosmetic!" replied Miriam with a smile to ease the clear difference of opinion but adding an animated voice to emphasize her point. "The sample size, the methodology, the things we check for are all the same. I don't believe we have looked at other scenarios in a long time."

"But the controls are the same," said Tony defensively. "Why would you change anything if the controls are the same?"

"Because the risks may change. The managers, and the quality of supervision has changed. Population size, the type of travel, all of that changes all the time," she insisted, now providing a rationale for her viewpoint and showing she was comfortable auditing business operations, and her expertise may extend well beyond IT.

"But the controls apply to the same process, and all of the transactions, regardless of type, go through those processes, so no change is needed. A few more hotel stays. A few less air travel. It doesn't matter!" said Tony, still holding on to his approach.

"OK," interjected John. "It looks like this subject has come up before?"

"Yes!" replied Miriam almost before John was done asking the question. "We have had many conversations about audit programs. T&E, Purchasing, AP, inventory. You name it. Same audit program every time. I don't," Miriam stopped mid-sentence realizing she was getting upset and didn't' want her new boss to see them fighting already; much less get overly emotional.

John noticed that Tony had now crossed his arms across his chest, was sitting back, and almost enjoying Miriam's outburst. He clearly supported the existing audit approach and John was now wondering if he wasn't just a supporter, but perhaps a key architect of it.

"Tony, what do you think about this approach? You think we should replicate the same audit programs if the controls remain the same?" asked John returning to a statement Tony had made, hoping to get confirmation about his position, but also hoping Tony would elaborate. John wanted to get a better understanding of how Tony thought.

"Of course! We check the controls, and if they haven't changed why should we change the procedures. Also. This I believe is also very important" Tony added, "the client knows what we check, so the process is smoother. They know what documents, reports, and files to have ready for us, so there is less disruption."

"And they know what to hide and how because we are so predictable" interjected Miriam again. "Sorry, I didn't mean to cut you off" she said putting her hands up in the air as an apologetic signal, but also clearly exasperated.

"You don't need to be sorry, Miriam," said John, "but let's back up a bit and examine our approach. We don't want to surprise our clients, but the term 'surprise' is interpreted differently among auditors. A good surprise is not necessarily bad. Right?"

"Right," said Miriam.

"And changing our procedures may be OK if it helps us identify areas for improvement. Right?" John asked again.

"Right," said Miriam and Tony in unison this time.

"That said, we should review our procedures periodically to see if conditions have changed. So, to Tony's point," now looking at Tony, "if nothing has changed, then nothing has changed. However, things often do change in organizations, especially organizations this size. For example, population sizes may increase, the type of transactions, the currency distribution of expenditures, the vendors used, the people who spent, all of those things may have changed. And equally important, the risks underlying these transactions," he said now looking at Miriam to show his acknowledgment of her perspective "risks often change, systems may change, the people working within the processes, may change, fraud risk and the fraud schemes people may perpetrate may change, and of course, we should be looking for best practices and ways that we may be able to identify ways to make the process faster, cheaper and better. Agree?" John asked and paused to let the message sink in, give them a chance to share their thoughts, and to catch his breath.

"Agree," said Miriam while nodding in agreement. Tony nodded silently while pursing his lips; a sign that his agreement might be underlined by some reluctance or anger about the way things were evolving on this topic.

As John made a mental note of their reaction to his words, he continued.

"In terms of methodology, we should be looking at our testing approach to see if we can find a better way of getting our work done, and the driver for what we do is risk. Not controls. We are going to spend a great deal of time talking about risk-based auditing and what that means. Questions before we move onto another topic?" asked

John giving both of his managers a chance to talk, but aware that this topic would likely be received differently by his two managers.

Since neither manager said anything, John continued.

"OK. Now. Let's talk about our seniors. What reaction do you anticipate from our seniors as we make these changes?"

Miriam spoke first. "I believe Rachel will do well with the changes. She has been begging for us to adopt some new practices for a while."

"She doesn't understand our company," said Tony abruptly.

"Maybe not as well as you and I do, but she has some great ideas. I think we should listen to her more," replied Miriam, once again showing the difference of opinion among them, but also her defense of their team member.

"We can't go chasing every audit fad out there. We have a methodology that works for us," insisted Tony.

"OK. We'll hear everyone out. We can't guarantee we'll do everything they want, but they deserve a hearing, and we'll do that going forward," explained John.

"That's good. I believe that's all she wants. Anyway, that's Rachel. Carolina is very smart. Kind of quiet when it comes to audit topics because she is new to the profession, and InSports, but also has good ideas that we could consider," said Miriam.

"That's good. Brian?" asked John about the remaining staff member on the team.

"He…" Miriam started to speak when Tony interrupted her.

"Brian is a good auditor. He is very bright. Good ideas and an up-and-coming IT auditor," said Tony about his close friend.

"Thanks Tony," acknowledged John. "Miriam, you were going to say?"

"Yes, thanks. Brian is smart and very motivated but doesn't have a lot of audit experience. He can do some great work but needs coaching. He usually thinks like an IT person rather than an auditor."

"Is that bad?" asked Tony.

"Not necessarily, but we are not doing IT, we are auditing and advising IT," explained Miriam.

"OK. I'll give you that, but knowing IT makes you a great auditor," said Tony defending Brian.

"Knowing IT can make you a great auditor" she said emphasizing the word "can." "He needs coaching, so he checks the right things in the context of risk, that's all," Miriam clarified.

"It sounds to me like we have a good team. We have a need for some coaching, but in general a good base to build upon," said John, bringing the conversation to an amicable closure noting the differences between his managers and the need to keep an eye for their interactions.

John woke up early as he usually did, ate breakfast, and went for a walk. It was a cold day and the wind made it even colder. "Invigorating," he said to himself; his coded way of tricking his mind into not labeling it cold outright and giving the whole experience a positive spin. He walked in the woods near his house that had become a good place to get fresh air, clear his mind, and get some exercise for himself and his dog.

When he returned home, he went into the kitchen and prepared a cup of coffee. He then walked the few steps over to his office and he checked the news feed online, read a motivational blog post from one of his favorite influencers, and then returned messages and e-mail. He learned to be very organized when he worked in business operations and subsequently as a management consultant; otherwise, as he would learn the hard way, things could, and would, quickly get out of hand. After being overwhelmed with work demands a few times when he was younger, he read and took some classes on time management, and since then his routine had been put in place. He crafted a rule that had served him well ever since: "take time for me to get a fresh and healthy start to the day, then manage my day rather than let technology and crises manage me."

One of the things he needed to do was get to a routine where he could set defined times to check e-mail, set goals for the day, then manage meetings, and pursue bigger goals and projects during the day. It was still early on in his new job, so he couldn't put that in place yet, but he needed to train his staff and his general work cycle to be organized and preventative.

Since he started, he had been flooded with e-mails and messages. Some of it was the "welcome to our company" types and the responses to his own requests to meet people to get acquainted with in his new organization. In time things needed to get into a better rhythm.

"Regarding e-mail, I don't want them to distract me throughout the day, but rather, I need to set four or so times a day to check them," he thought to himself while thinking about one of his main goals and the way he wanted to interact with most of his stakeholders.

He continued rehearsing his time management and management style policy, "staring at my phone or laptop all day is too distracting, hence inefficient. I need to get people around me used to the idea that I will be checking email first thing in the morning, before lunch, midafternoon and before wrapping up for the day. As far as messages, IM me if you need an immediate decision on something pressing and it will be a quick 'yes', 'no', 'wait' or 'contact so and so' – effectively refer or delegate. If it is a real emergency, call me. For everything else, make a note and let's cover it in one of our meetings. Oh, and let's use the subject line in emails to guide the reader so I can intelligently scan and prioritize them."

As he thought about his policy and described what the ideal state looked like, he smiled to himself because he realized an important exception existed to his otherwise universal rule: "If the chair of the audit committee or the CEO calls, maybe I should drop everything and attend to it!"

As he finished the first phase of his morning routine, he made a mental note of the fact that his team did a very poor job using the subject line in e-mails.

--------------------||--------------------

"Hello everyone," said John as he started the weekly staff meeting. "I am implementing one-on one meetings, so we get to know each other better and check in. We're mainly working remotely so I think it is important that we connect with each other weekly. I'll be setting up these meetings in your calendars so be on the lookout for them. I don't want them to be too formal, but I don't want them to be too fluffy either, so when you look at the meetings you will see that I have three bullets there for the agenda. First bullet, 'How are you?' That is meant to check in at a personal level. We have jobs to do, but I believe in the whole person concept. That means, the better you are doing as an individual, the better positioned you will be to work and excel at what you do for work. I don't want to pry, but I do care, so feel free to tell me how you are doing and if there is anything I can do to help.

The second bullet is how is the team? We are members of a team. Regardless of what I put in the annual audit plan, or what goals I tell the audit committee we are going to pursue, ninety percent of them will involve you to one degree or another. It is like the hand, while it is a unit, it consists of five fingers and if any of them is not well, the whole hand will have difficulties doing what it tries to do.

The third bullet is how can I help? How can I help you as a person and how can I help the team. A big part of my job is removing obstacles. I need to know how the team is doing so I can help you. Does that make sense?"

"Yes," the team replied.

"If you can't make a meeting let me know, but let's try to set that time apart and work around it so we don't neglect connecting with each other. Agree?"

"Yes, that's a good plan" was the response from his team.

"OK then, let's take a few moments to talk about work. Tony, Miriam, followed by Rachel, Brian, and Carolina, give us a summary of how things are coming along with your projects and what obstacles, if any, are in the way."

Each spoke briefly about their work and so John set a precedent for how he wanted his weekly meetings to run: organized, concise, and focused on performance.

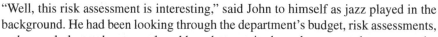

"Well, this risk assessment is interesting," said John to himself as jazz played in the background. He had been looking through the department's budget, risk assessments, and annual plan and was perplexed by what was in these documents, but more so by what was not in them.

He took a sip of coffee as he noticed the typical audits of traditional business activities like Accounts Receivable, Accounts Payable, Inventory, and Payroll, but not much from nontraditional areas of the organization. As he pulled up an org chart, he noticed there were several business units and product lines that had not been listed in the last five years' audit plans.

The risk assessments themselves were done once a year and there was no evidence of them being revised during the year, which was also odd, since dynamics for a company this size, in this industry, with a global reach often change quarterly, if not monthly or even weekly.

The risk rating was basic, if not rudimentary. High, Medium, and Low for risk probabilities, and the same three options for risk impacts. "Those are some very large buckets to be using for this," he said softly to himself. He looked for criteria that would further define these categories and found a similarly basic explanation for what "High, Medium, and Low" meant.

The definitions were largely subjective. "We can expand these definitions and add some more quantitative elements to this, especially the impact part of risk. Maybe make these 5-point scales rather than 3-point. That would give us more precision," he said to himself as he typed some notes. "There is a lot of manufacturing done too, so the EHS considerations should be expanded a bit too."

As he went from tab to tab on the spreadsheet, there was intermittent mention of who contributed to the risk assessments. He looked over at the files folder, which showed a similar lack of details. "Hmm, I wonder if this was done mostly by one person sitting alone. I only see a handful of key contributors. This is a big task, and quite a lonely one if done alone. I think a few more people contributing to this exercise would help," he said while typing a few more notes to himself.

He paused to gather his thoughts; "there are lots of bridges to build here. Lots of opportunity!"

He got up and went into the kitchen to get some more coffee. His mind was still focusing on the risk assessment. "I don't believe there was enough IT in there. Although InSports does a lot of manufacturing, virtually everything made has chips in it, never mind the many systems to run the whole organization. Then there is CAD/CAM to consider too."

As he put his Dunkin' creamer in the cup and some sugar he thought audibly "two IT auditor for a company this size." Maybe the risk assessment was done backward. "It looks like they assessed for the resource instead of finding resources to serve the organization and the expected results." He said walking back into his office. "Maybe the budget would add more clues to this."

He took his seat and opened the budget files. The budget seemed low, and as he looked through the line items and compared year over year, he noticed there was very little travel, but more worrisome was little spent on training or tools. Salaries were average at best, but likely a bit low, so he made a note to ask human resources when was the last time they had done a market analysis of auditor compensation.

"… so they performed … audits last year … and …" Jazz filled the silence with relaxing tunes while John calculated the average number of audits per auditor over the past five years. "…a little low I'd say. Quantity and quality, you can do five hundred lousy audits or twenty really good ones, but still, both elements matter…" as the rhythm livened the otherwise bleak numbers on John's calculator. "Oh, they did the math over here," he told himself as he moved across the spreadsheet and saw several performance indicators. "Did it seem low to them?" he continued his soliloquy as he opened the folder with the Audit Committee quarterly reports and a file with notes. "Nothing. That's interesting. Jim said performance was subpar, so they knew about it, but they just lived with it… OK, baseline John, here is your baseline" he said as he heard the doorbell ring.

Maybe this was the delivery of the book he was expecting.

As he turned to walk away from his desk, he heard the chime on his computer. He glanced at it and noticed it was a Teams message from Miriam; she wanted to know when the performance evaluation cycle would begin because that was typically done in January.

--------------------||--------------------

"Hmmm, said John as he looked through his staff's performance evaluations. Everyone gets a 5!, well, maybe not a five, but the average for the team is 4.84 even though the audit committee tells me they didn't seem to produce that many reports.

Let me see…," said John as he scanned the screen navigating the HR platform and dug into the specifics of each auditors' performance evaluation file. "Tony, 4.95. Miriam 4.85. Brian, 4.92. Rachel, 4.70. Carolina, 4.79."

"Tony is the most senior. A traditionalist, repeating and advising everyone to do the same thing year over year, and he has the highest rating.

Miriam with her IT background didn't get to do too many audits and seems to be bucking heads with Tony about our methodology. I wonder if the previous CAE didn't like her pushing back.

Brian has no audit experience but has an IT background. Smart, charismatic, and motivated. He got pretty much as high a rating as Tony, his close friend.

Rachel is the lowest rated staff member and based on Miriam's feedback she has probably been the loudest asking for change but has been kind of silenced for the sake of easy, repeat audits. The nail that sticks out gets the hammer.

Carolina, out in London. Relatively new, trying to get along. Mostly quiet. She gets 4.79.

Virtually no comments on what they need to improve on. Everyone gets an A. It is going to be interesting rating them in the future when their numbers have been so high for years, said John to himself as he thought about the past, present, and future implications of what looked like overly generous performance ratings. Gratuitous comes to mind. As Mother Theresa said "Honesty and transparency make you vulnerable. Be honest and transparent anyway. Here we go John," he said giving himself a pep talk knowing that this would also present some challenges when he tried to correct it."

--------------------||--------------------

"Hi Frank, how are you?"

"I'm well. Still trying to work off the million calories I ingested during the holidays!" he said cheerfully.

"I'm with you. Too much pie, eggnog, cakes, cookies, you name it."

"Butter cookies. Oh my. I can't eat just one. There is no such thing. Big weakness here," he said laughing loudly at his admission.

"Have you bought your gym membership yet?"

"I've had it all along, I just need to double down and go more often. Of course, I have two problems. I'm skiing in France where patisseries call my name and invite me in at virtually every street corner. And number two when I get back, I'll have to navigate a crowded gym with a hundred other people with regret-memberships."

"But many will be gone by Valentine's Day so just hang in there."

"Unfortunately for them and their resolutions. Good point. Lack of follow-through. Lack of consistency is the downfall of many people. OK. That was my first philosophical moment of the year. What's on your mind my friend?"

"As you know I'm the new CAE at InSports and one of the things that is already apparent is that I need to make some changes around here."

"That is often the case. Seldom does a new chief of anything come in to solidify the status quo. Quite often the new boss wants some changes made. The question is how many and how big?"

"Many and big. Now, as an auditor I'm familiar with being the change agent. That's the essence of every audit communication, or report: convey issues and make the presentation persuasive enough that they'll see the need to make the recommended and agreed-upon changes."

"So?"

"Performance metrics are down. Image is down. Relationships are down. I suspect even credibility might be hurting too."

"The bigger the challenge, the bigger the opportunity. I'm sure you can elevate the unit. I'm assuming you wanted more than a pep talk from me."

"I appreciate the positive reinforcement, and yes, I was wondering if you had a few words of wisdom as I take this on."

"Be sure you put your feet in the right place, then stand firm. That's from Abraham Lincoln. With that, and I'm sure you're under a lot of stress, you must balance the task with some humor. Something this big is not a straight walk up the hill. You will have to zig and you will have to zag. Did the board indicate you need to fix things?"

"Yes."

"How long did they say you..."

Silence.

"Frank? Hello?" John realized the call had ended abruptly. He called back but the call went straight into voicemail, so Frank was no longer available. There was a windstorm blowing outside and power outages had been forecasted, but both power and the internet router were up and running. So, the problem was on Frank's end. He was hoping he could get his call in before he lost his power, and it looks like Frank may have lost his power or internet access first.

Not wanting to let the moment be wasted, he went to his wine rack and picked a bottle of Malbec. He uncorked it, grabbed a wine glass, and poured a small amount so he could smell and taste it. Finding it to his liking, he headed for the fireplace in the living room not bothering to get a notepad because he kept one on the side table at all times. He had fire starter ready to go and there was wood waiting as well. He opened the flume, lit the fire, and sat comfortably in his armchair.

As he got comfortable, he brought his mind to attention. "OK now, John, on this fine Saturday afternoon, what was Frank thinking when the call ended abruptly?"

--------------------||--------------------

There are two types of winter people. Those who hibernate, anxiously waiting for the winter to end; they go outside only when necessary. Then there are those who have found enjoyment in winter in the beauty of trees covered in snow and snow-covered fields; and they go outdoors and enjoy the brisk air and quiet silence. They take long walks, may even go snowshoeing, downhill skiing, or in John's case, cross-country skiing. For him it was mind-clearing, but also a good way to exercise and stay fit during the long Northern winters.

He was truly enjoying the winter scene. Even though there was no snow, the leafless trees show their structure: massive trunks followed by branches that decrease in size until there are twigs at the ends where leaves once were. In the winter, the organic structure is evident demonstrating how oaks, maples, birches, and elms share their secret to withstanding whipping storm winds. Evergreens like red cedars, pines, and spruce kept the landscape colorful and are often used for privacy hedging.

"Tony, Miriam, and Rachel are like those tough, solid trees. Every department needs those team members that shape our structure and instill confidence. Brian and Carolina are my colorful evergreens, except in the fall; they'll be the colorful sugar maples. Nothing like diversity to make this merry-go-round enjoyable despite the whipping wind I'll have to deal with this year!"

As he climbed a long gradual hill and turned to make a slow descent toward the river on the far side of the woods it suddenly hit him. "Ah, that's what Frank was getting to, he was asking me how much time the board gave me to turn the department around. They wanted it turned around by yearend, but they didn't expect silence for eleven months then bam! Big reveal on the twelfth month. Change must start now, and they want to see results. They'll want me to show progress along the way."

"Create a sense of urgency," he said to himself.

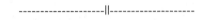

John got to the New York office Monday afternoon.

As he walked into the break room, he quickly noticed the refrigerator with the note on the door "Please write your name on your food items," and "Refrigerator is cleaned on the 15th and month-end. All leftovers will be discarded at that time." Over the sink, a more tongue-in-cheek message read "Your mother doesn't work here. Please wash your own dishes or put them in the dishwasher." There were two vending machines and, in the corner, a drip coffee maker, a French drip coffee maker, a k-cup coffee maker, and an industrial-size two-carafes coffee maker with hot water dispenser.

"Wow," he thought, "big coffee drinkers around here! The only thing we need is a cappuccino machine. I'm in good company!"

As he opened the cupboard looking for a cup, he heard two people talking as they entered the room. He turned around and noticed how tall both of them were.

"Hi," he said, using his search for a cup as an excuse to start a conversation. "Do you know where the cups are?"

"The cups are over here," as the younger woman reached into one of the cupboards and took down a roll of paper cups.

"Thank you. I see a dishwasher. Do we also have washable cups?" John asked.

"See?" said the woman as she put a handful of cups upside down on the counter. Nowadays people want washable cups, so we don't waste paper cups every time someone drinks a cup of coffee."

"Most people bring and use their own," said the other woman.

"I get it, but what if there is a guest in the office. Or someone forgets to bring their mug?" The first woman said arguing her point.

"OK, OK, I get it," said the other woman.

"I apologize if I started something," said John with a big smile. "It looks like this has been an ongoing conversation around here."

"Yes," said the younger woman. "I'm trying to get us to switch to re-usable mugs, and plates, but we haven't gotten that implemented yet. We now have a recycling bin, though," pointing to the blue container in the far corner of the room. "People are finally starting to use it," she said raising her arms as a sign of victory.

"Hi, I'm John," he said introducing himself. He was going to extend his hand for a handshake but had given up on that custom since the pandemic changed many social mores.

"Hi, I'm Terry and this is," waving to her colleague as an invitation to introduce herself.

"Hi, I'm Kathleen, the tree killer," she said with a smile. "I would shake your hand, but you know, COVID and all," she said verbalizing John's thoughts.

"I haven't seen you around here before, John. Which department do you work in?" asked Terry.

"Internal Audit."

"Oh, said Terry. New in the department?"

"He's our new Chief Auditor. You didn't get the e-mail?" asked Kathleen.

"Oh, well that's embarrassing. I…"

Kathleen saved Terry from further embarrassment and took over the conversation. "So, John, welcome to the company. How are things so far?"

"Things are going well. Getting to know the organization in more detail every day. There are the people of course, but the products and locations where we operate are quite diverse. I'm looking forward to visiting our locations to learn more."

"You can only learn so much through Teams and Zoom," offered Terry.

"Right. It gets you started, and then some, but for more in-depth understanding of what is going on, there is nothing like being there and talking to people."

"I agree. Being in HR has its challenges when it comes to that. We have adapted quite well to the work from home model, but there is still more to be done. COVID complicated things in so many ways," said Kathleen.

"Yes. The health issues are obvious, but at the organizational level we have team dynamics, communication challenges, coordination challenges, and process concerns."

"How are we doing in terms of corporate culture?" John asked.

"Corporate culture. She repeated with a big sigh while shaking her head slightly. We had some issues, mostly stemming from our fast growth and multiple acquisitions over the past five years. Bringing company cultures together has its challenges, but then not having people in the same buildings makes it harder because, like you said, communication, bonding, body language messaging, camaraderie, are all different. The new generation of workers may be handling it a bit better than older workers, but that is not always true. In fact, we have some younger workers who think they're Ok, but they're really not. We have managers who are still learning how to manage a distributed workforce."

"If I can't see them, how do I know they're working?" John contributed to the list of topics mentioned.

"Exactly! How do you measure performance? We have managers who are still searching for ways to assess performance and identify needs," she said sighing again.

"Do we have manager training for all of this?" John asked as he took a cup and walked over to the coffee maker.

"Some. We have had to ramp that up, but with so much turnover, even in HR, we are facing some challenges getting our initiatives completed," Kathleen replied.

"Any complaints from managers?" John asked.

"Yes"

"Complaints from employees?"

"Yes, again. I don't think an insurrection is on the way, but morale and engagement are being tested in some places," Kathleen answered as her body language showed that this topic was weighing heavily on her and likely a significant percentage of the workforce.

"Like?" John asked as he reached into the basket with the sugar packets and took two out.

Terry moved out of the immediate circle and was making herself a cup of tea with a bag of green tea she brought herself. She was using her own mug and while occupied preparing her drink, was clearly listening to the ongoing conversation.

"Well. We have some ideas, but don't know exactly. We do engagement surveys, and the numbers are OK, but I think there is more happening than the numbers show," Kathleen confided.

"Are you able to drill into the survey data to look for outliers and patterns?" John asked trying to get more insights into the engagement survey process and what it may be telling management.

"That is part of what I meant," said Kathleen. "Terry, what are your thoughts when it comes to the engagement surveys?"

Terry replied "The numbers look OK in terms of averages, and the survey application we use gives us range and standard deviation and I can tell we likely have some pockets. Mathematically. Anecdotally, I know we have pockets because I get complaints and turnover dynamics, but I don't have enough hard data or staff to crunch the numbers."

"So, you report on the averages?" John asked to confirm his understanding of the way this was working so far.

"Yes, but don't tell anyone about all the other stuff," Kathleen said jokingly.

John smiled. "I can't promise to keep secrets. You know I'm an auditor," he said smiling, which simultaneously clarified his obligation and his support.

"I know. I know. Listen. You are part of the team. Sooner or later stuff rises to the top. There is a lot being published in HR journals and talked about at conferences about the new generation of workers and WFH dynamics. Talent management. The Big Resignation, Quiet Quitting, Career Cushioning, who is leaving and why. There is so much happening and so much I want to do, but we have limited resources, and we are growing so fast," said Kathleen.

She added, "Terry is getting some more staff, but it is like playing catch-up with so much going on. It is exciting, challenging, and we're building an amazing company, so these are typical growing pains," shared Kathleen.

"I hear you," said John as he put some creamer in his coffee.

"Do you have people you can spare?" Kathleen said jokingly, but it was clear the comment was also a serious request.

"Well, not exactly. I am short staffed too. But I have some ideas that might help you," John said as he finished stirring his coffee and took a sip; "not bad."

"No, not bad. But if you're into coffee, we should go out sometime. There is a great coffee shop with a great selection of beans. If you want, they even draw little shapes on your mug too," said Kathleen. "It makes you feel guilty drinking the thing when you see the art in the cup."

"I know, right? I worked in Canada for a while and there was this chain where they did this, and I used to go there just for that. Maybe a little weird, but it was inspiring. I went back to work inspired after watching a barista being such an artist," John said as he shrugged his shoulders while putting a plastic lid on his unimpressive paper cup of coffee.

"BC? Vancouver?" asked John.

"No, Calgary," said Kathleen.

"Oh. OK. I was a consultant for a while and the shop I went to where they did this was Caffe Artigiano in Vancouver."

"That's it. Yes, that's them. They are in Calgary too," said Kathleen enthusiastically.

"Great experience. Such memories. Let's do that. We should chat some more about what's going on and how my team may be able to help you," he said while all three of them walked out of the break room together.

"Take care," said Kathleen.

"Bye," said Terry.

"Thanks. You too," said John, noticing that Kathleen left empty handed just like when she entered the room.

"Hello everyone," said John using his customary opening line when he started meetings.

He was welcomed on his computer screen with a variety of "welcomes" and hand gestures ranging from waves, open palms, and "Hi Johns." This time it was Carolina who started talking while her microphone was still in mute. Quickly Miriam alerted her of the problem.

"Hi everyone. Happy Monday and good afternoon," said Carolina after unmuting herself.

"Hi Carolina. Yes, it is afternoon for you. How was your weekend?" asked Miriam.

"It was good. We went hiking in Marlow, a small town not too far from London. We had two sunny days for a change. Amazing!"

"That's great. Would you recommend it if I visit in the summer?" asked Brian.

"Oh yes, very pretty town. Only around 30 miles west of London. Nice pubs too!"

"Sign me up," said Brian with a smile.

John rejoined the conversation and said "good tip and a reminder to take time to rest, relax, and get inspiration. On the topic of inspiration, let's talk about the plans for the week starting with Miriam, then Tony, Brian, Carolina, and Rachel."

As everyone spoke about their plans for the week, John thought to himself that the way they communicated the status of their projects and other work was a bit cumbersome and inconsistent. Not bad, but things could be organized a bit better for clarity and expediency.

"Thanks everyone. I appreciate all of your hard work and this relatively slow time of the year is a good time to review processes for when things pick up speed again. There's a simple formula I'd like to introduce for our weekly meetings that consists of four basic questions, What did you accomplish last week? What three things are you focusing on this week? What resources do you need to accomplish these goals?, and What blockers do you anticipate along the way? Accomplishments, goals, resources, and blockers. What do you think about that?"

"Sounds good," said Miriam.

"Simple; easy to remember," added Brian.

"Is that like a Six Sigma formula or something like that?" asked Rachel.

"Kind of" replied John. "It mostly borrows from agile development and the use of scrum meetings. It also focuses on what matters most in a short format that is consistent and sensitive to the need for efficiency and quick action. I like to focus on outcomes, so we start with accomplishments, so we recognize your successes, then focus on the upcoming week and what you need to succeed."

"Does this mean we don't need to produce status update reports?" asked Tony.

"Oh, yes, status update reports. I've been receiving those but not everyone seems to be preparing the reports. Is that correct?" asked John.

"No. They take too long to prepare," said Miriam.

"And no one reads them," added Rachel.

"I read them," said Tony, defending the practice.

"We were supposed to prepare status reports?" chimed in Carolina.

"You didn't know about them?" asked Brian.

As John watched the rapid exchange on display before him, he thought to himself about the inconsistent practices prevalent in the department.

"No, no one told me I had to prepare those. Is there a template I should be using?" asked Carolina.

"Yes, there is a template. And you're supposed to store weekly reports in the shared drive too," explained Tony.

"Where in the shared drive?" asked Brian, "I just e-mail those to you Tony. Was I supposed to also save them somewhere?"

"I've been saving them for you in the shared drive," replied Tony.

"Have you been preparing those reports Miriam?" asked Rachel.

"I either copy and paste your comment from the e-mail you send me, or I type it in based on our meeting conversations," explained Miriam.

"Miriam, do you do the same for me?" asked Carolina.

"Yes."

"Oh, had I known I would have done it myself. I didn't know you were doing that extra work by yourself," said Carolina showing sympathy for Miriam.

"That's Ok," said Miriam, "that's part of my job."

Having heard enough, John jumped back into the conversation. "Very interesting discovery, wouldn't you say?" he said asking rhetorically. "Tony, Miriam and I will review our project status update process, but in general, we need consistency, clarity and simplicity. I would like us to improve the template we have, because it is too long in my opinion. It captures interesting information, but it is not very clear what has been done with that information in the past. Tony, did you say they are being saved in the shared drive?"

"Yes, they are easy to find. Go to the admin folder, under each year, search by client, then project, then phase. There is one Word document per week," replied Tony.

"Did you say they are all Word documents?" asked John.

"Yes, they are easy to complete. Just need to fill in the fields," not realizing that what he was describing was an extensive collection of documents unfit for analysis and comparison.

"We may switch to a searchable tool where we can use the information to track and report our collective, and not just our individual, status," said John.

"Will we still have to record our work in 15-minute increments?" asked Brian, taking advantage of the opportunity to raise one of his objections with the current process.

"Yes," said Tony immediately, not waiting for John to respond.

"Let's think about that for a moment," objected John. "Why are we capturing time in 15-minute increments?"

"So, we can keep track of where we are spending our time," replied Tony. "We need to know what everyone is working on."

"Those are different things," said John. Keeping track of time, knowing what people are working on, and tracking progress on goals are different things. How many hours people spend working is not always a reflection of them getting work done."

"Amen," said Rachel.

John was taken aback by her response but was not entirely surprised. It was clear the current process had detractors and the topic of quantity of work hours and places where people choose to work had been a topic of discussion for years.

Without acknowledging her reaction, he added. "15-minute increments may be a lot. I worked in organizations where we charged our work hours back to the client, so we needed to be very precise tracking our time so our invoices would be accurate. It made sense there to track in small increments. I am not convinced that we need that level of detail here. At least not yet. If we decide to go forward, we will invest in a tool that helps collect all of this information more easily. That said, and this also goes back to your question Rachel about Six Sigma, we measure and track something because we will use the information to better understand something and make decisions. If nothing else, Excel would be a better tool and with some calculated summaries and visuals, we can track our progress towards our project goals," he said while taking a pause and a deep breath.

Then he continued.

"Well. That was enlightening," he said with a smile to ease the tension that had built up over the last minutes. I will add our formula to the meeting agenda for next time. Tony, let's start with you, then Miriam, Rachel, Brian and Carolina in that order. Last week accomplishments, three key actions for this week, resources you need and obstacles.

When they were done, John thanked the team and reiterated the plan for weekly meetings.

"Thanks everyone. Let me know if you need me to help remove any obstacles or blockers in your way, and have a great week," said John bringing the meeting to a close.

As he waved everyone goodbye and clicked the "Leave" button, he took another deep breath and thought to himself about the personalities he needed to lead and manage within his team.

--------------------||--------------------

John sat at his desk, put his coffee mug down, adjusted himself in his chair, and moved his fingers over the touchpad to get the laptop working. While he and his laptop were still waking up, he heard a ping on his phone. It was a notification from one of the social networks and as he looked at it closely, he noticed that it pertained to InSports.

The notification was a news update announcing the release of a mirror product that allowed subscribers to workout at home under the tutelage of an exercising coach. Exercise programs could be either standardized or customized by the customer and personal biometrics were captured, updated, and compared to others in various intervals.

"I don't remember reading about this product in the past three years' risk assessments or audit plans," he thought to himself. "I wonder if either Miriam or Tony knew about this beforehand."

He Teams messaged his two managers asking them if they knew about the development of this product. Miriam responded right away.

"No"

He explained how he found out about this new product, and she shared that the R&D group had grown recently in terms of budget and headcount. They had several products in development, but audit was not privy to what was actually being done there. Rumors were circulating that as much as they were developing and releasing new products, they were also running into technical issues.

"What kind of technical issues? Do you know?" he typed.

"Not exactly, but they are often running faster than the IT and cybersecurity groups, so they are always trying to catch up and provide the functionality that R&D envisions and Marketing supports."

"Do you know anything about the manufacturing and QA processes?" he kept the conversation going.

"Most manufacturing happens in Canada and Argentina. We have done some audits there, but the last one was a few years ago," she explained.

"I saw the report for the last audit in Argentina, but nothing about new or upcoming products. Canada was even older," John shared.

"Remember what I said in that meeting the other day? About cookie-cutter work programs?" Miriam reminded him.

"I remember that. Yes," he acknowledged.

"Lots of typing. Can we have a quick video call?" asked John.

"Yes," was the immediate reply.

As they got on an impromptu call, Miriam commented.

"We don't ask about new initiatives. I've told Tony that we should, but his opinion is we audit to the current process and controls, not to future processes. I still think we should ask. Do you agree?" she asked.

"Yes, we should ask. First at the risk assessment level. Were you involved in that?

"No, that was the previous CAE who did that alone. We got the results."

"Ok. So the next point is at the engagement level, and again, yes, any upcoming changes could impact the way things are designed and working in a way that makes the current structure and practices less relevant. Changes can result in poor controls and exposure to risks, so we could also identify opportunities to advise them about gaps they may not have thought about," he said.

"I agree. Changes can also impact any recommendations we make, right? If we recommend a course of action that a process or system change will nullify, we should know about it, so we don't waste our time or make impractical recommendations. Right?" she asked again.

"Yes, that is correct," said John approvingly.

"That's what I thought! but you can't convince Tony about that!" she said with a tone that suggested she had been having this conversation for a long time and had been blocked in her efforts.

"I will be providing more guidance in the coming weeks about our improved methodology," he reassured her.

"Thanks. That would be good."

"Thanks for getting on this call right away. I just wanted to get your input on this." John thanked her.

"No problem. Any time. Where's Tony anyway?" she asked.

"Not sure. He hasn't responded to my message yet. Probably in a meeting or something. We'll catch up later and I'll share with both of you what I hear about this new product."

"Thanks. Talk to you later."

"Bye," said John as he clicked the "Leave" button to end the call and wondered to himself what else the organization was working on that he should know about but didn't. He needed better and more timely information. He needed a seat at the table.

--------------------||--------------------

John sat facing his laptop as he waited for Frank to join. He enjoyed these meetings because they provided a safe place for him to talk about things and get candid feedback from someone who he knew and trusted. This was arguably one of the best decisions he had made; get a mentor. In reality, he didn't "get" a mentor; a mentor "happened." As he was remembering some of the events that resulted in him meeting Frank, he saw a black box appear on his screen indicating his guest's impending arrival.

"Hi John. How are you on this fine morning?" asked Frank.

"I'm well. A beautiful snowy day with blue skies. We had a foot of snow last night. Woke up to a winter wonderland!"

"Yes, that is beautiful. I remember how peaceful that can be until you have to shovel yourself out," he quipped giving him a hard time.

"We have snow blowers now, you know," said John returning the friendly banter.

"You softies. When I was young, we had to shovel our quarter mile driveway with a spatula," he said jokingly.

"Yes, right. You're just saying that because where you live now the coldest it gets is probably 50 degrees."

"You got that right! My neighbor is selling his house, so when you come to your senses you can move down here too and join me."

"Someday, but not yet," John said, pausing abruptly after his short sentence indicating he wanted to move to a more formal line of conversation.

"So, how are things at InSports?" Frank asked picking up on John's signal.

We're making progress, but just yesterday I confirmed something I had been suspecting and noticing for a while.

"What's that?"

"My predecessor didn't really have strong connections throughout the organization, and it doesn't look like he knew about major developments in the works."

"How do you know that?"

"Risk assessments and audit plans don't include things that not only you would consider standard items on these documents these days, but major projects and initiatives have not been mentioned at all as being in progress."

"That's a big oversight."

"Yes. And there is a lot of funding behind some of these initiatives and the risk that if these things don't work out, the strategic impact could be substantial."

Frank nodded as he heard John's description of the situation.

"How about unwritten indicators of awareness. Did your managers know about these things?"

"No. They were unaware. But interestingly enough, one of them knew that they should know more, but was kept back."

"And the other manager?"

"The other manager often acts as if knowing those things was not really that important to the role."

"Wow. Well John, you are describing the perils of not having a seat at the table. When you're not in the room, and at the table with the key decision-makers, those that visualize the future of the organization, allocate resources, and set goals, you end up hearing about things after the fact."

"That just about sums it up."

"But having a seat, or getting a seat as is often referred to, doesn't just happen. You have to work for it and earn it. Good, consistent work over time. Asking the right questions. Making contributions so the C-suite grows to seek your input."

"I agree, but can I merely invite myself to these meetings?"

"You should be getting invited to some of them as the new CAE. Are they inviting you?"

"Yes, for the most part, and while I take lots of notes and try to bring myself up to date, there is always more going on that keeps me getting surprised almost daily."

"That's understandable. It is a global company, so there must be many moving parts. Like drinking from fire hose, isn't it?"

"Exactly."

"I've been there on several occasions. Stay the course, be patient and take lots of notes that you review periodically and keep them organized."

"Good advice. I'm doing that."

"When people talk about 'the table,' Frank said making air quotes, "they usually think about a boardroom table. Lots of people sitting in suits and notepads. Let's change that up a little and think about it being a restaurant table instead," he paused to give John a chance to process the scenario he was creating.

"OooKayy," said John stretching the word out in acknowledgment.

"What usually happens during a meal at the table?" Frank asked with a smile enjoying the storytelling journey he was taking John on.

"I don't suppose you are still thinking about food."

"I'm always thinking about food" Frank said laughing, "but in *addition* to food," he said emphasizing the word "addition."

"I don't know. What?"

"Don't give up so quickly. Think ahead for a moment. What usually happens during a meal at the dinner table? How would you describe the dynamics around this table you are trying to get a seat at?"

"There is conversation."

"Exactly! Now imagine you get this coveted seat, and you are so unaware of the topics being discussed that you are at a loss."

"That would be awkward. Quite uncomfortable."

"Right again. Steering committees are particularly good if you can get on them. The name of the group may change, so don't just look for what's called a steering committee, look at what the groups do. But that's the formal or semi-formal channel. The informal channels are great too."

"Like which ones?"

"The grapevine. But I like to think of the seat at the table at the formal setting in the restaurant."

"I'm with you."

"Ok. Now think about all the things that happen *before* the big meal," Frank said as he pointed his index finger for emphasis when he said "before." "There is a whole crew in the kitchen that is also very knowledgeable about what happens in the organization. Talk with them."

"These are the operations and front-line workers?"

"Yes, exactly. They're cooking things up, see the ingredients get bought, inspected, stored, used, what's in the pantry. What's missing from the pantry. They may even know who takes without permission or swaps good for bad ingredients, waters down the sauce and all of that, if you get my meaning."

"I hear you," said John nodding in agreement.

"Similarly, spend time and talk with the wait staff. They often see, hear and in general, know what is happening too. They come in contact with those in the main dining room, so they see, hear and know things. They also interact with the kitchen crew. They are connectors."

"Hmmm. Interesting. Where are these people?"

"Some are just scattered around the organization. Some are secretaries, drivers, messengers, shippers, customer service, repair, and client support employees."

"That makes sense," said John showing deep interest in the conversation and expanding the scenario. "They may be privy to the sales tactics, shipping, delivery, returns, quality issues and customer complaints, so they know what works, what doesn't, shortcuts people take and places where the process breaks down."

"Exactly!" said Frank excitedly. "Some of the best information I obtained by talking to these workers, yet too often they are ignored because auditors follow what they call protocol, and that involves talking to managers and accounting staff. So, get into operations and meet First Line or front-line staffers. You will be surprised."

As Frank said this John heard a faint buzz and Frank turned his head to look down at something. His facial expression changed immediately indicating he was surprised by something he saw.

"Everything OK?" asked John.

"Yes, for me. Not so good for you."

"Oh?"

"I'm getting together with some friends to play tennis this morning. One of them wants a ride so I need to leave now so we get to the club on time. I have to go."

"No problem. Go ahead. Enjoy your game. You gave me some great ideas. Thanks."

"You're welcome. Talk again soon. Take care."

"I will."

With that Frank left the meeting and John leaned back in his chair reflecting on the conversation he just had.

--------------------||--------------------

As John logged into the Teams call, he noticed in Ken's background several motivational posters he had hanging from the walls. "Excellence," "Make it Happen," and "Above and Beyond." A trophy on the credenza suggested he ran, and won one of the top places, in a running race, while the three model-sized bicycles screamed of long, fast, and challenging road racing. The bookshelf had few books, but the ones he could decipher were classics and a completed Rubik's cube and a set of Newton's Cradle rounded out the display.

"Hi John, how are things in Boston?"

"Good. The weather is nice. Sunny, dry, not much snow. We're living the dream!"

"How cold is it?"

"Hmmm, let me check," said John as he looked at his phone and checked the Weather app. "15 degrees."

"And the Wind chill?"

"2 degrees."

"So, summer is around the corner," Ken said with a smile – a clear indicator he was not amused by those temperatures. "Gone skiing lately?"

"In fact, I did. Went to Maine last weekend and did both cross country and downhill skiing. There is nothing like looking at the world from up high. Blue skies, imposing mountain ranges, clean air. You should try it sometime!"

"Call me when you go camping after Memorial Day and maybe I'll join you. I'm a hot weather guy."

"I hear you."

"So, what can I do for you?"

"Risk assessments are one of our key processes to identify areas within the organization where company initiatives and strategic plans, resources and key deliverables converge as we go about our mission and goals. We will be performing a formal risk assessment in a few weeks, but I'm right now introducing myself and getting to know about the key initiatives that different business units have on their plate."

"A risk assessment?" asked Ken.

"You haven't been part of a risk assessment at InSports?"

"No, not officially. I was in a meeting with your predecessor some time ago and that came up in conversation, but he said he did that with the audit committee and together they decided what to audit. They never got me involved in that process and

I never asked because I'm doing just fine without being audited. Don't get me wrong, auditors play an important role, but no one asks to be audited, right?"

"Being audited is not so bad," said John with a smile.

"Yeah right, sure, says the auditor in the room!" replied Ken jovially.

"A risk assessment is not the same as being audited. We'll do a formal risk assessment later and I'll spend some time explaining that process, documentation and so on, but for now I'm just curious about the main things operations is doing. Ron said you have a number of big initiatives underway."

"Yep. We're quite busy here" he said as he proceeded to list no less than 10 multi-million-dollar initiatives that would result in the update, upgrade, and release of new products. There were another 10 mid-sized initiatives that were slated for introduction intermittently with the larger ones and several partnerships, where the R&D group was working with other companies to develop new products. Innovation was clearly alive and well.

"It sounds like several of these products use wireless technologies to interface with corporate and individual customers," said John.

"Yes," Ken replied excitedly as he described how some of the products would collect individuals' health and location information on wearable devices or on the exercise equipment, transmit to a central repository, and have it collected, analyzed, sometimes shared with third parties, and reported back to customers on the wearables, exercise equipment, or other devices of choice.

"That Project Delta that you told me about. Is that a new elliptical machine?"

"Yes," he again responded excitedly as he described the equipment's features and the built-in technology that captured health information and produced various statistics and lifestyle programs.

"Where are those machines going to be built? We currently don't make any of those, right?"

"No, we don't. Some will be built in Canada alongside some of our stationary bikes and others will be made in China with our rowing machines. Plans are to also outsource some of that production to a business partner in Costa Rica. Did they tell you about the factory we are building there?"

"No. I knew about the other locations, but Costa Rica is news to me."

"Great place! The facility is almost done, that's probably why they didn't tell you about that. We timed our design work with the construction project to make sure everything synced up. Should be going live by the summer."

"Is that connected to the Mexico business partner?"

"Yes. Our Mexican counterparts are expanding in Central America."

"Who is managing that construction project in Costa Rica?"

"Javier Gonzalez is our main contact. He is the project manager but it is really a fluid project team that checks in on things periodically. Finance is handling most of the monitoring because they pay the bills, but I believe that is being handled out of the Miami office. We also have a Panamanian construction company working with the Mexican partner and Costa Rican contractors. They're all good people. Honest, hardworking, friendly. Great team."

"What else are you working on?"

"A lot of companies are building apps that coach users to great health. No machines. Just software that can be deployed on a phone, watch, laptop, tablet and so on. We will be creating communities of users so people from the US can create running, rowing, hiking, rock climbing, you name it, different groups or clubs that exercise together. The software would count steps. Track hiking locations, check weight lost and so on. We collect and share results, so individuals can keep track of their own progress, but the really exciting feature is we can aggregate date, share date among teams and create competition among the various groups. That's a whole new level of community building. We collect all kinds of data like gender, age, nationality. Imagine 50-year-old Americans competing with their same age group friends from Germany, each hiking their own mountains, but keeping track of each other's progress. It's going to be like having our own multi-location Olympics!"

"That sounds like a really exciting initiative. Who are you working with on the cybersecurity requirements for … project … what is this one called?"

"Project Meta. We called it Meta because it is going to give us enough metadata to make that little company Meta cry! Anyway, we'll add the security later. People want to be free you know. It is a new world and people want to share info and do their thing and feel connected. We'll facilitate that and get oodles of data in the process."

"I'm assuming it will have a location tracker."

"Of course! That was one of the first features we put in there."

"We usually play the song 'Every step you make' around the office and sometimes when we start our meetings. It's almost a cult following now. By the time we're done we'll know every step people take," he said laughing.

As Ken described these ideas John felt a combination of exhilaration and concern. Great product ideas emanating from a high performing unit with a dynamic culture under the leadership of a charismatic and engaged leader. But the risk profile became increasingly concerning with every product description he heard. Virtually every sentence could result in a risk breakdown, and he had not heard much in the form of controls. What he heard often, though, was how people trusted each other and how being mission driven kept the company on a forward path. Trust is good for individuals and a great quality for an organization, but trust is not a good substitute for effective internal controls.

Avoiding immediate judgment, John replied "That is really good information and enough for now. I'll schedule a meeting later to get some more details and that risk assessment I told you about. We should do that soon."

"Sounds good."

"OK Ken. We're at time and it was good talking with you. Thank you for your time."

"You're welcome."

"Come over and visit us. Happy to show you around, show you some prototypes, some demos, introduce you to our team. You'll get a better sense of what we're doing. And you can get away from the cold for a while."

"I may take you up on that offer."

John ended the video call and took notes immediately. He needed to go to San Francisco and see for himself what R&D was doing. What he heard from the COO was worrisome.

--------------------||--------------------

"Hi Tony. How are the preparations for the T&E audit coming along?"

"Good!" Tony replied. "The audit program is done, and we are sending the notification to the client Wednesday letting them know when fieldwork will begin."

"When is fieldwork supposed to start again?"

"Next week. Brian is preparing the document and data request as we speak so that should go out right after the notification letter, so I would say, Thursday or Friday. We're really agile around here!" he said proudly.

"Wow, that would be fast, but let's talk about the process for a moment. Who is the project sponsor, or main contact for this audit?"

"We work with Dan, the Controller on this. We've done this audit many times before, so it is very straightforward," Tony responded confidently. "It is an annual review and we do it in February because things are otherwise pretty quiet around here. Also, Rachel was the auditor last year so she knows exactly what to do."

"OK. But who oversees the actual T&E process, I don't suppose Dan actually enforces the T&E policy and decides to pay or not pay the actual expenses. He's the Controller and I'm assuming he has a lieutenant handling that on a daily basis, right?"

"Oh, no. You're right. That's Mary who does that. She receives the expense reports from the field and works with the person's manager if there are any issues," he explained.

"Do you talk with her during planning?"

"No. She is really busy, so we came to an agreement a few years ago. We created a standard audit program and that's what we do every year. She loves the approach and Dan signed off on it,"

"Do you have the audit program handy so we can look it over?" asked John.

"Sure, but like I said, the Controller already agreed to it," Tony responded as his eyes moved around the camera while he searched for the audit program. "Here it is. OK … let me share my screen…. Can you see it?"

"Yes, I can. Can you make it a little larger. Just a bit… OK. Perfect that's it. Walk me through it please," asked John.

As Tony went through the audit program, John became increasingly aware that the audit program was indeed standardized and focused on basic compliance-related steps. It included things like checking that amounts did not exceed the daily meal limits, that receipts were provided, that the expense report was approved by a manager, and the disbursed amount matched the amount on the expense report.

When Tony finished his overview John asked, "Do we have preferred airlines, hotels or car rental agencies employees should be using?"

After a short hesitation, Tony said "No, we don't, the policy doesn't require it."

"How do we know we're not overpaying?"

"We don't know. Employees are supposed to fly economy class, but that's it. The cost for hotels and car rentals is supposed to be reasonable. That's what the policy requires."

"OK. How do we make sure gifts are not included in the expense report?"

"Gifts?"

"Yes, personal gifts, souvenirs, and the like," John clarified.

"Well, we don't check for that. That's the manager's job to screen for things like that."

"Does the policy say those items are unacceptable?"

"Yes, those would be unacceptable charges, but the policy states it is the manager's responsibility to check for that. They're the control point and they should be checking that."

"OK. I get it. How about personal expenses, kind of like gifts, but let's say to watch a movie, go to the theater, sporting events. Do we check for that?" asked John still using questions to help Tony identify possible limitations in the existing audit program.

"No. like gifts, the policy says you cannot do that unless the manager approves of it. You know, they could approve that for client entertainment in some cases, but we look for the manager's approval. We see some of that sometimes from the Sales group, but that's fine if the manager approved it," Tony explained.

"I see. How about when a group eats together, lunch or dinner, for example. Do we check who paid the bill and who approved it? I mean, let's say the manager was at the meal, does the manager pay and then submit for his or her manager to approve, or is that not checked separately?"

"No. We never check for that. That's too complicated!"

"Let me back up a little," said John still using a calm voice trying to keep his questions from unsettling Tony. "How many transactions do you check?"

"Oh, we are very thorough. We look at 100 items, a lot more than the typical 30 to 50 items for other types of testing. We take this really seriously, so we double the sample size!" he said proudly.

"What's the population size?"

"Something like ten thousand."

"Worldwide?"

"Oh no. This is the annual US audit. Foreign locations are done every two years when we travel to the locations," Tony explained.

"Are those audits done similarly?"

"Yes, we follow the same audit program so we can compare results. That was a strategic decision we made, and the Controller liked it when we proposed it a few years ago."

After a long and deep sigh, John said while shaking his head. "OK. A couple more questions. Would we know if an employee claimed reimbursement for the same expense multiple times?"

After a long pause while he processed the question, Tony replied sheepishly, "I don't think so."

John paused momentarily to let Tony realize the potential abuse this could entail and the fact the audit program did not contemplate this scenario. "I understand. Would we know if several people eating together claimed full reimbursement for the same meal multiple times?"

"Oh," Tony replied with renewed confidence "the expenses would have to be approved by the manager, and the manager would decline any duplicates."

"Unless the manager was in on the deal, or the employees worked for different managers," John said, reducing the strength of that argument.

After another short pause used to drive the message, John continued.

"OK. By now you probably agree with me there are a few additional things we should consider in the audit program. Some are compliance related, some are audit fraud steps, and some are potentially bigger impact items, like preferred vendors. Before we wrap up, let me ask you about the international T&E reviews. Did you say we do those every two years?"

"Yes."

"When is the next one?"

"This year. They should start around the same time. We're getting ready to kick off the UK one soon. Carolina is doing that one."

"OK. Two maybe three questions so I understand better what we do there. One, do those expense reports clearly and consistently show who attended the meal if the person does not work for InSports?"

"Usually. That is required per policy, and we often see a list of names."

"Do the names show what organization the person works for, or is affiliated with?"

"Hmmm," Tony paused to think for a moment. "Not always. I've seen some with and some without."

"I guess that was my second question, so I have one more. Let's make that a good one," John said with a smile to reassure his manager while looking up toward the ceiling. "If I lose my receipt, can I add a statement to the expense report saying so and do managers approve those?"

"Yes, it happens."

"Often?"

"Often."

"And the threshold requiring a receipt, as I recall from reviewing the policy is $100, correct?"

"Correct."

"What's the maximum without a receipt you've seen approved and paid? Roughly."

"The maximum was probably $300."

"How about a series of lower amounts, like let's say three $200 meals on the same expense report?"

Tony was silent for a moment processing the question and its implications in his mind, but silent nonetheless. After a prolonged pause he replied.

"I think I know where you're going with this. We should probably hold off on those audits."

"Yes, we should," replied John.

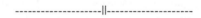

Flying into San Francisco is always a treat. After several hours in flight, two movies, reading, napping, snacking, looking at the diverse landscape below with green expanses, mountain ranges, desserts, rivers and lakes, the plane turns perpendicular to the coastline and approaches the city from the South. John enjoyed seeing the Dumbarton Bridge, San Carlos, Belmont, Foster City, San Mateo, and the San Mateo Hayward Bridge connecting the peninsula to the other side of the bay for the final approach. The windsurfers were out again at the Coyote Point Recreation Area adding even more color to this picturesque city.

Virtually every taxi is a hybrid vehicle in part due to the high gasoline taxes in California, which raises retail prices to one of the highest in the United States. "Steering people's behavior and purchasing choices by changing the price. I believe it's called Price Elasticity of Demand," he thought to himself trying to remember the technical name for something he learned in his economics classes at the university so many years ago.

He exited the plane and skipped the luggage claim area since his practice was to always do carryon. He went straight to the taxi stand and waited in line for a car. He often avoided Uber and Lyft, or at least tried to patronize both taxis and share ride services equally out of solidarity for the traditional taxi service providers. Disruption is a fact of life, but taxi operators had been nearly ruined by the entry of these transportation network companies and the rapid collapse of the value of taxi medallions, aggravated by the fact that many had borrowed to buy the medallions in the first place. He felt it was his way of helping them out and it wasn't going to add much to his travel time or cost anyway.

As the car raced by on the 101 then on Route 80, it wasn't long before he came upon Oracle Park. Too early for a baseball game since it is still winter. "I hope I can catch a game later in the year," he thought. It had been a while since he saw a game there and he wanted to relive the experience of watching the Giants play at home. It was always fun, like most baseball games, with an enthusiastic crowd cheering on their local team. An added bonus, and unique to this stadium, was the evening seagull display. Quite a sight with them flying overhead and making endless turns in the sky as if the birds enjoyed watching the game too. Whether they enjoyed watching the game was up for debate, but there was no doubt they were there for the food. They seem to like it as much as the fans!

The car turned left on 3rd Street and headed North toward Market Street and Downtown. Several streetcars were on Market Street, and it was busy as usual with cars, pedestrians, bicyclists, and skateboarders, all jostling for position to move up, down, and across town. "There are so many pedestrians!" he thought, half of whom were probably tourists.

The driver took several turns and as he got closer to his hotel, he checked the time hoping he would have enough time to go for a walk before dinner. "There's that restaurant near Fisherman's Wharf I would like to go to," he thought. He couldn't wait to get settled in his hotel room, then go for a walk in one of the most walkable cities in the country. After sitting on the plane for five hours, watching the movement and energy on the street made all of those hills very inviting. Going there by foot would provide some healthy exercise with amazing views as he walked across town for dinner.

"Maybe I'll take the Cable Cars on the way back," he thought to himself, "it has been a while since I did that. There are San Francisco visitors who are only tourists, and there are San Francisco visitors who are only workers. I'll be both!"

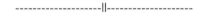

The next morning John got to the InSports San Francisco office early in the morning. Being from the East Coast he had a three-hour advantage, and although jet lag usually didn't affect him too much, he was up early and took advantage of his body clock.

"Good morning, Brian. How are things?"

"Good. Really good."

"What did you do this weekend? Any surfing?"

"Oh yes!" Brian answered immediately with a bright smile on his face. "I went to Ocean Beach with some friends, and we caught some good waves there. It was a lot of fun. The water was cold, but worth it!"

"I can't understand surfing in the winter, but I guess if you can't wait until summer that is one of the best and most accessible beaches near the city, right?"

"Exactly. You are from up North, so you know, there is no bad weather, only bad clothing. Put on a good wetsuit, go with friends, and keep moving!"

"Good for you. Not sure you could convince me to do that, but that's OK. As long as you're safe."

"I am. Always with company."

At this point Miriam joined the meeting via Teams so they proceeded to the review of the workpapers.

They spoke about the IT audit Brian was involved in. It was a carryover from last year, and although it was almost done, there were still a few things to wrap up. They discussed the observations related to change management and how informal the process was, resulting in issues over who requested changes, who approved and implemented those changes, and how those requests were subsequently closed. They also reviewed instances of developers moving their own code to the production environment, and while some organizations had come to treat that as an acceptable practice given limited staff levels and the need for speedy development and systems support, John was concerned about the lack of oversight, review and approval, and compensating controls. In effect, errors could and had been made, and if a developer wanted to do something inappropriate, there were few controls to stop that person.

In terms of logical access security, there were concerns there too. The lack of segregation of duties resulted in user access rights beyond the individuals' job responsibilities giving some people too much access. Upon further discussion, John learned that the change management policy was unclear at several levels, so they rewrote the observations and added a recommendation to review and update the existing policy, and follow those changes with communications, training, and supervision to improve the process.

Since Brian and Miriam identified segregation of duties issues and had a list of employees affected by this, John asked him if that included individuals in Accounts Payable. They reviewed the list and found four names of people still working there, and two additional individuals who had since transferred to Purchasing, another who transferred to Warehousing and the last one worked in Contracting. Brian was surprised by John's concern, highlighting Miriam's previous comment about him having and IT operator's mindset; not yet at IT auditor's mindset.

Another issue involved application controls and the trio spent a considerable amount of time there. As John applied a systematic approach to enquire about inputs, processing, outputs, and the quality of the system's audit trail, he kept finding issues with the existing process, especially related to data input quality. Problems here contaminated other aspects of the process downstream. There were issues with data completeness, accuracy, and even validity.

John was surprised that input controls over data quality were weak, or nonexistent. In several cases, previously existing controls had been turned off. Things like restrictions so only certain date or amount ranges, only numeric entries, or reasonable dates were accepted.

Knowing that input concerns existed prompted John to ask Brian about reporting issues, which he had not done. John explained the concern and the need to examine the underlying programming to ensure reports were complete and accurate.

They agreed on the next steps and Miriam signed off.

"Want to go out for lunch?" asked John since it was almost noon.

"Sure. Where do you want to go?"

"How about Little Italy?"

"Let's do it!" was Brian's enthusiastic response.

--------------------||--------------------

2 The Underperforming Internal Audit Department

"Hello everyone. Happy Monday!"

"Happy Monday," came the sleepy reply from the team.

"A few administrative things to go over. Time off. Please let me know when you plan to take time off so I can factor that into our audit schedule. You are entitled to time off, so take it. All I ask is that you let me know ahead of time.

Training. Let me know what training you would like to attend. I will be meeting with each of you to talk about your interests and skill gaps you would like to work on this year. If there is a training opportunity you would like to take, let me know so we can handle the scheduling and payment for it. I will bring in instructors from time to time, so let me know what training you believe we need, and I'll look at it in relation to skill gaps I notice among the team. I will be talking to Tony and Miriam about this later as well.

Projects. I will be sharing the titles of the audits we plan to perform this year. If there is an audit you have a burning desire to do, let me know and I'll try to get you on it. Given our small size, and your area of expertise, we have little wiggle room, but I'll do what I can to put you on the fun project of your choice."

"We get to choose what audits we want to work on?" asked Rachel.

"Not entirely. If everyone wants the exciting audits, we won't have anyone for the not-so-exciting ones," John said with a smile making the hard point with a bit of humor, "but I would like to balance the need to staff projects between the need and your interests. An important add on is the need to cross train or give some variety. I'm looking at previous audits to see who worked on what, but again, with our small department I can only spread things around so much."

"Tools. If you think we need certain tools, like data analytics software or something like that, let me know so I can look into it. I may not be able to give you everything you want, but I would definitely try to get you what you need to do your jobs. OK?" said John checking for understanding.

Heads were nodding at the directness of his comment and the fact that he was asking for their input over so many things, something historically unusual in this department.

"Getting together. We are a remote team, and we'll remain that way. However, I believe it is important to come together every once in a while to socialize, get trained, brainstorm and get to know each other better. That is part of socializing, but I think of those things slightly differently. Getting to know each other from a work perspective helps us work better with each other remotely. We get to understand each

DOI: 10.1201/9781003322870-2

other's humor, quirks, preferences for work product, and so on. Socializing is like what you're probably already thinking. Having fun. Eating together, maybe a field trip somewhere. Watch a movie. I believe in bonding as a group, so I'll ask you what we should do for work and outside of work when we come together."

"Escape room?" asked Rachel.

"Yes. Escape room works for me," said Carolina.

"Do we run the risk of getting on each other's throats if we can't get out?" Brian asked jokingly.

"Hopefully not. There is always an emergency exit so we'll do that if we must. But I think we'll survive it," said John.

"Do we have to do that?" asked Tony.

"Good question. We don't *have to*, but I would ask that you try some of these group activities. It is not just for fun or for work. I would also like you to think of some of these things as opportunities for you to get to know yourselves better too. How do you handle stress? How do you prioritize? How do you work through situations systematically and so on. If we're going to eat, how do we decide where to go and what food? How do we handle conversations? Now, we're all adults and professionals, but I remember early in my career and how business meetings became an important development thing for the entire team. When we traveled the Controller, CFO, Country Managers took us out to lunch and dinner. We needed to know when to say 'yes', and when to respectfully say 'no'. When to stay for a long lunch, when to put boundaries around where to go for dinner, and how to build relationships without losing your objectivity due to excessive hospitality. And yes, have fun."

"We never went out with your predecessor," confided Rachel.

"How about Tony and Miriam?" asked John.

"No. Never," said Miriam.

Tony merely shook his head also answering in the negative.

"OK. Well, I have a different perspective on this, so let's give that a try. Brian and I had lunch while we were in San Francisco and I think it was an enjoyable meal. Agree Brian?"

"Yes, we went to Little Italy. Talked shop, but also other stuff. It was fun," he replied.

"How often?" asked Caroline.

"I would like to get the team together quarterly, especially the first year, so we get to know each other better and as we introduce changes," answered John.

"Are we going white water rafting?" asked Brian.

"Maybe. On that note. We'll discuss plans as a team so everyone has a say and everyone can participate comfortably. I don't want to do something where anyone is so stressed or uncomfortable that we have the opposite effect. Like I said, let's try a few things, but I'm not going to agree to something so far out that you hate the experience," explained John.

"So, no sky diving?" said Brian.

"Maybe not," replied John.

"Definitely not," said Miriam.

"Where would we meet?" asked Tony.

John replied "Most often in headquarters. In New York, but if we have a project finishing or starting somewhere else, like London or San Francisco, and several of us are already there, we may get the rest of the team there for our get together."

With that answer the team seemed satisfied, and John was relieved that no one asked to meet in Hawaii. So, he continued.

"OK. Moving on. One on one meetings will be weekly. I will contact you to schedule those."

"Let's talk about what you're working on right now. Miriam, let's start with you." After Miriam explained her top tasks for the week, John asked Tony, Brian, Rachel, and Carolina for their respective updates.

--------------------||--------------------

"Hi Rachel," said Tony as he started the Teams meeting.

"Hi Tony," she replied unenthusiastically.

"I'm going to share the draft report so we can review it together," he explained as he looked around his computer screen to enable that functionality.

Before he was done, she said curtly, "I saw your notes and I responded to them already."

"I know, yes, I saw your responses and corrections, but there are still a few things I need to go over with you."

"Fine."

"There are several typos that you missed," he said while moving the document down to find an example, here, "there" and "their." In this sentence it should be "their."

"Any others?"

"Yes, he said again as he scrolled further down in the document. 'Its' without an apostrophe relates to ownership, but in this sentence, you say 'it's' which is an abbreviation for 'it' and 'is'. Since we don't want to use abbreviations in audit reports, it is best to spell it out, 'it is'."

"Got it. Are you done?" She once again said with a tone that was starting to irritate him.

"Yes, there are a few more unfortunately. Close to the end there were another two or three I saw," he said once again as he scrolled down the document, one is excessive wordiness, here. "'Due to the fact that' in your description of the issue could be said as 'because' and below when you were writing the cause of the issue 'one of the main reasons why' could be simply 'one reason'."

Rachel was silent as Tony went over these corrections, but her expression was one of annoyance.

"OK. I'll fix them. Highlight them and I'll change them the way you want them."

"I'm not mentioning these changes to be difficult; it is just a better way to write," Tony explained.

"Yep. Are there any real issues with the report? Substantive things I should fix?"

"No. Not anymore. There were two incorrect figures, but you fixed them, and one of the headings in an exhibit was confusing, but you already fixed that too. The other things you explained and clarified, so this should do it."

"OK. I have to run. Bye."

"Bye," replied Tony as the screen went black. He was trying not to scream at the way Rachel talked to him when he was doing his job and trying to publish a good report. "I don't know how much longer I can take this," he said to himself as he hit the "Leave" button on his screen.

--------------------||--------------------

"Hi Ken, how are things?"

"Good. Good. Keeping the lights on, you know!"

"That's always good, but I hear dark warehouses are quite the thing nowadays and they also save money on electricity bills!" said John jovially.

"True. We keep modernizing our warehouses, so we may very well do something like that soon, but we're not quite there yet. What can I do for you?"

"I'm spending time with the leadership team to get a better sense about your initiatives and how internal audit can better align its work with your priorities. My understanding is that this was not always practiced within internal audit, so we plan to change that."

"That sounds like a good idea, I suppose. I hear auditors like it when people talk about what keeps them up at night, so here are some of my concerns," he said in a business-like tone that suggested he was going to be direct. John was surprised by Ken's sudden willingness to talk, as if he had been waiting for such an opportunity, or perhaps he worked previously at a place where auditors did this habitually, or maybe…" John was about to continue exploring possibilities in his mind when Ken's voice interrupted him.

"We are having some issues with manufacturing quality. Nothing catastrophic, but as we look at trends and patterns, the numbers around waste, yields and rework are moving in the wrong direction, but auditors have never really talked to me about this."

"We're also having some Issues with construction projects," he continued. "I don't know what auditors can do for me but the word around here since I started a couple of years ago is that it is best not to ask Audit. From what I've seen they spend most of their time in the Accounting Department anyway. The truth is we are short staffed and some of the people we have lack some key skills, so we could use help with project management on the construction projects," he explained.

"What kinds of things worry you about the construction projects?" John asked.

Ken went on to explain that construction work was often late, cost over budget and sometimes workmanship issues were a problem, but he attributed this to typical construction project issues. Then he reassured himself and switched to ongoing manufacturing practices in their factories. They needed help with safety and gave several examples. In Thailand, a crane slipped and toppled. Some workers were injured. A digger broke a water main because they didn't check for utility lines beforehand. Compressed gas cylinders were not stored appropriately, so one fell, the cap broke and projectile, but thankfully no one was injured. Three workers had fallen – two on liquid spills and one off a scaffolding – because they were not wearing a harness like they should have been.

He continued.

"I would like some help there with a workplace safety review. Is that something you can do? Because I've been thinking about hiring a consulting firm to do that work for me. And that's just accidents in construction sites and manufacturing. Talk to Andy, he's one of our supply chain managers, we have some issues with safety in Distribution Centers too. Also some issues with stockouts."

"What kind of safety issues there?"

"Forklift and trucking accidents."

"Stockouts? Do you know what's driving them?"

"Probably poor forecasting."

"How about vendor management?"

"Some issues too. Vetting and contracting vendors. Follow through, you know?"

"I understand. Policies and training in place for what they should be doing?"

"Yes, for the most part. But I would appreciate you looking at it. Another pair of eyes, you know? They say the right things when I talk with them and when I go there. But the number and types of problems we're having tell me there's more below the surface."

"OK. Let me look into that and see what we can do."

"You have a small team don't you?"

"I do, we're trying to build it up."

"You might need a few more auditors to cover this company. InSports needs to look and operate with more precision. We're past being a small company. We need better oversight, in my opinion."

"I agree and appreciate the feedback," said John acknowledging that fact.

"I used to work in internal audit at one point, you know?" he admitted.

"You did?"

"Yes. I worked at a regional accounting firm until I got my CPA, then switched to internal audit. It was a lot of fun. I've been in operations for a while now and remember some of the things internal audit can do, but haven't seen it here," he paused for a moment, then added, "yet."

John took that to mean Ken was willing to support him transform the internal audit, and he was grateful for that.

"Thanks, Ken. I appreciate it."

"I need to run, but call me if you need anything. By the way, have you spoken with Brenda in R&D yet? You should. She runs a tight ship over there."

"I will," replied John as he saw Ken's eyes dart back and forth on the camera before the screen went blank.

--------------------||--------------------

John was walking toward the break room looking for some coffee but started thinking that perhaps going outside would be best. The coffee in the office was good, but he wanted something different and by going outside he would force himself to walk a little. As he waited for the elevator to arrive, he saw a young man holding a refillable coffee mug with the logo of a coffee shop.

"Where is…" as he leaned in to read the name on the mug.

"Sunflower Coffee House?" replied the young man turning the mug around for John to read it more easily.

"Yes, Sunflower Coffee House. Are they around here?"

"Yes, in fact I'm going there now. They're around the corner and they have something like 50 varieties of coffee to choose from around the world. Great place!" he said enthusiastically.

"Well, I'm looking for a cup of coffee; do you mind if I go with you?"

"Sure! No problem!" he replied as the elevator arrived.

When they got into the elevator John spoke first. "I'm John," he said introducing himself and waving in a way that had now become the common replacement for a handshake.

"I'm Randall. I go by Randy. I work in QA making sure our equipment works when it is supposed to."

"I like your description of your role. Short and clear."

"Thanks. That's my elevator pitch. Glad you liked it."

As they walked out onto the street and toward the coffee shop, Randy explained how he had been with the company for several years and was finding his role more difficult due to mounting quality problems. He was very forthcoming with his comments and examples, and John decided he should tell him about his role in the company lest Randy found out later and thought he withheld such an important detail.

"Just to be transparent; I work in internal audit," said John.

"Oh, OK. Good for you. We need more auditors around here."

"I'm the chief audit officer."

"Even better. You need more staff," said Randy, once again, readily sharing his thoughts. "I worked for a company where audit actually helped. They were tough, but their reports were helpful. And I don't only mean internal audit, where you are, but compliance, QA, all of them. It looks like that's not a big focus here," he said in an unusual display of candor for a new acquaintance.

"I see."

As they walked through the door of the coffee shop, John could smell the sweet aroma of coffee and a list of options that covered the larger portion of a wall. It was written on a chalkboard, which was probably done for ease so they could add and remove items easily.

"Over there on the left are the new arrivals and in the middle you find the regular items," said Randy pointing to the menu as he spoke. "To the right are decaf and chocolate, and way over there are pastries and desserts. When ready you order over there," said Randy as he started walking toward the Order counter.

As John scanned the menu trying not to get lost in the multitude of choices, he was simultaneously processing what Randy had said so far. He wanted to order quickly so he could catch up with him while he was still talkative just in case he decided to turn quiet. He decided to go with a Jamaican Blue Mountain coffee and two pastries.

By the time John got in line Randy was already at the door waiting for him. "Good, he is waiting for me," thought John.

"Thank you for the tip. Quite a place you have here," said John as they met at the sidewalk for their walk back to the office.

"I've been coming here for a while and if you're going to be here often you should get a mug. Refills are discounted and if you're on the rewards program you get free coffee after 10 cups. Worth your while."

"Loyalty is rewarded," said John.

"Exactly."

"I got two turnovers, one apple, one raspberry. Which one would you like?"

"You didn't have to do that, but if you're offering, I'll take the raspberry," said Randy, and John handed him one of the bags.

"You were saying that audit has apparently not been as much of a focus as it should be?"

"Oh, yes. We were talking about that. That's right. QA suffers when inputs and the production process are unreliable. We have shifted to low-cost providers to save money, and rushed to manufacture before everything was in place, so we've had an increase in QA problems."

"Warranty claims?"

"Warranty claims, repairs, complaints, give me my money back, all of that."

"Are these issues getting escalated for correction?" asked John.

"Oh yes. We have no shortage of reports. We talk about them every month, but things don't change. We also have some mistakes on the reports, which is another issue altogether," he explained.

As they walked into the building's lobby, they reached for their badges to wand their way through the turnstiles.

"When are you going to visit Argentina?" asked Randy using a very informal tone probably not meaning John personally when he said "you," but internal audit.

"I'm preparing our audit plan, but even after it is done, I want us to be flexible enough to adapt and go anywhere we need to go."

"Good. It would probably be good to go there," said Randy as he pressed the buttons to call for an elevator. "And it is summertime in South America," he said as the doors opened and they walked into the elevator.

They were joined by a couple of people as the doors closed and the conversation ended as everyone turned their attention to the little TV monitor in the upper corner displaying weather, news, stock market information and an ad encouraging people to go to Puerto Rico on vacation.

--------------------||--------------------

"Hi Nihal, how are things?"

"Nice to meet you. We're doing OK. Lots of work these days with our tech stack. Technology is always changing so always something to upgrade, add, and sometimes retire. How can I help you?" he replied pleasantly.

"Nice to meet you too. I am getting acquainted with dynamics within InSports and technology is obviously pivotal to everything we do. That said, I need to better understand some of our tech priorities and ways that I can support your goals and our strategic direction."

"Sure. Well. Let me give you a little context here. I've been in this role for five years, which is an eternity for CTOs, but my job has changed almost every three months. We're on a rollercoaster as the company grows and technology changes, but we've also had some turnover issues."

"Have you had a chance to work with audit during all of these changes?"

"Yes and no," he said with a head bobble. "Over the past five years all I get from audit are forms to fill out. Auditors have mostly only asked me to fill out forms, but they don't seem to test much. The forms ask about protecting our hardware so that only authorized personnel have physical access to it, intervals for requiring password resets, backup procedures whether we do them at the few data centers remaining or by contractual obligation with cloud providers, if we have reviewed our policies and procedures in the last year and things like that. I've come to think of them as more of a formality that they go through once or twice a year."

"I understand. Those are standard general IT controls. Have they been following up on your responses?"

"No, not really. I would have asked me some follow-up questions, quite honestly, but I don't get much of that. Or any of that."

"I see. What else?"

"That's just the paperwork part of it and it is something I know I'm going to get around January and June or July every year. What I could use help with is IT project management. We have some big projects coming online as part of our DevSecOps initiatives where we have tight deadlines and some big budget implications, and it would be good to have someone make sure we are OK before we spend a lot of money. Most people don't want auditors looking over their shoulders, but there is too much money on the line and I would rather have the auditors check things out first before something happens and I have Ron asking me about it."

"We've released several systems lately. Did audit do what you just said in terms of financial and operational controls for those projects?"

"No. Bonnie, who works here with me asked me about three transactions last year or the year before because those payments came up during an AP audit. We gave the auditors the information and they were gone as quietly as they came."

"So you could use some support for project management?"

"Yes, but not about the technical aspect of project management. I have good IT brainpower. I'm talking about culture, documentation, collaboration, communication, soft skills. Like I said, we've had some turnover issues and onboarding is still a work in progress, but you know what, I suppose auditors don't look into those things. Maybe I should be talking to HR about that?"

"Not necessarily. I mean, talk to HR, but we can also help with soft skills and communication. I'm still building my team, so I need to look into fitting that into our plan, but yes, internal auditors do that."

As Nihal shook his head as a sign that he was processing that piece of information, he said, "well, ITIL covers all of that, so there are crossover points between various frameworks, management tools, and what you and I do."

"Exactly. Our approach is risk-based so there are risks associated with people and their interactions. Not only about the technology and whether it is working or not working, the payment of bills, and so on."

"I understand. The risk-based approach argument is not new to me. What is new is auditors doing things differently. Like I said, I've been getting forms to fill out for five years. The same forms, mind you. So, I could copy paste my answers and they probably wouldn't have noticed. I don't do that," he said showing and exposing both palms as he smiled, "but you understand my point."

"Of course," said John, also smiling. "We're going to make some changes in our approach. We are implementing an objectives and risk-based approach to better align what we do with your priorities."

"Miriam is a good auditor," he said with a head bobble again. "We have spoken a few times, but I always felt like she could, and wanted to do more, but she was being held back."

"Yes, she is good."

"She is really good," now shaking his head up and down in a "yes" motion. "Like I said, auditors didn't go much past the forms they sent, but even the few times Miriam and I spoke I could tell that she had some good ideas and things she would like to work on, but was not at liberty to take those ideas further. I was tempted to poach her from audit you know!"

"Excuse me?" said John raising his eyebrows to reciprocate the challenge implied in Nihal's statement.

"You heard me. If you don't take good care of her, I may bring her over here. We are short staffed!" he said with a light tone while indicating the deep respect he had for Miriam.

"So am I. I guess I better keep an eye on you and treat my people well."

"You do that. Now, I don't want crazy audits. I need audits that support what we're trying to do and helps us avoid problems. Miriam has the right ideas from what I can tell. If she is willing to act on that approach, send her over here and we can figure out some things that need to be fixed in our projects."

"I'll do that. Thanks Nihal. I appreciate your time and candor. Even if you try to grab the few people I have."

"I'll let you keep her ... out of common courtesy... but watch out. I'm always fishing..."

"See you later."

"Talk to you later."

--------------------||--------------------

"Hello everyone. Happy Monday. Did anyone do anything fun this weekend?" said John kicking the weekly team meeting into gear.

"Mostly cooking and eating," said Rachel.

"I went on a hike," said Miriam.

"I watched football most of the weekend," said Brian.

"Not much. Mostly slept," said Carolina with a shoulder shrug and in a dismissive tone, then in a more animated way added, "can we go back to cooking and eating? What did you cook Rachel?"

"I made some hominy for breakfast Saturday, which is made with evaporated milk, condensed milk, coconut milk, vanilla, and nutmeg. Then I made some rice and beans in my slow cooker. That has coconut milk, thyme, and other spices," she shared.

"Did you cook chicken with the rice and beans?" asked Miriam.

"Yes, jerk chicken. It came out really good!" she said proudly.

"It sounds like the perfect Caribbean dish!" Miriam added.

"Do we have a chef on the team?" asked John rounding out the conversation. "It sounds that way to me," he said with a congratulatory air verbalizing what he thought the rest of the team might be thinking.

"We certainly do. Before we had to start working from home due to COVID she brought food into the office all the time. That is one of the things I miss the most about being remote," confessed Miriam.

"Second that," said Rachel.

"Yes, the pandemic changed so many things about the way we interact and the things that brought us together. On that note, I wanted to share a thought with the team. How about we roll out a book club? It would be a way to do something together as a team even if we're remote."

"Interesting," said Miriam. "What types of books would we read?"

"I'm thinking we would vary the list. Sometimes business related, sometimes more literary. Self-help or personal improvement?"

"Just for fun?" asked Brian.

"It is always just for fun," said John, "but if you mean like light, beach reading, we could slide in a couple of those too … sporadically. In general, lest we get carried away or miss the big picture, the idea is to do something together as a team, but we should think about topics of interest, another way of training and developing ourselves. Two criteria, relevant and engaging."

"How many pages?" asked Brian again. "I'm not a big reader. Sorry."

"That's OK, John said in a reassuring tone. We should look for books that we can break into chapters or segments because they might be easier to discuss and you," he said making a circular motion with his hands to indicate the collective "you" and not just Brian who asked the question, "can jump in and out as your availability permits."

"Shakespeare?" asked Tony.

"I'm thinking not," said John.

"Thank you!" said Rachel. "Shakespeare? Really?"

"While I like Shakespeare, and recommend you read his work if you haven't or if it has been a while, for our book club we should probably stick with some lighter reading," explained John.

"How much time to read each book?" asked Brian again.

"Good question. How about a month each? This would keep Brian from suggesting War and Peace or Don Quixote," John said jokingly. "But here's an idea so we don't have to wait a full month to talk about the books, how about we have a Teams or Slack channel where we post discussion questions or if there is a nagging question or observation you can't wait to share? Also, we can post links to the author's TED talks or interviews if those are available."

"I like that," said Brian, suddenly sounding interested.

"Good. I think this could be fun. I'll facilitate the first two or three meetings, then we'll rotate the role of facilitator. We'll set up a schedule for the entire year, so you know when your turn is coming up and for you to prepare. Also, we should agree on the books a month in advance so everyone can get a copy."

John continued. "Since some of you may be wondering, I'll go ahead and say it now. Participation is not mandatory. I would like everyone to participate for the reasons I mentioned earlier, but you are not being forced to join. I believe it will be worth your while at several levels, and we'll be having fun, so perhaps you don't want to be left out," he said with a suggestive rising of his eyebrows, which the team was starting to understand meant the sincerity of his words and the determination to move ideas from words to action.

--------------------||--------------------

As Dan came online, John immediately noticed he had a worried expression on his face. Or maybe he was simply stressed. Either way, he looked tense. John also noticed some of the knick knacks on the shelves behind him. There were the three see no evil, hear no evil, say no evil monkeys, which he thought was an interesting choice for a controller. Maybe he was reading too much into that. One shelf below that were two balls.

"Hi Dan, how are things these days? Is that a cricket ball?"

Dan started speaking almost before John was done introducing himself "things are OK. Chugging along," he seemed to have heard the latter part of the statement because he seemed to break into a smile as he turned to look over his left shoulder.

"Yes, that's a cricket ball. I lived abroad for a while and learned to play. Good way to make friends and a good alternative to baseball I suppose. Did you know that approximately 500 million people follow baseball?" and before John could answer he continued, "but there are more than 2 billion people who follow cricket! Crazy, isn't it?"

"It is. I can't keep up with all the rules, especially the scoring, but I sometimes watch it on TV. Not much coverage in the US, unfortunately."

"I know. It's a shame, but things are getting better. You can stream matches online and watch on cable. There are live games too depending on where you live." By now Dan was quite animated and relaxed. He was now describing the cricket league in the New York area and the US tournaments. As he was talking about the international world cup and world Test championships, he realized that he was monopolizing the conversation.

"Wow, got carried away there. Next time you are in town we can talk more about this. What can I do for you?"

"No problem," said John reassuringly, having succeeded in building a connection with Dan at a social level. "I wanted to introduce myself, but also to talk about your initiatives and how audit has worked with you in the past."

"I worked with Nick, and he kept reviewing payroll, T&E, AR and AP. There were never any significant findings. We could have used a little more help with cost accounting and why departments submitting invoices for payment were doing so incorrectly. A common problem here is departments charging to the wrong cost center, which drives my team crazy. With AP, why is it that Operations isn't creating POs and putting in requisitions so when invoices arrive my team has to chase people around the company for the corresponding PO before payment? You know what the result is? We can't take discounts! Vendors are unhappy and yell at my team! Why are there so many vendors so that similar items cost different amounts? I told you about the need to manage our costs, right? But audit claimed, when I brought those things up, that those were operational considerations and they couldn't look into those things because of their independence mandate. I hated that. Also, the numbers out of Argentina seem out of whack. Lots of losses, but management attributes them to their slow start since they opened their facilities last year, so startup costs and inefficiencies. We need someone to look more closely at things there." Then he stopped suddenly realizing again that he had monopolized the conversation.

"It looks like there are a few things we can partner on. My approach is collaborative and you are describing what I was going to ask you next, what are your priorities and concerns. So, I took notes while you were talking. I'll go over those and circle back with you in a few days. Sounds good?"

"Yes, sure. Any time, bye" he said looking as tense as he was when he first joined the call as he logged out of the meeting.

"Wow," John said to himself. "It is going to be interesting working with the team there," as he logged himself out of the meeting.

---------------------||---------------------

John started the meeting and noticed he was the first person in the room. While he waited for the rest of the team to join, he noticed that a new Teams message arrived.

"Can we meet to talk about the AP audit? Matt is asking questions about the audit report."

"Put a meeting on my calendar," he replied.

A thumbs-up emoji appeared next to his message.

"Hi John," said Tony joining the call.

"Hi, how are things in New York?"

"Good. No complaints."

"Is Rachel joining us?"

"Let me ping her." After a brief pause. "I just messaged her. Ah, she said she's running late from her previous meeting and will be here shortly."

"OK. Thanks. So, did you tell her why we're having this meeting?"

"Yes, I explained to her that we were going to revisit the T&E audit program and" as he was still in mid-sentence, Rachel appeared on screen.

"Hi, sorry I'm late. My previous meeting ran a little longer than anticipated. Matt in AP is driving me crazy. He just keeps asking questions about things we already discussed."

"Did you discuss these things during fieldwork?" asked John.

"Yes, he agreed they were issues. I just sent the meeting invitation and agenda for the exit meeting, and he is now asking all these questions. He even wants to see the workpapers."

"We should have them sign off on every finding when we discuss with them," offered Tony.

"Is this new or has he always been like this?" asked John.

"More so recently. He was OK and then last year he flipped on us and now he questions everything we do."

"Did something happen to make him change his attitude towards us?" asked John.

"Do you want to tell him or should I?", asked Rachel.

"You tell him," replied Tony.

"OK. Well last year we had an auditor who has since left. He told us he briefed Matt on issues before the exit meeting, but didn't. At least not all the issues. We went to the exit meeting, and it was nothing short of fireworks in there. It was a mess. Lots of arguing about what we did and who we talked to. They questioned our data, our methodology, our results, the conclusion. Everything! He questions everything we did!" Rachel said with very vivid hand motions. "It was terrible, and he was terrible!"

"Was he right?" John asked, which caused the conversation to take a sudden pause. Tony and Rachel seemed surprised, if not a bit embarrassed by the question. Tony spoke first.

"He did not want to listen to us even though we tried to explain our methodology and that we were right."

"Was he right?" John asked again.

Tony spoke again. "I guess so, but he should not have talked to us like that in front of the Controller!"

"That sounds like a lack of professionalism, and we can address that separately. Let's stay with the quality of our work," replied John. "And the report?"

"Yeah, the report," Rachel jumped back into the conversation. "We probably re-wrote that draft 20 times. It took us months to finish it."

"Why so many re-writes?" John asked again,

"Well, there were some mistakes," acknowledged Tony. "But they weren't our fault."

"So, we made mistakes not keeping him in the loop during fieldwork and going to the Exit with surprises, that were incorrect after all. Then the draft report also mis-stated conditions and had to be corrected after long deliberations. Did I summarize what happened correctly?" asked John.

After a pause Tony spoke again.

"But it was not our fault" Tony stated holding his ground. Larry didn't manage the audit and then he left us holding the bag. Why are we now having to clean up his mess?"

"Not the way we want things to work out, but it is what it is. We need to make it right now. It is up to us. So, were you just talking with him now before this meeting?"

"Yes, we were editing version 50 of the draft report!" We've been in the Reporting phase for months trying to get that report out."

"I thought you said you were up to version 20. Now they're 50?

"20. 50, It could be 100 for all I know. I just don't know how much longer I can work with him. He questions everything!"

"Understood. I hear what you're saying, but we can't blame him for everything, right? We messed up. We now need to fix this. I need to talk with him anyway. I believe I have a meeting with him later this week, so I'll see what I can do, but in general, we need to rebuild our trust. If you were in Matt's shoes, and the people auditing you did this, wouldn't you be upset too?"

John then moved the topic of the meeting to T&E.

"Tony and I were reviewing the T&E audit program and I thought we should revisit it. I understand it was agreed upon a while ago and we have been using it ever since. Is that right?"

"Yes, the Controller signed off on it and that's what we use. It works well. It's a good program!"

"To some extent," said John refuting Tony's assessment of the quality of the audit program, while Rachel remained silent. "There are a few additional things we should consider doing that would give us better insights about that process. Let's start by breaking it down into strategic, compliance, and operational objectives, and risks. Can I see the risk and controls matrix for this audit?"

"The silence and blank stares John witnessed told him there was much work to be done."

"We don't create one for this audit because we already have a work program. We just follow it," explained Tony.

"We should anyway, because conditions can, and often, do change, even for the same process from one year to the next. A risk could be low one year and increase the next, so it is an important exercise. So, can one of you please open a blank RCM template and we'll start creating one together," John asked.

While Rachel searched for a blank template, John added, "and we should be discussing the RCM with the process owner, so they have input into this," which resulted in Rachel, who was searching for the template, to freeze temporarily and blink in rapid succession, while Tony's eyebrows rose so high John thought they might touch his hairline. Their body language told John that collaboration was another practice he would need to foment in the unit.

After a moment, Rachel informed everyone she was ready and proceeded to share her screen.

"Good, let's begin with the objectives. What would you say the T&E process is supposed to achieve? What would constitute success?"

"They meet the T&E policy," said Tony immediately.

"Yes, that's good, but we may want to be a little more specific because we need to identify some risks that jeopardize their achievement of that objective, so saying they meet the objective is a little vague. What do you think would be a more specific objective?"

Tony shared his idea "They perform reconciliations monthly. That is something they are supposed to do."

"OK, yes, they're supposed to do that monthly, but that reads more like a control," replied John. "Other ideas?"

"They only pay for legitimate business expenses," said Rachel.

"Yes. That's something they should be aiming for. Exactly. They only pay for legitimate business expenses. Go ahead and write that down."

John continued, "What type, or category of objective would you say that represents?"

"Compliance," said Tony.

"Financial reporting. Only appropriate transactions are processed and those will flow to our financial reports so we have integrity there," said Rachel.

"We could argue it meets both, so let's go with that for now." As John waited for Rachel, who was acting as notetaker to type the information in the RCM, he was making a mental note about their demeanor during the exercise. Rachel seemed to be enjoying this and her body language was relaxed and engaged. Tony, on the other hand, acted as if this was unnecessary and he was an unwilling participant.

"Let's do three for now, then I'll have you work on your own. What would be a second objective?"

"They process transactions promptly," said Rachel.

"That's a good one. Speed is important."

"Do we need to indicate what 'promptly' means?" asked Rachel furthering the conversation.

"Do you mean units of time, like pay within 5 business days?" asked John for clarification.

"Yes."

"We could but I don't believe that is necessary. The objective can be a bit broad at this point. We can find out later, when we get to the controls, what standards they have in place and make a note of the number of days they are aiming for," John explained.

"OK."

"How about a third objective?" asked John continuing the exercise and helping them gain familiarity with the methodology he wanted them to adopt.

"Payments are reflected accurately in the financial statements," said Tony now joining into the exercise.

"Internal or external financial statements?" asked John, which gave him pause because he wasn't expecting that question.

"I don't know. External? Wait, we also produce internal financial statements, so I guess both."

"Right. Yes, both types," said John as he repeated Tony's objectives for confirmation and prompting Rachel to write down the answer.

"Good! OK. Now let's think of a risk for each objective. Again, this is just so you get started, but we should think about a couple more risks to fill this out. So, the first objective was that they only pay for legitimate expenses," he repeated to refresh their memory. "What could go wrong that impedes their ability to achieve this objective?"

They spent a few moments identifying the risks and talking about the risk level they should assign to each of them, discussing the probability, then the impact. "At some point we may want to also consider velocity and persistence, but for now, let's focus on probability and impact. How likely is it that this would happen?"

As they discussed likelihood and impact, they also spoke about the need to clarify the three levels attributed to each and John's desire to increase that to five levels.

"It looks like we need to document our expanded definitions because the existing descriptions were too vague," said John. "I'll expand on those and add it to the template for future use."

"Thanks. That would be very helpful. We should also describe in more detail what Strategic, Compliance and Operational mean," John added. "Another thing. We should add a couple more categories to the template. I believe IT should be there. It is important and will continue to be so in the future. Any other categories come to mind?" he asked encouraging them to think further on the subject.

"Cybersecurity?" said Rachel.

"That is important and we could. Let's make a note of it, but for simplicity we can leave it within IT. But good point and important that we always remember cyber as we look at risk. Any others? I'm thinking about acts characterized by deceit, concealment, or violation of trust that is done by individuals or organizations to secure an advantage."

Neither one of them responded as they were still processing the clues.

"Required by the IIA."

"Are you referring to fraud?"

"Exactly! We should evaluate the risk of fraud and how the organization manages that risk. If we don't have it as a category, we might forget to do it. For example, we're talking about T&E, where fraud can occur, and unfortunately, often does.

So, by putting a fraud category at the top it would remind us to include fraud-related risks."

"So should we add one now?" asked Rachel.

"Yes. What do you think could happen in the form of fraud?" John asked, encouraging further exploration.

"During the last meeting you asked what if several people expensed the same meal" shared Tony.

"That's a good one, not only because it was my idea," John replied playfully, getting some smiles in return from his staff, who were now more relaxed and seemed to be enjoying the exercise.

"Yes, let's write that down. It is an OK idea, but it will do for now," said Rachel sharing in the good humor, as they continued filling out the RCM.

--------------------||--------------------

"How is the AR audit coming along?"

"It's coming."

"What's wrong?"

"We're not getting the information we need. They are stonewalling so every request takes a long time, and when we get something from them it might be a question asking for clarification or the wrong stuff."

"Is this new or have they always been like that?"

"They've always been like that. We audit them every year, so I don't understand why they can't just send us the information like they're supposed to. They should know by now that when Audit asks for something they should provide it immediately!"

"OK. That's true. But aren't they the same people who have a huge work backlog and are now working with a new computer system?"

"Yes, but..."

"I also heard they have been dealing with some turnover issues. Is that right?"

"Yes, but, that's their problem. We tell them we are going to do an audit. Annually, I must add. And it is pretty much the same reports, documents, and data. Why can't they just do it?"

"Have you tried getting some of it yourself?"

"Not my job."

"What do you mean it is not your job?"

"It is not my job. We audit them. They are the keepers and owners of the information. It is not OK for me to go around getting information that they should be providing us. Independence. Separation of duties. All of that!"

"I understand, Tony, but we also need to understand their situation. Do you think they don't provide the information right away because they don't want to or because they can't get to it?"

"I don't believe it matters. They should fix their processes so they can get these things done. Not my job to fix their problems, or in this case, pull the information we need for an audit."

"What do you believe we should do?"

"Write them up! I think this qualifies as a scope limitation!"

"Let's think about this for a moment before we talk about writing them up for anything. Just so I understand. You haven't offered to get any of the needed information yourself. Is that correct?"

"That's right, I shouldn't have to."

"I hear you. Do you know where some of the necessary information may be located?"

"Some of it, but I don't have access to it."

"Policies and procedures are in a shared drive, right? You should have access to those."

"Well, yes, but…"

"Are any of the data or reports we need available by running queries ourselves, or by working with IT?"

"Yes, I guess so."

"Good. For stored images, where are they stored?"

"In SalesForce, but that means I have to pull it myself."

"Who can help you expedite that process? Anyone in the department or in IT?"

"I guess there are some people there that can get that."

"What else do you need?"

"List of transactions and authorization limits. But I don't know what parameters to use."

"I believe we already defined, communicated, and agreed with the client what the scope for the audit was, and the location and specific query details should be similar to what was done previously, so the prior year workpapers should have that. I believe you did the audit last year, so that shouldn't be too much of a problem, right?"

"Yes, but that's me digging around and rounding up different people to do what is rightfully the client's job. That's why it is called IPE, Information Provided by Entity!, or client, in this case."

"I understand, but we can help them given the issues they're experiencing. What if you tell the main contact there what you are going to do and have them agree to it so there are no questions about the type and manner of getting the information."

"OK," Tony said reluctantly.

"Good. I understand this is not standard procedure and not what you, or we, are accustomed to do, but given the circumstances we should meet them halfway. We can, and should, try to help them out."

"I guess so. I think they're holding out, but I'll do what you ask."

"Thanks."

"No problem. Are we all set?" Tony asked attempting to exit the meeting.

"Yes, we're done. Let me know how it goes. Bye," said John.

With that, Tony clicked the Leave button and put an end to what was a testy exchange.

"Wow," John sighed while shaking his head in disbelief. "So much for customer service. We have some work to do here," he thought as he made a note to include an agenda item about the role of internal audit at the next staff meeting.

--------------------||--------------------

"Hello. This is Frank," said the voice on the phone with a cadence that made him sound pensive, as if he were being interrupted from a deep thought or perhaps just being awakened from a nap.

"Hi Frank," said John returning the greeting. "Hope I'm not bothering you."

"No, no."

"How are you today?" asked John, starting the conversation with some pleasantries.

"I'm doing well. Working on a 1,000-piece jigsaw puzzle. Too much sky, John, too much sky. I have 999 blue pieces to work with!" Frank responded jokingly.

"Start around the edges, that's what I've been told."

"I'll keep that in mind. How are things at InSports?"

"Well, I'm trying to figure out some puzzle pieces of my own over here. The budget is low, staffing is limited, and public opinion is not all that favorable."

"For how long has this been going on?"

"Apparently for several years. Well, decreasing over a number of years to the very thin resources we have available today."

"How many FTEs do you have?"

"Six, including me."

"And in your view that is not enough to cover InSports?"

"Right."

"Why do you think that's the case?"

"The low regard or the low resources?"

"Both. One may be causing the other."

"I believe the low regard for internal audit is a big factor here. They don't see it as much of a value-adding unit within the organization."

"I see. And what about the people, your staff, what have they been working on the past couple of years?"

"Typical AP, AR, T&E, payroll. Mostly focusing on compliance."

"How effective are they doing these projects? Before you answer, you understand I mean how much value are they demonstrating with these audits?"

"Not that much. I reviewed the audit reports for the past couple of years and nothing significantly being reported. Softball issues."

"Have they exhausted all the low-hanging-fruit topics and issues in those areas?"

"I wouldn't say so. They repeat the same audits and repeat the audit procedures, so not finding much of anything really."

"SALY, eh?"

"Sallie, like the mortgage company?"

"No, S.A.L.Y, same as last year."

"Oh, yes."

"Maybe even jelly."

"What? Jelly? What's that?"

"Just Exactly Like Last Year," Frank explained laughing. Sorry. I couldn't help myself. I know this is stressful for you, but I hope you forgive my humor."

"I understand. I don't mind. You taught me the importance of humor when things are tense. I probably need to laugh a bit more myself. So, are you saying that the problem is audit doing the same-old reviews year after year?"

"In part. I think there is a more fundamental problem and what you are telling me are symptoms, or at the very least, downstream manifestations of the bigger issue at the source."

"What's that?"

"Tell me about the risk assessment they have been performing the past five years."

"Funny thing you ask, because I looked at them and they are relatively simplistic and did not include all the stakeholders I was expecting to see engaged when those risk assessments were being conducted."

"Go on."

"Yes, so only a handful of people, and mostly in Accounting and Finance. The Controller for example. But mostly prepared by the audit director with limited involvement of the audit managers."

"Were they all accountants?"

"Yes."

"So, they were probably working in an echo chamber. All of them thinking about accounting and financial reporting risks and auditing what they were familiar with. What about the measurement or rating of the risks?"

"Those were relatively simplistic too – a 3x3 matrix without very clear or detailed descriptions of each rating score on the scale."

"I wouldn't imagine they were very quantitative."

"No. Mostly subjective."

"OK. I think we can see the source of the problem."

"The risk assessment?"

"That is a part of it, but there are aspects of risk assessments that auditors often ignore to their detriment. They need to start at the beginning. At the top, if you will."

"Like what?"

Silence

"Frank? Are you there?"

"John, can you hear me?"

"Yes, can you hear me?"

"I can't hear you. John. Hello? John?" and with that the call ended abruptly.

"Call Lost" was the message on display on John's phone. He called back twice trying to connect, but instead heard Frank's voice inviting him to leave a voicemail message.

"We lost the call, Frank. I'll try back another time. Thanks for chatting with me. Good luck finishing the puzzle," was the message John left for Frank.

John wondered what "at the beginning" or "at the top" meant. He would have to figure that out himself for now.

--------------------||--------------------

"I don't like him either," said Rachel.

"Hi everyone! What am I walking into today?" said John as he joined the meeting.

"It's Sam in IT, again. Every time we send a data or document request, we either get the wrong information back or a question for clarification."

"That's not a new person we work with over in IT, is it?" asked John.

"That's the thing. No, we have been working with him for years and it is almost always the same problem. 'What do you mean by ...', or 'How do you want that exported', or 'By when do you need this?', I mean, stalling, stalling every time. I'm so sick of him!" she said while holding her fists up in the air and clenching her lips.

John thought to himself, "this sounds like the problem we're having with Nancy in AR, now it is IT."

"OK, let's slow it down a little. I can see we are frustrated with IT about the request, so let's think this through," suggested John as he tried to mediate the situation and find a possible solution to this new revelation. "Root cause analysis, right? We have heard that expression before, so let's apply the technique here," he said.

"Why are they responding the way they do?" asked Miriam.

"They are lazy," responded Brian immediately.

"That could be a reason, but reports I've seen and heard from the management team is that they have a very long list of action items. Is the long list of action items believable?" asked John.

"I think it is," replied Tony providing support for the thought and a bit of defense of the IT department. "Systems are breaking down all the time and they have process problems over there. Just about everyone in the company agrees that they are under-staffed and overworked," he said.

"OK, so it looks like they are overworked. Any other possible reasons for their behavior? Any thoughts?" asked John again.

No one said anything, so John shared another thought for their consideration. "How do we request things from IT?"

"E-mail, like everything else," replied Brian. "I'm assuming they can read," he said still furious and not trying to hide it.

John chose to ignore the sarcasm and continued. "Do we follow up that e-mail with a phone call, or better yet, have a meeting or call with, what's his name, Sam? To explain what we need, when, why, and how it should look when returned to us?" John asked.

"Kind of. We write a comprehensive e-mail with all the details, so we give them the what, and how for sure. Besides, we need to document the request, so we have a record of it," said Miriam. "That's how we know who is not responding and how long it takes them to act. I have to say, I don't understand why they can't read the e-mail and follow the instructions. It's all there!"

John took a few seconds to process what he was hearing, and was a bit perturbed by it. "Could it be that with all they have going on, a very lengthy e-mail may not be serving its intended purpose? Maybe they're not understanding the questions. Perhaps a legitimate gap in understanding what we need?"

Miriam's facial expression changed to one of surprise, or perhaps it was recognition. She seemed to have gotten the message right away and realized the merits of the comment. Tony and Brian were silent; apparently surprised by the idea.

"Let's try having a request meeting with Sam to explain what we are asking for. That way you can talk it through. Go over the list of items you are requesting so you can check for understanding. It often takes less time to talk through the request than it is to write it all down anyway. Which begs a question. How long does it usually take to write these comprehensive request e-mails, anyway?" John asked his team.

The group remained silent, now contemplating the benefits of this new approach, and a bit embarrassed by the amount of time and effort they had been putting into these lengthy e-mail requests.

"Maybe a couple of hours," said Brian sheepishly.

"A couple of hours as in two or a couple as in several," said John with a smile trying to soften the tense climate that had been building up to this point.

"Several" clarified Tony. "We work really hard to write a comprehensive e-mail so, yes, it eats up a big chunk of a day just to do this so that's why we're so frustrated by this."

"I've been there. Your frustration is understandable but continuing to do the same is probably not our best solution. Set up a meeting with Sam to talk it over, and let's see what comes of it. OK?" instructed John, turning the situation into a call for action. "Let me know how it goes."

"OK" said Miriam. "By the way, writing a comprehensive data and document request has been our required procedure, but having a call makes sense. I'll set it up and invite you, Tony and Brian because we're working on the audit together. You can come or not," referring to John, "but so you have the choice and you know I'm handling it."

"Sounds good. Thanks" replied John.

"Now to our regularly scheduled programming" said John as he turned the group's attention to the staff meeting that was the original reason they were there."

--------------------||--------------------

As John walked through the woods, he kept thinking about Frank's words, "At the beginning," "At the top." What did he mean by that? The board? Maybe, but that's to be expected. The external auditors also ask the board for their thoughts on financial risks for the preparation of the financial statements. Maybe he meant that.

As he walked a bit further up the trail, he noticed there were a few rain dark clouds building in the horizon, but overhead the sky was blue with a few scattered white clouds. There were patches of snow on the ground, but this winter did not have a lot of snow to speak of. Too bad. He enjoyed cross-country skiing, or Nordic skiing as was sometimes referred to, so a good snowstorm made it easier to get to the woods, put on his skis and go. With so little snow accumulation he would have to either go to a golf course where they made snow or a long drive to the nearest mountains. "I remember when snow was abundant and predictable," he thought to himself and as he was reminiscing about those days another thought came to him.

Maybe the operational objectives. Well-prepared risk assessments should begin with the business objectives for the area being reviewed. We spoke about the risk assessments focusing on accounting and finance, and they were talking to the people most experienced in those topics. In this case, the Controller, so that may or may not be it either.

"Come!" John called his dog who had wandered off a bit and was almost out of sight. She came back running happily to his side expecting a treat for doing as told, but then quickly turned and continued sniffing and enjoying the adventure.

The risks that jeopardize the achievement of objectives. Maybe other types of risks, so beyond operational and financial, maybe looking at IT and fraud risks in more detail and with more emphasis. As he thought about this some more, he stopped and looked through the trees at the river down the hill, the peaceful environment with no sounds other than the gentle whistle of the wind. Perfectly blue skies above and a happy dog zigzagging all over finding scents left by other dogs, deer, squirrels, foxes, and untold other animals. As John took a deep breath and savored the physical and emotional benefits of being in the woods, he said to himself, "what a sight!" and suddenly he realized what Frank was suggesting as the likely problem the internal audit department was facing.

"They had no vision!" he said thinking out loud. Internal audit has been performing risk assessments without placing their sights on the mission and vision of the organization or their own department!

--------------------||--------------------

"Hello everyone. Happy Monday. How was your weekend? I hope you rested and did something fun?" said John as he started the weekly staff meeting.

"How was your weekend?" asked Rachel turning the focus on her boss.

"Thanks for asking. I went for a walk Saturday and it was quite pleasant. Beautiful blue skies, relatively mild temperatures and very peaceful. I had some great ideas. By the way, folks, walking in the woods or sitting by the beach can turn out to be quite healthy for you mentally, spiritually, and physically. It can also be dangerous if I get some new wild idea, but these usually turn out to be productivity and effectiveness leaps, so I've learned to welcome them," he said jokingly.

"In the woods, we return to reason and faith. There I feel that nothing can befall me in life, no disgrace, no calamity, which nature cannot repair," said Miriam.

"Emerson. Very good, Miriam," said John raising his eyebrows and his coffee mug, showing admiration.

After reviewing some housekeeping topics and getting an update on the audits in progress, John turned their attention to a new feature he added to the weekly staff meetings, a training and development segment.

"For this week's T&D topic, I would like us to talk about the risk and controls matrix, often referred to as the RCM.

Some internal audit departments have moved away from creating Risk-Control Matrices (RCM). I still believe they are relevant and useful. Without them we may not understand the objectives of the activity under review; fail to identify the risks we, auditors and audit clients, should focus on; and fail to identify the controls that help us mitigate the risks and increase the likelihood of achieving the objectives.

Furthermore, without the identification and rating of risks we may be relying, focusing, and testing less-than-critical controls or fail to see that some significant risks have no controls in place. All things worth knowing before we perform any testing and they could also indicate a possible design deficiency."

"Design deficiency?" asked Carolina.

"Yes, a design deficiency is a situation where the structure of the program or process does not meet specifications, or we are missing a control where one is necessary. In Sarbanes-Oxley parlance, it is when a control necessary to meet the control objective is missing or an existing control is not properly designed so that even if the control operates as designed, the control objective would not be met."

"Is that AS5?" asked Tony.

"Yes, Auditing Standard number 5 for audits of internal control over financial reporting integrated with an audit of financial statements."

"ICFR," said Tony again showing his familiarity with Sarbanes–Oxley regulations and his preference for compliance standards.

"Correct again. Although it relates primarily to external financial audits, we can use the same concepts in internal audits. There could be great observations to share with management before we do any testing whatsoever. So, a well-developed RCM aligns tests to key controls; key controls to relevant risks; relevant and significant risks worth worrying about with true objectives. This way we focus on what matters most and don't' waste our time testing things that are non-key. Then, if we identify something out of place, by definition it will be important to the stakeholders we aim to serve.""How much time should we spend creating RCMs?" asked Tony and in so doing made John wonder if he was asking because he was a big fan of the tool and wanted everyone to invest more in it or he was not a big fan of the tool and was hoping for a ceiling so he could fly below it.

"We shouldn't spend an inordinate amount of time preparing an RCM. However, without it, we are merely improvising; keeping ourselves busy while hoping we are on the right track. We can't do that. We will be spending a little more time becoming more familiar with their creation and management.

When completing Risk-Control Matrices (RCM), many people start with the risk, but they should start with the objectives of the activity under review. If you don't know what our clients are trying to accomplish, how do you know which risks are relevant and key? How can you help them succeed and make useful recommendations?" asked John rhetorically. "Start with objectives!"

He continued, "there are three types of objectives per COSO IC-IF. Anyone remembers those?"

"Operational, reporting and compliance," replied Tony."Exactly. Yes, thanks. Objectives can be operational, reporting, which breaks down into four types; internal or external, financial or non-financial. The third type is compliance. I mention compliance last on purpose because organizations and their underlying processes are not created to comply," John took a pause to allow the words to sink in.

He continued, this time speaking more slowly for effect.

"Organizations are created to pursue a mission. A vision. To address the needs of a target market, taxpayers, or clients. These are all operational objectives. Organizations must move information within and outside the organization, which is what reporting is all about, and yes, they must also comply."

Having made his main point clear, he resumed the typical speed of his speech. He also smiled remembering that his preferred leadership style was to convince his staff of the merits and benefits of going forward so they did so willingly, rather than sternly pushing them.

"So, you don't start with compliance! It is part of what organizations must do along the way, but focusing on compliance from the beginning is like walking while staring at your feet. If you do this, you are likely to fall off the road or run into a light post. Look up!" said John injecting some humor into his directive.

"Questions about RCMs?" he asked inviting his team to share their thoughts.

There were no questions or comments, so John ended the meeting explaining to them that his philosophy was to provide learning opportunities throughout the work-week and not to limit these to designated training events only.

--------------------||--------------------

The team got together again on a scheduled meeting to review the risk-control matrix. They had been working on it for several days, so it was time to check the progress made.

"When we met last time, we were filling out the RCM and we got some objectives, risks, and controls, and you were going to fill it out more. Right?"

"Yes," the team replied.

"Before we take a look at your work, I want to add something to what we're doing here. Remember, a risk assessment typically starts with the business objectives of the area being reviewed. There is another step before that. At the enterprise level, a risk assessment typically starts with the strategic, operational, compliance and reporting objectives of the organization. But there is also another step before that, and it is often forgotten."

"What's that?" asked Rachel.

"The mission and vision. At the enterprise level the organization has documented those somewhere. There are also values statements. But we usually don't visit those when doing an enterprise risk assessment, we usually just jump into risks. Some auditors start with the objectives, which is better, but not the mission. What are we here trying to accomplish? It sets the tone and direction for every objective. If it is not aligned with the organization's mission and vision, why is it an objective in the first place? It helps us find our North Star. Our raison d'être."

Brian looked surprised at the French expression and before he could ask what it meant, Carolina spoke "our reason to be, or to exist."

"Exactly. It defines what is important. The overarching purpose. So, let's practice that here. What is the mission of the T&E process?"

"Pay expenses promptly," said Rachel.

"That is an objective, not its mission. Why do they exist?"

After thinking for a moment, Carolina said, "reimburse employees?"

"Not quite. That is along the lines of the objective of paying accurately. Keep thinking."

"How about facilitating the payment of needed business travel," said Miriam.

"I think that's a good one. We can circle back with Mary who runs this process, but I think that is a good start for their mission. With 'facilitating' you make it easy for everyone connected to this process, employees, record-keepers, disbursers, and accountants. 'Payment' is straight forward. 'Needed' because we don't want unnecessary or frivolous travel and 'business' because it has to be not only needed but needed by the business; business appropriate."

The mention of words that could readily connect with compliance themes seemed to resonate with Tony, who finally joined the conversation.

"That seems to work."

"I think so too. Let's go with that. Now, let's take a look at your objectives," said John directing the group to the originally stated purpose of the meeting.

"Yes, we got together and did some more brainstorming on that, and this is what we have. Can you see the spreadsheet?" asked Rachel.

"Yes," replied John. "I can see it." After a moment he added, "good, I was just going to ask you to make it larger, so you read my mind."

As they reviewed the expanded list of objectives, risks, and controls, John made some adjustments. "This one is a broken control, remember? We shouldn't write it down as 'they don't reconcile travel advances' but what that could cause. What do you think might be an effect of not reconciling travel advances?" John asked prompting them to think through the scenario.

"The employee could keep the money indefinitely, which is the use of a company asset," Carolina replied.

"Exactly!" John responded as Rachel updated the control on the RCM.

"What do you think about the last control?" John asked. "Management avoids paying the same expense more than once."

After a short silence, Carolina responded, "That sounds like an objective?"

"Is that a question or a statement?" asked John.

"A statement?"

"You're doing it again. You say it but you don't sound like you're sure of your answer. You're correct. It is a statement, and it is more of an objective than a control. Remember, a control is a process or action to help achieve an objective. It is something that is done, so what might they be doing to avoid paying the same expense more than once?" he asked.

"Someone should be checking receipts to make sure they are originals. That's how we did that at my previous company," said Tony.

"Yes, we used to do that too. That's a good one," said Carolina.

"Yes, that works when you look at physical receipts, but if people are submitting scanned images, there are no little pieces of paper to look at, touch and verify they are original documents," said John challenging them.

"Ooops, that's right," said Tony scratching his head before lowering his hand slowly and letting his jaw rest on his open palm in a sign of frustration.

"Maybe the system used to process T&E has a way of checking for what might look like duplicates, so put that there for now and we'll check, but I'm guessing it is up to the approving manager to somehow check for that," John said helping them out.

"Hold on. How does it check for duplicates if they are scanned images?" asked Brian.

"Good question," acknowledge John. "Who can answer that question? It is a very good question and one that applies to AP and other functions too."

"What do you mean?" said Rachel asking for clarification.

"The question, and problem, of duplicates remain. In the past people, auditors, operators, managers would look at payment requests and try to verify that the document, whether invoice or receipt for reimbursement, was an original. They assumption was that there was only one of those documents in existence, and a copy was an anomaly that could result in us paying once with the original document and again with the copy. So the policy, and practice was to only pay on the original. But now with scanned and electronic documents, there can be hundreds of those," Miriam explained.

"Exactly," said John. "So now the question is, how can we, in today's world, determine that we are only going to pay once for a transaction, even if copies are in circulation?"

"Copies made by mistake or intentional?" asked Brian.

"It doesn't really matter. Well, I'll take it back. By mistake is unintentional and intentional could be an attempt to defraud, so it does matter. But the answer is the same. The process should avoid paying for the request more than once," John explained.

Tony seemed frustrated by the back-and-forth; it looked like he just wanted John to tell them what the answer should be.

"I guess so, but for years I've approved T&E for our department and the system doesn't check for that so there is no mechanism to avoid paying the expense twice. No plan A. We rely on plan B, the manager," said Tony.

"That might be a potential recommendation after we dig deeper and confirm that the system can't do that. There are ways for systems to check text and figures on scanned images. But maybe someone in accounting checks every so often looking for duplicates," said John.

"Accounting?" said Rachel surprised, "They don't do anything like that!"

"I'm getting lost. Do anything like what?" asked Tony feeling lost at the speed of the conversation and the multiple scenarios being discussed.

"Processes should have a way of comparing new requests to older requests to determine if the incoming transaction is a duplicate, or a repeated request for payment. Someone remembering if they saw that request before is not a good system because the person is likely to forget over time and with large volumes of transactions, they will likely forget fast," explained John.

"And if they do it as a periodic reconciliation?" asked Carolina.

"That is a good and common technique," said John. "But there is a downside to that. Anyone knows what that is?"

The resulting silence made John realize that they were either getting tired or were so accustomed to periodic monitoring techniques that they were struggling to think of continuous monitoring, so he helped them out, "because by the time the review is done several transactions may have been processed. Continuous monitoring through automation is a better solution."

"All good, but they don't," said Miriam making a short yet confusing statement.

"Because they don't know how, or they don't know they should?" asked John.

"I don't know why, but they don't," she explained.

"Ok, well, that might require some more research as to the root cause, but in the end it sounds like another recommendation for management," said John. "For now, though, that could be a good audit procedure, what do you think?" asking a leading question.

"Data analytics," said Miriam.

Happy that the team was following along and arriving at the procedures he thought they needed to adopt, he replied, "Yes, that would be a nice check to see if that risk is actually happening. So, this brings us to audit procedures. Add that to the Column for procedures, Rachel. Which one is it for audit procedures?"

"M," answered Rachel, as she started typing the audit procedure.

"Good. Let's go to the top of Column M and read across. We always start with the objective, ask what can go wrong, check the control, and think of an audit procedure that would help us determine if the risk is happening or the control is working." As John leaned into the screen to see the words, he rubbed his chin and read the objective silently mumbling the words to himself, "So ..., compliance and fraud ... Objective ..., how would we know if multiple people are expensing the same meal?"

"Objective ..., how would we know if the same person is expensing the same transaction multiple times?"

"Objective ..., how would we know if transactions without a legitimate business purpose are being expensed and paid?"

After reading quietly to himself, he raised his voice now addressing the team again.

"Here is another question for you. Maybe we should look to see what the range of hotel costs is. Now, understand that hotel prices change, sometimes substantially, but maybe we can do some analytics to look at the average, minimum and maximum for the same location to determine if there is a lot of fluctuation in prices paid."

"That would suggest an opportunity for cost savings!" said Miriam.

"Exactly. We don't want to be overly restrictive and sound unreasonable, but at the very least, if InSports negotiated prices with several hotels so employees have a choice, that could be a very interesting observation," John added.

John continued reading the RCM and prompting his staff to think through risky scenarios and how they could determine if those issues were occurring or not.

--------------------||--------------------

Tony and Rachel were already in the meeting when Dan and Mary joined. As soon as they joined Dan started talking.

"Hi Rachel and Tony. Tony I'm glad you scheduled this meeting before the audit started because I was wondering what this was all about."

"Hi Dan," Tony replied. "We have been doing some brainstorming and want to go over this with you before the audit starts. We are changing up the audit approach a bit and want to show you what we're thinking about, but more importantly, work with you and maybe someone else in your group who is very familiar with the process to update the matrix as necessary."

"Well, I appreciate you asking me before you start doing any work, or even asking us to pull data, which you also mention in the attachment to the meeting invitation. We can talk about that later, but what are you trying to do here?"

"We have been doing the same audit year after year and we usually don't find anything significant to share with you in T&E. Not that we want to find anything wrong, but our new CAE wants us to rethink our approach and see if there is more there to learn and maybe share some opportunities for improvement by revamping our procedures," explained Tony.

"CAE, do you mean John?" asked Dan.

"Yes, exactly. Sorry, yes, John is our new Chief Audit Executive, and he has some new ideas on how to perform audits," said Tony.

Noticing that Tony's tone and demeanor were not particularly positive, Rachel took control of the meeting. "It is not really new, new. It is what auditors have been doing at other organizations, but we weren't doing that here. So, we are going to start here now," she explained.

"OK. Does that mean more work for us?" asked Mary.

"Maybe, but also for internal audit. But more importantly, it is not just about more work, but better results. The goal is not just to scratch the surface on audit areas but do meaningful work that helps you achieve your mission and us better understand the process, see if what is happening is what *should* be happening and help make the process better. We also want to know if there are any strange things happening so you can focus on that if anything comes up. It is about risk. If we find nothing, you sleep better. If we find something, you know what to focus on," explained Rachel.

"Sounds lofty. Good, but lofty. But first, what about the way you have been auditing T&E all these years?"

"It was not wrong, but the audit program we agreed to use years ago focused primarily on controls, not risks. For example, we looked to see if the amount paid equaled the amount of the expense report, so we were checking the mathematical accuracy of reimbursement. We'll check that now too, so don't worry about that, but we hardly ever found anything wrong there. We also looked at the approver to make sure the right manager approved the expense report. Again, we never found any issues there because employees sent the report to their managers, so that was very straightforward and almost always correct."

"So, what are you going to do now?" asked Dan.

"We'll walk you through our thoughts, and just a quick checkpoint here is to make sure we understand, and that our work is aimed at helping you, achieve your mission. Mission and objectives, those are the drivers for what you do, and now for what we do too," said Rachel sounding like a confident salesperson.

"OK," replied Dan with a skeptical tone while nodding in agreement. Both Tony and Rachel noticed his behavior and were encouraged, as they thought he might judge their approach not practical enough.

"The way we see it," continued Rachel, "your unit facilitates the payment of needed business travel. The reason we want to capture that is that the starting point for what we do is making sure you and us, we, agree on the value you provide the organization. You and your team probably deal with a lot of challenges."

"Do we ever! You call them challenges. We call them headaches!"

"Yes, a lot of challenges, sorry, headaches, along the way of supporting the organization's need to engage in needed travel. Business travel helps salespeople, engineers, designers, senior management, and others go where they need to go to facilitate our overarching goal of designing, making, inspecting, selling, and otherwise moving the company forward. This is an important activity in the organization."

"It is, and often not seen that way."

"Exactly. So we want to make sure we as auditors recognize that and don't just come here and start turning the place inside out without appreciating your overarching mission."

"Ok. You got it. I like how that is worded. What's next?"

"Our approach is now also focused on the objectives you pursue. We have traditionally looked at accuracy of payments and accuracy of recording on the corresponding general ledger account, so basically, the accounting side of things."

"Yes."

"There are other objectives you also have on your list of priorities. Like paying promptly. When there are delays, employees get upset and that is not 'facilitating' things in employee minds."

"Right."

"Another objective is to only pay legitimate expenses, which would fall under 'needed'. If there is abuse, we wouldn't want to pay it. We don't have the word 'appropriate' in the mission because that is a bit of auditor jargon, but the point is, you are watching for legitimate or appropriate payments and only paying those, legitimate meals, legitimate hotel, legitimate car rental, and so on."

"I'm with you. I like this. Go on."

"Now about the risks. We will perform what is called risk-based auditing. So, we will then look at the types of risks or concerns that get in the way of you achieving your mission and objectives. For example, your mission and objectives also include meaningful concerns like finding out if several employees expensed the same meal individually. Imagine four employees go to dinner, and each submits an expense report for the same dinner. Or an employee pays for a meal with the P-card, then submits the same dinner through T&E and gets reimbursed personally, even though the P-card process would pay for it."

"How would an employee submit the same receipt more than once?"

"They don't really submit receipts. Employees scan them. So, they send one image to the P-card reconciler and another one goes with the T&E report."

Mary seemed to lose a bit of color in her face when she heard this. "Can they do that?"

"Technically, they could. They could submit the same expense a third time through an open PO, and that would be paid by yet another person in accounting, that would be Matt, I believe. We have Sarah processing P-cards, Mary processing T&E, and Matt processing vendor invoices."

"I don't like how that sounds," said Dan.

"We don't know if that is happening, but that is how we are thinking about risk and a recommended approach to doing an audit like this one. Looking at things like that helps us identify anomalies that would be of concern and that the organization should prevent and stop immediately if it is happening. I'll give you another example about something where there could be bigger dollars at stake. We don't have a clear policy on hotels, car rentals and even airline carriers, only what class of travel, economy, with a few exceptions for international travel over six hours long. So, how much are we paying for hotel stays and car rentals? Could employees be overspending and stay where they like and driving up the costs to InSports unnecessarily above what we think is necessary? We want employees to be comfortable, but there are limits."

Dan responded: "actually, that is a question I've been wondering about for a while. I can tell you that our expenses have increased over the last couple of years, and I just never had anyone free to do analysis about that. I've been meaning to do that, but we're understaffed."

Piggybacking off her boss's comment, Mary added, "yes, that would be helpful."

Seeing the opening, Rachel added: "we can work with you to do that during this review. That is part of what we are going to start doing from now on, and one of the reasons why we wanted to meet with you today. To tell you about our new approach and explain our new focus."

"Will you keep us updated as you proceed?" asked Dan again.

"We will. We'll let you know what we find and what we don't find."

"What do you mean?" asked Mary with a suspicious tone.

"The focus of internal audit is to communicate results, not only what we have historically referred to as findings."

"I still don't understand. What's the difference?" said Dan looking at Mary, Tony, and resting on Rachel.

"Our goal is to provide reasonable assurance. That sounds like more auditor jargon, but what that means is we strive to answer questions about whether we as a company are achieving our objectives, managing risks and if controls are working."

"So?"

"If you are achieving your objectives, managing your risks and your controls are where they are supposed to be and are working like they should, then that's fine. We'll tell you. We'll tell senior management and the board, and we move on. We don't have to find problems to issue results," said Rachel with a confident tone, happy to share the news about the new approach. In the meantime, Tony looked on silently feeling that things were changing rapidly around him.

"Oh. Wow. Well that's different!" Mary said enthusiastically, relieved that this new approach may be a bit less stressful than the traditional approach.

"Yes, different indeed," agreed Dan. "I thought you got paid based on the number of findings you reported!" he said jokingly while Mary wondered if there wasn't a bit of truth to that unfortunate, but widely held myth.

"No. No bonuses for findings," said Rachel with a smile.

"Well. You said you were changing what internal audit is all about. This sounds different for sure. I like what I'm hearing. What's the next step?"

With this invitation, Rachel explained the approach in more detail, focusing on the adoption of a more collaborative approach, and more frequent and clear communications.

"The department does not have a policy or a means to monitor and correct deviations from expected practice," read Tony during the exit meeting with the department head, the division head, and the plant manager. The plant manager had had enough and interrupted Tony by saying angrily:

"What do you mean we have no means to monitor and correct? Of course we do."

"We reviewed your policies and there was no document related to," Tony tried to respond before being cut off again.

"Yes, we do. Alex, didn't you give him the memos and e-mails we have sent about this? I told you to," asked Justin. "Did you?"

"I did. Over a week ago. You said you got them," Alex said now turning his gaze to Tony asking for confirmation.

"Yes, we received the documents last week Tuesday or Wednesday, but the…"

"So why would you say we don't have anything. You just said you got them over a week ago. This is what I don't like about auditors, they do this 'gotcha thing'. This is not even gotcha. This is, and I hate to say it, like lying guys, what is this?" Justin said getting angrier by the minute.

"No, we are not lying, and we are not saying that you don't have..." Tony tried again to explain the observation, but was once again interrupted by Justin who had lost the patience to listen.

"I think I may have a solution," said Rachel joining the scuffle and trying to calm things down.

"What if we re-wrote the observation so we give you, let's call it credit for having some of the elements of a policy, but not yet publishing a formal policy as such?" she said in a calm voice in stark contrast to the angry crescendo in the meeting.

"I'm listening," said Justin encouragingly, but with an air of suspicion in his reply.

"Yes, so we say you have issued, how many notices, four or so? so we quantify the communications, summarize like I just did that the elements of expected performance have been shared with the staff and so on. Now, about monitoring, Sandra told me you do a monthly reconciliation but that is not exactly documented anywhere in the procedures manual, so you are doing it, and we saw that. You saw that, right Tony?"

"Yes."

"We received nine months' worth. Was it nine months? Tony," Rachel asked again.

"Yes."

"Good. You have copies going back at least nine months. Completed, reviewed, and signed off by the plant manager," Rachel confirmed even more upbeat about the way the conversation was going.

"OK," said Tony now attempting to take the reins of the conversation once again and using his hands in a gathering motion said, "so we state you have been performing these reviews consistently and they have been reviewed and approved by management," motioning with his open hand at the plant manager and the department supervisor in acknowledgment, then turning his gaze and hand gestures toward Justin "and we encourage management to update the department's policies to reflect this expectation and the monthly monitoring cycle it requires."

"Hmm, that might work," said Justin nodding his head.

"Yes, I think this might work," said Rachel. "We acknowledge what you have and are doing, and state what is needed for this to be formalized. I think it is more accurate and senior management, you know, Ken and Ron, will see that you are getting some really important things done, but true to life, there is room for improvement," she concluded.

"When will I see the observation rewritten like you just said?" asked Justin.

"By end of business Friday," said Rachel.

The group reviewed the remaining observations, and while the tension had subsided significantly, the feeling was unfortunately still like that of rivals. There was much work to be done to build trust and a friendlier relationship between them.

---------------------||---------------------

3 Building a Coalition
Outreach

"Hi Brenda, Thanks for meeting with me."

"Sure. Good to meet you. How are you enjoying San Francisco?"

"It's been good. Went to North Beach and had some amazing Italian food, but I guess that's to be expected there."

"Yes, that's the best place for it."

"First of all, I want to officially introduce myself, but also spend a few moments talking about your group, what plans are underway and how I can make sure our risk assessment and audit plan can best sync up so that we can focus on what matters most to you and InSports," John said explaining the purpose of the meeting.

"Well John, first of all," she said repeating his opening statement, "that's the best introduction, or maybe overall statement, I've heard from audit in years. I won't go over past grievances, but to keep a long story short, they only contacted me when they wanted to show me the final risk assessment, which undoubtedly suggested everything was OK in R&D. Occasionally someone would escalate a request for some vendor or consultant document, but it was a byproduct of another audit, typically AP. No one goes around asking to be audited, but even though I know my team is doing a great job, I would like the confirmation from an independent party sometimes."

"I'm working on changing that, so we include senior management more in the risk assessment process and audit planning."

"That's good, so what do you need to know and how can I help?"

With that John and Brenda spoke for much longer than the half-hour the meeting was initially scheduled for and discussed R&D's objectives, main initiatives underway, a high-level overview of their review and selection process, and the names of key project managers she relied on for oversight.

"Thanks Brenda. I appreciate your time and insights."

"We're having a birthday cake for one of our team members tomorrow. Come over if you're still in town. I'll introduce you to the team and to some of the people I mentioned so you can arrange meetings."

"Thanks again. I just might show up. It's hard to say 'no' to cake."

"Come for the food. Stay for the fun. We have a great team and maybe there are some best practices you can take from what we do and help some other units. Some people are struggling a bit out there."

John left the meeting thinking to himself that R&D might be an internal center of excellence and IA could possibly help disseminate best practices with their support. That's the kind of environment he hoped to create at InSports.

--------------------||--------------------

DOI: 10.1201/9781003322870-3

"Hi Tanya, how are things?" asked John starting the conversation.

"Good. It is a nice, sunny day here, so I'm happy to live in Florida. A little nicer than up North, I tell you that!"

"I can imagine."

"Where are you?" she asked and before John could answer she kept talking "I believe they just had a bomb cyclone last week. I thought I saw some really low temperatures around Minneapolis. Like negative numbers. That's cold!"

"Good for ice fishing!" John said before Tanya started talking again.

"I miss that a little, but not enough to return for that!"

"I hear you. Florida can be appealing."

"Hot with humidity, or hot with less humidity," she said laughing at her own joke.

John smiled broadly at the description of the Florida weather, but also at the very energized person on camera.

"I wanted to talk with you to ask you a favor. We're making some needed changes in internal audit, and I need to upskill our auditors a bit. One area where your staff excels is in project management, so I was wondering if I could have one of your senior PMs present at one of our staff meetings what your group does, how they do it, and how they stay on task and on budget. You're creating some great products, so you're doing a few things right from what I can see."

"Thanks. Appreciate the feedback and the request. Brenda told me you would contact me. I don't have a problem with that. Glad to help. When would you like this? How long a presentation?" Tanya talked so fast it reminded John of a podcast playing at 2x speed.

"Two weeks from now. It's during a staff meeting, so not long. Let's say twenty minutes," he explained.

"Yeah, I think that's doable. I don't see a problem with that. Do you have a template you want me to use? How many slides?"

"Any template you like. I don't have a preference on the number of slides, but not too many."

"OK. If I have questions, do I ask you or is there someone else in your department I should contact?"

"No, just me. I'll send you a meeting invitation. If you need anything let me know."

"Got it. Talk to you soon. Bye."

"Phew," John thought to himself as the camera went blank, "that is one energized project manager. I wouldn't mind if some of that energy rubs off on the team here."

--------------------||--------------------

"Hello everyone and thanks for joining us for this presentation. I'm John Taylor and I'm the chief audit executive, or CAE, at InSports. I'm your friendly and helpful general auditor as some like to call me," he said injecting some humor into his introduction.

"Internal audit has been a part of InSports for many years," he continued. "It has helped the organization identify areas where weaknesses in our processes, systems and compliance infrastructure could expose the organization to loss, fines, penalties, and other negative consequences. Some of you may have been audited in the past and met the staff in that department. Others perhaps not. We are conducting these aware-ness sessions to explain who we are, what we do, and how we can help you. Before I proceed, I would like to introduce my two managers, Miriam Abrams, who is our IT auditor," he said as he looked to his right where Miriam was standing. "And to my left is Tony Barone, our Business Processes manager," he said looking over at Tony with a hand gesture to move the group's attention in that direction.

"Miriam has been with InSports for five years and Tony twelve years, so together they have a great deal of experience on our company, the people, processes, and sys-tems we use. Miriam, please tell us more about your background at and before InSports so we have a better understanding of your background."

After describing her experience and credentials, he did the same with Tony, who introduced himself and described his work at InSports in lengthy detail.

The group consisted primarily of operations personnel, but there were also a few financial reporting and IT operations personnel.

John then proceeded to go over some administrative matters related to breaks, lunches, invited everyone to ask questions at any time and not to wait until the end unless that was their preference. He reviewed the agenda and once again asked the group if there were any questions. When done, he proceeded with the orientation ses-sion starting with the definition of internal auditing, with special emphasis on the words "advisory," "add value and improve an organization's operations," "help," "accomplish its objectives," and "improve the effectiveness." The group was silent at first, but questions started soon after he began his focus on these words, because "advisory" was a new concept they had never associated with internal audit, much less at InSports.

John then described the audit methodology cycle, and once again, spent consider-able time explaining risk assessments at the enterprise level and then at the project level, the importance of planning for effective fieldwork and how more efficient, effective, and focused fieldwork reduces the disruption to operations staff.

Next, John explained what internal controls were. The group had a lot to say about segregation of duties, documentation requirements, and their actual practices espe-cially related to approvals because decisions were sometimes made with insufficient information or by someone who was too removed from the actual activity that was being approved. They also had a lively conversation about their challenges with rec-onciliations and addressing reconciling items when they were overworked and found it difficult to research and review those items for resolution. One of the longest serv-ing employees in that unit asked about the challenges that staff turnover presented because it set them back in terms of their productivity. He explained the exposure to the organization but also to him personally if there was ever a problem and it went unnoticed for long, how that might be viewed by others as his lack of follow-through on his role.

When John suggested raising the issue with the manager, he said he had in the past with no corrective action taking place, but he had never included ideas to hire tempo-rary help for this task or a statement about the implications to the organization. He liked that and asked about additional resources at least to do the reconciliations.

When John explained monitoring, the group had a lot to say about the quality of data and reports, and the challenge of establishing accountability for corrective actions to address issues identified. The frequency of monitoring activities was also of special interest because some thought some monitoring was too frequent and focused on relatively unimportant aspects of the business while others thought it needed to be improved because in some cases it was too manual. The current ad hoc and exception-based manual approach was viewed as inadequate when more focused and exhaustive approaches were feasible and available.

John then spoke about safeguarding of assets and records, and linked that to supply chain flows. The group was attuned to his description of the inputs and outputs along the supply chain and how external parties played a role whether they were vendors, customers, or other InSports subsidiaries.

IT security was not received with the same enthusiasm because many of the features and expectations were thought to reside with, and be managed by, the IT and the IT Security departments. When John mentioned that many security incidents are caused by human activity and the importance of employees knowing what controls they needed to oversee, they pushed back saying that they had received limited cybersecurity training and even less IT controls training.

John explained The Three Lines Model where the questions focused primarily on roles and responsibilities.

The last item on the agenda was a description of the COSO IC-IF model and how it was an integral part of the work of internal and external auditors. John concluded by explaining its use and the importance of seeing it through the lens of a management tool for better decision-making and management.

The road show orientation session concluded with John sharing a link to an online class evaluation and a request for feedback on how the program could be made better.

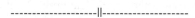

"Hi Dianne. How is the world of Supply Chain Management treating you?"

"Not too bad, other than high-flying inflation, and recalculating our supply chain costs every three hours given the craziness in South America and Asia Pac," she said.

"I heard. Currency devaluations and some street closures due to protests."

"Yes, and we're watching a couple of big monsoon storms that already shut down one plant and the other one is probably going to have to close temporarily too. Flooding issues."

"Wow. Not good."

"But don't worry about us too much. We don't need an audit just yet. We have contingency plans in place and that includes sourcing from other providers, so we'll still make our numbers."

"Well, that's part of the reason I wanted to talk with you," said John. "I'm making some changes in internal audit and would like to upskill our auditors a bit about supply chain management."

"You want me to train your auditors so they can audit us?" she said smiling. "Audit never comes around here!"

"I know, that has been..." John said before Dianne interrupted him.

"John, I was only kidding. Listen. I've been in supply chain for over twenty years, and five years here at InSports. I'm telling you, audit has never showed up here, but

I don't understand it, because that was standard practice at all the manufacturing companies where I've worked before. Supply chain is supposed to be a big deal, you know. I almost feel neglected. I guess I'm not that important around here!" she said jokingly.

"We'll make you feel special again. We'll get to you," John said keeping the light mood going with some healthy banter.

"I'm happy to talk with your team. But don't audit me until your people are ready. I may get upset if they don't know what they're doing. But once we work with them, and you get them trained, we can work this out together. We can always use a different perspective and another pair of eyes. In my previous companies the auditors usually saw things we missed and helped us identify weaknesses, so we kept things working smoothly. Few people like to be audited, so maybe I'm weird like that, but if your team is knowledgeable, glad to have them help us out over here. We have a million moving parts, literally, and we could miss something, you know?"

"I appreciate your thoughts about this. That's the goal. Provide another pair of eyes and insight that balances our expertise on risks and controls, with your operational expertise while together we focus on achieving business objectives."

"When would you like to do this?"

"How about three weeks from today? Not too long. A twenty-minute presentation during a staff meeting."

"Sure. Do you want me to use a certain template or just bring what I have?"

"Just bring what you have."

"I have a short presentation I use while onboarding new staff on my team and a few spreadsheets, so people get a flavor for what we do and how complex it is. Nothing scary, but a lot of people don't fully appreciate what it takes to get all the parts to the right place to build our machines."

"I know. I appreciate you."

"I know you do. You'll send me the invitation, so it gets on my calendar?"

"Yes, I'll send that today."

"Good. Nice chatting with you. Anything else?"

"No, that's it for now."

"Take care. Talk to you soon. Bye."

With that, John made notes and sent out meeting invitations for his guest speakers. He was excited about the lineup he had already secured: Dianne from Supply Chain and Brenda from R&D would help upskill his team, while he built a coalition of knowledgeable and respected business partners to move audit to the next level. Good things were in motion.

"We would like to give you an update on the modified T&E audit we are performing. It is a split audit this time around. One phase now, as initially scheduled and agreed last year, and we'll do the second half later in the year. So, we ran some numbers, and you may find some of this interesting," said Rachel as she got the meeting started. Dan and Mary were joining the video call from Dan's office, while Rachel and Tony were joining from their home offices.

"OK, let's hear it," said Dan.

"This chart shows how our expenses for air travel, hotel and car rental has increased."

"How much of it is due to inflation and just people needing to travel more for business?" asked Dan.

"Good question. This other chart shows the average cost per stay, and that has increased. But it doesn't quite answer your question. But *this* one provides an interested perspective. It shows the number of trips per year over here, per quarter over here, and per month over here. The frequency of travel has not changed much, but costs have increased."

"OK"

"We were curious about the change in expenditures, so the next thing we wanted to do was to see what happened during each trip. We grouped the travelers by trip. It took a bit of work, but it wasn't' really all that hard to do. We grouped the travelers by trip, and noticed that for the same trip, the variance in hotel stays could vary by fifty percent or more. That's the percentage. Over here is the dollar figure. Per trip. Per month. Per quarter. For all of last year."

"What? 175 thousand?" Mary almost screamed when she saw the number.

"Yep. Replied Rachel shaking her head giving the figure some time to sink in further. After a few seconds she continued. "And over here is another thing we looked at. Remember when we met the last time and we were going to look at the possibility of the same person expensing the same item, meal, hotel, car or even airfare multiple times?"

"Y e s," replied Mary and Dan almost in unison slowly dragging out the word.

"We found twelve employees who did that. Several times so maybe they made a mistake, but they made the mistake, let's see, a minimum of six times and a maximum of thirty-two times. That could be a recurring mistake, but we are starting to doubt that. It looks quite suspicious," said Rachel.

"That is no mistake," Mary said pursing her lips. "I need their names."

"Yes, we can provide that, but we should probably get HR involved too," said Tony responding to the alarmed reaction from both Mary and Dan.

"Yes, we should," said Dan. "What's next?" with a deep sigh.

"OK. We also looked at people paying for insurance on car rentals. Company policy says renters should decline that. We paid $36,000 last year in car rental insurance."

Mary closed her eyes as Dan's neck started to turn more pink than usual.

"What else?" asked Mary again now worrying what Dan thought about her work overseeing this process. She asked while rubbing her hands as she tried to release some of the tension that was rapidly rising.

"The last time we spoke about the possibility of multiple people at a meal, each person expensing the same meal and the manager approving the same meal multiple times. Does that make sense?" asked Rachel again.

"Yes," Mary said, closing her eyes and nodding in agreement. "It makes sense. Don't tell me you found that too."

"Unfortunately, we did. Three locations in Florida and two in Illinois. Total 12 people, 48 meals, $12,000 dollars."

Dan leaned back in his chair with his arms closed and said "OK. So, 175 plus what was it, 36, and now another 12, what's that, $223 thousand?" said Dan adding the figures in his head.

"Yes, that's correct," confirmed Rachel.

"I don't know if I should ask you this, but is that it? Is the audit done?" asked Mary hoping for a "yes" answer.

"No, that's what we have done so far. We have a few more audit steps coming up. We'll update you as we do and learn more."

"I can't wait," said Mary with a deeply worried look on her face.

Tony spoke next. "We can provide the detail behind these numbers. While we are still conducting the audit, perhaps you should be familiar with our observations in detail as we notify HR and our investigative team."

"Agree. Let's meet tomorrow. Let me look at my calendar so we can schedule that right away" said Dan as he looked at his computer in search of a time slot when they could continue the conversation.

---------------------||---------------------

Yesterday was momentous. The alarm rang at 5:00 AM and John rolled over to turn it off. For a moment he pawed his way around the night table until he realized that he wasn't home. It took a few seconds to get his bearings right. Sleeping in a hotel room was a nice treat, with a heavy comforter and more pillows than he would ever have at home, but also disorienting when woken up. "Where am I again? Oh, yes, Buenos Aires."

He wanted to go for a walk, so he dressed quickly, stepped out of the hotel, and turned West onto Avenida Córdoba. He was enjoying the architecture and was reminded why it was referred to as the Paris of South America. Shortly after San Martín he crossed Avenida Florida committing to walking on it on the way back, but he wanted to get to Avenida 9 de Julio a little further ahead. The widest avenue in the world was as impressive as he remembered it with up to 14 lanes of traffic in some places.

He thought of the many changes he needed to make in his department. Ironic, he thought as he came upon it, "I need to cross a major divide in my department and perhaps act as the Moses of sorts, leading my team across the big expanse," he said with a small smirk on his face.

Upon crossing the road, he took a left turn on it heading south. He knew what he wanted to see, and it didn't take him long to come upon the Teatro Colón, one of the best in the world with an ornate façade outside, exceptional acoustics inside, and beautiful architectural details throughout. He sighed thinking about the rich theater history of Buenos Aires and he made a note to try to watch a show while there. "Inspiring just to walk by it," he thought to himself.

Two more blocks further south, John admired the Plaza de la República to his left as he approached Avenida Corrientes. There he turned east and waited for the traffic light to change so he could cross Av. 9 de Julio at the Obelisco, all along thinking how this monument represented Independence Day and the place where Argentina's flag was raised in the city for the first time. The obelisk is 67 meters tall, or almost 220 feet tall and it reminded him of the Washington Monument.

"Hmm, the symbolism of it all," John thought again giving himself a pep talk. "OK John, raise that internal audit flag at InSports, 'tall and proud'," he thought to himself, "tall and proud."

As he gazed at the menus of the numerous pizza, ice cream, coffee, and other food eateries along the way, John was grateful it was early Sunday morning and the stores were still closed, but he knew he would gain weight, probably a lot, by the time he returned home. In particular, that hot chocolate and churros.

He soon came upon Calle Florida again. As a pedestrian street he could admire more of the storefronts and zigzag as much as he wanted while window shopping for souvenirs. He turned left heading north and few blocks later he turned right onto Tucumán reminding himself that as much as he enjoyed the walk his goal was to get to Puerto Madero.

He took a deep breath when he came to the water and as he looked to his right he saw the Yacht Club, exactly where he remembered it, to his right and across the waterway. He smiled to himself as he thought of what he would see across from it on his side of the waterway.

He decided to walk that stretch. After all, the point was to enjoy the views, exercise, do some sightseeing, and feel the ambience of Buenos Aires. He passed Lucciano's then the restaurant he felt obligated to dine in before he returned home: Cabaña Las Lilas. He remembered dining there with a former audit team many years ago and how the memories had been seared in his heart and mind. "I shall return" he told himself many years ago, and here he was. Dinner plans must be made.

He returned to the hotel refreshed, excited, and very hungry.

After a quick shower it was time for breakfast of bizcochos and a medialuna rellena, with some hot chocolate. Not wanting to waste any time after eating, he asked the concierge for help getting a taxi and after a few minutes he was in San Telmo, the site of antique shops and the notorious flea market where he browsed through stalls and meandered in and out of stores for hours.

He later made his way to Recoleta and by then many stores were open and families were out and about. It was as impressive as always. Restaurants, shops, and families enjoying the warm weather. It seemed strange to be walking around in the middle of the summer when at home it was still winter. Winter eventually becomes summer. Remember that. The shortest days and darkest nights eventually turn into the longest, warmest, and brightest days.

Just stay the course.

--------------------||--------------------

Monday started just fine.

"Good morning, John. How was your trip?" asked Pablo, the local controller. Pablo was a young, energetic, and friendly asset to the company. A Big 4 alumnus, he had made significant improvements to the company's accounting processes since he joined five months earlier. He implemented several new reports and was making almost daily improvement recommendations to the CFO and country manager.

John's first appointment of the day was at 10 AM and he was glad. Dinner last night did not end until midnight and consisted mostly of picaña and morzilla, which he appropriately accompanied with some malbec wine. He felt like he was still digesting that heavy dinner, but he had few regrets. It was a wonderful night.

"I'm well thanks. Had dinner in Puerto Madero. Incredible food! Wow."

"Yes, we have good food here," replied Pablo happy that his visitor was enjoying the wonderful Argentinian cuisine.

As John described his Sunday adventures, it was evident that the audit would be a partnership as together they evaluated conditions and discussed concerns.

John was offered a workspace down the hall from the accounting office, and he settled into a comfortable cubicle with a window overlooking a small park below.

Pablo and his assistant, Carmen, provided most of the files he requested immediately and promised to provide the remainder that afternoon. John also received access to the accounting system so he could view records on his own and reduce the disruption he might cause during the audit.

As he looked at equipment inventory, he reviewed what was added, what was shipped, and what was on hand. He verified both quantities, the valuation, and status. The reconciliation did not show any discrepancies, but he noticed the type codes of retail, wholesale for distributors, and a third category for demonstration items. While the movement in and out of retail and wholesale items could be traced and reconciled without exceptions, he noticed a pattern of demo items entering the warehouse, being removed by salespeople, but only a fraction of them were returned into stock.

A closer look at the salespeople who were withdrawing items as demo equipment showed that the practice was widespread; virtually all salespeople did this, so it was commonplace. What was unusual, though, was that the majority of items outstanding were attributed to two salespeople. How far did this practice go for?

As he checked the previous year. Same pattern.

As he looked at the year before that. Again, the same.

This practice went back three years, month after month, quarter after quarter, the same two employees had demo inventory assigned to them and virtually none of it was ever returned. They must be very successful salespeople, because demo items were intended to allow prospects to use some equipment temporarily so they could decide if they wanted to buy it. If they did, the equipment was already on site, so they just had to pay for the items and continue using it. Hopefully they would buy more.

This goal of buy more is what made John look back at all the data. These two salespeople were OK, but they were not showing as top overall salespeople because most of the other sale items were distributed across all salespeople with little difference.

As he was turning his observations into Pareto Diagrams showing the patterns over several quarters, he decided to also take a look at the serial numbers. So far, he had been looking at the model numbers, but he knew the machines' serial numbers were also captured in sales orders as part of the service warranty, in case there were recalls and so on.

As he looked at the sales orders, the serial numbers were not showing up there. Were these machines giveaways? Donated perhaps? The demo period was not supposed to be more than 60 days, so they should either appear as returns or as sold, so what is happening?

He worked on the data the entire day and halfway through the following. He was getting increasingly worried about this and the possibility that this was a serious problem. He sent a meeting request for that afternoon to provide Pablo an update and talk about the results. In the meantime, he went outside for lunch and a walk.

Lunch in Argentina is often long due to the tradition of siesta. It provides enough time to eat and John took advantage of it to get some fresh air, enjoy the sun, and mull over the strange results his data analytics was uncovering.

"Hi Pablo, I'm noticing something rather strange and was wondering if you have a few minutes to tell me if I'm missing something here."

As John described the situation, Pablo also became increasingly concerned. The items were clearly disappearing, and their collective value was now in the hundreds of thousands of dollars.

They decided to ask Carmen about this apparent discrepancy, and she agreed there was no clear answer as to what was happening. They decided to call a couple of the gyms that bought the equipment. Tell them they were checking up on it, if they liked the machines, and when the loaner period would be over.

In both cases, the gym personnel indicated they paid for the equipment. First for the demos, and subsequently for additional machines, but they shared that the sales agent asked them to pay for the items separately, which they thought was strange.

With this revelation, additional locations were contacted over the next two days, and some patterns emerged. In some gyms, rehabilitation centers, and apartment complexes, only demos were sold this way while in others there were demos first and additional items bought subsequently. In all instances, the payments were by check and the salesperson requested the check be hand delivered to the salesperson. If there were a combination of demos and regular items, there was some breakdown, but the demos were always paid separately and by hand-delivered checks.

A review of the locations where these discrepancies were noted showed that they corresponded to the territory for these two salespeople.

Thursday afternoon Pablo, Carmen, and John agreed they had enough information to alert Loss Prevention. They met immediately and reviewed the information they had.

"Should we include HR too?" asked Carmen at the end of the meeting.

"Yes, this might turn into an investigation right away so let's loop them and Legal too," replied John.

They decided to meet with HR Friday morning.

"What time Friday?"

"Let's try for 11 AM or so. See if we can get them all together before lunch."

Friday morning the group assembled in the conference room. Since everyone arrived at about the same time, there was little waiting around and after some initial pleasantries, John described the situation.

"So, these salespeople are pocketing the sale proceeds?" asked the Sales Manager.

"Yes," replied Eduardo, the Loss Prevention Officer. "Let me show you what happened and how John, our chief auditor from headquarters, found this out."

With every sentence the Sales Manager grew increasingly angry at the betrayal. These were salespeople he knew and in the case of one of them, he hired himself.

"We'll take it from here," said Eduardo as the meeting adjourned. "We'll work with Legal and HR on the next steps." Everyone understood that given the amounts involved, and the duration of the fraud, termination and prosecution would likely follow. If there was any way to recover some of those losses, that should be attempted as well. They shouldn't get away with this.

-------------------||-------------------

"Hello everyone. Thanks for making the time to meet with us as we take a look at the results from the T&E audit. We modified our approach in consultation with Dan and Mary so we would address business concerns better," said Rachel kicking off the meeting. Even though Tony was the manager, Rachel was taking the initiative and embracing the new methodology, and newfound professional freedom, much more readily.

"We have some interesting observations to share with you. First of all, let's review our objectives. One, review T&E transactions by region to identify and review outliers. Second, search for opportunities for cost savings by region, especially related to air travel, hotel, meals, and car rentals.

Regarding our first objective, we used a technique called a Z-score. It is a statistical tool to help us identify outliers, which is important because we want to look through the entire population and identify any transactions that look strange or suspicious."

"You don't look at samples anymore?" asked Mary.

"Good question. Sampling has been a very common technique among auditors for decades, but as organizations digitize and software tools become more powerful, it is now possible to review all transactions instead of just a few. Let me back up a little. Sampling was usually done because as a reviewer you couldn't review all transactions, so you selected a subset and looked at that with the expectation that what you saw in the sample was a reflection of what was happening in the population."

"But if you can look at the entire population, looking at a sample becomes somewhat unnecessary" said Dan finishing Rachel's statement.

"Exactly. So it is now possible to look at the entire population in some cases as quickly or even faster than if you select a sample and review those transactions individually or manually. So back to the Z-score. It allows an analysis of the entire population and a comparison of each value, or subset if you want to, against the arithmetic mean, or average of all the other values. So, this way you can systematically look for outliers based on a mathematical, or statistical, criterium."

"Without eyeballing each number," Dan once again ended the statement for Rachel.

"Exactly," replied Rachel smiling as she spoke acknowledging Dan's comment.

"I worked in manufacturing, and we adopted Six Sigma. I am a Six Sigma Green Belt and my project used Z-scores," Dan explained.

"Oh, OK. Good! So, you can relate to our methodology!"

"I do."

"So, we ran the numbers and found some interesting results. We used MCC codes to determine…"

"What?" asked Mary.

"MCC codes, Merchant Category Codes. These are codes assigned by the credit card companies to different merchant types, like hotels, airlines, restaurants, etc."

"OK. Thanks. Go ahead."

"Yes, so ... I should probably show you the charts," said Rachel as she put the slide up on the screen. "Here are the top ten most widely used MCC codes. Nothing unusual. Not by location. Not by percentage or amount because the top ones are what we would consider legitimate travel-related transactions, airfare, hotels and each of these, restaurants, car rental, trains. However, after you go past the top ten, we noticed item 16 was code 5531, automotive supply stores, item number 17, 5533, automotive parts and accessories, number 18, 5541 service stations. Then over here we have items 5713 Floor covering stores, 5714 draperies and window coverings, and 5937 antique reproductions, and 7623, air conditioning and refrigeration repair shops. Looks like the person was doing home repairs. As we look over here, we see some more interesting items, 5551 boat dealers. The employee bought a boat and supplies. Then 5598 snowmobile dealers. Questions?"

Rachel stopped for a moment to let the information sink in. She had noticed Dan's neck turning pink as she went over the observations and by the time she got to the end his neck and ears were red. He was furious. Mary was sitting on her hands by now to hide her incessant fidgeting.

Rachel continued.

"The Z-score helped identify anomalous amounts and another procedure was to identify unusual codes. What I shared with you is the result of both procedures. We contacted Loss Prevention and shared our findings, so they went ahead and investigated these items further. These were either salespeople or accounting staff who made personal purchases and had InSports pay for these items. In all cases the amounts were low in terms of individual transactions, so they did this to avoid detection but when the amounts are added together, they figures are substantial."

"How much?"

"We broke them down by location, so Chicago was 40 thousand, Miami was 38 thousand and the boating another 22 thousand. The snowmobiles were in Vancouver for 12 thousand, so everything totals 112 thousand dollars."

"Over what period?"

"Three years, but the investigation is ongoing. Several people colluded in several of those frauds and some of them had been employees for between five and ten years, so we believe the amounts may be higher. Loss Prevention is now working on this and going further back to see if they can determine when each of those frauds started and the total amount."

"So, the amounts could be higher?"

"For these, yes. But there is another strange situation we uncovered."

"There is more?"

"Yes, unfortunately."

"There is a salesperson responsible for large accounts out of New York City who may have violated anti-corruption rules."

"I'm listening," said Dan closing his eyes and throwing his head backward. "Go ahead."

"He has been buying jewelry, watches, and things like that and either have them delivered to the office in Manhattan, to his home in New Jersey, to various office locations where he has them held until he arrives and, in several instances, shipped to client locations. The items were paid by the corporate card and later we found two transactions through Purchasing near the holidays, so we believe there are more yet to be found."

"Oh my. How bad?"

"Over sixty thousand. He generates a lot of sales, so his manager didn't review things too closely and he worked largely independently. But the bigger issue is who got these items. For all the other people, it appears they took possession of the goods they bought. Bad? Yes, but for personal use so a fairly clean fraud situation. This salesperson appears to have been buying gifts for clients."

"You said large accounts. US or foreign?"

"Thankfully, only national so no apparent FCPA implications. Foreign transactions all checked out when we looked at them."

"Phew. Who is investigating this?"

"We brought Legal in, and they are handling this."

"Keep me updated on what they find out and do. This Z-score technique is quite a thing. So, what else do you have for me?"

"That's it for Objective One. So if you don't mind, let's talk about Objective two, which pertains to opportunities to save the company money."

At this point Rachel and Tony described some policy recommendations that if enacted would result in InSports negotiating preferential rates with hotels, and car rental companies, and partner with a travel services provider to funnel all reservations and negotiate rebates.

"I don't like what you found, but I'm glad you did. And we need to find a way to prevent this from happening again," said Dan.

"Or detect it sooner," said Mary realizing that existing procedures allowed abuse to exist for long.

"Yes, both things."

"One of the new initiatives within Internal Audit is to support other monitoring units within InSports, so we would like to finetune the procedures we performed and create some scripts so they can run automatically or with minimal intervention. As soon as that's done, we can hand it over to Corporate Compliance, for example, or the operating units, so they can review the transactions periodically and address anomalies immediately."

"I like that. How soon can that be done?"

"A couple of weeks for the scripts to be written and one or two cycles to make sure they work like they should. We should also work with someone in Compliance so they understand how they work and be ready for us to hand these off to them when done."

"Please do it. In three months, this should go to Compliance for them to monitor, and Mary, work with them. Coordinate and make this a priority. This observation, when communicated up to chain is going to be ugly."

"You got it. We'll let you know about our progress and when the handover takes place. This concludes the initial phase of the T&E audit. We'll resume in the summer."

"Thank you. We need time to work through your observations. I have to say that as unhappy as I am with the fact that you found these issues, I'm happy you did, so we can put a stop to them. If this is what happens when you change audit programs, go ahead. See you in the summer," and with that Dan abruptly ended the call and Mary, who looked a bit shell-shocked, logged out shortly after him without saying another word.

"I feel badly for Mary, and to some extent Dan who I think is angry and embarrassed," said Rachel reflecting on the meeting.

"Maybe we're changing too fast and alienating auditees?" said Tony.

"I don't think so. We needed to change and I'm glad we're finally doing some more robust work. It was long overdue. We found all of these things because John suggested we perform these procedures."

"Fine," said Tony sounding exasperated at his colleague contradicting him. "Talk to you later."

"Bye," said Rachel wondering if Tony would continue being a guardian of the status quo, or move on and embrace the changes John was implementing.

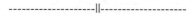

The next day, shortly after lunch, Tony and Rachel received an e-mail from John. In it he congratulated them on the work they did on the first phase of the T&E audit. John shared that he had spoken with Dan that morning and during that meeting he expressed gratitude for the work the two of them had done and apologized if he appeared angry or rude. He explained he was unhappy with the results but appreciated them for discovering the problems that can now be fixed.

John ended the e-mail with the note, "He specifically wants you to know that he supports the new approach."

"I wanted to meet with you because we noticed some accident numbers coming out of the Georgia facility and we wanted to chat with you about it."

"Sure. Yes. How can we help?"

"We have benchmarks, we explained our procedures to the workers, conducted training, but continue to have people getting hurt on the job. Thankfully they are not very serious requiring hospitalization. We would like to have zero incidents, but near zero would do for us," he said smiling trying to add a bit of lightheartedness to a serious situation.

"I understand," replied John. "Let's see what we can do. Can you give us some figures first?"

The two reviewed the incident data. They reviewed the number, the categorization of these incidents focusing on severity. During the conversation, it became evident that categorization was not very clear or consistently applied across facilities. When discussing the location of the incidents, there was no clear way to pinpoint production lines and information about the shifts affected was inconclusive. John also asked about the tenure or amount of experience of those injured, and information was not readily available either.

"Wow. Those are great questions too. Sorry, you are highlighting the need for better information on our part. Maybe you can look into that too?"

"Yes, sure. I ask these questions to help us get a sense about what we already know before we move into what we don't know. But that's fine. Let's do this. I'll draft a scope memo. Short, just something defining what we are looking into, your role, and I'll leave a few placeholders for you to indicate who our contacts would be for information, interviews, site visit, and so on. I'll put a projected duration and estimated date for a results document; a report of sorts, you know? How does that sound?"

"Sounds good. Thanks for your help, John."

"Sure. Glad to help."

"I'll be on the lookout for that draft scope letter and we'll finetune things from there."

"Perfect. Talk to you soon."

"Bye now."

"Bye."

As John ended the call, he thought to himself, "was that Operations soliciting audit's consulting assistance? It sure looks like it!"

--------------------||--------------------

"Are you sure that is a good idea?" asked Tony.

"Yes. We have been focusing on compliance-type work, but internal audit is much more than that and this is an opportunity for us to go there. What's your concern?" asked John probing.

"I just think that this might jeopardize our independence."

"Not necessarily. I agree there is a line we don't want to cross, but consulting or advisory work is OK if it is well defined. We just have to be clear about our role, and the role of our counterparts. That's why we'll prepare a scope document outlining the work, so that will serve as our project charter and expectations document. This way we draw that line and don't compromise our independence."

"Will we also include recommendations?"

"Probably."

"They'll treat those as audit requirements."

"Not if we explain in the beginning. When we publish the results of our work we will explain they are recommendations in the true sense of the word. Is this a common issue where management treats recommendations as a mandate?" John asked for clarification about the culture at InSports since he was still relatively new to the organization.

"Well. We haven't been doing consulting work, but when we tried it in the past, that is what happened."

"I understand. The way I think of it is that if something good went poorly we should examine it to see why it didn't work rather than walking away from the practice completely. There are good ideas that don't work at the implementation phase, not because they were not good ideas, but because there is a difference between strategy formulation and strategy execution that sometimes doesn't get enough attention."

"OK. Well. Maybe."

"I understand your skepticism about this, but we need to modernize internal audit. If this works, it will help us in that transformation. Since the department doesn't have a lot of experience with this, I'll be involved along the way. What do you think. Up to the mission?" John said attempting to encourage Tony.

"OK," he replied with a lukewarm, non-committal tone.

"Good! I'll start a draft and show it to you, so you see what it looks like. We'll talk about the proposed scope and timeline based on what we heard, and send it over for their reaction. Sounds good?"

"Sounds good."

"All right. I have to go. I should be sending that to you by end of day tomorrow. Bye."

--------------------||--------------------

"Hello everyone. We're very happy to have with us today one of the best project managers at InSports. Her name is Tanya Mendoza and she is joining us to talk a bit about what she and her team does, how they manage projects, KPIs they depend on, and how results are communicated. She can answer questions along the way during her presentation, but if you can, save them for the Q&A at the end so she can cover the topics she prepared for us today." With that, Tanya introduced herself, addressed the topics John mentioned, and answered questions for the team. The main takeaways were that systems, processes, and the people involved were working well together to understand what customers needed and wanted and then developing products and services that met those expectations.

There were questions about analyzing data from current and prospective customers, testing prototypes, designing, and conducting surveys and focus groups, and reviewing market research information.

The team was impressed by the speed at which they operated and got things done. They were known to develop products at a fast pace, but they also supported existing products providing updates, and their quality control unit was scientific and well-respected. A key takeaway was the use of KPIs to track the progress of their projects and the way they managed change orders, both challenges for other units within InSports.

The main weaknesses noted involved the transition from R&D to manufacturing and finding suppliers that would meet the requirements outlined in their specification documents.

At the end Tanya, who was as energetic during this meeting as she was when she met John initially, finished with a joke. The subsequent Q&A portion of the meeting was relaxed and productive. She answered their questions with detailed answers.

After she left, John engaged the team with some discussion to link what they had heard with what he hoped internal audit would do. They talked about the importance of innovation, helping InSports stay relevant, providing superior customer service, making sure testing was purposeful, that they pay attention to quality in all they did, and protecting sensitive information.

When they were done, John felt the team had been positively impacted by the experience. He finished by reminding them that as much as people generally embraced the phrase, and he saw a great deal of wisdom in the expression "don't reinvent the wheel," he wanted to impress on them that it was not always true. Whether it is incremental improvement, or an outright overhaul, there is always room for improvement even in internal audit methodology.

"Had people not reinvented, or improved, on the Egyptian stone wheel, horse-drawn wagons would be impractical, and we would be driving some very clunky cars on our roads."

The meeting ended with a good laugh as John displayed the pictures of a Flintstone car next to a Porsche Macan.

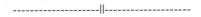

The accident data from the Georgia plant arrived, and John put Rachel and Brian to work on that review.

They had three days to go through the data. The instructions were fairly simple: the first phase involved understanding what data were provided, verifying the data were reliable, and then identifying and noting issues with data quality.

When done, move to phase two: perform analytics focusing on outliers, determine maximums-minimums-ranges-means, and perform comparisons by month, week, and day; daytime vs. nighttime; each shift; each product, every production lines, number of years of experience of the operators; categories of accidents; and training statistics. They were also to compare production orders, delivery dates, and accident figures.

The pair was done in two days and presented their results on the third day. They found a concentration of issues on the second and third shifts, overseen by two out of the eight managers, and the accidents correlated with newer employees and large rush orders. Training frequency and quality had deteriorated as of late due to turnover among the trainers.

John, Rachel, and Brian presented the results to Ken who was delighted with the speed and the focus of the review. He asked them to present the results to the EHS team at a later date as a potential training opportunity for them to collaborate with internal audit and adopt a more quantitative approach in their oversight capacity.

Since the staff were available that same week due to the slow activity levels during winter, the meeting with EHS occurred two days later. Only Miriam was missing from internal audit. Two managers represented EHS.

During that meeting the groups discussed the work of internal audit, the quantitative analysis done, and what the two groups typically focused on during their respective reviews. Several ideas were floated, but in general they agreed to discuss scope and review procedures in the future to minimize overlap, and for EHS to incorporate more analytical procedures, like Ken requested. Another important takeaway was the plan to review benchmarking data across locations.

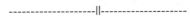

John opened the company's HRIS system to take a look at his team's skills inventory. He recalled how little information there was about training, and he wanted to make sure to tie any skill gaps, present and future, with training opportunities for the team.

The list was incomplete, focusing disproportionately on accounting and compliance topics: "Financial Accounting," "Financial Reporting," "Payroll," "Taxes," and "Contracting" stood out to him.

"All important, certainly, but I believe our external auditors should be handling some of these things and we should broaden our work to look at more operational, IT, knowledge management, and corporate culture topics." He made a note about these other categories, which were presently missing from the list.

He clicked on the next tab labeled soft skills. He noticed there was an extensive list more in line with what he was looking for. It included "teamwork," "verbal communications," "written communication," "time management," and "negotiation techniques," but none of the auditors had selected items or filled out their proficiency levels there. John made a note to include conflict resolution, persuasion skills, work ethics, and collaboration.

He went into the kitchen to make a cup of coffee. As he waited the recommended four minutes for the coffee to brew in his French press, he was looking out the window and realized he needed to add critical thinking, problem-solving skills, and adaptability to change to the list of soft skills.

He returned to his desk and more topics came to mind. He made a note to also add data analytics and creativity.

He noticed the five-point scale to rate proficiency levels. "The scale looks good and the descriptions make sense."

"Very good. Now where are my staff's entries referencing all of this?" He noticed that only Carolina and Brian had entries completed for their skills assessment. "Hmm. Maybe because they are the newest hires."

With this John started to cross reference his entire team and made an assessment based on what he knew so far. "I need to chat with each of them and have this updated, but I need some placeholders. We can't continue to have the skills inventory skewed towards accounting and compliance, most of the team hasn't completed it and my goodness, big miss on interpersonal skills!"

--------------------||--------------------

John settled into his seat and joined the Teams meeting. "Hi Kathleen, how are you?" he said as soon as her image appeared on screen.

"I'm well. Working on a few fun projects to keep our employees happy and reduce turnover. How are you?"

"I'm doing all right," he replied. "Trying to grow the team."

"That's what we do," she said with a cheerful voice.

"How busy is your recruiter?"

"Our recruiters," she corrected him. "We have several at different locations, and we're trying to develop them into specialists, so we'll have a go-to person for manufacturing and supply chain, someone for more creative fields like R&D, design, and advertising. For you, I think Linda would be best."

"How busy is Linda?"

"She's busy. We've had some turnover issues in a few areas within the company, but we may still be able to help you. How many people do you need and where will they be stationed?"

The conversation went smoothly as John explained he was looking for just one auditor for now. No preference on location, but in the United States. Now that work from home was commonplace it broadened the options for searching, and finding, the needed talent. Compensation options were also more flexible to accommodate different experience levels and cost of living scenarios, but in general, he was looking for someone with two to five years of experience. Everything was making sense to Kathleen until the conversation turned to the job description and in particular the needed credentials.

"What do you mean a degree in accounting is not required? I thought that was a requirement for audit jobs."

"Not anymore."

"Is that a decision you made or something bigger happening in the world of audit?"

"One impacted the other, but yes, the world of audit has been changing and I've decided to get on board with that."

"I was always told that auditors focused on accounting transactions, and they audited financial statements and the process to prepare those financial statements. In fact, we had a few auditors take a look at some of the things we do here in Human Resources, like payroll, which isn't exactly financial statement related, but is accounting related. Isn't it? Oh, and they reviewed some compliance things too like credentials, identification papers, and immigration status."

"What you're describing is the traditional focus of internal audit. It centered on accounting, financial information, and compliance. We will continue to do that, but our scope as a profession is broader now. Our scope of work now includes operational efficiency, IT, cybersecurity, and management practices that can lead to reputation damage. We still look for fraud, but not only economic fraud like embezzlement and tax fraud; we also look for leakage of PII."

"PII?"

"Personally identifiable information"

"Oh, yes. I forgot the acronym for a moment."

"No problem."

"IT and cybersecurity make sense. I just remembered, we helped to hire Brian, your IT auditor. But tell me more about the management practices and reputation damage? Those are outside what I have ever heard auditors do before."

"Yes, the key driver of what we do is risk. Let me give you an example. If we have a manager misbehaving in the company, like engaging in harassment, and we have a lawsuit on our hands, we have a major problem. Expensive for sure, but if there are several employees affected, it could hit the news and turn into a class. That's ugly, expensive, distracting and could affect our recruitment, retention, public image, you name it. So, auditors recognize that as a risk, so now, as a profession we have started doing culture audits. We look at training and the support managers get so they know what acceptable conduct is and what is not. Also, we check to make sure employees know what to do if they encounter a problem like this so someone can intervene immediately before the problem festers and goes from one person to another eventually turning into a larger problem," John explained.

"That's interesting. We would be involved in such audits, right? No disrespect, but one of your auditors going around the company asking employees about harassment could cause some waves, do you agree?"

"Agree. We're making big changes in internal audit and one of them is to increase collaboration with our audit clients. More specific to this type of audit, absolutely. We realize it is a very delicate topic, so we would work with you to make sure it is done well."

As Kathleen nodded in agreement, it was evident she was processing this new information. Her eyes glided across her desk, then over the monitor into the distance, and then back to John as her eyes refocused on him.

"John, did you say auditors now also look at processes? Did you say operational efficiency is part of your scope of work?"

"I did. Why?"

"Well, we have some recruitment problems here in HR."

--------------------||--------------------

"Hello everyone and Happy Tuesday. Hope everyone enjoyed the long weekend," said John getting everyone's attention.

"Too short, even with the extra day," said Brian, verbalizing what everyone was thinking. The work pace had been increasing and while the extra day was a welcomed respite, the team was still getting used to the accelerated work pace that was now becoming the norm.

"Yes, I agree. Time goes by too fast sometimes, so we must make every moment count. Whether it is work or personal time. I don't want to say 'time is money' because I don't believe everything should be reflected in monetary terms. Better, I believe, is to say 'time is precious,'" John replied.

"Work hard and play hard," said Brian again.

"Yes, indeed. Work hard and enjoy your moments of rest and relaxation in a healthy but determined way," said John acknowledging Brian's point, but adding a reflective tone to the "play hard" part of it.

"I usually start by asking Tony and Miriam about their upcoming week, what resources they need to accomplish their goals and any blockers. Today we'll start with Carolina, then Rachel, Brian and wrap up with Miriam and Tony. So, Carolina, the floor is yours."

When everyone had provided their updates, John turned to skills and training.

"OK everyone. I took a look at Talent+, our HR information system and noticed a few things I want to, one, consult with you about, and two, start working on some gaps I believe exist. So, one, did you, collective you, use this and enter your personal skills assessment?" he asked.

"No. We didn't use that. We only used the payroll and benefits section," said Miriam.

"And the time off, PTO, request forms," added Tony.

"Interesting. There is a whole section on skills there that no one ever used," John said.

"I saw that and filled some of it out, but I don't believe anyone looked at it," said Carolina.

"Me too. I was browsing through the platform one day and just started filling it out. I was hoping we would have a conversation about that, but we never got around to it. I was going to ask him about it before year-end last year, but next thing you know he was gone," explained Brian.

"No one said to fill it out, so I didn't," confessed Rachel. "I thought we should be doing that. At my previous company that was an annual exercise with quarterly updates."

"Thanks for helping me understand what was done, and not done, in the past. I agree that we should have a conversation about training and development and how I can help you advance your skills and your career. So, here's what we'll do. I want each of you to log in, go to the Skills and Talents section, and do a self-assessment. I expanded the list by the way, to include a more accurate list of the skills I believe internal auditors should have. Based on that and our conversation after you fill that out, we'll work on individualized training and development plans for the year. Sounds good?"

"By when do you want this done?" asked Miriam.

"A week should be enough time; today being Tuesday let's go with next week Friday, so you have a few extra days. Try not to be late so we can get this moving and we can talk about a training plan. Ok?" John instructed.

John explained the importance he attributed to training and development and how hiring people with the requisite skills was just the beginning; "you must remain knowledgeable, so continuing education is key," he told them. He also explained the value of being certified and recalled certifications were not shown in Talent+. It turns out only Miriam had a certification, CISA; that was it.

He encouraged the team to consider traditional internal auditor certifications like CIA, CISSP, PMP, and CFE and surprised them by also recommending they consider nontraditional ones related to cloud, networks, Six Sigma, and quality assurance, and construction contract administration. He also encouraged them to consider attending internal audit conferences and local chapter events.

He surprised them again by suggesting they read more about the fitness industry and that attending a fitness and health conference might be appropriate so they gained a better understanding of their industry.

--------------------||--------------------

After Kathleen explained the recruitment issues in New York, John called on Carolina to work on it. The problem consisted of delays finding suitable candidates.

"Hi Carolina. I have a project for you. You took Operations Management in college, right?"

"Yes, I did."

"Good. There is a situation in New York where recruiters are having difficulty finding candidates. Kathleen Meadows is the head of HR and she asked us to take a look. We have some data and I'm sending you a link so you can review it. Kathleen said that if you have any questions to contact her directly. Three days, two phases. Phase one, understand the data. Kathleen already told me she checked the data and it is reliable and there are no issues with data quality to worry about.

"For phase two, you move to perform analytics focusing on outliers, determine maximums-minimums-ranges-means, and perform comparisons by month, week, and day; job categories, number of calls, interviews, hires and for how long do those hired stay. Break those figures down by recruiter, number of years of experience of each recruiter and training statistics for each recruiter." He also told her to pay close attention to recruiter notes in the hiring platform.

Carolina was done in three days. She explained that her work moved relatively slowly because she had to read through many comments and she also had some difficulties reaching Kathleen, who had a very busy calendar.

She found that issues were of three types. The first involved poor job descriptions, so after the recruiter identified and spoke with leads, candidates either backed out when they spoke with the supervising manager or they resigned within a few months upon discovering what the job was truly about. The second type of issue involved delays sending offer letters and candidates often accepted other job offers they received sooner. The third type of issue involved low overall compensation, which was noted because many of the candidates who accepted the delayed offers, declined them because they were considered too low.

Carolina presented the results as John looked on. The recommendations included more detailed job descriptions and in-depth conversations about expectations of the role so recruiters could better screen and explain requirements with candidates. Another recommendation was for better timelines and deadlines for recruiters and managers to track cases moving through the recruitment process, and thirdly a market study to evaluate compensation levels because the last study was several years old.

Kathleen was very pleased with the quick turnaround, the quality and focus of results, and viewed the recommendations as being in line with her suspicions. She had found herself struggling to convince operations managers they needed to be more involved in the recruitment process but instead saw them take a hands-off approach then blame HR for the results.

As John was reviewing e-mails and catching up with some action items from his to-do list, he received a Teams chat message asking if he had a minute. It was Miriam and there had been some issues lately. Lots of fires all over the place and it kept everyone busy and on edge.

"Yes," he typed back. "What's up?"

"Can we do a video call?" came the reply almost instantaneously.

Less than a minute later they initiated the call and John noticed that she seemed upset.

"What's going on?" John asked. "It looks like this is not your favorite day of the week," he said trying to lighten the mood a bit and get the conversation moving positively.

"Well, Brian was asking for and reviewing some of the information we received for the IT audit and our contact there sent an e-mail to his boss asking some questions. His response, the boss', was really rude. Brian says he can't work with anyone in that department anymore!" she said while scratching her head, or maybe she was pulling her hair.

"That doesn't sound too good. Tell me more," replied John trying to be helpful and knowing that with sensitivities being where they were, he had to be careful to sound empathetic while helping his manager solve the immediate problem and improve her people-management skills.

"Like I said, he was reviewing some of the information and he needed to ask some follow-up questions, so he sent Kate an e-mail asking for clarification. The response came from Kate's boss, Barry. Brian says the response was very rude and unprofessional."

"Did you see the e-mail?"

"Yes, it was very detailed. The response sounded curt. Really abrupt."

"We have had problems working with people in IT. Zach treated IT poorly, so now everyone over there treats us poorly. It is unacceptable!"

"I hear you. I just want to make sure we understand the situation before we come to any conclusions. Zach was the IT auditor before Brian, right?"

"Right."

"He is gone because of behavior like that?" John asked so he would better understand some of the surrounding history.

"Yes, and more, but he wasn't really fired. He quit. He was rough around the edges. Very smart but had a bit of a chip on his shoulder. Anyway, that's in the past. Why are they treating Brian like that? He didn't do anything wrong?"

"Sounds like we're still dealing with the fallout and poor relationships around InSports. We'll need to work on that. We need to reassure Brian that we're working on it. Be empathetic and positive. Make sure he's Ok. Schedule a video call for later today so we can talk this through, see the e-mail, understand this as best we can, then I'll work with IT if I need to get involved. Before I call them though, I need to understand this better so we handle the situation the right way," John instructed.

"I will," she replied.

"Thanks. The takeaway here is that we need to be careful about hasty generalizations. That happens when we don't have enough data or information to formulate an opinion, but we do anyway. We'll work on making things better, but we need to be careful given the history around these relationships."

That afternoon John met with Miriam and Brian. They heard Brian's explanation and reviewed the chain of e-mails between Brian and Kate. She was Sam's counterpart in IT and had a similar attitude to Sam's toward internal audit. There was some confusion and Kate escalated the request to Barry, who then exchanged additional e-mails with Kate and Brian. In the end, after many e-mails moved back and forth among the three of them, Barry responded in what was clearly an exasperated tone.

By now Brian had calmed down. His explanation was a bit disorganized, but Miriam had succeeded in calming him down, so he was composed. Then John asked.

"Brian, what do you think of the number of e-mails exchanged?"

"I guess there were too many."

"I agree. What do you think of the way you explained what you needed and why?"

"I could have been a bit clearer about what exactly I needed and when."

"Again, I agree. I asked about 'what' and 'why'. You answered about 'what' and 'how'. What do you think of the 'why' of your request?"

"I get it. I never explained why I needed those things."

"What about the 'when'. They explained they needed more time to provide the information."

"It always takes them too long. I just wanted them to hurry up so we could get our work done."

"How about the way you needed the information submitted?"

"Yes, that too. There were nuances to the information request that were not very clear. But I didn't know that. I was just requesting information I was told we needed."

"I believe I saw somewhere in the e-mail chain that they objected to the files being provided via e-mail. Did you respond to that?"

"Oh yes. They did say that. I forgot. I guess I didn't respond to that. I missed that in the back-and-forth."

"Let's summarize this then. If you were in IT, or any department for that matter, and were asked these things as written, the what, why, and how. Might you be confused? Given the 'when', or deadline, might you be taken aback by what seemed like an unreasonable turnaround time? Before you answer, and this is difficult, but think about it for a moment because you wrote with the benefit of knowing what you were requesting. So, do you believe you explained the request clearly enough?"

Brian sighed before answering, "no."

"Ok. This is a learning opportunity. We'll get through this, but we need to think this through a bit more. So, what do you believe you might do differently next time?"

"Explain the who, what, when, where, why and how better," he replied.

"Yes, that is good. How about the medium you used. I mean, is e-mail the best tool for this?" John asked again.

"I don't understand," Brian responded.

"Email is a great tool, but not the best or only tool for everything all the time. In this case we can conclude that e-mail was probably not the 'only' tool we should have used here."

"I'm in New York, I can't go into Kate's office. She's in San Francisco," Brian replied, not quite defensively, but locked in his conviction that e-mail was the tool for the job.

"How about a phone call or better yet, a video call, like we're doing right now. When you write you only have the words. When you talk on the phone you have the benefit of tone and voice speed, so you can convey your meaning better and hear confusion or hesitation in the other person's voice. Signs you are probably facing an issue. Then when you can see the person, like a video call, you can see some of the body language. Not quite as clearly as being there in person, but facial expressions, posture and hand movements may tell you things aren't going well."

"But we need written evidence of the request."

"Yes, you can still do that. You can send an e-mail and schedule a call to discuss or have the call then follow-up with an e-mail as confirmation."

"That makes sense," Brian agreed.

"I've been there. E-mail is a great tool, but not the best for everything. Same about instant messaging, which tends to be even shorter of course. Quite cryptic sometimes. Keep this in mind and we'll provide some guidance for the entire team; it is a learning opportunity for everyone."

"The two of you should contact Kate and smooth things over. We need to get the audit moving again," John instructed.

Through it all, Miriam watched the conversation thankful she had not sent that e-mail she had been writing for another audit. She had spent a lot of time drafting it and she now decided to schedule a meeting instead. The e-mail could wait.

--------------------||--------------------

The next day Miriam, Brian, Kate, and Barry met and they discussed the situation. Barry didn't realize his e-mail had sounded that harsh, but he admitted to being taken aback by the e-mail tennis he was pulled into. By the time the call was over, they were talking about other IT audits underway and how InSports needed help managing the growing list of IT risks.

Subsequently, Miriam shared her observations with John, who added notes to update the risk assessment on file. Miriam's observations were shared via e-mail.

--------------------||--------------------

John started the weekly staff meeting with a quote: "Failure is the opportunity to begin again more intelligently. Henry Ford." He said it again and waited a few seconds for the words to sink in. Then he continued.

"Everyone. All of us want to be successful. We want to do a good job. Excel. Prove ourselves. Even if it is just to preserve our jobs so that we can protect our basic needs and our lifestyle, or to prove ourselves so we get rewarded and promoted later on; we want to do well. However, life is complicated and there are challenges. Some of our own doing, some caused by external factors. Either way, we may fail at times.

Our culture and organization celebrate success and accomplishments, which is to be expected. But I want to also highlight the fact that even Henry Ford, one of the most successful entrepreneurs, business leaders, and business influencers, recognized failure as a possibility. An opportunity. A development to be viewed and treated as an opportunity. A chance to get up, brush yourself off and get going again. This time with lessons learned so we can move forward more intelligently. We try not to fail catastrophically, so we plan, strategize, anticipate, and plan again. Then we act, check on the results. Go back to the planning board and keep going. There is a technique called PDCA that is widely used in manufacturing and quality assurance. Anyone familiar with the acronym?" he asked after his short presentation.

"Plan, do, check, act," replied Carolina.

"Exactly."

"Plan is about setting objectives and processes that are necessary to deliver the results we want according to specifications.

Do is about implementing the plan and making the product or delivering the service. One thing that is not mentioned often is that during this phase we should be collecting data, which becomes important for the next step, Check.

Check is about studying the actual results collected from the previous phase and comparing those results against the expected results or objectives that we defined in the Plan phase. This helps us identify gaps and determine what differences exist between the plan and actual results. The last phase is act.

Act is where we request corrections to the main deficiencies between the planned and actual results. Here we also analyze the differences to determine what is, or are, the root causes of the gaps identified. PDCA."

"A few weeks ago, we had a situation where we decided not to write lengthy e-mails to IT because long e-mails lend themselves to misunderstandings. We fixed the situation by talking to the client then and that review moved forward. This week it happened again. Another lengthy e-mail to IT that escalated to the person's manager, and we resolved it by talking it over. This is a reminder about the importance of not repeating actions that we determined are ineffective. We need to learn from our mistakes and move forward trying not to do the same thing again. Understood?" said John speaking firmly and making it known that he was not pleased by the repeated behavior that created avoidable complications. Miriam, Rachel, and Brian knew that he was talking about them and appreciated not being singled out by name.

Having made his point, John changed the topic so the group could move on.

"So, we will continue trying things as we create a better internal audit department. Don't be too afraid to fail. We may from time to time. We'll just try not to cause catastrophic failures, but beyond that, it is OK to try new and different things. We're moving forward. Sounds good?"

"Sounds good," came the collective reply.

"Well then, let's turn now to the rest of our agenda," John said as he led the team through a discussion of the projects in progress.

--------------------||--------------------

"For book club this month, how about we read Good to Great? I read it in college, and it was very interesting. I liked how practical it was and I believe the recommendations would be good for us as we assess our processes," said John. "Any other ideas or suggestions?"

No one said anything for a while until Miriam replied, "I like it. I never read it, but I've heard a lot about it over the years."

"Well, I was afraid to say that myself, but I never read the book either, so thanks Miriam for confessing to this one. I like the recommendation too," said Brian.

After a pause to allow others to opine, John said, "Ok. Since I don't hear other suggestions, raise your virtual hands everyone who likes this book," as he was first to raise his virtual hand. Promptly, Miriam, Brian, Rachel, and Carolina did the same, but not Tony. His hand protruding from a long-sleeved shirt was visible on camera voting in the affirmative too.

"Since all hands are up it looks like we have a unanimous 'yes', so that's our book for March. Thanks everyone. Let's now talk about how our projects are coming along. Miriam, lead the way."

--------------------||--------------------

Summary
Winter

The first audit committee meeting of the year started amicably, but there was an evident tension in the room. John knew that his bosses were assessing his performance in light of the tenuous situation under which he was hired. They wanted an update on his progress because they wanted to make decisions about him, his team, and their own reputations.

The meeting started with a very direct question that clearly set the tone and mood for what was clearly a no-nonsense meeting – "You have been in your role for three months now. What do you believe needs to be fixed?" asked Jim.

While John preferred more relaxed and friendly interactions with the audit committee, he knew their relationship wasn't there yet. He was asked a direct question and he needed to provide an answer to match. "Here are some of the areas where I believe we need to improve. The audit plan is not as risk based as it should be. We need to diversify the risk areas we review and we've not been doing any consulting or advisory work. I already delivered two consulting projects that resulted in immediate positive results. We'll do more later, but I believe we should focus on and get comfortable with compliance, or assurance first, so we'll tackle a significant increase in advisory work down the road. Another area of focus for me is skillset development. I am working with the team assessing their competency levels, doing a gap analysis, and preparing a training and development plan tailored to each auditor, that is also collectively geared towards upskilling the unit."

Finding that answer satisfactory, the next question was a relatively innocent one, but one with very serious and consequential implications. "Is the internal audit department following the Standards?" asked Jim again.

"That is a very good question and one that I started asking myself right away when I started working at InSports. Here's my take. Generally speaking, yes. We have some room for improvement, but we are righting the ship and so far, some of the key requirements and arguably, some of the most important, are being met. For example, we are having this conversation because internal audit reports directly to the AC. That focuses on our independence, and we don't have operational responsibilities. We are documenting, and communicating the results of our work, and following-up on management's action items like we should."

"How about the relationship with management?" asked Sanjay touching on the strained relationship that existed between audit and management.

"Yes, I was getting to that because you're right, and you did warn me about that during the interview process, there is room for improvement there. I've met with everyone on the executive leadership team and key players mid-level too to patch

DOI: 10.1201/9781003322870-4

some of those relationships and rebuild a few bridges. They have been very candid with me, so I believe we're addressing these challenges honestly."

"What are some of the other things that need to be done so you can provide us the information, and assurance we need about what's happening at InSports?" asked Jim again.

"For you to rely on the information we provide, everyone on the team must understand and follow the Standards. We must execute as professional internal auditors and some things to address are for example the need for a more risk-based approach, having a better understanding of the objectives of the areas we're auditing, and incorporating that knowledge into the way we audit; the methodology. I noticed that audit programs, an important component of our methodology were too repetitive and scripted, so they were no longer meeting the current needs of our clients, so I changed that. This will provide a better alignment so we act like a service unit within InSports, helping management understand, or I should say, verify, that what should be happening is happening and we are helping them succeed. Again, independence and objectivity reign supreme, but this alignment helps us avoid auditing in a vacuum."

"This sounds good. We've heard the term control-based vs. risk-based. You have been talking quite a bit about risk-based. What is your understanding and the difference and how are you going to move from control to risk-based?" asked Sanjay.

"The explanation can be a bit lengthy but in summary control-based is prescriptive, reviewing controls because they're there and following scripts and checklists previously created. Risk based is more fluid so the focus is on understanding what the objectives are for the area under review, what can get in the way of achieving their objectives and what measures are being taken to protect the organization from the downside while increasing the likelihood of achieving the stated objectives. It is not only about protecting value, but also about helping the organization create value. It requires more thinking, better alignment, and more flexibility. It also requires higher-level skills and thinking, but the result is much better; far superior. You will feel more confident in what we're doing and what information we're providing you as this approach becomes more ingrained in the department."

"Ok. Thanks John," said Jim as he redirected the meeting. "Let's take a look at your quarterly report." With that the group started reviewing performance metrics looking at audits in progress, audits planned, number of hours spent on each by phase, and projected completion dates. At the end of that review, John wanted to ask the AC if the report's format was meeting their needs, but he decided against that; "too soon," he thought to himself. "I'll bring that up at the next meeting or the fall. I'll focus on substance, and get their confidence first, and we can address form later."

There was a lull in the conversation as the audit committee members seemed to be digesting the information received, what they heard, and whether they still harbored any reservations about the progress they were hearing about. The next question suggested the tone was turning a bit friendlier now.

"How are the auditors doing in the work-from-home arrangement? Is that going to affect the quality or quantity of work?" asked Sanjay.

"Not really. I don't think so. Working from home is a reality in many organizations. The key is how you manage the group. There had been a trend towards remote work for auditors for quite some time, even though some organizations were reluctant to embrace it. Of course, the pandemic accelerated that shift, and some may argue pushed us there. We'll be fine. I manage by objectives and output is not driving performance assessments, outcomes do," said John confidently.

"We're running out of time, but before we go, I have one last question for you. Do you have any new ideas you are working on?" asked Jim.

Before answering the question, John wondered if this was actually a test. Was he focusing on fixing the fundamentals or was visioning potentially going to distract him too much and confuse the team leaving them without a clear path forward? He already knew the pitfalls of moving in too many directions at once, so he explained his approach.

"I have a strategic plan and a tactical one. They're connected, but I want to make sure that I don't confuse or overwhelm the team. We are going to get them upskilled and tighten our methodology, so you are more confident in what you are getting from us. By year-end, we will have some bigger items on display. I'll update you every quarter, but the process is gradual, yet decisive. I already spoke with them about the need for change and how it will impact them personally as we rebuild the team. So far, their behaviors are lining up toward that transformation," John answered reassuring the AC that he was in control of the situation and leading the team in the right direction with the right approach.

"Do you have what you need to make this happen?" asked Jim.

With that question, the team discussed the budget now that John had been on the job for three months, the audit plan and the need for a flexible one, and changes that were possible given the changing conditions at InSports.

As John walked out of the building, he felt the cold chill still in the air. NYC is always intriguing and inviting, but today he was feeling tired. He started heading North, turned East on a street that was going into evening mode, and entered the subway station. He would take the train back to his hotel, eat dinner at a pub nearby, and get to bed early. He was exhausted.

The team met in New York for their quarterly meeting. The first activity was a social one the afternoon of the first day since most of them arrived that same day. They met at the hotel's lobby and walked over to an Italian restaurant. Dinner was uneventful except for a debate over what type of wine to get; Carolina wanted an Argentinian Malbec, Rachel a French Chardonnay, Miriam didn't drink alcohol so she abstained, Brian wanted beer but for wines he preferred South African Syrah, and Tony said he would drink whatever the team chose, so he didn't help much. John had a preference but in his role chose to observe their behaviors rather than get too involved and steer the voting too much, so he chose a neutral path – he asked the waiter. In the end, the team shared two bottles: a white Pinot Grigio and a red Chianti; they were at an Italian restaurant after all.

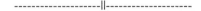

As the group settled in for their meeting, John started.

"Hello everyone. Good morning. Nice to see you. Hope you slept well." Everyone nodded in agreement, although they seemed a bit tired from the travel and late dinner the night before.

"Earlier in the year I told you I was not going to ask you to return to the office. In fact, few organizations do. The work from home arrangement is fairly standard and I believe we can do most of our work remotely. However, I also said at the time that I believe there are times when coming together would be good so we can review company and departmental news together, connect with each other better by socializing, meet some of our clients, and have some training added to the event," he said as he counted with his fingers the four key goals of meeting in person. "So, how did we do with number 2, socializing?" he asked with a smile.

After a short pause while the team processed the four objectives, but also realizing their boss was starting the conversation with the most casual of the four items, Miriam responded, "it was good. The food was great and so was the company." The team reminisced about the day before, which made it clear to John that getting them together was a good idea. A considerable amount of time was spent talking about the pros and cons of working remotely, and individually, for months during the winter. They spoke about wellness; ways to improve and maintain work–life balance; the importance of exercise for physical, mental, and spiritual wellness; the need to be on the lookout for symptoms of extreme isolation in themselves and their teammates; and the lack of sunlight during winter.

The group then reviewed company and department performance over the quarter, projects in progress, and planned to begin in Q2. They spent a considerable amount of time talking about the work on the improved T&E audit and the recruitment process improvement project.

Lunch was delivered to the office, which provided additional opportunities to socialize. The afternoon was split between time to work side by side with each other on ongoing projects, and time to meet and greet others at InSports. That evening they went to a sports bar, where they had dinner, played some games, and, with dozens of TVs all around, it allowed the team to watch the sport of their choice.

For Day Two, John conducted three short training sessions on ways to add more data analytics and add fraud audit steps to audit programs. For soft skills, they learned interviewing techniques.

The group had lunch delivered to the office again, and after eating, John engaged the group for a recap of the quarter's work. "Let's revisit some of our accomplishments for Q1. One, I joined this amazing team and thank you for welcoming me into your group. While there is a lot of work ahead, which I told you when I started, let's take some time to celebrate what we have accomplished. I'll start by saying that your willingness to try new things is commendable and appreciated. That's one of the first things necessary to bring about change. We also agreed that our metrics needed to be revisited so they more accurately reflected where we're going, what we're doing and how far along we have come, in other words, what was accomplished. What else did we accomplish this quarter?"

"We improved our process for selecting training. It used to be very ad hoc, with each person asking for what they thought they needed and often not getting it. It looks like we're focusing more on training now. I found Tanya's training on project management also very helpful," said Miriam leading the way.

"Yes," acknowledged John, "training is very important to me and will be for our department going forward. I can't expect you to do something if you don't have the knowledge and skills to do it." John then paused briefly as he thought about the potential underlying message in Miriam's words; then he added, "training needs to be focused; strategic. We are creating a new vision for the department, so the training needs to align with your and our department's current, combined, skillset, our individual and combined strengths, and weaknesses, but equally important, our future, combined, skillset. We will work together to make sure all of this is aligned. Thanks Miriam, good highlight."

John continued, "On the topic of skills, it has come to my attention that some of you may be feeling a little uncomfortable and stressed by my approach when we're analyzing a situation and trying to figure something out because I ask a lot of questions rather than telling you directly. I realize that telling people what to do is a common management approach, but I have a different philosophy. I prefer to follow the Socratic Method, which consists of dialogue based on questions and answers that stimulate some debate, but also critical thinking. In my experience, those involved understand the goal and approach better through inclusion in the process rather than being passive and only receive instructions to-go-and-do. It also makes everyday activities and decisions learning moments. Lastly, the top-down approach of telling people what to do is very autocratic and hierarchical; with such a small team, I believe in including people as much as I can. Does that make sense?"

After a brief moment while the team processed John's explanation and what in their unit was an unconventional approach, Miriam replied.

"Yes, it makes sense and while we appreciate the learning opportunity, we ask that you understand it can be tough since we are not used to that approach."

"I understand and I appreciate this being brought to my attention. We are a team and communication in all its forms, whether it is concerns, instructions, questions, or suggestions should flow as freely and often as possible. Back to our list of accomplishments," he said directing the group back to the agenda item.

"We have a say in the projects that we want to work on," shared Rachel, following Miriam's lead. "Previously we were assigned to projects without much of a chance to give an opinion. Don't take this the wrong way Tony and Miriam, I believe it was the Big Boss who decided for all of us," she concluded trying not to blame the two managers present.

"The Big Boss, like you call him, told us, so we just passed the message down," said Tony defensively trying to avoid being blamed for that past practice.

"That's what I said, Tony. I wasn't blaming you," she said with a similarly defensive tone.

With this John sensed a theme and the lingering tension between Rachel and Tony. He recognized the need to address the latter problem, so a few words were necessary.

"It looks like decisions were made at the highest level with limited input, even from the managers, so we'll work on that. In fact, my view is to engage with as many people as possible, and with a team this size, I would be remiss in excluding all of you unless the situation specifically warranted a level of confidentiality and I had to exclude someone. Otherwise, you have my commitment to include you in shaping your work life. I can't promise to give you everything you ask for, but I will hear you and we'll work things out together. Sounds good?"

"Yes," came the response from everyone, either visually with nodding heads and smiles, or audible "yeses."

"Other wins for the quarter?" John asked again, re-engaging the group in the exercise.

"Yes, we have been working on restoring the confidence of our auditees," said Carolina.

John took the opportunity to expand the conversation because this was one of his most important goals, and accomplishments so far, but also to encourage the most junior auditor in the team to speak more, "tell us more about that Carolina."

"We were not in very good terms with several people in Accounting, Operations, and other areas, but while they still seem suspicious, I've noticed a slight change in their attitude towards us. Maybe just giving us the benefit of the doubt again, but I'll take it! I believe you speaking at the company's quarterly town hall meeting was good for all of us," she said finishing her statement with a smile.

"I'm glad to hear that, Carolina. Even if all they've done so far is given us the benefit of the doubt, it creates an opportunity for us to redefine the relationship and turn things around. Now we need to convince them that we're the new and improved internal audit department," replied John with an enthusiastic tone trying to lift the mood of the meeting after the exchange between Rachel and Tony.

"We delivered the first Road Show presentation," said Tony with a serious tone.

"Yes, the Road Show. Tell us more about it, Tony," John asked.

"We created a presentation that explained what we do, and we delivered it to one of our key clients," he said in a matter-of-fact way.

"How would you say we did?" asked John trying to get Tony to elaborate.

"We did Ok. They understand we do more than compliance," he said with limited emotion.

Realizing that Tony's stoic attitude was not likely to change, John decided to move on hoping to regain some more positive energy in the meeting. "Brian, we can't leave you out. What say you?" John asked in an upbeat tone inviting the free-spirited Brian to take his cue and hopefully reply in kind.

"Well, you didn't tell us to return to the office to work, that's a win. You got rid of the 15-minute increment time-tracking thing. That's another win. You are looking to hire some new people, I believe that's three. We also learned about PDCA. That's four. We learned not to send extra-long e-mails to IT. That's five. And we now have book club. Minus one, so we're back to five because I don't like to read," he said with a big smile. "Just joking, that's six and I like to read."

The entire team looked at Brian surprised, no one more than Rachel.

"Wow, thanks Brian. That's quite a summary. Fewer administrative requirements, plans to expand the team's number, new collaboration tool and your favorite club," John said acknowledging Brian's contribution and using his energy to rally the team.

After some unstructured talk where they covered miscellanea, there was one item left on John's mind, so he asked the team for their feedback on their first get-together. They discussed their objectives of reviewing company and departmental news, socializing as a team, meeting clients, and getting some training. The feedback was very positive, and they said they were looking forward to getting together again. With that, John brought the meeting to a close, they said their goodbyes, and left headed to the airport and train stations to return home.

--------------------||--------------------

4 Creating a Vision and Strategy

John was in the office and asked his team if they wanted to come to the office for the day. Tony, Miriam, Rachel, and Brian joined him there, while Carolina joined remotely.

"Hello everyone, how was your weekend?"

"Good," said Rachel right away and asked a return question immediately "how was yours?"

"Mostly good. I went running and had to drop out," said John.

"What happened?" asked Rachel and Miriam in unison.

"Cramps. I could run 10Ks no problem, but it is getting harder to do every year."

"Did you stretch?" Brian asked.

"That was my mistake. I got there late, barely warmed up then started running too soon. Once upon a time I could just lace up and go, but now I have to spend as much time warming up and stretching as running. Crazy, eh?" he said with a smile trying to lighten the mood since everyone seemed concerned about his health.

"Well, at least you can still run. My knees won't let me, so I bike instead," shared Tony.

"Risk management, gentlemen, risk management," said Carolina.

"You and your risk management line. You crack me up!" said John.

"Yes, but am I right or what? Celia Cruz has a song where she says 'Si quieres llegar primero, mejor se corre despacio. Disfruta bien de la vida, pero tomando medidas.' 'If you want to get there first, it is better to run slowly. Enjoy life, but take preventive measures,'" she said, quoting the Cuban Salsa singer's lyrics before translating them to English for her co-workers.

As the team laughed at the Salsa singer's words of wisdom, John interrupted the group "on that note, excuse the pun everyone, let's get started. How about a quick exercise. Think of an object that we can say represents internal audit."

"A snail," said Rachel.

"A snail?" asked John.

"Yes, we're slow and over the past couple of years we got offended by the feedback we got in our post-audit surveys, so we got rid of it; so, we are slow, fragile and can't handle a little salt thrown our way."

"Hmm, wow. well, that's interesting, but not quite what I had in mind," John confessed.

"How about a rock," said Brian. "We are hard to deal with, we don't move easily, and we use it to beat people when they don't do what they say they'll do."

"That's graphic and not funny," countered Tony.

"I'm just joking Tony, well joking about the beating people. Of course, I wouldn't do that, not with a rock, maybe a stick, but never a rock. I'm joking. I'm joking,

DOI: 10.1201/9781003322870-5

but not about the hard to deal with and the don't move. We are a boulder," now shifting his tone to a more serious one.

"Ok. I get your point, Brian," said John, inserting himself into the conversation. "Let's hold onto some of those thoughts and let me tell you what I had in mind. How about an object that represents *what we would like to become*. Is that a little better? Let's do this. How about we take 5 minutes to work individually. Think about that and why you chose that object," said John providing better guidance and instructions for them to work on an exercise.

As the group went to work, John thought how the team was talkative, had a nice way of bantering with each other, and used some humor while working. "That's a good base to build upon," he thought to himself.

When done he gave them some more assignments to be done individually, in pairs, and for the entire group to work on. They reviewed and wrote aspects of their mission statement, vision statement, and values.

"What do we want to do for dinner?" asked Miriam.

"Let's go to Times Square. The N, Q, R, S, W, 1, 2, 3, and 7 trains stop there," said Tony.

"M I C K E Y, M O U S E. Which one from here gets to Times Square Tony?" said Rachel sarcastically.

"Not necessary, Rachel. There are trains to get us there and I am not that familiar with the train system in New York yet. Thanks Tony," said Brian defending Tony and trying to smooth things over with Rachel.

Rachel apologized and explained she was having some family issues and was under a lot of stress. The team rallied around her as John watched how they supported their colleague.

"Let's go to Times Square and have dinner on Restaurant Row, or maybe dinner first. We can also buy some same-day discounted Broadway tickets," offered Miriam providing more options the team could choose from as they continued bonding and finding enjoyable things to do together.

As everyone stood up and started gathering their belongings to head out, Tony looked at his phone and immediately sat back down. "Oh great!"

--------------------||--------------------

"Hi Frank, how are you?" asked John.

"I'm well. Just getting back into the house. Betty and I were out playing tennis," came his reply as he seemed to be ruffling the phone against his ear.

"Good for you. Did she beat you again?" asked John.

"Of course. I don't know how she does it, but she does. She's a much better player than I am. She makes it seem effortless. Anyway, I promised her I would grill for dinner, so that's what I'm working on now."

"Is this a good time to talk or should I call you later?"

"No, no. no. Go ahead. Meat is already marinated and getting the fire going is quick. It's always good hearing from you. So how are things at InSports? Getting by?"

"Things are coming along. As you know I need to turn the unit around. There are lots of legacy practices, and some mindsets within the department and throughout the organization that need refocusing. I'm running into some resistance. I was thinking I might call you for your thoughts."

"Sure. I understand. That can be difficult. Remember that a change initiative can be very complicated as it impacts people and processes. Even the tools you use. All of it can be hard for people to understand, especially those employees at the lower end of the hierarchy. Have you been telling them about your vision?"

"Yes, I've been seeding their minds with it for a while, so they are ready for the transformation that's coming."

"Is it working across the different levels in your department?"

"Not equally. I have some at the top that are very set in their ways and some at the bottom who can't quite seem to grasp what it will look like. They are new to this."

"I see. You have a vision in your head, but you may want to create a vision statement that is easy to understand and captures the overall goal. Something they can read, reflect on, revisit periodically. Is it written? Before you answer, I'm grilling now, just so you know."

"It's OK if you need to go, I understand. Regarding your question. Not yet. I've been talking about it, but nothing in writing yet. I guess you're suggesting I do, and while I'm at it, to pay very close attention to the language?"

"Exactly. You need support from everyone, within audit and outside. Using complicated language would be counterproductive, especially if it has a lot of auditor jargon. Keep it simple, positive, and understandable. And don't forget inspirational or it may not generate the effect you're aiming for."

With these words John realized that the team exercise they did, and the draft vision statement he was writing lacked some of these positive qualities and had some of the negative ones. As he repeated it in his mind, he identified some words that should be replaced.

Frank and John discussed the qualitative aspects of the vision for some time. They discussed the internal and external elements of the vision, collaboration with other assurance providers and management, adding value and what that meant in measurable terms, and what a reasonable timeline was given the small department, limited resources, and needs at InSports.

At the conclusion of their conversation, Frank said, "You are working on item number one. Congratulations! However, you are missing two equally important things here," after a brief hesitation as if someone else were also trying to get his attention.

"What am I missing?" asked John.

"Oops, I've got to go. Meat's about to burn. Always important to move things along John. Don't let things cook for too long." As John tried to figure out if there was some connection to Frank's earlier comment, the last thing he heard Frank say was "Yikes."

"I hope he didn't burn the steak," he thought to himself as he pondered what the other two things he needed to do next were.

---------------------||---------------------

The next morning, as John opened a new bag of Colombian coffee and poured some into the French press, he kept thinking about the next steps Frank mentioned before the call ended abruptly. He was thinking out loud when he said, "I'll edit the vision statement and share it with the staff at our next meeting."

He poured some hot water and walked over to his desk. As he was preparing the agenda for the meeting and still thinking about Frank's word, he thought he might have figured out what he was alluding to.

"I can't just tell them people in the organization about this. They will forget by dinner that very same day. We need something better organized. Creating the vision is not enough to get the support we need for it. We need a good mechanism to communicate it throughout the organization." As he thought about this, he had an idea. "I'll use the coalition that's emerging. They are all connected and part of the InSports network throughout the company. I also need to communicate this message often because I'm up against competing messages."

He returned to the kitchen to the scent of fresh coffee, pressed it, and poured some into one of his souvenir mugs with the London Underground map on its side. As he paused to reminisce about The Tube and how much he enjoyed London he had a thought that made him freeze.

"Aha! I'll post this in our Teams channels, through some selected e-mail messages, I'll have it posted on our website too." As his enthusiasm grew, he started thinking about the individuals that would best help support this transformation. "Kathleen in human resources, Ken in operations, and Brenda and Tanya in R&D." He listed the names of his key allies in his head. "Having Dan from the controller's office in my corner would be good too. I'll call them selectively but in general they already seem pleased with the changes I'm making here. They may have some insights to project the change throughout InSports."

As he opened his laptop to create a list of To Dos and write down the names of his coalition members, another thought ran through his head. He leaned back as he took a sip and thought, "People are anxious to talk face-to-face. I need to see my staff and several business partners in different locations. I need to expand the Road Show to additional locations! That will help communicate this vision even better. All of this relates to a singular category, so this must be Frank's number two. What is number three?"

At that moment he heard a notification on his laptop; a quick glance revealed a situation needing his immediate attention.

--------------------||--------------------

As John was preparing the plan for his Road Show, he thought about his team and more specifically his managers. Miriam was ready for change. She understood the need and was pushing for it. Tony, on the other hand, seemed to be struggling.

"I need to get Tony on board. He needs to understand the goal, become an advocate for it and support the change through action. How do I get him to replace old-school auditing and managing with the new methodology I'm putting in place? Maybe training, but I guess I'll have to coach him, help him re-skill and develop," he thought to himself.

--------------------||--------------------

5 Updating the Methodology

"Good morning, everyone! How are things?

"Cold, said Rachel. It was in the 30s this morning!"

Somehow a statement like that acts like a trigger for everyone to look at their phones to quote their own temperatures.

"That's not cold. It was 25 degrees in Chicago," said Brian. I went to visit some friends over the weekend. I thought it would feel like spring by now."

"Chicago is cold even in the summer," replied Rachel.

"Maybe, but San Francisco holds the title for being cold in the summer. Who was it, Mark Twain who said "The coldest winter I ever spent was a summer in San Francisco?"

"There is some question as to whether he actually said that, but whoever said it first, I am always cold in San Fran no matter what time of year I go," said John. "London. What are things like where you are, Carolina?"

"Well, it is 13 degrees, but that's Celsius, of course."

"How much is that in Fahrenheit?" asked Brian.

"Around 55 degrees," she replied.

"How can you convert these temperatures so fast?"

"When you grow up and live outside the US, but spend as much time with Americans you develop this superpower," she said jokingly.

"OK, folks. Nice to see and hear everyone," interjected John. "Everyone has their coffee and blankets to stay warm? We need to get the meeting started, but make sure you're comfortable. Scarves are OK too," he said jokingly. "As I indicated in the meeting agenda, we should spend some time thinking through our methodology, because there are a few things we can improve upon there."

He continued, "as I reviewed the annual plan for the past 5 years, audit reports and related workpapers, I noticed an interesting pattern. Most audits were of T&E, AP, AR, and payroll. And although the reports shared only a few findings, and none particularly serious, we kept auditing the same areas."

Tony noticed that John said "we," which he thought was good because when the meeting started, he feared this would turn into a "who do we blame" session.

As John described the prevailing approaches used in traditional auditing, he explained how the profession moved beyond auditing those processes that relied primarily on accounting topics, and shifted to the modern embrace of risk-based auditing.

"We've been to training on risk-based auditing but our previous director wanted us to do those audits," said Tony.

DOI: 10.1201/9781003322870-6

"I understand," replied John. "I'm not trying to blame anyone, either here or departed. But let's think ahead because we're going to go beyond talking about what we should do and we're going to actually do those things from now on."

He continued. "From a definition perspective, what is risk-based auditing? Since all of you took that class, I saw your personnel files, anyone wants to explain it so we're all on the same page and starting from a point of common understanding?"

"I'll give it a try," said Miriam. "It focuses on the analysis of risk as the basis for all audit work, so instead of going straight to controls, we look at the risks that are more significant and then look for the controls that mitigate them."

"We should be studying, understanding, and testing risks and not just checking to see if the controls are working," said Rachel.

"Anyone else?" asked John.

"Well, I guess the difference from traditional auditing is that instead of testing all controls in a process, you only test those that relate to the most important risks. Most important meaning key," said Miriam.

"All of this is true," said John. "Think about your house and the fact that you have a lock on the front door and on your windows. The locks are controls. The risk is that someone gets into your house and steals your valuables. Or hurts you. The objective, and no one mentioned objectives, but objectives are key to risk-based auditing. The objective, like people often say, is for your home to be a safe place for yourself, your loved ones, and your belongings. Are you following?"

"Yes," they said in unison.

"You can test whether there is a lock on the door and the windows. That is the test of design. If there are locks, some auditors would check the box indicating they found the control. But is that enough?" John asked.

After a brief pause, Brian said. "Not really."

"Good. Why?" asked John.

"Because having locks doesn't mean the homeowner is using them."

"Exactly! So, we should check to see if the locks are being used. We can select a sample and test 25 days to see if the locks were used. Is that enough?"

After another pause, Brian spoke again. "What if the lock is not a really good one. It locks but you push the door lightly and it opens?"

"Good! That refers to effectiveness, so we can see if it's a hard lock that sustain some pressure. What else?"

Rachel added her thoughts. "Testing for 25 days doesn't mean the lock is always used. Maybe they locked the door those 25 days, or some subset of those, but they habitually leave the door unlocked otherwise."

"Very good. Exactly, so we could test a few instances and say we determined that based on our testing the lock had been engaged x number of days or y percentage of the time, but the goal of securing the house begs for the locks to be engaged all the time. If we sample statistically, we could draw some conclusion about the totality of days within our confidence level, which is usually 95 percent."

After a short pause, John continued. "Imagine the house has standard doors to the main portion of the house. There is a front door, a back door, a car door to the garage and another door from the garage into the house. A little door for the dog that a person cannot fit through. There is also an old door to the basement that has been nailed shut but still has a lock on it. Then as far as windows, we have double hung sliding windows all with a catch, so they only open six inches. We have some jalousie windows…"

"What?"

"Jalousie windows are the type with many parallel slats of glass that open like a set of blinds. They work with a crank and the slats tilt to the side. They are popular in coastal areas. May be old-fashioned but they are still around."

"OK. Thanks."

"Sure. No problem. So, windows. and we have casement windows that open to the side, but no more than six inches. Now. Absent someone breaking the windows, we're only looking at entering through spaces large enough. Do we test all doors?"

"Yes," said Tony.

"Not the one from the garage into the house. You have the big car door and the other door, so both limit access," said Rachel.

"Good. We might test the inside door, but only if we determine that those garage doors are locked inconsistently. That other door could be like a compensating control, right?"

"Right."

"When do we test?"

"Do you mean like during fieldwork?"

"No. Do we test to determine if the doors are locked during the day or at night?" John explained his question.

"At night," said Brian.

"Thieves don't steal during the day?" asked John.

"Not where I live!" Brian said trying not to admit the flaw in his answer.

"Smart guy," said John acknowledging Brian's humor. "If you have to sample, you may select more instances at night rather than day because the risk of someone getting in is larger at night, right? Thieves tend to work when it is dark."

"Is that like stratifying the sample?" asked Carolina.

"Yes, you can say that, and we're describing risk considerations in your sample selection. We are testing based on risk. Now. Windows. What do you think?"

"What about the boarded-up door?" asked Tony.

"Oh yes, about that door. Do we need to test it?"

No one answered, so John asked differently.

"Do we need to walk by the door 25 times to see if it is still nailed shut?"

Carolina was taking a sip from her water bottle and almost choked when she heard John's question.

"I'll take that as a 'no'. Are you OK Carolina?"

"I'm Ok," she said amid coughs.

"Now, those windows. What do we do about them?"

After a while with no answers being provided, John gave the team a tip. "Based on my description of the windows, can anyone fit through any of those window openings?"

"I don't think so," said Carolina, now composed.

"So, if a person cannot fit though any of the windows, do we still need to test them since they have locks?"

"Don't we need to verify that there are locks?" asked Tony.

"Do you mean document that there are locks?" asked John coaching Tony's thought process and word choice.

"Well, yes, verify," Tony said again.

"We can determine there are locks for the record, but that is just a notation based on observation of the type of windows in place. You can tour the house or do a walk-through if you will, but you don't need to test multiple instances to determine whether the locks are activated or not because no one can fit through the windows. There is no risk of entry and our objective of securing our assets is safe."

"Assuming they can't break into through the window," said Carolina.

"Yes, we established that earlier. A person cannot fit through the windows because they only open six inches."

"OK. In that case, we only test some of the doors," said Rachel softly because she was verbalizing her thoughts, but she was speaking for the entire team, except Tony who was still processing the example.

Miriam was the first to react with a big smile.

"Why are you smiling?" asked John.

"Because you are describing a debate we have been having for a long time about testing controls or risks. We have been testing controls for the longest time and not finding problems, but there are still problems at InSports that we don't catch."

"Are we testing the wrong controls?"

"I think so."

"Are we testing the right controls the wrong way?"

"Often, she said again."

"Are we testing the right controls insufficiently?"

"Right again," she said still brimming as if she had arrived at the end of a long difficult hike and was greeted with a splendid vista of the mountain range and a pitcher of refreshing lemonade.

"Well. We're going to fix that," said John confidently.

As John continued explaining risk-based auditing and the systematic objective and subjective elements involved, a spark lit in his head. He made a quick note not to forget what it was, then resumed his conversation with the team.

After the meeting, John went into his kitchen and while making another cup of coffee he looked out at his garden. He saw the rows of plants he had and how years ago he had come up with a vision for his flower beds. He wanted a garden that would flower throughout the year, and he also wanted to have some order if possible. Plant heights should complement the garden and work with each other.

He took a sip of coffee.

"So, shorter plants would be in the front, followed by taller ones, then the tallest ones in the middle of the island flower beds. Or the back for those set against the property lines. That was during the warmer months. Now, this early in the spring, there were crocuses, tulips, and some daffodils out. Neatly arranged by color and clustered for visual effect. This had not happened by mistake."

He took another sip of coffee.

"I started with a vision. Got some help building a coalition that included my sister who gave me some ideas of what types of plants may be suitable for those places, then, as he looked to the far side of the yard at the forsythias he froze suddenly; Yes! He said out loud, startling the dog who raised its head wondering what was going on."

"That's the third step, prepare a strategy! You can't just wish it. It doesn't matter how well you sell the idea, at some point you need a strategy to go with it. In fact, some people won't come around to the vision until they see a plan."

John turned to the dog to explain what was going on, "For my gardens I drew up maps and sketches, indicated what plants I wanted where, how many should be planted and how they would be spaced." The dog looked attentively as if it understood and was following the train of thought.

"That's what Frank was talking about! I need to prepare a clear and compelling strategy and share it with the team! Third item, check!" he said throwing his head back as a sign of relief and accomplishment. "Phew, that one took some time to figure out," he said and as he took another sip of coffee and relished the aroma the dog put its head back down to resume its nap.

"Thanks Costa Rican Tarrazú!" he said as he walked back into his office to start working on the strategy.

--------------------||--------------------

"Hi Rachel"

"Hi Tony. What did I mess up now?"

"What do you mean?"

"If I didn't mess anything up, then why do we have to rewrite so much of the report?"

"You do good work. My notes and comments are to clarify some of your points, but it is very good. For example," he said as he scrolled the document onscreen looking for a correction he wanted made. "Here, in your recommendation, talking about the enhanced procedures, which, by the way, you got them to agree on, it says 'on a regular basis' you should replace that with 'monthly' since that is what they are going to do."

He continued: "On the other finding, the one right below it, you said 'we were able to complete' and it would be clearer if it says 'we completed' and as you explain the discrepancy in the figures it says 'It is apparent, therefore that there was a discrepancy.' In other words, just say what you want to say. 'There is a discrepancy between' and off you go. Simple, right?"

"I guess."

"Lastly, and I'm highlighting these separately because I know the client. I've worked with her in the past and she does not like us very much, so she picks at individual words and the last two audits she took offense at the wording of our findings, so let me show you."

"She wasn't that bad with me."

"Good. I'm glad. She was OK with me when I spoke with her and during our meetings. She was cordial, but the last time that is how we started then when we sent her the draft report it was fireworks all over the place; and not the good kind."

"Yikes. OK."

"Here. Close to the top where you say, 'clearly evident', it is best to change that to something like 'we observed' or the 'report shows' and state the facts. 'Clearly evident' can be read with an unfriendly tone, if you know what I mean."

"Yes, I guess so."

"There is one more. This is in the middle, when the manager finally agreed with the facts and that the changes needed to be made to the floorplan in the warehouse, it says 'The manager finally recognized'. The word 'finally' and even 'recognized' can be read with a figurative dagger, so how about 'the manager acknowledged' which says the same thing plus it almost gives them credit for getting on board with the facts. What do you say?"

"I like it. OK. When do you need these back?"

"A couple of days. We're still on schedule so make the changes and I'll give it a final read through before sending it to John. Ok?"

"Ok. Bye. I have to go. I have a meeting to go over a data and document request."

"Bye," said Tony as he rested his chin in his palm. "That went better than I thought it would."

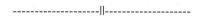

Tony and John joined their weekly scheduled one-on-one meeting and John asked his now typical question, "How are things?"

Tony seemed pensive today and replied after a moment, "I'm OK. Things are going well. We're getting our projects done and they're moving according to schedule."

"Your body language and tone betray you my friend," replied John. "What's on your mind?"

"OK. I guess I'm not that good hiding how I feel," said Tony.

"That's not necessarily a bad thing. So, tell me, what's going on?"

"Why can't we get people to work harder?" asked Tony.

"That's a broad statement. What do you mean?" asked John.

"When I started working, even before I went to college, we were glad to have a job. After college, I took a job as an accountant in a manufacturing company and we worked long, hard hours. Closing was crazy! At first, I wasn't directly involved in the closing, but I did later, and we had numbers coming in from the different divisions and consolidating the numbers was a nightmare. We had computers, it's not like we were using an abacus, but still, system data, spreadsheets, all of that were rudimentary. Anyway. I did that, got promoted a few times. Left to go to work for an insurance company; a little better, but still long hours and month-end and especially quarter-end, were a mad dash to get the numbers in. Couple promotions and I moved into audit. Did that for a few years before coming here, and again, put in the work, put in the hours, prove yourself, and eventually you get promoted."

"I hear you," said John showing empathy. "My experience was similar to yours. It was a gradual process of proving yourself, learning, taking a promotion, and repeating the process. The expectation was that employees would be patient."

"Exactly! Young people today want a promotion after a few weeks of working. They want pay raises right away. They want all this time off so they can bungee jump, sky dive and they can't find themselves in New York or London, so they try to find themselves in some Mediterranean or French Polynesian island. They want constant feedback; everybody gets a medal. And if the company doesn't give them these things, they quit," he said sounding exasperated.

"Sounds like you've been thinking about this for a while."

"Yes. Not just me, right? I would imagine you've been watching the lower work ethic. All the time off companies have to offer. I don't think productivity is going to catch up to all of this. What do you think?"

"You know Tony, I'm glad you're paying attention to all of this. Not that it is easy to avoid or ignore, but you are also thinking about these dynamics. Here's my take. We have gone through several workplace eras, or phases. The industrial one, or Industrial Revolution occurred when people moved from the countryside and replaced farming and rural living with factories and city living. There weren't too many choices in terms of places to work and getting promoted took a long time, if at all. Mostly one or two levels to supervisor or manager. But in general, you worked hard to survive and to have the necessities of life. You needed a house, and you probably rented it. You needed food and clothes. The fundamental needs of life. Bosses could also be unpleasant to work for, to put it mildly. So, people stayed in their jobs to build a foundation for their children, so they had a better life. That was probably true until the Sixties and early Seventies, when World War II ended and due to higher education, more diverse and larger companies, bigger government, there was a hierarchy to climb. Managers became better, but workers had to put up with a lot due to inflation and some job scarcities. Another thing is that the need to be skilled often made people a bit nervous to quit. They had pensions too, which obligated people to stay but was also seen as a reward. This was the information technology era from the Seventies and Eighties, until more or less 2008. Up until then, people worked to have a better standard of living. A nicer house, a nicer car, go on vacation if only once a year. I don't know if this describes you, but people in our generation probably lived according to this general framework. Are you with me still?"

"Of course. This is interesting and you're right. That describes my family. I'm with you."

"OK. So. Now. Around 2008, maybe a little before, but definitely after 2008, we move into the third era or workplace revolution. That is where we are now. Social media takes off as a new generation of people join the workforce. Millennials are joined by Gen Z who saw their parents get laid off from companies and their parents told their children not to be too loyal to companies because companies are not guaranteeing employment for life like they used to. Another important dynamic is that these new workers don't have to work for survival. Their grandparents did that. They don't have to work for a higher standard of living. Their parents did that. This new generation is looking for a higher quality of life. Remember what I said about knowledge and skill in the first Era? Most of those workers did manual work. For the second Era, or revolution, what do you think were the knowledge and skill requirements?"

"Something more specialized? IT? I believe you called it the information technology era," he replied.

"Exactly! So, more people are getting college degrees and that gets you through the door into companies. A Master's Degree gives you a shot at outpacing your competition in the workforce so you can move to manager, director and higher. But now, in the Third Revolution or Era, going to college is almost assumed or at least expected of most workers going into professional jobs, but there is a countercurrent questioning college degrees and promoting certifications. In general, however, we have fairly successfully separated manual, trade or blue-collar jobs from professional, or white-collar jobs. Knowledge is decentralized and almost or completely free. You can learn a lot of what you need to know at a very low cost, or even free, from YouTube, Coursera, edX, and other platforms. So now workers want quality of life and you mentioned some of the things some of these workers want, but that is not a complete list."

"I didn't mean it to be an all-inclusive list."

"I know. I understand. I'm agreeing with you that those behaviors are new, and I get that. Workers also want to work remotely. So, Industrial revolution? Work was mainly in factories. Information Revolution? Better, safer factories," he said using air quotes with the word "factories," "and offices. For the third revolution, work for many people is remote and schedules are flexible."

"Was that caused by the COVID pandemic?"

"To a large extent, but there were people working remotely long before that. Salespeople, call center workers, some repair technicians, and some IT workers, these are some professions where people have been working remotely for a long time, but now it has become commonplace. Partly due to the pandemic, but also technology caught up with the needs. We now have faster computers, readily available cameras and microphones on laptop computers, very powerful cellphones, and of course, broadband, and increasingly 5G. These things made remote work feasible and in many ways seamless. Video conferencing is easy and convenient with few delays, fuzzy or jumpy video streaming and so on."

"So, what do you call this Third Revolution?"

"The social revolution. Not just social media, that is part of it, but social because we socialize differently, we bond differently, we define friendships, co-workers, or collaborators differently and of course, we also work differently." After a short pause, John added, "and we measure performance differently." He waited a moment to let the concept sink in and Tony to make the connection.

"So, we don't measure performance by people being in the office. I remember seeing people sitting in the office from early morning until late in the afternoon or evening, yet had little to show for work. I would assume you witnessed that too," asked John.

"Yes, I did. We worked hard but others seemed to sit around a lot too."

"That's right. Some people would read the newspaper at their desks then go around talking to others so they couldn't get their work done either. We used to joke that some people should pay rent because they were there so long, using water, drinking the coffee, enjoying the AC and heat, and having a place to park their car that they might as well pay rent!" John said jokingly.

Tony reacted with a broad smile, now more relaxed and clearly enjoying the candid conversation with his boss. "I saw that too. You know what's funny? There was this saying, 'get there before your boss and leave after your boss leaves.'"

"That's right. I remember that too. Even college professors would say that as a form of advice. It wasn't all bad advice because that was the common view at the time, and like I said, to a large extent, managers equated number of hours clocked with performance. You were working long hours, which was a way of showing you were committed to the company. We sometimes knew that was not always true, but promotions in many cases were given based on that false equivalency that more hours clocked meant more performance. It was an attempt to replicate the industrial era connection between hours and output. In other words, effort, and output."

"I guess that's not the case in the social era," asked Tony.

"That's right. It is not. The change started toward the end of the information era when performance and productivity experts using techniques like Six Sigma and quality control separated output-based metrics from outcome-based metrics. Looking at effort vs results. Quality of the end product and the satisfaction of the customer with the product or service delivered."

"So, are people more productive now?"

"We are living through a period of change. Fundamental and significant change. We need to redefine work in the context of work-life balance and how they coexist. We need to get work done, but we are more than workers, we are people who happen to work. In audit, there are many things we do because that was the traditional approach to auditing, and we need to examine those. We don't need everyone logging in or 'punching in' at the same time necessarily, but we need to come together at certain times to collaborate more effectively. If someone has a doctor's appointment or child-care or elder care responsibilities, they should be able to do that as long as they get the work done by the deadlines we set up and the work is done with high quality."

"That seems weird to me, probably because I had to go into an office for so many years and we had set work hours," said Tony with a thoughtful tone in his voice as if reminiscing about the way things used to be and reconciling those memories and experiences with current workplace practices.

"I understand. We're all understanding this new reality better every day and adapting to it. I'm sure you can too," said John slowing the speed of his speech and the tone of his voice to provide reassurance and indicate that the conversation was winding down.

"I guess."

"I know you can. Hang in there. I'm glad you brought this up. It is an important topic. Does it make more sense now?"

"Yes, but I still need to reframe my thinking."

"I know you can. Oh my! We're out of time. I have another meeting to get to. I enjoyed our chat, Tony. If you have any questions, let me know. We will be working through this as a department, so we'll work on it together. OK?"

"Thanks John," said Tony with a satisfied smile. He enjoyed the conversation and the counsel of his boss and was especially happy the conversation was ending on such a positive note.

"Thank you, Tony. Asking means you care. That's one of the things I want from my managers. Caring, thinking, exploring, and of course working. Talk to you soon."

As the call ended, John thought about the conversation with Tony and he hoped this would help him change and improve. Tony wanted to do better, but was a product of old practices and limited training. "There is will and there is skill. I continue to believe that Tony has the will deep down inside, he just feels awkward not having the skill to carry this through."

--------------------||--------------------

John was back in Argentina. After the discovery of the sales fraud, he decided to return to finish another key portion of his audit program. He was intrigued by what Randy had told him in New York, and, after reviewing some operational reports, thought a deeper dive might be good. He asked Carolina and Brian to meet him there for a weeklong review because he wanted to teach them the new audit methodology he wanted the team to adopt.

They started the review on Monday.

They toured the facility earlier that morning and the size and palpable energy emanating from the facility were impressive. It was a sunny day with warm temperatures and people walking and jogging on the many trails in the area was a welcomed sight especially since so much of the work was done from home and John missed the direct human interaction.

Employees of the facility indicated the traffic was much heavier in the past, but since the pandemic and the widespread adoption of work-from-home arrangements, the traffic was lighter as fewer people needed to commute to work. This being a fulfillment center, though, it still buzzed inside with a significant number of employees to receive, process, and forward new and pre-used equipment.

The walkthrough of the new equipment process went well. They had seen videos of the entire facility and that process in particular before arriving on site. The most recent audit of this process was three years ago, and it focused on the related accounting and inventory activities. That review found no anomalies, but John noticed from the videos and video meetings with the staff that there were some inefficiencies that were troubling workers and delaying deliveries. Workers indicated the problems started five years ago when volumes increased as a result of new product introductions, and the acquisition of Sports World.

When asked about the equipment received under warranty for repairs, the manager explained a complicated process with what appeared to be some weaknesses in identifying, segregating, counting, and routing the items.

The workpaper review showed that auditors did not include operational dynamics in that audit, so the inefficiencies had not been treated as in-scope. According to staff, the problem had increased significantly since then.

John followed up on that information and by Tuesday afternoon confirmed the accuracy of their assertions. There were issues with shipping items on time, shipping to the correct address, too many partial shipments, backlogs, and backorders. Customer dissatisfaction had also increased significantly.

John, Carolina, and Brian met with Ken and explained the focus on this audit, how previous audit teams had done some cursory reviews of inventory totals, but John thought the focus should not be excessive there since previous audits had not found any significant issues, and external auditors reviewed those activities quarterly as part of their financial reporting review.

As the audit team discussed their observations so far with Ken, who was in New York, they wondered how reliable returns and refurbishment activities were.

Wednesday, they asked warehouse staff about this and employees' body reaction differed by individual, but were consistent in the aggregate in that they pointed toward pleasant surprise and relief at the new line of questioning. Responses included "Yes, that is a mess," "Oh, good, glad you know about that. Who told you?" and "You have a nose for problem areas. How did you sniff that one out?"

When meeting with the plant manager, his response was, "If you can help us fix that mess you will make a few friends around here."

Wednesday morning's tour of the facility included the Returns Department, and several employees appeared nervous to have the auditor inspect the facility, while others seemed almost indifferent. The problems were widely known, but the manager shrugged them off and told employees to just carry on doing their best.

In addition to the visual inspection, John decided they needed to do some data analytics of items returned for repairs and their disposition. Carolina and Brian performed the analytics work, and they noticed some strange things first. They shared their concerns Wednesday late afternoon.

"John, we pulled data for the past five years since it really doesn't require much more work to do five than one. The data is all there. We looked at trends and the number of returns has increased at close to the same rate as the increase in production and sales, so nothing strange there."

Carolina continued, "the types of returns remained somewhat similar and distributed across all inventory types, with minor fluctuation the first three and a half years, but for the past 18 months there is a noticeable spike. I stratified the value of the returns and for those valued between $100 and $500, the rate was several times over, and for those from $400 and $500, most seem to simply disappear. What I mean is, the customers returning the items indicate they send the items as shown in the customer service email account, and I can trace the items to the warehouse. So, they arrive on site. I can reconcile the shipping costs for those returns too because we pay the return shipment. But that's it. There is no record of them getting into the refurbishment cycle."

"What do you think is happening?" asked John.

"They are disappearing."

"Like gone? Lost? Stolen?"

"Looks like they are being stolen."

"Do we have cameras in the vicinity of the Returns and Refurbishment areas?"

"Yes. I thought about that, so I got the files with the images. I received access to that information at the start of the audit, so it was easy to do. I noticed some strange things."

"Like what?"

"A couple of employees on the second shift; there is no third shift; carried what looked like heavy boxes to their cars close to the end of their shifts between 9 and 11 PM. Not all at once, but they take a few trips out to the parking lot and returned without the boxes a few minutes later."

"Same people?"

"Yes, the same two employees."

"How do you know it is the same people?"

"From the clothes they were wearing, but also because the images are really good. Whoever put up those cameras did it right. We have a front view on one and a slight profile on another. Close to the door, high resolution, and good lighting."

"Good!"

"And ... I pulled up the access records. Each door has a badge reader, so I got the list of badge readings for the doors letting out to the parking lot. They used the same door out the back from the warehouse, so they made it easier for me. I have their names and exact times of exit and entry."

"Did you match that to the images from the cameras?"

"I thought you would ask, so yes, I did. Exact match every time. All we need is to have someone else positively identify them, but we have the same two people. Basically, the same faces match the names, which match the badge numbers matching the time in and out for the movement through the doors."

"But we can't see what's inside the boxes or know for sure that it is company equipment. That is anecdotal at this point."

"Yes. You're right."

"But that's OK. We have enough to refer this to the Loss Prevention Unit and they can work with Legal and HR to hopefully get to the bottom of this."

"And maybe confessions if they did what I unfortunately suspect happened," added John.

"Good work Carolina. I'll take it from here. Really good work."

Thursday, they shifted their focus to vendor selection and management. After talking with staff in the purchasing department and discussing the process of selecting and contracting with vendors, they matched their observations with the data they received that morning. It was requested before their arrival and was provided Wednesday, so it arrived just in time.

Carolina and Brian performed the analytics again, and the data highlighted some concerns. Too many vendors were labeled sole providers for years without documented attempts to find other providers recently, documentation of the selection process was shoddy, and rates charged sometimes differed from contracted rates. Other concerns included the discovery of two vendors with names and addresses matching that of employees and recurring short shipments, faulty inventory, and freight charges not allowed per contract terms. The quality issues related to faulty merchandise, missed deadlines, and short shipments aligned with some of the concerns Randy raised weeks before.

John reviewed the work Friday morning, and Friday afternoon the team met again with Loss Prevention to share their newest findings. These were added to the previous issues for resolution by management, while the team prepared their report for Ken.

--------------------||--------------------

Back at home, John sat at his laptop with his coffee mug and two hamantaschen. He arrived from Argentina Saturday and slept most of the day. Sunday, he went into town and visited a bakery he had been to before, but not recently. As he got closer, he recalled the long lines and the wonderful pastries they sold and as he turned the corner, he saw an equally long line.

"Wow. I guess they still draw a crowd. A line outside usually means good food inside," he said to himself.

He joined the line that snaked outside but consistent with his memory, moved fast. Soon enough he was inside staring at a long glass counter with a multitude of pastries, racks of breads against the back wall, and on the far side away from the entrance, a separate counter where they prepared bagels – seemingly a hundred different types, but the main draw was the smoked salmon with cream cheese and capers; sometimes referred to as lox or nova. When asked by the friendly, but efficient clerk, what he wanted, he ordered muffins, bagels, apricot, and lekvar hamantaschen, a loaf of rye bread, a bagel with smoked salmon, and some coffee. After a short wait, he was back on the sidewalk heading for his car while shaking his head wondering why he bought so many things. "Don't go food shopping when you're hungry," he told himself and he realized he was whistling. Clearly a case of impulse shopping with no regrets.

He started typing an e-mail for his team.

"Hi. I am going to schedule a meeting for us to brainstorm ways to update and improve our methodology. There are things we can do to make our approach faster, cheaper, and better, and I would like you to think about what we do and how. I'll put it on your calendars for next week, so look out for that. I'm letting you know now in case you need time to process this and start brainstorming on your own. Sounds good?"

He received several "yes" replies right away, with Rachel adding in her response that she was happy and grateful to hear about this initiative and that it was long overdue.

--------------------||--------------------

"Good morning everyone. Last week we spoke about our methodology and how we want to adopt risk-based auditing. We defined it. Explained it. Discussed it. Any questions?" John asked, and the response was silence and heads indicating no, so he proceeded with another question.

"Anyone familiar with SIPOC maps?"

There was complete silence as this was undoubtedly an unknown tool to the team. After a few seconds John continued speaking.

"No problem. I'll explain it. SIPOC is actually an acronym that stands for Suppliers, Inputs, Process, Outputs and Customers. The map serves to organize some of the key elements that are very important in understanding activities within organizations. This is something we need to do whether we are auditing or performing consulting or advisory activities."

Turning to the graphic projected on the large monitor, John continued.

"Here is a conceptual representation of a SIPOC map. You'll notice that Suppliers, Inputs, Outputs and Customers are generally lists. The P in the middle is usually a seven to nine step, high-level, process flow. Just enough to get a high-level understanding of what happens in the process. Questions to this point?" John asked encouraging discussion with his team.

"Yes, I have a question," said Brian. "Are these internal or external things that we capture on the SIPOC map?"

"Both. The map can be drawn for a process that consists exclusively of internal components. It can be for external components, like when you receive parts that go into one of our products. Or it can be a combination."

"Would most of our SIPOC maps be of the combination type?" asked Carolina joining the conversation.

"Probably. For many of our processes there are external parties that play a role in what we do internally," replied John.

"Let's go over an example to illustrate this a bit further, then we'll have an exercise," said John showing a completed SIPOC map.

"This is the map for the process of repairing a car damaged during a collision. I would imagine all of you have some knowledge of a process like that, hopefully you haven't been involved in a collision."

He was interrupted by Rachel who decided to share a personal connection to this topic.

"Brian was in a car accident last winter, so he's an expert at this, right Brian?"

"I'm an expert at crashing and fixing cars," replied Brian. "I had to fight with the shop to fix it right, but now I'm a subject matter expert on this," he said pumping his fist for emphasis, which made several people in the room laugh.

"So," interjected John to make sure the meeting didn't drift off topic too much, "Brian, you can tell us if this sounds right. Everyone, you'll see under Suppliers a list of entities, or organizations, or people, so we have the car owner, the insurance company since we're assuming this is an insurable claim, and the car parts supplier."

"Under Inputs, you notice that these are things, so here we see a list with the car and car parts. Outputs is also about things, so here we see the repaired vehicle. Lastly, for C, customers, we have the car owner, the insurance company, the repair shop and the part supplier or suppliers. Does this make sense?" asked John checking on his team.

"Yes," they replied.

"Let's go back to P now, and see what a high-level process would look like for this," as John read the key activities starting with the customer bringing the vehicle to the repair and the assignment of a mechanic to do the work, followed by the inspection of the car, the preparation of an estimate and obtaining approvals, parts being ordered and installed, the vehicle being test-driven, and culminating in the customer picking up the vehicle.

"Questions?"

"You have the insurance company under suppliers and again under customers Is that OK?" asked Carolina.

"Yes, good observation and yes, it is OK. A party in the process can play multiple roles," John explained.

"Any other questions or comments?" John asked the group, and everyone shook their heads in the negative.

"Well then. Let's practice this for an activity you are familiar with here at InSports." "Here are the instructions," John said as he displayed the instructions to the exercise.

"Tony, Rachel, and Carolina, you will work together. And Miriam and Brian, you will work together on the other team. You have 30 minutes to prepare a SIPOC map. You can choose any process within the organization you are familiar with. Decide amongst yourselves in the team. When you're done, choose a spokesperson to explain it to the rest of the group, so be ready to present. Questions?"

Since there were no questions, the two groups went to work. With this exercise, John wanted to see decision-making skills, time-management skills, possible conflict resolutions skills, and organization skills. When the team returned, they shared the results of the exercise and their takeaways. Asking no one in particular, John said.

"What uses, beyond what I've already described, can you think of for this tool?"

Miriam responded quickly, "It can help us define where the process starts and where it ends."

"It can also help us gain a better understanding, even if at a high-level, but we sometimes struggle understanding the key activities in a process, so the major things that happen along the way," said Rachel.

"Good observations," replied John.

"I think its ability to help us capture key inputs, like activities, tasks, even materials used, who provides them, all of that is helpful too," said Brian.

"Are you thinking about identifying who plays a role in the process?" asked Miriam.

"Yes, exactly. We are sometimes surprised by people who we find out later in the process that played a role, and we didn't know because no one told us."

"We are going to focus more on success factors in our reviews, so SIPOC maps also help us identify the key inputs required for the process to succeed, so those are talking points we can, and should refer to while auditing or consulting with our clients," added John.

He continued, "To your point earlier, Miriam, I'm thinking this also helps us define who the process is for. The customer. We usually capture the 'what' along the way, but the 'who' can be unclear sometimes. This should help clarify that too."

"Let's take a break, and when we return, we'll learn about RACI Charts and how we can use those in our work."

--------------------||--------------------

After the break, John started the next session with "Who is familiar with RACI diagrams?

Rachel was the first to answer, "it is an acronym for a matrix that shows who is responsible, who is accountable, those that are consulted and those that are informed about various tasks or activities."

"That's right. Thanks Rachel. Now, Responsible. Who is that?" asked John.

"The person who does the work," responded Carolina.

"A?"

"Approver or Accountable," replied Rachel. "The person who is ultimately responsible for the completion of the deliverable or task. It is the person R is accountable to."

"Exactly," said John. "There are two common labels for A. You got them both. Consulted?"

"The person, or people whose opinions we need for two-way communication?" answered Brian.

"Yes. Note the two-way communication mention in the description. Thanks Brian."

"I?"

"Informed," replied Miriam.

"Yes?" said John prompting her to elaborate.

"Oh, yes, those that must be kept up to date on the progress of the activity."

"Are they expected to be told every day what is happening?" asked Tony.

"Not necessarily, but that is a great question. The interval of communication is something that should be agreed upon. Quite often they are informed upon completion of the task or deliverable and sometimes as an announcement because this notification is the trigger for the next, or another task to begin."

"One-way communication?" asked Brian.

"Yes, quite often one way."

John proceeded to show the team a completed RACI chart for a small IT project as an illustration to better understand its contents. No one had any questions at the end, so John divided the team into groups and once again asked them to apply the tool to a process they were familiar with. This time, he mentioned they could use a process within internal audit, like report writing or conducting data analytics for a project. With 45 minutes allocated to the exercise, the team dispersed to work on the assignment. This time John paired Miriam with Tony, while Rachel, Brian, and Carolina formed the other team. This decision was made so they could work with other team members across specialties.

After the allotted time, John welcomed the team back.

"Welcome back everyone! How did it go?"

"It went well. We thought it would be a good tool for report writing like you suggested, so that's the process we chose," said Carolina.

"Good. Walk us through the results of your work."

When Carolina was done, Miriam described their work and used the creation of business accounts.

"Thanks Miriam. So, questions, comments, thoughts?"

"Could this be added to the policies and procedures in a department?" asked Miriam.

"Yes. Absolutely. The illustration I used was for a project, which is arguably the classical example for a RACI chart, but both of you used processes to illustrate its use. Was this an observation while you were working on the exercise?"

"Yes, Tony is the one that mentioned it. He was telling me how some units have a big problem with accountability so this could help clarify who is responsible for what. Responsible as in accountable, consulted, etc, not just Responsible as per the definition. Know what I mean?"

"Yes, I understand and both of you are correct. In fact, it is sometimes referred to as the Responsibility Assignment Matrix or RAM and can be used to help alleviate accountability issues in departments."

"Would it be added to the policies and procedures documents?"

"Yes. I did that several times when I worked in operations and later as an auditor and consultant. The RACI or RAM matrix helped address that issue very nicely."

John continued, "since everyone is in a thinking mode, which I love by the way, are there other people in departments who may not fit into the RACI letters?" Then he waited silently while his team thought about the question. After a short while, Brian responded.

"Some people may be on the project team or in the department who are not involved in the activities you list."

"Exactly!" replied John enthusiastically. "For that, and if you rotate the letters a bit, you have CAIRO where the O stands for Omitted. That's for those out of the loop. That may not sound very nicely to some people, so another option is RASCI, where the S stands for supportive."

"A little nicer," said Rachel.

"Right. Now remember, this is not meant as a tool to blame people. It is best when used as a tool that helps the unit going forward so there is clarity around roles and responsibilities, and to reduce the likelihood of key steps being forgotten."

"The problem may have already happened, though. Right?" asked Tony.

"Yes, that is true. It could be the solution to a problem, but when introducing it, describing, discussing it with the client, it is important to be sensitive to the dynamics if the problem is already there. It is used to improve processes, reassigning responsibilities if over time the load has shifted and accumulated on someone, or as general reference as to who does what, like for us to document, and for our clients to keep."

"An organizational tool," said Brian.

"Yes. Not a substitute for management, and again, not a tool to assign blame or give credit."

"I've seen teams very frustrated because they don't know who does what, or who is supposed to do what," said Miriam.

"Issues in IT and IT projects?"

"Yes."

"I've seen some issues in operations too," said Rachel. "Some manufacturing issues, shipping, repairs. Some areas have people putting out fires all the time and this could help them a lot!"

"Good. This could help them reduce frustration levels."

"Could this help with people who simply forget to do something?"

"Yes. That too. Not only due to procrastination, being overworked or distracted. But because for any of those reasons, someone realizes the problem at the last minute and guess what, now everyone is scrambling to fix something and of course, 'so and so was supposed to do it, but didn't' or 'we decided and agreed that Bob was going to get that done by Thursday' but Bob was overloaded, never heard about it, or, and here is another interesting one, Bob is the most experienced person on the team so most tasks fall on poor Bob. This way we can look down the column and see that Bob has too many responsibilities, so a manager or team leader can reassign tasks."

"What if Bob is shy and doesn't speak up enough?" asked Brian.

"You have some good emotional intelligence skills Brian. Yes, if Bob doesn't speak up, the work could flow quietly in that direction and before you know it there is too much resting on him, leading to burnout, resentment, or just simply what some may describe as 'it is too late to reassign and get all of these things done now,' and Bob could get blamed. So, in summary, a RACI, RAM, CAIRO or RASCI chart can help address these issues, either through prevention or early detection of these scenarios."

"Would we do it on the computer or on a whiteboard?" asked Brian again, this time interrupting John, who was surprised by the question, but not in the least annoyed.

"Great question. We talk about being more collaborative with our clients. These charts, we'll decide which one we want to adopt for our team toolbox, but it can be done on a whiteboard, on a simple spreadsheet, word processor if you like or using some other group facilitation software, and there are several in the market. But this is so simple, you can be creative and spontaneous. You start this with the client upon hearing about their issues and they will likely jump in immediately to fill it out."

"Can this be used for segregation of duties?" asked Tony, gravitating toward compliance as he usually did.

"Yes, we can use this to check for segregation of duties, who is responsible and who is accountable, or the approver. By the way, you must always have an R because someone always has to perform the task. You also always need an A for accountable or approver. And this can be the same person so always an A, always an R and it can be the same person. So, in terms of segregation of duties, make sure the activity, if it is a control activity, is not going to be impaired by this. If the R and A are the same for an important control, we just spotted a conversation topic with management!"

"A finding?" asked Tony.

"Yes, an observation. We're trying to get away from calling these things findings, but yes. It could indicate a concern. I just thought of something else," said John. "Back to Inform. Are there times when people don't inform someone of something then later say they did?"

"Absolutely," said Carolina. "I just had that happen in my last audit. They dropped the ball and started pointing fingers. Someone asked to see the e-mail and she couldn't find it, so she apologized, but that was a heated discussion among them."

"Not good to see, but good that we have experienced it so you understand the value of the tool. It can correct some poor team dynamics, so that's another benefit. Hopefully less in-fighting for some groups, but don't only think of the toxic environment and bad feelings that can be created, think of the inefficiencies."

"That was part of the problem. They were constantly going back and forth on things, making decisions as they went and others not knowing. Then the communication thing I just mentioned happened. I wish I had known about this tool then," said Carolina.

"Let's talk about that audit later and see if there is something we can do to help them there."

As the meeting adjourned, the team discussed places to eat and settled on the Seaport area to start with. They would eventually eat in Greenwich Village.

--------------------||--------------------

"I'm telling you, people would steal anything, including ice cream trucks."

"No way," replied Carolina.

"Yes, look it up. Thieves will do crazy things. I mean, how fast and how far can you go with an ice cream truck? But it happens," said Brian trying to convince his colleagues.

"He's right. I'm looking at several stories from Florida, California, and Ohio," said Rachel defending Brian as she read the results of her Google search.

"Good morning, folks. What am I walking into this time?" asked John.

"We're talking about asset misappropriation," said Brian, making his story sound more upscale and serious.

"He's telling us that if he left internal audit he would go live at a beach and for money he would give surfing lessons and drive an ice cream truck."

"But my experience in audit would go to really good use because they wouldn't steal my truck, you know."

"Ok. I'm glad you're learning some very valuable lessons," said John enjoying the camaraderie among his team members.

"I would then franchise. How many beaches are there in Florida, California? The Carolinas. I'm telling you, it's a gold mine waiting to be discovered."

With a smile John added, "I can see you building an ice cream empire Brian. You'll probably find a way to sell advertisement on the side of the trucks so in addition to ice cream flavors the sides look like NASCAR cars. How was your evening?"

"I like that! I'll hire you as my CFO John. We'll go into business together. About yesterday. It was very good. Lots to see and do in New York," said Brian as he switched topics and started narrating the places the team went and what they saw. After a few minutes of conversation to let the team get settled in, John started with a question.

"Anyone familiar with Cause-and-Effect Diagrams?"

"Yes," replied Carolina with her customary enthusiastic tone. "It is a tool to help identify the root cause of problems."

"Exactly. Cause and Effect Diagrams, also known as?" asked John encouraging discussion.

"Fishbone Diagrams," replied Brian.

"Fishbone Diagrams, yes, why the name?"

"Because when completed they look like a fish," replied Brian. "I'll sell fish and chips at the beach too. Cornering the market with food trucks."

Tony was not amused and turned into the disciplinarian. "Can we get back on topic guys?" he asked.

John didn't need help redirecting the group but took the help anyway and built on Brian's earlier response. "Yes, they look like a fish. Root cause analysis is important for several reasons. Why is that?"

"Because you otherwise document symptoms and we should avoid that," said Rachel.

"True. We'll talk about why in a moment. Let's talk about the model for documenting issues, or observations. Remember the CCCER model? What does it stand for again? Let's begin with the first C."

"Criteria," said Tony, and before he could name the next item, John asked, "and what does it involve?"

"The standard of performance. What should be happening," replied Tony.

"Who or what defines the standards of performance?" asked John again.

"Rules, regulations, policies, procedures, laws, contracts," said Tony proud to enumerate all of these compliance items.

"Good, exactly. Internal and external requirements, including benchmarking, best practices, our values, and even our mission defines our standards of performance. Very good," which made Tony more proud yet.

"Next?" asked John, holding up two fingers to indicate he was inquiring about the second element.

"Condition," replied Rachel.

"And what is the condition?" asked John.

"What we observed. What we found as a result of our work," replied Rachel.

"Very good. Only our work?" asked John prompting them again.

"Yes," said Carolina.

"Mmm, not quite," he responded bobbing his head indicating the answer was not entirely correct. "It doesn't have to be only our work. If we are going to work collaboratively with our clients, then it is what we, as in the audit team finds, as a result of the work done, but as we adopt Agile auditing, the audit clients are also going to contribute to this discovery of the condition. How about the third element," said John now holding up three fingers. "What is the third C?"

"Cause. It is the root cause of the problem," said Miriam.

"Root cause. Yes. We try to stay away from listing just the symptoms. Why is that?"

"We have been told for years that we shouldn't just list symptoms, but I don't know if anyone ever said why," replied Brian.

"Think about our overall goal, which is not only to list issues, but also make recommendations for improvement. What happens when you fix the symptom of a problem?" said John looking directly at Brian indicating he wanted him to answer the question himself.

"I guess it comes back," said Brian.

"Exactly. Fixing the symptom does not make the problem go away permanently. It is likely to recur. So, getting to the root cause will help us make recommendations that get to the heart of the problem and management can fix the problem where it started, at the source. Our recommendations would be more effective this way."

"Are we supposed to do that or is that the client's responsibility?" asked Tony.

"To identify the root cause or to fix the problem?" asked John seeking clarification before he answered.

"Both."

"They are responsible for fixing the problem, but we should be helpful and make recommendations," replied John.

"It is in the Standards," said Miriam.

"Exactly. And it is also good business practice," added John.

"OK. But it would take too much time. We don't have time to get into all of that when we are trying to finish an audit," replied Tony.

"It is a requirement and something we need to do to improve our image. We need to make the time. It is worth it," said John admonishing him.

"Do we allocate time in our audit program?" asked Carolina.

"Yes, we must avoid getting ourselves scheduled so tightly that we can't do this. Also, we'll continue to learn about new techniques and as you get more familiar with them, you will be able to get to the root cause faster. We're up to the fourth element here. 'E'," said John as a statement but clearly asking for input from his team.

"Effect?" said Carolina.

"Are you asking or answering?" said John.

"Saying? Er answering?" she replied.

"You are correct, and I was trying to help you answer with more confidence," said John smiling as he made his point.

"Thanks," said Carolina appreciating John's development help.

"So, Effect. What is that all about?"

"It is the consequence of the issue. For example, if the organization is not conducting cybersecurity awareness training, employees may be careless in their handling of data and we as a company could be exposed to fines and penalties by a business partner or a government agency, like in the case of GDPR non-compliance," said Miriam.

"Exactly! Good point and I appreciate you using an example to illustrate the concept. That is exactly what Effect is all about. In fact, we used to refer to it as the 'so what?' aspect of audit observations. We treated it as an internal QA, or quality assurance, technique to check ourselves. Why should the client care about the observation we are bringing to their attention? If we can't articulate the 'so what?' we should pause to think whether we truly have an observation that is meaningful, or a preference or an ancillary topic that we could possible handle verbally during the audit and present at the exit meeting, but not put in the report."

"How do we determine that? What's the rule?" asked Tony.

"It depends. There is no hard and fast rule to make that determination," responded John.

"Hard and what?" asked Carolina.

"Hard and fast rule is an expression meaning there is a rule firmly set in place that we can use. These rules don't change often or easily," said John explaining the reference.

"Oh. Ok."

"So, there is no definitive rule per se, so we look at the context of the situation. Good to consult with your teammates and as we build a better relationship with our audit clients, it will also help us gain a better appreciation for that. I'm not saying we do as they say necessarily. We are not surrendering our independence and objectivity and leaving it up to the audit client to decide what is and isn't an observation, or how critical it is. We share in that assessment as a go/no-go, and welcome their input on how concerning it is, but we remain the Third Line and final decision makers. Just give them the courtesy of consultation, conversation, and consideration. Does that make sense?"

"I still think we should put everything in the report," said Tony holding his ground.

"We need to make sure only significant items make it into the report. It goes to operations management, the people that you likely worked with day in and day out during the audit, but it also goes to upper management. The C-Suite including the CFO and CEO. And it also goes to the audit committee of the board. At the board level they don't want, or need, to see minutiae. They expect management to handle the smaller items. They only get the bigger items so they focus, like they should, on the most important things," said John explaining the rationale for that practice.

"What if it is a smaller item that keeps coming up?" asked Tony again.

"Ok. Maybe. If it indicates a bigger problem, like an organizational culture problem, I can see that. We may need to present it as such, so the audit committee understands why this matters. That's the key. Context."

"Could smaller items, or recurring smaller items also indicate that management is not doing their job?"

"Yes, that could be it also. You are raising very good points about context and that's what we need to be clear about. So what?" using his hands with the palms up motion for emphasis as he asked the group. He promptly answered it himself indicating it was a rhetorical question, "there is a cultural issue where this is indicative of a larger problem we should address globally. Get the point?"

"Yes," everyone nodded except Tony, who was rocking his head side-to-side indicating he was still on the fence and processing the philosophy. John noticed Tony's reaction and decided to address this privately with Tony later to avoid a public confrontation. For now, however, he would continue the class.

"This brings us to the last letter in CCCER, the R. What is that about?"

"Recommendation," replied Brian.

"Good. We should make assessments and make appropriate recommendations."

"Some internal audit departments don't write recommendation anymore," said Brian.

"That's right," agreed Miriam. "I thought that was weird. So, you agree we should make recommendations?" she asked.

"Yes. It is in the Standards, it is good business practice. It also helps to elevate our jobs. You are not here only to write a laundry list of problems. You are here to help the organization improve by developing observations, recommendations and conclusions. We help achieve the organization's objectives. Also, we don't have to formulate all recommendations by ourselves. Yes, we will research and leverage our collective knowledge. But we will work more closely with the audit client to find a corrective action that is practical, cost effective, and realistic. We want the audit client to understand the issue, and get invested in the corrective action. By the way, you hear me say corrective action several times. The CCCER model is sometimes also referred to as the 5Cs model, where the first three Cs are the same, Criteria, Condition, and Cause, but the fourth one, E instead of Effect becomes Consequence, and the last item, R, instead of Recommendation becomes Corrective Action. Questions? I've enjoyed our conversation. This is good."

"It makes the time go by faster," said Brian.

"That's right, and more relevant to your work. On that note, it is time for lunch. Let's take a break and let's be back in one hour."

John was looking out his window admiring his garden. An object of love. He was always battling bugs, rabbits, squirrels, deer, and occasionally some fungus that tried to undermine his efforts, but all of that was worth it. How can you put a price on the joy he got from the flowers? Tulips and crocuses were always first as they welcome spring after a long winter and portend the opportunities that the changing seasons represent. As the weather warms, bright yellow marigolds like the sun. Colorful coleus with their bright reddish leaves look very cheerful. Puffy and proud hydrangeas and of course the very regal lilies and roses. That and more made the summer a special season and something worth looking forward to.

Suddenly he got a Teams video call request.

"Hi Rachel. Hi Carolina," he said after accepting the call.

"Hi John. Do you have a minute?"

"Of course. What's up?"

"We are reviewing their processes and one of the employees mentioned a lot of issues. Later, when Carolina and I were facilitating a meeting with the other 4 employees in the unit that came up again and there were more stories of disfunction. So I was writing it all up and it is unwieldly. I was just wondering if you want us to write a comprehensive narrative of the issues."

"How about drawing a flowchart?" he suggested.

"Yeah, that might work. I haven't done one since college. We were discouraged from drawing them here."

"Why?"

"They always said it took too long to draw and they never had enough details anyway, so after spending a lot of time drawing them, we ended up with a narrative just the same."

"Understood. Yes, they can take a while to draw, especially early on when not very familiar with how to draw them, or the process is very complex, but flowcharts can be very useful to see the flow of activities in a program or process. They get easier to draw the more practice one has. What are some of the issues they are telling you about? Think categories of issues," he explained.

"Hmm. Let's see. I have my notes right here," she said as her eyes shifted to look at another document on the other computer screen.

"Rework. They return items often because they are incomplete or incorrect in some way."

"OK. That's a back flow. An arrow going in the opposite direction of the expected flow." "What else?"

"Bottlenecks. Things getting stuck along the way then having to wait."

"There is a symbol for that. Try the Delay symbol. What else?"

"Things taking too long for completion, so a very long cycle time," she replied.

"OK. There are different things we can do for that. One is noting the average, minimum and maximum times for all the transactions during the period under review, or a stratified analysis showing let's say the monthly average, max and min if there is variability over time. That way we can show the process is getting worse. For each step, especially the major ones, can we find out how long they take?"

"Yes, they use a workflow application to process these documents, so the system captures all of those details."

"Perfect! Note that on the flowchart for each major step and later we can review with the staff to see if the durations make sense. What you're hearing is anecdotal, right? They experience these issues, but they don't have the data to back up those statements. Now we will. Are you OK with all the things I'm suggesting?"

"Me to some extent, but more so Carolina. What did you tell me, Caro?"

"Yes, I did several case studies like this in the university, but when I got here, they discouraged doing this kind of work. I'm glad you're giving us the OK to do it."

"Good, I'm glad. We're looking at bringing in those techniques. Going back to the flow and backflows. You have the population number, right?"

"Yes."

"OK. Now see if you can get the number of transactions that are in those back-flows, where they go from and to, and why. Once you have the number of transactions, you can calculate the percentage of the total transactions that are subject to rework. Same for the bottlenecks, see if you can find out who or what is holding up the process. We need to know so we can get to the root cause and make useful recommendations. Just telling management 'the process has a bottleneck that needs to be fixed' is not particularly useful," he said with a smile both on his face and in his voice.

Carolina replied: "We agree. What you just said that was not particularly useful is what we have been doing since I got here. Glad to see we're digging deeper into operational issues. I was starting to second-guess myself and wondering if I had wasted my tuition money when I took Operations Management at the university!"

"You didn't waste your time or your money. We just need to rethink how we use these tools," John replied reassuringly. "Go ye therefore and wow our clients!" John continued, with a flourish in his hands.

"We will. We'll let you know how it goes," Rachel said as the call ended.

John looked out into the garden just as the white tail of a rabbit disappeared into the bushes. The cute brown thief was headed for the woods.

--------------------||--------------------

"We just found out that a salesperson temporarily lost his laptop. I say temporarily because it turns out he took it to his beach house to work on some proposals over the weekend. Misplaced it in the house and couldn't find it. Returned to his main residence on Monday in a panic and as he was getting ready to call IT and his boss to report the missing device, his wife, who had stayed at the beach house with the children found the laptop and told him she found it. He was relieved, but this incident raises some questions about the level of awareness people have about cybersecurity. I'm not only talking about knowing where your equipment is. I'm talking about preparing the device so that if it were ever lost, we can minimize the likelihood of important data being compromised. Or when they are using the device, the information being compromised."

John continued. "It turns out he used the device at a coffee shop during the weekend, so he didn't know if he had left it there or what. So, let's take a look at how we can help InSports on this topic."

"Are you thinking about a vulnerability assessment?" asked Miriam.

"Yes, but before that, there are a number of things we should be looking at, starting with the devices themselves. How they are configured. Then how people use them to make sure they are being street smart, let's call it that. Then we can address vulnerability assessments and eventually we'll need to explore penetration testing. So, where should we start?"

"How about awareness training?" said Miriam again.

"Good. What do we do there?"

"Make sure everyone attended," said Brian.

"Good. What else?"

"How long after hire did they attend?" said Brian again.

"How about recurring training, like annual refresher training?" added Miriam.

"Good point. It shouldn't be just once and done, right?"

"Exactly, things change."

"And people forget, so they need refreshers."

"OK. Anything else?" said John prompting his IT auditors further.

"I believe that's it. Who attended and when. Is there anything else we can look at?" said Brian, showing his limited knowledge of audit procedures.

"I think so. How about the contents?" said Miriam.

"The contents?" Brian asked.

"Yes, the fact that people attended training doesn't mean they learned. And Learning has to do with the content and the teaching methods."

"So are you thinking about an exam at the end?"

"Yes, that is part of it. Is there an assessment and how did people do in it?"

"What if the questions are super easy? Then everyone passes and we get a false reading on knowledge gain."

"Good point. That is a subjective topic and very important. We should look at the content and the questions to make sure there is substance to them. How about before the assessment, what can or should we look at?" asked John probing further.

As they thought about the answer, John gave them a hint. "How can we tell if the materials have substance?"

"We have traditionally assumed that going to training was 'it', but if the materials are terrible, just going may be pointless, or at least, not very productive," said Miriam.

"Exactly."

"Wait a minute. Is this computer-based training or taught by a person?"

"We don't know. But that is important too. If by a person, are they qualified and were there opportunities for interaction?"

"Questions and answers, explanations, and examples!" Chimed Brian.

"Exactly. Now, does instructor led means we don't need to look at the materials?" asked Brian.

"I think we should still look at them because workers may refer back to them in the future if they have questions, so we should look at materials regardless of delivery mode," said John. "Agree?"

"Agree," said Miriam.

"What topics do you believe should be covered in a well-developed cyber awareness training like the one we're talking about?" asked John.

"I think it should include things like travel safety. Keeping an eye on the equipment, like at airports, hotels, and coffee shops," said Brian now understanding the value of this approach.

"At airports make sure they see the devices go through the scanner before walking themselves through screening machines, so the devices are in front of you and not behind you," said John sharing an example and practice from his many years as a business traveler.

"Good tip. Yes, we learned about that when I started in audit years ago. A simple thing, but very important," added Miriam.

"Yes, and making sure you check before you walk away from the security checkpoint and at hotel lobbies," added John once more. "So, safety practices on the go. Hotels, restaurants, security checkpoints, ride share services and taxis. Lots of good ideas, team. What else?"

"Ok, so that's the on the go, part. How about let's call it stationary. Things like hackers intercepting information while using the device, so encryption, don't use unsecured public WiFi, don't charge your phone using the USB connectors in public places…," said Brian.

"What?"

"Yes, hackers can tamper with the endpoints of USB connections in public places and access your information while your device is charging. Have you noticed that when you plug in your phone into the car or a laptop it tries to read the contents?" Brian explained.

"Ow," said Miriam pursing her lips as she understood the dynamic.

"Yes, so only use power chargers either as a power cord or a USB to power adapter, but never USB straight from the wall to your device."

"Gotcha."

"Well, this is turning into a learning moment even for us. I love it!" said John.

"The device should be protected too with fingerprint ID or multifactor authentication. Also, do workers know to avoid free WiFi and hotspots, and avoid accessing important information while connected to these?"

"How about having reliable anti-virus software?"

"Yes, that too. And making sure that and their operating systems are up to date."

"We can't ask people because they wouldn't know. That's an IT question."

"Yes. Right. We need to check that updates and patches are pushed immediately. There's zero-day exploits, so we need to move fast when there is a new vulnerability identified and communicated."

"Got it."

"Bluetooth can be troublesome too."

"Yes, Bluetooth connectivity should be turned off as well as turn off the WiFi auto connect feature. Travelers should know what networks they are connecting to and do it themselves after they determine it is OK to do that."

"What about VPNs?"

"Good point. We need to check with IT about that too and verify that InSports provides encrypted VPN that turns on automatically when connecting to WiFi while on the road."

"Back to hotels. How about checking the door before you leave the room? I've noticed doors at hotels that don't close fully if you hold it close to the threshold before letting go of it."

"Yes!, I was in a hotel where I actually had to pull the door shut. The arm didn't pull the door hard enough to shut."

"OK. I'll add that," said Brian as he served as the note taker for the exercise. "Are we forgetting anything?"

"Auto lock feature on laptops and phones," said Miriam.

"Yes, password lock after a while and encryption of the device so even if someone takes a hold of it, they can't make sense of any of its contents."

"We mentioned encryption earlier, didn't we?"

"Yes, there's encryption of the data at rest, which is what we're talking about here, there is encryption of the data in motion, and encryption of the data while being processed. We need all three."

"Got it. That will make for an interesting conversation!"

"Agree. It can be a bit difficult to explain, but for most people, we just need to let them know what it does, and the IT and cybersecurity folks need to make sure it happens. We don't want to confuse people during training; we want them to know what they need to do and what others are doing to help protect them."

"Good point. So maybe a roles and responsibilities section in the training program too, then?"

"Absolutely."

"And while we're on that subject, maybe explain The Three Lines Model. It applies in many ways to different things and often used to explain the role of auditors, compliance, risk management, cybersecurity, and so on, but the goal is to raise awareness and explain how everyone is working together to help protect data, so a quick overview," suggested John.

"Some may have heard about the model by then, or even use it."

"Right, so they can help others understand it. The rest will be new to it, so everyone walks away with a solid foundation."

"Good folks. I think we have a very good start to this review. Brian, you have been taking notes; can you share them with Miriam and me and all three of us can review them and add new items as needed; then we'll talk with Cybersecurity about this."

"Should we also talk to HR since training and development reports into them?" asked Miriam.

"Yes, let's tackle the primary connection with cyber and as we get buy in, we'll bring in HR and TD. I'm referring to a 1–2 approach, but there won't be much gap between the two. We need to move fast, like always."

"Got it."

"I have another meeting in three minutes. Need to go. See everyone later."

"See you later. Bye."

--------------------||--------------------

6 Improved Reporting

"As I look at our audit reports, I noticed a number of things that we could improve upon," said John getting his team's attention immediately. "Our reports have been too long. They ramble too much. Can be confusing and don't always explain what the issue is that we're suggesting they fix. Do you agree that our reports are too long and there is room for improvement?" he asked aiming for an early point of agreement.

"Yes," came the reply from his team verbally and using head nods.

"OK. So, there are a number of things to keep in mind when we write reports. First of all, reports are not the place to explain our methodology. We can give a high-level view into what we did so the reader has some context, but we don't need to explain everything we did."

"We used to avoid that in the past and they used to ask a million questions about how we got that information, how we found this or that issue, how do we know it is really an issue, etc. etc.," said Tony defending the current practice.

"I understand, but in my experience those types of questions are because we haven't explained the process and our observations along the way, so they are suspicious of the information we used and how we arrived at the results at the end of fieldwork. I believe a good rule is to focus on what we want to make sure the client knows, which is different from all the things that we may want to say. Those are two different things. Does that make sense?" asked John emphasizing the difference between what the client would be interested in as opposed to what internal auditors may consider important.

"Not exactly," said Tony.

John chose to use a bit of levity to clarify but he still wanted to make the point clear that change was necessary. In the end, the goal was to get the team to change and especially Tony, who had been struggling with this. Calm but determined, John replied.

"Sounds like something Confucius would say, doesn't it? Let me explain. As auditors we may want to describe all the information we received, the people we talked to, the documents and reports we reviewed, and especially the very extensive procedures we applied, but the report is meant to communicate results. We must communicate the results of engagements," and he emphasized the word "results." "We include objectives and scope, for context, and where applicable, we may add an opinion and do so in a way that is clear, accurate, objective, concise, complete and so on. Those are key attributes of effective communication. But describing procedures is a bit much. It is not necessary."

After waiting a moment to let this information sink in, he added, "your reports just got shorter!" what was undoubtedly a benefit of following his instructions.

The team smiled at this, and noticing the receptive mood, John continued.

DOI: 10.1201/9781003322870-7

"That being the case then, we should focus on what the report readers need to know."

"Is there a roadmap to do that?" asked Rachel.

"The way I do it, I focus on some key questions; What is the problem? How serious is it? So what? why should the reader care? and lastly, what should or could be done to fix it? Does that make sense? Would it help?"

"Yes," said Rachel, while Tony and Miriam nodded their heads in unison.

"OK. Now, back to those attributes of effective communications, which as I mentioned previously, are also in the Standards, so concise comes to mind. And by the way, that one is central to what we're talking about here. There is another important rule we should adopt and that is that we must do what we can, so the report is actually read."

"We can't force them to read the reports!" said Tony.

"That's true," agreed John, "but we must try. So, how do we try?" said John stopping suddenly, which took his team a minute to understand this was not merely a rhetorical question, but rather one he wanted them to answer.

"Well?" John asked again after a moment of silence.

"By making it concise?" said Miriam.

"Yes," encouraged John, "how else?"

"Constructive?" said Miriam again.

"Yes," said John again. "I believe both help a lot in making the report something they want to read. Let's expand on constructive. Constructive means it is helpful to the organization and the person, and will result in improvements where improvements are needed. When they realize there is useful content in the report, they will want to find out what we have to say!" John said emphatically. "We write not to explain what we did, but to convey what they should know because it will help them in their work."

All heads nodded as they silently agreed with John's words. The upward glances and squinting eyes told John they were processing his words carefully.

After a few seconds, Rachel interjected. "Would making the report short help make it desirable to read?"

"That's what concise means," answered Miriam instead.

"That's right. Duh," replied Rachel realizing what she had just asked. "Sorry, I'm processing all of this," she said apologetically.

"No worries. You are thinking about it and that's what I want you to do right now. Ok. So, new rules on reports?" asked John recapping his points with the team as he raised his thumb indicating he wanted to count.

"Are we focusing on what they need to know?" answered Miriam.

"Good! And number two," said John as he put out his index finger asking for the second rule.

"Is it constructive?" said Rachel.

"Very good. Is it constructive so the readers would WANT to read it," John said expanding the answer for emphasis. He noticed that Tony was mostly quiet during the conversation, and John wondered if he was buying into all of this, but he needed to move on. He would bring this up again during their one-on-one meeting later in the week.

"All right. Let's go onto the next item on our agenda and take a look at those audits in progress."

--------------------||--------------------

"Hi Tony, how are things?"

"All is good. The audit is coming along well, we're about two thirds of the way done with the testing and the auditee has agreed to all of our findings."

"So, the client is agreeing with the issues. OK. That's good," said John correcting Tony.

"Yes," replied Tony not getting John's hint.

"Let's call them audit clients rather than auditees, and let's call these things issues or observations rather than findings. It makes a difference in the end," John explained.

Tony looked on a bit puzzled and shook his head in what looked like passive agreement. Noticing the lukewarm reception to the idea, John decided to probe further.

"What do you think our relationship with our audit clients is like?"

"We audit them, and they respond to the reports we issue," he responded matter-of-factly.

"Yes, that is true, but we work for the same company, so building relationships and aiming for collaboration are also important," John added.

"That's true. Is changing what we call things going to change the way they interact with us? I ask because they don't always respond to our requests and some audit issues remain outstanding way too long," Tony said.

"To answer your first question, maybe not. Just changing labels is not enough. Changing how we treat them, clarifying our role and the benefit we bring to the organization might make them more responsive before, during, and after the audit," John explained.

"I hope so. Otherwise, we may need to be tougher to get them to respect audit more," Tony said surprising John with the authoritarian tone of his voice.

"Respect is earned. Demanding compliance or directly and indirectly threatening them may backfire, do you agree?" John asked trying to get Tony to think about his approach and its consequences.

"Yes, I guess so," he replied after a short pause as he thought about this.

"It often does. The goal is not to be feared. The goal is to be respected. We'll start with changing our mindset about the people and units we serve, and how we interact with them. That means minding our words, our attitude, our impression of them, and what we want the relationship to look like," John said firmly and with conviction, which didn't leave much room for Tony but to appreciate how important this was to the new chief audit executive.

With that, the conversation turned to training and the absence of a strategic, well-coordinated, training approach in the department for many years partially explained why Tony acted the way he did; but keeping the status quo was not an option. Tony had to change or move on. They also talked about the rapid growth of InSports and how Tony was feeling left behind by the rapid changes.

--------------------||--------------------

"Happy Monday."

"Happy Monday," the choir responded.

"How was your weekend?" asked John to everyone and no one in particular.

"Yard work the entire weekend. Getting the garden in shape," said Tony.

"Nice. Good to be outside even if it is to pull weeds and clean up after the winter," said John.

"Yes, glad to be outside except for the allergies," said Rachel.

"Do you take anything for it?" asked Tony.

"Yes, I just wasn't expecting them to hit so early," she replied.

"Sorry to hear that. Hope antihistamines will help with that so you can enjoy being outside even more. Some suggest locally harvested honey helps too," said John injecting himself in the exchange so others could also join in. "Anyone else. What did you do Carolina?" he asked.

Carolina seemed to have been waiting for the opportunity because she became talkative immediately. "We went to Amsterdam for the weekend. It is so pretty. A million tulips out. I just love the city architecture, the canals, the countryside, the windmills. I'm tired from doing so much, but it was worth it," she said with a wide smile.

"Did you go to Zaanse Schans?" asked Rachel.

"Yes, that's where I saw the windmills," replied Carolina.

"Sounds great. Maybe Tony will be inspired by your tale of a million tulips now that he is working on his garden," added John.

"I have daffodils and tulips. Those come early, like crocuses. Then it's on to primrose and forsythias. My garden keeps me busy, but it returns the favor just when I need some color after a long winter," said Tony sounding animated, which was rare.

"Gardening is a good hobby. Maybe a lifestyle. Well. It sounds like several of you had nice weekends and got to do some fun things. Some of it was work, but good and fun types of work. Talking about work and fun. The summer will be here before we know it. Let me know, if you haven't yet, when you plan to take vacation time off. Now, something very important. You go on vacation, you're on vacation. No checking emails, no IMs. No checking voicemail for work. When you're out, you're out," John instructed his team.

"What if I'm working on an audit?" asked Tony.

"Let's plan ahead so you either finish it, hand things over to someone else while you're away, or leave it at a good stopping point until you return," replied John.

"Are you sure you don't want us to check our emails?" asked Miriam.

"Yes, I'm sure," came John's emphatic reply. "Is that a problem?"

"We always checked email while away. Maybe except for Carolina and Brian, but no one was ever that emphatic about that," said Tony referring to their previous boss.

"You. We, all of us need time to step away and rest. Vacation is important and we want you to treat it like a vacation," said John with a serious look on his face for emphasis.

"Withdrawal problem over here," said Miriam.

"OK. We'll work on that together then. Are you worried of stresslaxing?" asked John.

"Stresslaxing? What's that?" asked Miriam.

"It is when relaxation causes anxiety. People get stressed to the point where relaxing makes them more stressed because they're not working on what's making them stressed," explained John.

"That's exactly it!" said Miriam. "I have these audits. I have a to-do list and I feel like I need to get things done for the audit. What if there are questions? What if someone sends a file?"

"Let me stop you there Miriam. I appreciate your dedication. By the way, I'm saying this for everyone's benefit. You know I appreciate your hard work, but let's notify our contacts so they know when you'll be out and when you'll be back. Tell them, then turn on your out of office notification. Then walk away," said John providing hints on how to make the transition that in his mind would help his team improve their work–life balance.

"Carolina is good at that!" said Brian adding levity to the situation.

"Hey. In Europe when we're on leave we are on leave," she explained.

"All of August!"

"Don't blame me!" said Carolina defending the practice. "People in the US work too much. That's your fault."

"Carolina has a point. We historically work too hard, and we are fixing that. It is a cultural shift for many, but as a company we're encouraging the practice and within internal audit, I'm telling you to take your time. Spend it with your family, friends, significant other, pets, garden, however, whatever makes you happy and helps you rest."

"Surfing?"

"Surfing. Yes Brian. Where are you surfing this summer?" asked Tony.

"Costa Rica."

"Pura Vida," said Carolina cheerfully.

"Yes, indeed. Living life," said Brian.

"Nice. OK everyone, let's take a lesson from Brian. Are you taking your laptop to Tamarindo, Carmen, or is it Dominical?" asked John showing with his question his familiarity with Costa Rica's beach hotspots.

"Heavens no! No work laptops for me, John. Sorry. And by the way, I'll be down the road at Mal Pais," replied Brian.

"Good. It was a trick question. I wouldn't want you getting sand all over your laptop there. Enjoy yourself, be safe, and you can send pictures as an incentive for the rest of us to get outside too."

"I will," he said with a beaming smile at John's instruction. In doing so, Brian was expressing the team's appreciation for the instruction to work on their wellness, something the previous CAE was silent about.

--------------------||--------------------

"I read through your audit report and I wanted to talk with you about it," said John as he started the meeting with Tony and Rachel.

"The draft report. Yes. We issue the draft report first, get the auditee's responses, then issue the final report," said Tony explaining the standard practice.

"Yes, that's a practice that many organizations follow and has been around for a long time. Decades, actually. I have some feedback on it, some thoughts and I would like your thoughts as well. But first, I'm assuming you cleared all of these items with the client already?" asked John.

"Yes, the auditee was told about these issues during fieldwork and agreed with them during the exit meeting," replied Tony.

"Good. Can we call them clients rather than auditees?" asked John.

"Ah, yes, sure. Clients," Tony replied.

"Good. OK. So, the report comes out to what is it, 41 pages?"

"Yes, that's correct," replied Rachel right away but her tone left John wondering if she was proud or disappointed by the length of the document.

"There are 24 issues here. And you went over all of these with them?" asked John seeking confirmation.

"Yes. And they agreed with all of them. We had to fight over a few of them, but they eventually agreed that those were in fact correct," said Tony with a proud tone in his voice.

"Why were they, 'fighting' the issues?" asked John making air quotes.

"They said they were not important issues, or they were already working on them," replied Tony while Rachel looked on.

"And what did you say to that?"

"Standard practice is those items still make it to the audit report because they were identified during fieldwork. They fixed a couple of items, so we gave them credit for that, but they're still in the report. We can't take those items out, you know," said Tony explaining the practice.

"I understand. I'm not suggesting, or asking, you to take them out. I am still trying to understand the dynamics better. As I read through the draft report, I only saw one item where it was clear the client fixed the issue during fieldwork."

"It's in there. I'll have to find you the exact one and the language I used, but I said so in the report," Tony replied a bit defensively.

"OK. Was it one, a couple or several items they corrected?" John probed for clarification searching for an accurate response since Tony had said, "a few."

"Several, like five or six," said Rachel firmly.

"Five or six. OK. We'll come back to that. In terms of the number of items and the risk rating, or severity of the observations. We have a rating matrix, right?"

"Yes, we have a matrix we use to determine if the finding is insignificant or all the way up to catastrophic," said Tony.

"I thought the ratings were minor, moderate, significant and extreme," John said with a tone implying it was a question.

"Yes, same thing; small, big or catastrophic finding," replied Tony sounding a bit frustrated.

"We should refer to these as observations instead of findings, especially if they are not entirely new or very significant. For more significant observations, issue is a good word choice."

"OK."

"Same for the ratings. If we refer to the level in our matrix, we won't confuse terms or descriptions. OK?"

"OK," came his unenthusiastic reply.

"About those ratings. How many are extreme?"

"Let me look," said Tony as he scrolled through the draft report. John let him scroll and count, and after a while Tony provided the answer.

"There are three."

"OK, how about significant?"

As Tony was counting after almost a minute, John interrupted him. "You can tell me later. Do you know how many minor and how many moderate are there? I'm assuming you will have to scroll through the report and count them as well, right?"

"Yes, I guess so," said Tony not fully understanding what John was teaching them.

"All right, so let's put ourselves in the client's shoes now and pretend we are receiving this report. We open it and start reading it, and have the same questions I just asked you. How would they get that answer, which I believe most executives would have, right? They need to assess the situation and make quick decisions about what they really need to focus on," said John prompting their thinking through questions.

"They should read the whole report," replied Tony.

"I hear you. But they also have limited time, and they are always forced to prioritize things. If you want them to read the report, we need to make it easy to get through."

"The findings are in descending order by section of the audit, so all related findings are in the corresponding section and the most important ones are at the beginning of that section."

"So, they would have to flip through, or scroll through while counting issues themselves," said John as a question but also a statement.

"I guess so, but that's why they're paid the big bucks," said Tony with a forced smile in an attempt to justify the approach.

"Not really. They are not paid to do that, and we don't want them to spend their time doing that. We need to think of ways to help them navigate the report better. We have an executive summary, which is good. Three pages may be a little long for that, but there are ten findings here out of twenty-four. So, ten findings are extreme?"

"Ten findings are either extreme or significant."

"How many of each?"

"I would have to go back. I believe it was three and seven."

"Three extreme and seven significant?" asked John seeking clarification.

"No, seven and three. Seven extreme."

"Ok. I read them and, can you pull the executive summary and share it with me?"

As Tony moved the document back to the top, he then had to scroll down two pages to the executive summary.

"Thanks Tony. We'll need to take a look at the opening two pages to see if all of that is really necessary. Let's jump to the observations in the summary and review them together. I looked at the items on the executive summary before our meeting and it looks to me like items 2, 5 and 6 are related. Could they be consolidated into one?"

"Maybe, but I believe it is best to break them down, so it is clearer to auditees that there are three issues there."

John didn't acknowledge or dispute Tony's answer but made a mental note about this perspective on things.

"How about items 8 and 10? I believe those are related too."

"Yes, they are related. But again, we should separate them, so they see there are two issues."

"What do you think about the executive summary being three pages long?"

"I needed that much space to explain what we found."

"Usually, the executive summary describes the issues briefly and what management is going to do about it. Do you think there might be too much detail there? For example, the first item gets into why this issue is happening. Isn't that better left for the body of the report?"

"Maybe," Tony replied with a tone that suggested he was starting to see there might be another way, but his noncommittal tone also indicated he didn't have a remedy to the issues John highlighted.

John asked Tony to go to the detailed portion of the report and walk him through the individual items. The results were the same. Tony did not consider simplicity and brevity sufficiently and thought his detailed descriptions were important. His tone was starting to sound more doubtful, but not sufficiently so.

At this point John had seen enough and needed to move Tony into solution mode. "There is a technique, and a resulting diagram called an Affinity Diagram that can be used to consolidate items like this. It becomes handy when there are many items to go through because sometimes items are not necessarily separate from each other, but rather they may relate. Several of the items here are likely symptoms of a bigger issue. For example. Items 8 and 10 are things that happen when training is not provided promptly and effectively to workers. So, the issue is about training deficiencies that cause damage to inventory and misplacing inventory items, and workers end up running around the shop floor looking for the items they need. Inventory locations are labeled, and they are spacious enough, from the description of the issue in the report. The problem seems to be that they don't know about the procedures, and act in ways that cause inventory to be misplaced or damaged due to poor handling and storage practices."

"I guess so," admitted Tony moving his head side to side showing lukewarm agreement with what John was explaining.

"Let's move to another topic. How about the methodology section? That adds three more pages to the report. What do you think about keeping or removing that?"

"I realize it adds three more pages to the report, but auditees are always asking how we do our work, so five years ago we included this section. We hardly get any questions now!" Tony said with glee.

"Has this methodology section always been three pages? You know, from the time it was introduced five years ago?"

"No. It was only one page, then we made it more detailed because they kept asking questions. Now, it looks like we got it right."

"Do you think it would have been better to explain our methodology some other way rather than adding all of that to every report?"

"Maybe," said Tony thoughtfully.

"I'm going to write my observations about the report as review comments, so take a look at those. A focus point will be conciseness; brevity without sacrificing clarity. Schedule a meeting to review the edits next week. Monday afternoon or Tuesday so we keep this moving and publish it soon. As far as the Affinity Diagram and consolidating observations, also about the methodology section; we'll revisit that as a team, but I believe we can do without it by communicating and explaining our methodology some other way, so the report is shorter. I'll add a quick explanation of the situation in our Monday morning staff meeting and we'll have some training on that. This report, and two others I've looked at recently show a similar pattern in terms of number of observations that can be reduced and other wording that makes them longer than necessary. Anything else about the report that we should talk about before next week's follow-up meeting?" asked John inviting Tony and Rachel to add any last words before closing the meeting.

"No. That's it," said Tony feeling that the methodology he was accustomed to was about to be altered and he was not very comfortable, much less excited, about that.

"OK. Thanks for walking me through the report."

"Bye," said Tony waving at the camera before he quickly hit the Leave button.

Noticing that Rachel was not leaving the meeting, John asked her, "you were mostly silent during today's meeting. What do you think about what we discussed?"

"I believe this change is long overdue. Our reports are too long and cumbersome. Tony likes to explain everything in far more detail than necessary. Miriam and I have been talking about making them shorter, but the old boss and Tony insisted on doing things their way."

"Thanks for providing some background to this. You can tell what I think of the way reports are being written, so we're making changes now. Let's be patient with Tony. He's a good writer, but we need to help him move forward and away from that old lengthy writing style. I believe he's turning the corner on this," John said making sure to encourage Rachel while showing both understanding and emphasizing the need for change.

"I'm with you on this change. Count on me!" she said enthusiastically.

"Thanks."

"Bye," said Rachel with a hand wave and a broad smile suggesting she felt a major victory had been achieved. Then the screen went blank.

As John saw the second video screen disappear, he signed off as well and scratched his head. There were so many things that should be changed about the audit reports. "Too long" summarized it, but the issues included too many observations, too many words, that methodology section; even the executive summary needed to be summarized further. "We need to overhaul our reports," said John taking a big gulp of water. "I need to go for a walk," he said as he turned in his chair and walked toward the door to get his walking shoes, sunglasses, and the leash for his dog.

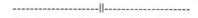

"Last week we spent some time in our weekly meeting talking about our reports and how we can make them better. I would like to talk about that again. Did everyone read about the Affinity Diagram? I sent you an e-mail with a link to a video and a description of the tool. I also added that link to the meeting invitation. Did everyone have a chance to read it?" asked John.

"Yes," was the reply from the entire team.

"I read it, but it is a bit confusing to me," said Carolina.

"I understand. We will cover it in more detail and practice using it at a training session I'm arranging for the team. For now, do the mechanics of it make some sense? List the items. One item per sticky note. List goes on the wall or tabletop. Each person takes a turn silently arranging the items as they believe they relate to each other. When everyone is done the group talks about the clusters and gives each cluster a name. Did you get that when you were reading the piece?" John asked checking with the group.

"Yes. Can I ask a question?" said Carolina and without waiting for a response or permission continued with the rest of the question. "What if we're not in the same location when we try to do the exercise?"

"That is a great question Carolina," replied John, "and for that we have technology; like so many things in our lives these days. There are several tools we can use online to do this. A few that come to mind are Miro boards, Creately, and Lucidchart."

"OK. I thought there might be something. Thanks."

"Which reminds me, we need to consider ways to get our work done remotely since that is the trend and I don't see that reversing direction anytime soon. Onto another topic," John continued asking no one in particular, "you are familiar with the 'So What?' concept of audit reports, right?"

"Yes," said Rachel as the rest of the team nodded in agreement.

"Good. So, along those lines we need to make sure our reports explain to the reader why the issue is important. We have the ratings, but the wording of the issue should also convey that importance. Not alarmist, just direct. There are a couple of things I believe would help improve our reports," said John as the team listened intently.

"One. The e-mail about the report must include the report summary paragraph so readers can quickly determine what the report is about and if they need to read the entire report, which would be attached."

"So, we are going from concise to uber-concise!" exclaimed Rachel enthusiastically.

"I guess that's a good way to put it," replied John.

"Why? Aren't they supposed to read the report because it is important? We are already making it shorter and adding an executive summary. That's one to two pages. Are you saying we should go even shorter?" asked Tony.

"Yes, for the reason I mentioned above, but also because most people now read their e-mails from a cellphone. People scan e-mails on tiny screens before they read them, so we need to help our readers scan it, and prioritize our communications. Basically, help them understand what the report is about. What they need to know to prioritize its contents appropriately," explained John.

"Wow. I guess it's true about the cellphone thing. All of us do it so I'm sure they do too," said Brian.

"Exactly."

"And some people don't have the ability to read really tiny print either, so we need to have a conversation about accessibility too," added John.

"What do you mean?" asked Miriam.

"For example, can readers using cellphones enlarge the font on the report's text? Can they enlarge our graphics if they launch the actual report? We need to be careful about our choice of color in our charts and graphs," explained John.

"I had never thought about that," said Miriam.

"Good points," Tony agreed in a low voice.

People support what they helped to create, so John had an idea. He decided to give Tony an assignment that would make him own part of the process of changing the report.

"Tony, please contact Corporate Communications and tell them what we want to do about accessibility and see if they have corporate guidelines and suggestions. Also, it would be very helpful if you could find best practices that we can adopt right away and share those with the team next week. If Corporate Communications doesn't have anything, see if you can find some information online for us to get started. Look at the ADA, WCAG, and Section 508."

"OK. I will," Tony replied with uncharacteristic enthusiasm at the assignment.

"Thanks."

"All right. Now on to the other topics on today's agenda," said John as he redirected the team.

--------------------||--------------------

"Good morning team!" said John. "Nice seeing everyone again. Let's try something different for this weekly meeting. Instead of going in hierarchical order starting with Tony and Miriam, let's do it alphabetically. So, Brian, what did you accomplish last week, three things you're working on this week, and what obstacles do you anticipate that the team needs to know about so we, or I, can help remove them?" After a pause without Brian joining the conversation John asked again. "Brian?"

Brian was surprised by John's alphabetical order approach. Consistent with Brian's very open personality he commented instinctively, "I'm like the lowest ranking person on the team. Why did you choose me first?"

"Luck of the draw Brian, your name is first alphabetically. Then Carolina, who is also one of our newest hires. Then Miriam, Rachel, and Tony will come last this time around."

"Why change it?" he insisted.

"Three reasons. One, Why not? I don't like the expression 'if it ain't broken don't fix it', we should always aim to improve on current conditions and processes, within reason of course, but there is usually a benefit to improving what you currently have. We should always innovate, so we're innovating our weekly meeting order. Two, we must have a hierarchy for administrative purposes, but I am interested in what everyone does. Like your hand, we need all five fingers to get a good grip on InSports," John said enthusiastically and pausing as if done with his explanation.

"And three? You said there were three reasons," Carolina reminded John.

"Oh yes, three. Keep everyone on their toes. If you were waiting for Tony to take the heat first while you rushed and prepared your notes for your turn, you're now in trouble," he said with a smile on his face.

With this, Brian nodded in a slow rhythm as he smiled. "Cool," he said while thinking how much he liked his boss's freedom from tight boundaries. He presented his four agenda points confidently, followed by his peers who also enjoyed going before Tony for a change. Tony, for his part, liked the idea and said so when it was finally his turn. The team was coming together.

--------------------||--------------------

7 Training, Development, Coaching, and Mentoring

In preparation for the upcoming training in New York, John reviewed the team's skills inventory to make sure he was clear about their strengths and weaknesses. He was still working with HR to clarify some of the roles of internal auditors and how their skillset differed from what most people thought auditors did. The platform had the skills separated by technical and soft skills, and now the department was using InSports' HRIS' Talent+ system to track and monitor all of this.

The technical skills section of the platform included topics like IT, cybersecurity, project management, data mining, data analytics, and, he added, supply chain management.

Next, he looked at the list for soft skills. He disliked the term "soft skills."

"There is nothing soft about them. They are essential business skills, without which, all the analytics, reporting, visioneering, and other things people do would probably be dead on arrival. How many plans turn to nothing for lack of effective communication? How many collaborative possibilities are blown for lack of effective teamwork? How many disagreements, or outright fights are due to poor communication? The list goes on and on. These should be labeled essential business skills. Enough philosophizing, John," he said forcing himself to get back on track.

He had submitted his comments to HR weeks ago, and they updated the list. It now included topics like conflict resolution, persuasion skills, work ethic, and collaboration. His team had filled out their skill levels for these and the ones that were there when he arrived at InSports: teamwork, verbal communication, written communication, time management, and negotiation techniques.

"In today's work from home, or rather, work from anywhere world, auditors need to be familiar with online tools like Slack, Asana, Office 365, Google Workspace, Trello, Notion, and video conferencing tools like Teams, Zoom, and WebEx. I'll check with HR to see how to add items to these lists too. They'll love hearing from me again, but the list needs to adapt to new developments," he mused.

He noticed it included time management. "Great! When you're managing people remotely you can't spend your time chasing them around to get the work done. They need to meet deadlines without someone looking over their shoulder. It is never a good thing, but much less with such a small team."

John made a few notes before hearing a chime. It was his reminder to "contact a stakeholder" meeting. It was the CTO's turn then; it was followed by "contact a manager." It would be Miriam's turn. He implemented this practice to make sure he reached out to key people within InSports and his unit.

------------------||--------------------

DOI: 10.1201/9781003322870-8

"Hello everyone. Good morning. So good to see all of you here in New York. It was good to get together last night for dinner and get all of us socializing a bit. Like I said last night. Our team is not only about finishing projects. I believe it is important that we enjoy working on, and finishing, projects. I would like us to do a professional job, but also to have fun while working. Third point, get to know each other better because it makes our interactions more productive. You get to understand the person behind the e-mail. You get to understand the person at the other end of the camera. Work from home is great in many ways, but it can create some isolation, and one of my goals is to reduce the likelihood of this happening in our team. You may be alone working from home, but you are not alone in internal audit. You may be alone working from home, but I hope you are not feeling lonely. If you, or one of your colleagues seems to be emotionally affected by our geographic distance, bring it to my attention as a caring act so we can help you. And with that, Brian, I knew you were funny, but wow, you had me in stitches my friend, and I believe everyone in this room will agree with that."

"He could moonlight as a comedy act," said Carolina.

"Well, we are in New York, and Broadway is just down the road," added Miriam with a smile while pointing out the window. She continued, "nice blouse there Rachel, I like the colors. Very spring-like!"

"Thanks. I like to wear lively colors. They brighten my day," Rachel accepted the compliment gladly.

John added, "Yes, they are cheerful and puts us in a happy mood. Good way to start the day."

Now with the icebreaker phase over having done its job, John brought the meeting to order. "Let's go over some administrative things before we get into the class itself," said John as he went over expectations that his team would not get too distracted with their phones, that they would pay attention and be active participants, and return promptly after breaks. He also covered the evening plans for additional social activities among the team members and told them there were a few meet-and-greet opportunities with audit clients while everyone was in headquarters.

"Let's begin with the Affinity Diagram. A very interesting and practical tool that I've used many times to organize things when I have a long list of items to work with, like after a brainstorming session with clients. I've also used it with previous audit teams. In one instance, we were trying to figure out why a manufacturing unit was having so many turnover problems. The client had almost grown accustomed to the turnover, but the number was inching up and they were building an army of trainers to onboard the waves of new hires. We said, let's take a look at the situation and see if we can find what is causing the problem, in effect, let's get to the root cause of the problem. We assembled a workgroup with the HR team, receiving, warehousing, manufacturing, and shipping and the results helped us help them lower the turnover problem significantly."

"That sounds like a success story," said Rachel.

"Yes, it was, and we did it in one session! We started going over the scale of the problem, we established some ground rules, helped people really introduce themselves, because even though they worked in the same plant, many of them just walked past each other. We then did the brainstorming session as a workshop. They learned a lot about each other and the problem, and after organizing the results we developed action plans. It worked very well."

"Where do you do the actual work?" Brian wanted to know.

"Do you mean the documenting of brainstorming items and so on?" asked John for clarification.

"Yes."

"You can do it against a wall, on a tabletop or on a computer with tools like Miro, Creately, or Lucidspark, for example," said John naming a few of the tools that facilitate this work electronically.

"Today we'll practice creating an Affinity Diagram to organize multiple items. Tony, we did this for your audit. Can you explain how Affinity Diagrams are constructed to the team to bring everyone up to speed?"

Tony was surprised by the request, but John was deliberate in his approach; he wanted Tony to explain the tool, which would remind him of it and solidify his knowledge, but also see if he would sell its benefits too.

"Affinity Diagrams are used to organize lists of items. Sometimes relationships are not apparent, but with this tool we can consolidate similar items and arrange them based on common characteristics. In my case, we reduced the number of audit findings from fifteen to seven."

"How did we do it?" John asked.

Tony explained the process but missed a few steps. John didn't interrupt while he was talking, but waited until he was done. No one asked any questions, leading John to assume, as he suspected, that perhaps they weren't fully understanding how to create the Affinity Diagram.

"OK, let's do an exercise where we practice creating one," said John as he handed the team a write-up of a case study involving a manufacturing organization that created a list of key performance and risk metrics for their operation. "Read the case study for the next ten minutes or so, then Tony will lead us on the work towards a solution as a team." The team read the case study silently, and when John saw them finish reading, he nodded at Tony to get started.

The team got together to discuss the case study and list the metrics indicated in the case study. They wrote the items on the whiteboard, so they worked from the same list.

"Do we have post-it notes, John?" Tony asked.

"We do. Yes. Right here," said John handing Tony pink, green, and yellow stacks of adhesive notes.

"So, let's see if I remember. We write each item on its own card," he said taking the yellow stack and splitting it in two by giving the other half to Miriam. "Do you want a stack too?" asked Tony realizing he was leaving John and the rest of the team out of the exercise.

John thought quickly then replied, "sure, I'll take some. We'll leave Rachel, Carolina, and Brian out of the writing part of the exercise for now." He decided to get involved in the handwriting part of the exercise to support his manager, but also to show his team that everyone chipped in. He recalled his early days in consulting when the company founder told his employees that everyone should be prepared to sweep the floor or empty the trash bin.

"OK, let me give you some," he said splitting his stack in half and sharing it with John. He then started writing items from the list not realizing that Miriam and John sat there watching him work alone.

"You can split the list in three and each of us can write some items. That way everyone gets involved," John suggested helping and coaching Tony along the way.

"Good idea. OK," he said as he eyeballed the list and split it into three groups.

When they were done writing the items on the sticky notes, he started explaining the next step. "Now each person puts their notes on the wall, and we see what categories come from it."

As he said this Miriam's face looked confused and both John and Tony noticed that. "Sorry Miriam, I'm still learning how to do this," Tony said apologetically.

"I'll help," said John. "A little background. We put all of the items on the wall, and we take turns arranging them the way we believe they should cluster. One person at a time. Silently. So, Carolina, you go first."

With this Carolina walked up to the board and spent a few minutes moving the items around and creating clusters based on her opinion.

"Thanks. Now Rachel. Your turn. Move them around as you see fit, and if you agree with any part of what Carolina did, you can leave them where they are."

With this Rachel walked up to the wall and both Brian and Miriam started commenting on what Carolina did and how they should rearrange the items.

"No. No talking. This part of the process is done silently," John instructed the couple.

"Oh, sorry," said Brian as they became silent.

When Rachel was done, it was Miriam's turn followed by Brian and Tony was last. At this point, John told the team to get together at the wall, review the items, and do a final review and decide if the arrangement reflected their collective view on the items. "You can talk now," John explained.

After about five minutes discussing the items, Tony turned to John and said, "we're done. We agree on this arrangement. The next step is to label the groups, right?"

"Exactly. Now you put a label that best describes or names the group. Do it for every cluster."

The team went back to work and labeled the seven groups they had created and labeled them with another sticky note color.

"We're done. Now what?" asked Miriam.

"Great," affirmed John. "Let's now think what we need to do to address each cluster. For example, who would own the metrics, where the data would be generated from, how often it would be produced, who would receive the results, and what escalation mechanism might be put in place if the metric deviated from its expected values."

The group went back to work and after 45 minutes or so, they indicated they were done. The group discussed their results.

Next, John reminded the team of the SIPOC map, and again, spent time describing it, explaining its uses and his experience with it, followed by an exercise and a debrief session. Positive feedback once again was obtained from most of his team, while Tony's enthusiasm level gradually increased. Mild enthusiasm was arguably a good descriptor, and John accepted that. "He's getting better and slowly falling in line," he thought. Brian was a keen participant; he was very engaged during the activity and more so during the debrief sessions where the team discussed ways to incorporate the tool in their day-to-day activities. Miriam, Rachel, and Carolina were also very animated and shared insightful perspectives on things. John was particularly pleased at the work Carolina was doing and how she interacted naturally with her teammates. He was generally concerned about her since she was the most junior member of the team and because she lived in the UK she was constantly adapting her schedule to meet her teammates and clients. But seeing the team's dynamics put him at ease.

After lunch, the team returned and this time company colleagues from financial reporting, quality assurance, EHS, and corporate compliance joined for the afternoon sessions. The group discussed The Three Lines Model, the importance and benefits of providing assurance to InSports' stakeholders, and during breakout sessions talked about ways to collaborate.

---------------------||---------------------

"Well, that was a very productive meeting with the Second Line yesterday!" commented Miriam as the group assembled for the second day of training.

"Yes, I enjoyed talking with them and getting their perspective on things. I never really understood what they did. I had some idea, but their work writing policies and training people was a surprise to me," said Carolina.

John walked into the room and saw his teammates involved in what sounded like an important and animated conversation. He needed to get organized for the morning's training session, so he let them talk among themselves while he prepped and eavesdropped casually.

"Yes, I believe those are some of the reasons why we should continue to work with them," said Rachel joining the conversation.

"Does this compromise our independence?" asked Tony.

"Why would it?" replied Miriam with a question and a quizzical look.

"Because they help write and interpret policy, they are not the best people to do testing. If we work with them maybe, we would also compromise our independence," he said explaining his viewpoint.

"I don't think it does," replied Miriam, again trying to understand how something that seemed so positive could be viewed as a problem by Tony.

"I think that if we clarify our role from the beginning, we would be OK," added Rachel. "We work for the same company, so there is an inherent challenge to independence there, but we can work around it if we distance ourselves from day-to-day activities and explain that we are testing, or assessing, what operating units do."

"What about getting too friendly with them," insisted Tony. "Wouldn't we be compromising our objectivity by being too friendly with them if and when we have to audit them and their work?"

John saw through the corner of his eye that Rachel was giving Miriam looks and nodding with her head that she should ask him to settle the debate.

"What do you think, John?" asked Miriam, acting on Rachel's prodding.

"The simple answer is that all of you are correct. I'll explain. Yes, we could lose our objectivity but only if we lose sight of our role and responsibility as internal auditors. It is OK to work with the Second Line units. We are all assurance providers, but we are the Third Line, and as such, we need to balance collaboration with independence and objectivity. It can be done; we just have to be clear who we are, what we do, and what our stakeholders expect; then act on that realization. With that, we should, well, we must collaborate so that we avoid overlapping our work unnecessarily, wasting time, disrupting our mutual clients by auditing them on the same things or excessively, and generating multiple reports for the audit committee and senior management."

When John was done, the room fell silent as everyone processed his response. John waited a moment deliberately in case anyone had a question, and after a brief pause, he continued.

"It looks like we're in agreement?" he paused briefly again, and no one said anything.

"OK, then. Let's get moving on today's agenda. I would like to spend time talking about communication skills. As auditors we tend to default to technical topics, tools, IT, cybersecurity, data analytics, etc. etc. I believe soft skills, or business skills as I prefer to call them, are equally important. So, let's take a look at verbal, written communications, and body language."

With that John started a presentation and the team discussed techniques to improve their communication skills and covered visual, verbal, and written approaches in depth.

--------------------||--------------------

"Hi," said John addressing the InSports employees assembled in the large auditorium. It was a gathering of managers going through HR training and John had been asked to speak to them about diversity and inclusion. He chose to do so as another manager interested in the topic rather than addressing the topic as an auditor focusing on compliance. He had suggested to Kathleen that addressing new hires would help them become aware of the role of internal audit, and how they were a resource within the organization.

"Unlocking team productivity is a daily pursuit. Most managers would believe that giving employees the right tools and healthy processes, they will become very productive automatically. While that is supremely important, more is needed.

"We increasingly see evidence that a team with a strong sense of belonging among its members will be more creative, cohesive, and resourceful while showing lower turnover levels."

"A diverse team is one with different personal, academic, and professional backgrounds, genders, and ages, and such diversity will be more likely to generate a wider spectrum of ideas. Racial, physical ability, and economic background diversity can produce surprisingly fresh and innovative ideas too."

"How should we handle our team members' individuality?

"A good starting point is realizing that some of our colleagues seek stability and predictability. Others are givers and need to understand how their work improves other people's lives and the organization at large. Another group wants to be career auditors because they want to master their work. There's also those that seek variety and autonomy. Lastly, we should remember the innovators and trailblazers who are constantly looking to the future and are our allies shaping our company and our industry."

"Treating everyone fairly is essential. Equity and merit in recruitment, hiring, promotion, compensation, and assignments will encourage healthy competition to improve oneself, learn, and perform at the highest level possible. We should look at past performance, but don't forget to consider people's potential."

"By including everyone, we create a great sense of the collective, where the entire team works together to support each other and achieve the organization's mission of protecting and enhancing organizational value by providing products and services that enhance our customers' lives. Within audit, we provide assurance and advice by looking at past performance – hindsight, current practices – insight, and the future – foresight."

"Diversity, equity, inclusion, and belonging (DEIB) should be viewed as much more than a fad. While the acronym may be relatively new, I've seen what the adoption of its principles has done for audit, compliance, and other units within organizations for decades."

"As we empower our team members and show them that we want them to bring their genuine selves to work, we will unlock team productivity and be surprised by the amazing things they will accomplish in the short and long term!"

"Thanks! I really appreciate your time. We are in a great position to elevate the quality of our team's work and create a very healthy and productive work environment along the way at InSports."

At the end of his short speech, there was a 20-minute Q&A session where John was able to elaborate on the work of internal audit and broadened the audience's understanding of the profession. Tony and Miriam sat in the back of the room feeling like they were part of a great and exiting transformation experiment.

-------------------||--------------------

8 Communicating the Vision
Outreach

"How would you like getting involved in a road show?" asked John.

"A road show? What is that about?" asked Tony.

"Internal audit organizes a few events and invites members of the InSports community to attend. During these sessions we talk about who we are, what we do, how we do it, and try to convince them that we don't bite," replied John.

"Sounds like the presentation to the management team last week. They seemed very impressed."

"Were you impressed?"

"I was. You have a very different philosophy for our department than we had in the past. I'm starting to get it."

John wondered why Tony used the words "get it," but he liked it because that was his concern with Tony – did he "get" what the vision was for the department and was he on board with it?

He continued, "that's an interesting idea. How many sessions?"

"I'm not sure yet. I'm thinking five virtual and five on site at our main locations."

"How long would each session be?"

"One hour. We keep them brief. We talk for no more than forty minutes, and dedicate twenty to Q&A."

"When would we do this?"

"Soon. I would like us to get these scheduled in the next couple of weeks and the first session happening no more than two weeks after that."

"This could be good! I think it would help get the word out. What would you like me to do?" asked Tony showing interest and a willingness to participate.

"Prepare a draft of an agenda and a presentation. A few charts and graphs."

"A short video?" asked Tony surprising John.

"Sure. Yes, let's add a video or two. The tone should be light and engaging, but professional. Can you show me something in a couple of days?"

"You got it! I'll have the agenda and a presentation. Those videos will take a little longer."

"Sure, sure. Of course. Yes, but give me some ideas of what those videos might look like. Like an overview or summary of scenes, you know?"

"Yes. I can do that."

"It would be fun to have the entire staff involved."

"That's what I was thinking."

"Thank you. Anything else going on I should know about?" asked John.

DOI: 10.1201/9781003322870-9

"No, not at the moment. Everything is moving along nicely and the rest I can handle on my own," said Tony confidently.

"Good. Thanks for all you do. I appreciate it."

"You're welcome. Bye."

"Bye," said John as he paused for a moment to take in what he had just witnessed. Tony had been the slowest team member to embrace change, in fact, for a while he was reluctant to change his traditional ways and the approach the department had embraced in the past. He seemed to have turned the corner today.

--------------------||--------------------

"Hi Kathleen. This is John. How are you today?"

"I'm well. Excited about the new employee survey that we spoke about. It should be going out to all employees Wednesday."

"That's really good. I look forward to getting my invitation."

"Let me know Thursday if you don't, because that means something went wrong with the distribution."

"Will that go out to everyone globally?"

"Yes. The default will be English, but if anyone wants it in Spanish, they can choose that instead. When we spoke about it a few weeks ago you offered one of your auditors strong in data analytics to help us look through the data. Is that offer still on the table?"

"Yes, when would be the best time to send someone over?"

"Let's see. It goes out Wednesday with a 10-day window to respond. That puts us two weeks out, so how about the fifteenth? That's two and a half weeks from today."

"That works for me. You got it. I'll let Rachel know. Who on your team is leading this project?"

"Sarah Faulkner."

"OK. Could you tell Sarah to contact Rachel and copy me, so I know when this gets going?"

"Sure."

"Good. I have an idea I want to run by you. It is actually an offer."

"I'm listening."

"When we had coffee a couple of weeks ago you told me you were looking at the onboarding process and management development program because you wanted to make some changes. I believe you mentioned more coverage of our values, code of ethics, and so on."

"Uhm, hmmm."

"Would it help if during the onboarding process one of our auditors spent some time with new employees explaining who we are, what we do, how to contact us if there are issues and so on?"

"How much time?"

"Twenty minutes or so. No more than thirty."

"Go on."

"We could have two different presentations. One for non-management employees, and another for managers. Slightly different content. For example, many managers approve budgets and timesheets, get involved in selecting vendors, they authorize access to computer systems, monitor controls and so on, so the presentation would help to explain some of their responsibilities as they relate to these topics."

"I like it. I heard about the presentation you made at the management meeting. I got some good feedback."

"Thanks. We want to include some videos too to make it more engaging and interesting, so I'll record a short piece and maybe have one or two of our auditors also record a short video explaining what we do, what modern internal auditing is all about, how we can help them if they need help with strange transactions, if there are ethical issues, and so on. We also have an auditor that speaks Spanish and another that speaks Arabic, so we can make it more interesting for our international operations too. I'll work with the Instructional Design group to make sure it is done well. Maybe we can have a fully recorded session, but for now I'd like to have a person present it live, so we personalize it for new hires, and also to answer questions."

"When would you be ready to roll this out?"

"I want to fast track this, so about four weeks. Can you help me move it through the Training group?"

"Yes, sure."

"OK. Thanks. That's all."

"How are your auditors doing?"

"They're doing fine. I'm implementing a number of changes and so far they're coming along with them. They're not complaining much, so that's good. I need them on board, and they are. On a separate note, I will need to fill a vacancy, so I'll get back to you on that."

"OK. Let me know how we can help."

"Not that I want you auditing me, but are you going to audit Payroll again?"

"We'll visit payroll, but the review will be different. We're implementing a new auditing approach called risk-based auditing. It is not new in the profession, but from what I've seen it would be new here. The focus is on auditing the topics of highest risk, or concern. Auditing what matters most to you, which is what should matter most to us too."

"OK. Payroll has come out fine in the past audits, but if you are going to do it again, let us know."

"I will."

"Bye."

--------------------||--------------------

"Hello everyone. Thanks for attending this orientation session," said John as he brought the meeting to order.

"Internal audit has typically supported management on the topic of fraud from an investigative perspective. While that has been very good, like it was when we recovered twenty-five thousand dollars from an inventory employee who had stolen and was selling our equipment, and when we helped to stop a fraudster outside the US who was steering business by granting contracts inappropriately. While good, these are examples of investigative work. Our goal is to take the fight against fraud one step further. We already enhanced our methodology to incorporate more detective techniques."

"Wasn't that a standard practice among auditors?" asked the corporate controller.

"To some extent. Let me explain. We test internal controls to identify anomalies. Many of those will be errors, omissions, and lack of compliance with our policies and procedures. External auditors perform testing related to the preparation and signoff of our financial statements and they focus on materiality. From our perspective as internal auditors, we do some testing to help them and reduce our overall fees to the CPAs.

What I'm sharing with you is that we will include more robust anti-fraud testing procedures in our audits, and that also means some more pointed questions during our interviews as well.

As a matter of company policy, it would be beneficial to also let units being audited know that we need their support as usual, but that the questions asked are not an insinuation of guilt or wrongdoing, but standard procedure to meet and strengthen our anti-fraud goals and integrity values.

We are also going to conduct an orientation session online and a Road Show to several locations."

The controller's group, as this meeting was often referred to, consisted of accounting and financial reporting staff from InSports' global operations. These meetings were held quarterly as a mini conference to review strategic initiatives, discuss performance metrics and common issues, search for solutions that sometimes were thought to be isolated but crossed divisions, and search for best practices. John wanted to share his vision outside the department as much as he wanted to share it within. He was succeeding.

--------------------||--------------------

"Hi John."

"Hi, Tony. I'm looking forward to those ideas for the Road Show."

"I think you'll like this. So, let's begin with the agenda. Let me share my screen and we can edit as we go along." With that, he shared the screen and described how the Road Show meetings would begin with an introduction of the team, their roles within the department, its reporting to the board of directors, the definition of internal auditing, the code of ethics, the three phases of audits, how internal audit did compliance and IT work, and the focus on risks and controls. The presentation then included short videos from each auditor introducing themselves, their professional backgrounds, an interesting personal anecdote, and "a day in the life" to highlight the types of work they did.

"I like it," said John enthusiastically. "I like the description of our function and who we report to, the balance of professional and personal, and I also like 'day in the life' feature." Then using the Sandwich Approach to feedback, he added what he wanted changed.

"Can you go back to the section on how internal audit does compliance and IT work?"

Tony moved the presentation to that section. "Here it is."

"Good. Let's change that because it is a bit limiting of what we cover. In addition to compliance, we should add operational and fraud reviews. With IT, let me turn my thought into a question, is there something technical we should add there?"

"Um," Tony thought for a moment, then uttered "cybersecurity?"

"Exactly. Yes, they are separate fields so let's be explicit and include that there," as he made the changes immediately.

"Now, go to the section on 'risk', he instructed." When that section was on display John asked, "what should come before looking at risks?"

"Hmm," another moment went by as Tony thought about the question. "It's not controls, I know that much."

"That's right."

"Objectives?"

"Is that a question or a statement?" John asked prompting for a confident answer.

"Objectives," said Tony with a more confident tone.

"That' right!" John replied congratulating him. "Business objectives should always come first. Beyond putting that as a bullet, let's add why each element is important. Objectives, risks, controls and how we then use that understanding of the program or process to develop audit steps."

"OK," was the reply.

"Another thing we should add, which I believe is also very important here at InSports is that we're becoming more collaborative, so add something about our approach to risk assessments at the enterprise and project levels, how the three phases of planning, field-work, and reporting are opportunities for collaboration, and how we also want to col-laborate when we do follow-ups of outstanding issues that needed remediation."

"We haven't been very diligent with follow-up audits," he said.

"I know. We're changing that," John replied. "This is as much what we're doing as what we're going to do. Can you make the internal audit phases into an infographic? Are you comfortable doing that?"

"You mean a diagram?"

"Yes. A visual representation of the process, which can also look like a cycle because we do recurring reviews, so our audience gets the information clearly and quickly. Bullets are good, but a diagram may be more helpful."

"Ok. I should have thought about that."

"That's why we talk about these things before going live. We check each other's work! One last thing. Go to the section where we mention compliance and IT audits. Add that we also do consulting or provide advisory services. We need to do more of that, and we will, but it should be in the presentation now."

"I'll add it."

"Thanks. Let's talk about it tomorrow. I would like us to start thinking about the videos because those will take a bit of time. Find some time on my calendar, OK?"

"No problem. See you tomorrow."

"Yes, thanks. Bye for now."

--------------------||--------------------

John arrived a day early for the quarterly meeting with the audit committee. He typi-cally arrives in the evening, but today he arrived earlier so he could talk with Ken. They walked together to Sunflower Coffee House and chatted about company initia-tives and several operational challenges impacting InSports.

"I heard from EHS that they have been chatting with audit about accidents and workplace safety," said Ken as they settled in his office with coffee and pastries.

"Yes, we met in the winter, sometime around February, and showed them some of the work we did. They liked it and we have been collaborating since."

"Good. Their new reports include some interesting stuff. When I asked them about it they credited you and your team with the analysis. I particularly liked the benchmarking section, they said you suggested it and they now include it in their monthly reports to me. Help me understand this, you are emphasizing what can and must go right, not only what goes wrong?"

"Yes. What must go right for the group to succeed. In the case of Georgia, you remember that's how we started looking at that facility, right?"

"Right."

"When we compared the results with Illinois there were certain things they were doing that made them successful, including training, flexible procedures, internal safety competition with rewards, a buddy system, and several very visible metrics so everyone there knew how they were doing at all times. So Georgia adopted those practices too and now their numbers are much better."

"Well John, that vision and approach work and I like it. Thanks for helping EHS out."

"You're welcome."

"Now, I have to kick you out of my office because I have another meeting coming up, but come by before you leave town, OK?"

"I will."

--------------------||--------------------

Summary
Spring

"We've noticed a change in the work of internal audit, and not only based on what you are telling us, but we're hearing some good things from the CEO and CFO. We like what we are hearing, John," said Jim starting the meeting.

"Thank you."

"Now, to the business at hand. What are, or how, is internal audit identifying new areas of concern that we need to be on the lookout for?"

"Internal audit needs to align itself with the risks that are critical to InSports. Business dynamics, and external dynamics, are changing constantly, so internal audit needs to adjust too. We need to be risk-based, and since the risks change often, we also need to be flexible," said John.

"What are some of these dynamics you are thinking about?" asked Jim wanting to expand the conversation further.

"Things like cybersecurity and data privacy, those are big topics because we collect, process, and disseminate so much data within InSports, with vendors, and with our customers. Another is ESG, which has been getting a lot of attention lately from governments and investors. While we're not publicly traded, there are rating agencies still looking at some of those metrics. The media, consumers, and other special interest groups are also watching."

"Any others?" asked Sanjay.

"Outsourcing and our supply chain. We depend on third parties and one of the things we and so many organizations around the world found out the hard way during the pandemic and the war in Ukraine, was that our supply chains are very vulnerable. I looked through previous years' audit plans and noticed that these topics were not audited as much as they should have been."

"They were not audited at all. There were peripheral, but related, reviews like AP and contracts, but an in-depth review was something we talked about but never got on the audit plan," confessed Jim.

"So, we're on the same page on that one. I will be directing some in the team to look at that," said John using that as an opportunity to show that his role was to provide assurance on what mattered most to the organization.

"Are you going to assign the audit to someone on the team?" asked Sanjay.

John realized that this was a question with a potentially hidden agenda. If InSports, and more specifically the internal audit team, had never audited these things before, what would be the result if he merely delegated it to people who had no experience on that subject? John knew there were two options: either he was actively involved in the audit directing and coaching the team or he would need to co-source the review. He took a balanced approach with his answer while signaling he had deep knowledge on the subject.

"I will work with the team as we review this. I've audited this before. We should co-source some audit work, but I don't think this is the project we should do that with. I'm thinking we can co-source something more IT or cybersecurity related."

"I would like to hear more about that. We have two IT auditors, right?" asked Sanjay.

"Yes, Miriam and Brian. They're both good auditors but need some upskilling. As we look differently and more deeply at subjects, some outside help would help and we would also benefit from some exposure. When they see what other auditors are doing it will give them some fresh ideas and help me with the training process."

"Makes sense. Does all of this mean less financial, legal, and regulatory compliance reviews?" asked Jim.

"The way I see it, yes. But we won't ignore it. We will continue to monitor those too, but we have focused on those for many years and things seem controlled there," said John reassuring the committee.

"But the topics you mentioned look like bigger exposures?" asked Jim again.

"Yes, in the short and longer term," explained John.

"Any others?"

"The organizational culture."

"I've seen that mentioned in various publications. I suppose that is associated with HR," said Sanjay.

"Yes, HR plays a key role when it comes to the organizational culture, but so does executive leadership and management, and the alignment between our mission, values, policies, and practices. We also need to look at how we do grooming, deploying, rewarding, and disciplining managers in terms of culture because that affects our image internally and externally, recruitment and retention, motivation, management practices, and so many other things. It affects our collective performance but yes, HR plays a key role, and we would work with them if we reviewed that topic."

"Good. I don't believe I've ever seen an internal audit report that touched on HR but the whole world seems to be talking about corporate culture these days," said Jim showing support for what John stated.

"Work from home arrangements, flexible time off policies, inclusion, and diversity programs, the list goes on and on," added John.

"What else?" Jim wanted to know.

"Basically, all threats that can keep us from achieving our strategy, affect our performance or affect our reputation should be on our priority list," said John.

"So, what, roughly, would you consider your priorities?" asked Jim.

"First, we take care of the obvious, things related to internal controls, fraud, and theft prevention. For example, we need to make sure the math is right on financial reporting, but also the related disclosures."

"What about non-financial disclosures?"

"Yes, there is a growing demand for transparency about corporate responsibility and sustainability. Investors, activists, and rating agencies are watching this closely, so ESG-related disclosures are a top priority. Even the SEC has issued climate and ESG disclosure requirements so other stakeholders are paying attention and demanding high-quality and transparent information."

"Do you think benchmarking is necessary?" asked Sanjay.

"ESG benchmarking?"

"Yes."

"Probably. We are just starting the journey ourselves, so to not make avoidable mistakes and see how we compare, I think we should consider hiring some external consultants to help us benchmark against our peers and the standards that ESG rating organizations use."

"In terms of financial reporting, what is happening with tax? I heard there is a proposal for a 15 percent global minimum corporate tax rate. Is that right?"

"Yes, the OECD is driving some of that minimum tax rate conversation and to some extent it is related to ESG since stakeholders expect corporations meet certain conduct requirements, including how we handle tax matters."

"So, we minimize our tax liability like everyone else is, pay what we owe, and we're done," chimed Sanjay.

"Yes, but there is more to that. As the audit committee, you should assess our tolerance for reputational hits based on the tax choices we make and how those choices can affect our sustainability scores. We can save money by doing what we have always done, which is tax avoidance, but consider the penalties, headaches, and bad press that companies like Google, Apple and Amazon endured in Europe."

"Is that related to the Double Dutch thing?" asked Jim.

"Yes, 'double Irish' and 'Dutch sandwich'. That was Google. So, tax reporting for many stakeholders now means good tax reporting."

"Another topic I don't believe has been looked at is the whistleblower hotline," said John.

"We have one, don't we?" asked Sanjay.

"Yes, we do, but I don't believe we have ever reviewed it. We need to make sure all allegations are dealt with fairly, expeditiously, and ethically. Sarbanes-Oxley requires we have the hotline and the NACD states the board is responsible for that too."

"That's the National Association of what again?" interrupted Sanjay, while John was mid-sentence.

"National Association of Corporate Directors," explained John. "They state that boards must ensure compliance and ethics are an integral part of how organizations operate and if these programs are driving long-term positive behaviors."

"That is a squishy topic!" said Sanjay sounding annoyed.

"Yes, unfortunately but that is the reality. So, the key is to demonstrate our efforts in that regard in case anyone comes asking," said Jim defending John's argument. "Wasn't there a scandal over at GE over some reputational issues?" he added.

"Most scandals cause reputational damage. In the case of GE, there were accounting issues in the billions of dollars, and the issues with operating results also involved insurance projections and estimates related to insurance liabilities, so their ethics and compliance failures were material. My point is, the audit committee needs to drive, and internal audit can assess, whether management has designed, implemented, is actively monitoring, and taking remedial action where needed so an ethics and compliance program works to enable a healthy organizational culture and objectives."

"Anything else?" asked Sanjay almost sounding frustrated, or maybe overwhelmed, by the long list of requirements.

"Another thing I believe is important to consider is IT. I mentioned cybersecurity and data privacy, but on a general level, IT drives most of our company and we need it to improve processes and productivity while reducing costs. So, in general, IT is part of our overall strategy and we need to make sure there is alignment among systems, that the money is spent well, and projects are completed on time and achieve their objectives."

"We may need a PMO," said Jim thoughtfully.

"That may be true. But also, we need to make sure we have the talent to adapt to changing demands and needs," said John.

"Talent management?" asked Jim.

"Talent and knowledge management, yes. We're talking about it in the context of IT, but that is a broader topic impacting InSports at multiple levels, from design, to sales, manufacturing, etc.," explained John as Sanjay seemed restless. Jim seemed to have noticed Sanjay's behavior, so the following comments seemed aimed more at him than to John.

"This has been very helpful, John. Thanks for listing these areas of interest so we can work with you to prioritize them. You have been more flexible when managing the audit plan, but how is completion of the audit plan coming along? We're halfway through the year, do you think you'll be able to do all the reviews?"

John noticed Jim's eye movement and his tone while asking the question. It sounded to him like an indication this was an opening.

"Yes, we'll be able to meet the audit plan I started with six months ago. I'm looking forward to revising the process, so we are more tactical. That does not preclude our ability to be strategic with the audit plan, it just means that we become more flexible and adapt to the needs of InSports. We become more agile. As we do that, we would talk about what I'm seeing and what you need assurance on, we evaluate our resources and deploy. That said, I'm submitting a request for an increase in our budget that would add one full time equivalent to our staff this year."

With that, the focus of the meeting shifted to a discussion of increasing productivity, enhancing the coverage and how internal audit would demonstrate its value more visibly to InSports. They discussed the road show and how it would enhance the image of internal audit, which was a concern the committee mentioned when he was hired. They also reviewed the status of audits in progress and planned for the next quarter, the need to upskill the staff, and concluded with a discussion of the company's financial results. They didn't agree to hiring a new auditor.

After the meeting, John walked outside onto 5th Avenue feeling good. The meeting had gone well, even if they had not agreed immediately to hiring an additional auditor for his department. They embraced his plans and complimented the improvements made to date. He remembered how different everything felt on that same sidewalk three months ago when he stepped out on a cold, windy, and dark March afternoon. He wanted to go to his hotel, change, and go for a nice long walk, but that required a train ride first. He didn't want to wait.

It was late spring and a lovely day. There was a cool comfortable breeze, so he took off his jacket, threw it over his shoulder, and decided to walk for a while around midtown. This was an afternoon to enjoy. He would get to his hotel later.

He saw the sun setting through some buildings on Manhattan's West side and thought how if he didn't know the time of day that image of the sun could be a sunrise as much as it was a sunset.

Today he would treat it as an evening sunrise. The sun is rising on internal audit!

The team met in New York again and overwhelmingly voted to meet at the same sports bar as they did during their previous get-together. John noticed the higher level of comfort they seemed to have with each other. The next morning started with John bringing the noisy group to order.

"Hello all. Welcome to our state of the unit address," he said starting the team's spring quarterly meeting. "We're halfway through the year, can you believe it? We're staring at summer in the eye. The year is going by so fast. So, let's review the agenda, shall we? What we've accomplished. What we're working on. What's coming next. Challenges and obstacles. First, what we've accomplished, and we have a lot to list and be proud of."

"We're wrapping up the second quarter of the year and we're starting to see some significant improvements in what we do and how. Colin Powell said, 'A dream doesn't become reality through magic; it takes sweat, determination and hard work.' I want to thank all of you for your hard work and for all the things you do to elevate your team – our department. I also realize you are sacrificing your time and your significant others' time, so thanks for all you do." John paused to let his recognition sink in, then he proceeded.

"Let's do a bit of inventory, shall we? We've accomplished several things, right? Let's enumerate some of those great things you are doing. I'll start; we created a vision statement that is informing our strategy, so we have a clearer sense of where we're going and why. Next?"

Miriam spoke up next. "We updated our methodology by moving from traditional auditing to risk-based auditing, so we are focusing on key risks and controls."

"Yes, good. Starting with?" asked John prompting some more discussion on the topic that Miriam was sharing with the group.

"Objectives," said Carolina.

"Exactly. We begin with objectives, identify the key risks that can have the biggest influence on the achievement of those objectives, then controls. By linking the corresponding controls on key risks, you should be focusing on key controls only. Nice. Other accomplishments?" said John creating an opening for someone else to share.

"We improved reporting because we now have a better understanding of what CCCER is really all about and how to incorporate the seven communication attributes from the Standards," said Brian.

"Yes. What are those seven attributes again?" asked John furthering the conversation.

"Clarity, conciseness, completeness," said Brian immediately since he was already on this topic.

"Accurate, objective," said Tony.

"Clear," said Carolina.

"Constructive," said Tony.

All along John was counting visibly with his fingers. The flow paused indicating the team had exhausted their collective memory on the attributes and one was missing, so John helped them finish the list. "Brian, you said 'clarity' and Carolina said 'clear', which is effectively the same thing, so we're still short one, 'timely'," he said solving the puzzle. "So, we improved reporting, did we accomplish anything else?"

"Can I add something?" asked Tony.

"Of course, go ahead."

"Over the last few weeks as we've talked about the attributes of effective communication and ways to improve our reporting, it struck me that we need to focus especially on 'constructive'."

John found the comment peculiar and thought there was a personal element to Tony's comment, so he asked him to elaborate. "Why is that?"

"Because the Standards state that constructive means our communications help the engagement client and the organization, and lead to improvements where needed. Since our focus is now far more than listing issues and on helping the client succeed, this seems really important to me," he explained.

"Good points," John acknowledged Tony's remarks and was pleased because it suggests Tony was continuing his embrace of the change.

"We learned about the Affinity Diagram and how we can use it," said Rachel.

"For example?" inquired John.

"To cluster similar items when we're writing an audit report, so we present the information more logically," she replied.

"Very good," acknowledged John.

"And make the reports shorter," said Brian.

"That's right. You're the one who said 'concise' earlier, so here's a tool for you, Brian."

"Exactly. I'm paying attention! He said with a proud tone on his voice."

"I know you are. What else?" John continued prodding the team to recall more items.

"SIPOC. Which stands for Suppliers, Inputs, Process, Outputs and Customers. The S and C are typically organizations or people and the I and O are usually things," Carolina said almost at a hurried pace as if trying not to forget anything. She continued, "we can use it to define the boundaries of a process, which can be useful when setting the scope of an audit, or any review really, identify stakeholders and key items flowing through a process for significance. We also get a high-level understanding of the process itself," as she took a deep breath.

"Were you trying to avoid me asking you a question?" asked John jovially. "I think you were."

She raised her hands as a sign of feigned defeat.

"I'll give it to you. No follow-up questions for Carolina. Unless someone wants to ask something and ruin her happy moment," said John with a big smile. Silence. Everyone thought she had done it good naturedly and the group should move on.

"Anyone likes to travel?" asked John giving the team a hint about the next item he wanted recalled.

"I do," said Brian. "I'm not sure where you're going with that … oh wait … yes, the road show. We organized and delivered a road show to management."

"You got the answer by accident," said Tony joining the conversation.

"Better to be lucky than smart," replied Brian.

"What?" asked Rachel.

"Just kidding, I'm wicked smaht and also lucky. Luck of the Irish," he said as he leaned back in his chair.

"Smaht, I see what you did there Brian," said Miriam repeating Brian's words emulating a Boston accent.

"OK everyone," chimed in John choosing not to indulge the conversation and keep some decorum. "Good memory of the concepts and tools. Good review of ways to apply the concepts and tools. Remember, the goal is not only to list, recall, or know things, we are also doing things. Knowledge in action."

With that John shared with the team some company news about key developments, the status of several audits at various levels of completion, company financial and operational results, and industry and economic dynamics that had an effect on InSports. They then talked about projects that would continue or launch during the summer, and the challenges and potential obstacles anticipated. After the serious items were properly addressed and questions were answered, John relaxed the tone of the meeting once again, led the five of them through some casual conversation by talking about summer plans, the weather, baseball, and the hurricane brewing in the Gulf of Mexico.

Lunch was delivered to the room, and in the afternoon, they worked side-by-side on current and upcoming projects. Later they split up as they went to meet and greet some audit clients throughout the building. Dinner was at a Brazilian Steakhouse, and while the evening was uneventful, the discussion as to which steak was better was the highlight. Brian argued American, Tony and Miriam thought Brazilian, Rachel shared her experience eating steak in Japan, and Carolina argued in favor of her Argentinian Gaucho heritage.

Day Two began with three short training sessions. For the first session, they invited someone from the Legal Department to review contracts, common risks associated with business contracts, and the controls the Legal Department had in place to protect the organization when working with large suppliers and customers. John delivered the second training on occupational fraud, focusing on asset misappropriation. Miriam delivered the third training session, focusing on IT general controls and what steps could be included in operational audits to make them better integrated with IT.

Lunch was delivered, and a bit of sadness was evident in the room as the team's behavior showed that departing would happen soon. John thought this was bittersweet. He enjoyed watching the camaraderie that had strengthened among the team members and the fact they were sad to leave meant they enjoyed each other's company. After all, building a cohesive team was one of his goals.

Before they left, John asked for feedback from the team on their second get-together. They discussed their objectives of reviewing company and departmental news, socializing as a team, meeting clients, and getting some training. The feedback was again positive, and they said they were looking forward to getting together again next quarter.

--------------------||--------------------

9 Measurement and Methodology Changes and Performance Evaluations

"Hello everyone!" said John as he started the meeting. "I sent an e-mail Monday with some information on what I noticed about performance metrics and what I would like to see us do."

He continued. "Thanks to everyone who submitted some ideas on this. What you indicated in your feedback was generally in line with what I was thinking, which is, in some instances we have been measuring the wrong things. It is not surprising, because audit departments have been focusing on traditional metrics for decades, so some of these old habits are hard to shake off, but we should take a hard look at them now."

"What do you mean?" asked Tony.

"Well, for example. When I arrived, I noticed that every Monday we had a haphazard process of Word documents and Excel spreadsheets with the number of hours worked the previous week in 15-minute increments. These were broken down nicely by project and phase, but I couldn't find what anyone did with all of that information. Remember?"

After a brief silence, Rachel chimed in, saying, "I remember, and we got rid of that practice. It was a waste of time."

"Correct. The practice was to document how many hours people worked, which did not correlate to outcomes. Talking of outcomes, we also tracked the number of findings each team and each auditor found. Correct?"

"Yes," said Tony. "I had the highest number three years in a row and got a trophy too!"

"OK. Yes, I saw that," said John wondering how acute the misplacement of priorities in the unit was.

"What happened to the post-audit questionnaire? I saw some old ones but nothing in the past couple of years," John asked already assuming the answer in his head.

"We stopped sending them out two years ago because clients were not filling them out. And a few of our clients gave us bad scores, so we stopped," said Tony, recalling the related history.

"Exactly," said John. "This is something many audit departments do. They stop using surveys due to low participation rates or poor evaluation scores, even though both of these dynamics are actually worth a ton of gold in terms of feedback value."

"Are we going to re-introduce post-audit surveys?" asked Miriam.

DOI: 10.1201/9781003322870-11

"Yes, we're going to re-introduce post-audit surveys. We'll explain the purpose and value they represent to us from now on, first at the beginning of the audit and again when we're done. It is about feedback. We'll also ask our clients what the best way is to get that feedback, by phone, video call or survey, which is electronic of course. We won't assume that everyone wants an electronic survey because some people may not want to type their thoughts down. If clients don't respond, we'll call them. If they give us low scores. We'll call them. We'll work at it together. Oh, we should also not think of scores as good or bad. They're either high or low. Artificially high scores look good mathematically, but we don't want clients lying to us and giving us high marks if we didn't earn them. Those are high mathematically but bad. And very low scores, can also be bad. But they can be good, if the client tells us honestly and accurately that we did a poor job, but those are good scores because we get useful feedback that we can work with. So, let's think high, medium, or low and always aim for honest feedback. What do you think about that?" John asked to check for understanding among the team.

Everyone nodded, except Carolina, who took the opportunity to ask a question.

"Are survey results going to play a role in our performance evaluations? Would bad, I mean, low scores, reduce our pay raise or lead to getting fired?"

"No. We are going to use a composite approach. Like the balanced scorecard that you've probably heard about. We won't make decisions only based on one variable, because high performance, or success, is defined by the achievement of multiple things. For example, identification of the objectives and key risks of the area under review and using those as our North Star during the review. Presentation of all audit observations to the client during fieldwork, and I don't mean the evening before the exit meeting, I mean as fieldwork was progressing. Working with the client to get their agreement and acceptance of the issues and preparing action items with them. Notice I'm not just talking about the number of findings. We're talking about the quality and communication of the findings too."

"How about the number of hours of the audit in relation to the budget?" asked Tony focusing the conversation on a topic that had been discussed extensively but never resolved in the unit over the years.

"Yes and no. Yes, we need to manage the budget and manage to the budget, but I don't want us to say things like we have to stop because we are out of hours."

"So, we keep going?" asked Rachel.

"If there are issues that need to be looked at, let's talk about it and see if we are going to address those things during that review, bring in additional resources or table those topics for a future review, but in general, if the issue looks important enough, we'll search for a way to look at it then. If there's a significant risk, we want to examine it," explained John.

"What about continuing to test if we have found nothing?" asked Miriam.

"Good question," said John. "If you are testing and finding nothing, and you're done verifying that things related to the key objectives, risks and controls are in order, let's talk about it because we are probably going to stop and move onto something else. No need to keep testing as if we're hoping to find a problem. That's not our goal. We can stop early, or we can go longer, based on the reality on the ground."

"Well, that's good because in the past we were locked into the budget," said Rachel referring to one of the points of disagreement with Tony, who was usually enforcing such measures.

"So, no more eating hours?" asked Carolina.

"What's that?" asked John seeking clarification.

"If we had to get a lot of testing done and we used up our budget, we continued working but didn't log in the actual hours, because we would get dinged for blowing the budget," explained Carolina.

"You used to do that?" John asked again to better understand her point.

"Yes, I believe everyone did it," said Rachel. "Carolina wasn't impacted by it much because she is a relatively new employee, but yes."

Tony's complexion was now changing as his face turned increasingly red. He was either angry or embarrassed, but it was clear this action was done to circumvent some of the department rules.

"I was just making sure we followed Nick's requirements," he said referencing the previous CAE.

"OK," said John gesturing with his hands for emphasis. "I want to make this point very clearly so please listen carefully. No more eating hours. Work what you record and record what you work. I expect you to work diligently and smartly, so if you are doing that, log in your hours accurately. If you're goofing off, then we have another issue to address and you saying you're working when you are not, is a case of dishonesty we won't accept. But working extra hours without reporting that is a disservice to you the worker, but also complicates things for your manager and me."

"How so?" asked Brian getting into the conversation.

"Every time we do a review, we want to know how long it took to see how accurate our planning is. If we do a similar review in the future, we usually assume that those working on it will benefit from the accumulated knowledge and be able to do the review faster the next time because now you know the people, the process, you have a running start on the objectives, risks, controls, key reports, data sources, and so on."

John paused giving his team a chance to process what he had just said. He wanted to be clear about this because he vehemently disagreed with the practice. Then he continued.

"I also found out that promotions were awarded based on time on the job, so staff are promoted to Senior Auditor after two years, and Senior Auditors are promoted to Manager after three more years. I believe in rewarding hard work and accomplishments, but we should be careful granting promotions only based on a calendar. I don't want to scare anyone, we're not just throwing everything you are accustomed to out the window without thinking it through," he said explaining the rationale. "We want to make sure you have the tools and knowledge to get ahead. We'll work through this intelligently. But here are some of my thoughts."

The team was silent as they heard this from John. Expectations were clearly being changed, and they were wondering what this meant for their career progression at InSports.

--------------------||--------------------

"Hi Frank!"

"Hi John, how are things at InSports?"

"Things are going well, but I have a question for you. There has been a practice in many organizations, especially professional service organizations."

"Like audit firms?"

"Yes, like audit firms, to promote auditors based on seniority. After two years, promote to senior. After two more years, promote to manager, and so on."

"OK, yes, I'm familiar with the practice. It is quite widespread I believe."

"Yes, in some cases the attached phrase is 'up or out'."

"Yes, that's true. So, what's the problem?"

"I have a very small department. We only have five staff and me, so not much room to promote my team. There aren't enough positions to create a ladder up."

"Do they have to move up all the time?" asked Frank.

"Not really, but they have learned to expect it."

"I see. The problem is not your creation, but you now have to deal with it and address it somehow."

"Exactly."

"True professionals are less fixated on titles. While important, titles don't tell the entire story. For example, have you ever met a staff auditor who was doing what in other organizations was being done by a senior auditor?"

After a moment thinking about the question, John answered, "yes, I have. Like leading exit meetings keeping track of the team's progress, and so on."

Frank asked another question, "How about a senior doing what a manager at other organizations did?"

After another moment thinking about the question, John again answered, "yes, I have too. I've seen seniors prepare audit programs and write audit reports, which in some organizations is done by managers."

"And we can continue up the line, with managers managing multiple projects or creating audit plans for the entire department, even presenting to the audit committee. In fact, I remember one organization where the chief audit executive's title was actually Senior Manager. Now, I have an issue with the CAE's title not being on par with the other 'chiefs'. This person has to work with and look them in the eye, but you understand my point."

"That people do work that may differ from their title? That role does not equal title?" asked John.

"Yes. That's it. Now, learning, growing, becoming more marketable, building your brand, these are things professionals should focus on. They still need a decent compensation package because they have to live and take care of their families, but there is much more to it than the salary."

"Yes, I agree. In fact there are many people leaving organizations even when the salary is very high."

"Exactly, I remember during the Iraq War a conversation in a classroom where people were complaining about what they described as low pay and another student jumped in after a few moments and said something that dropped like a bucket of cold water, or a whiff of fresh air, depending on how you want to think about it."

"What did the student say?"

"If you want to make a lot of money, get a truck driver's license, and go drive big rigs in Iraq. They need truckers and they're paying them well over $100,000 a year. You can also go work on a drilling platform in the Gulf of Mexico or the North Sea. You can work really fast and long hours on a union assembly line. You'll likely make over $100,000 in any of those jobs. There are ways to make a lot more money if you really want to, but would you trade..."

"Trade what?" asked John.

"Can you hear me?" John asked again.

"What?... not again. Yes, no problem. I'll be right there," said Frank clearly talking to someone else and needing to leave in a hurry.

"I have to go," said Frank, now speaking to John. "Think about that because I believe you can take care of that issue to everyone's benefit," he recommended.

"OK. Thank you," said John, grateful for his time, albeit limited, and now with some additional ideas to better address the coaching of his team on title vs. role, pay and work satisfaction, and career management.

--------------------||--------------------

John called his dog, and it popped its head by the door threshold with an inquisitive look on his face as if asking "did you call me?" John had been walking more since he got the dog and was thankful for the company from his exercise buddy. He called the dog again, and, now having its suspicions confirmed, it came jogging when he saw John holding the leash.

They walked down the street and into the nearby woods taking one of the many familiar trails. As John was walking his dog he thought about Frank's words, and the example he gave about working on oil rigs and driving trucks in dangerous places. There are ways and places where you can make a lot of money but those working conditions may not be what auditors have in mind for work.

I remember my Organizational Behavior class where we learned about Herzberg's Hygiene Factors. The fact that there are certain things in the workplace that cause satisfaction, and others that cause dissatisfaction. Motivators include things like challenging work, recognition for one's contribution and accomplishments, amount of responsibility, opportunity to do meaningful work, and having a chance to be involved in decision-making. Things that are labeled hygiene factors include status, salary, benefits, work conditions, and vacations are to some extent expected so they don't give satisfaction, but in their absence, they created dissatisfaction. These are outside of the job itself, or extrinsic as my professor described them.

He also thought about Maslow and the Hierarchy of Needs, where individuals need to have their physiological needs met first. These were about basic survival and include food, water, shelter, and sleep. Once that was met, then individuals could pursue safety needs, and that included security of employment, of body, health, and property. Above that was the need for love and belonging, where individuals need friendship, family, and intimacy. Next, esteem, where individuals yearn for the respect from others, and confidence that comes from self-esteem and recognition by their peers. The fifth and highest-level needs were referred to as self-actualization, where creativity, spontaneity, problem solving, and the acceptance of facts results in the lack of prejudice and a high-level view of camaraderie and solidarity with others.

"This is all good," he thought to himself, "I suppose that's what Frank had in mind. Could that be it or is there more?"

John was thinking about this as he walked on the riverbank and started reminiscing about his career and one of his favorite jobs early in his career. He started doing the same type of work day in and day out, and at first it was interesting and exciting. He built an expertise in his tasks, but the pride of expertise was starting to turn to boredom. Then his boss gave him additional things to do. He started broadening his duties while continuing to do what he had become an expert in, and colleagues came to him for assistance and advice. He loved the widening scope of his role, and how he was learning new things. The pay was good, but more importantly, he was carving out a place in the department and the organization as someone who was knowledgeable. And the emotional pay was great.

Then the job changed again. This time, tasks previously reserved for "higher-ups" were shared with him. He described this as shared because he was part of the team and he assisted, but those with more experience and knowledge still owned these tasked and were responsible for them. He was brought into that circle, and he loved the exposure. He was learning how decisions were made and how some of the things that he had been doing related to these more important and influential actions. He now understood the process better and how decisions upstream affected activities downstream. He was getting a panoramic view of the operation and rubbing elbows with people whose title he wanted to have someday.

As John walked out of the woods and onto his street he was thinking about his dog and how he sniffed and stopped sometimes at the same spots, but sometimes at new ones indicating a new scent was left there. Then suddenly it dawned on him.

"Frank was talking about job enlargement and job enrichment!"

The clarification of this nagging conundrum made John smile, and he was deep in thought processing the implications of this revelation. As they walked home, he saw his neighbor in his backyard with his new puppy. They were too far back in the yard for John to say anything to them. Besides, Carl's back was toward the street, and the dog was the one facing John. John thought the dog might be interested in his dog, lose focus, and run toward him to play with his dog, but the dog didn't. It was focused on Carl and apparently doing everything Carl asked so it could earn a treat.

"Dogs can be the son or daughter of the family, and at the same time play the role of watchdog, companion, play pal, or worker based on how you frame their roles. They can also change roles throughout the day as the owner or situation dictates. Not to dehumanize workers, but their role can change as the case warrants, independent of their title.

"So, my staffer could act like a senior, and my senior can act like a manager. It is all dependent on their role. But the role is best performed when properly trained. Carl is teaching his new dog to sit, lie down, roll, and fetch. But the dog will probably also figure out that just lying at your feet or on your lap is what the moment requires, like when someone in the family is sad or ill, and just needs company. The dog can also learn to fetch and treat it as work or as play, but that doesn't change the fact that it is still the dog, companion, or watchdog in the family. There may be a main role, but then there are many other things the dog can perform joyfully and competently.

"Maybe this is what Frank meant. Teach them new skills so they can do different things regardless of their title. Role is more important. Even if I can't elevate their title, professionals value the ability to learn, do more, and accomplish different things as they grow in their careers.

"I need to redefine career advancement at InSports. Your worth is not determined by your title, it is determined by what you learn to do and your ability to expand your job so you enjoy what you are doing. On that note, there's job enrichment and job enlargement, so I have options!"

--------------------||--------------------

"The idea of Agile Auditing has been around for a while now. I noticed in your file Miriam that you took an Agile Auditing class, is that right?"

"Yes, it was an online class, and it covered the methodology in detail."

"Did the department consider implementing it?"

"We talked about it but thought it would be too difficult to implement here."

"Why?"

"We knew that clients wouldn't cooperate. They don't want to get involved in the audit. They just want us to hurry up, finish the audit and hopefully write a report that has no findings. They keep referring to themselves as 'wanting to pass the audit' and us 'passing them' as if it were an exam where they are the students, and we are the teacher."

"Did we explain the methodology and the benefits to them getting involved?"

"The chief's view was, why bother? He was convinced they wouldn't be interested."

"I understand. How about the length of the reporting cycle? Average time from the end of fieldwork to publish the draft report is two months and another 2 months for the final report to go out. Did the long cycle time factor into the decision, as in, why does it take so long, and can we shorten it?"

"The clients argue with us all the time and keep asking questions about the methodology. They want to see the documentation. They want to know who we talked to and what they said. They come up with new evidence that they claim they didn't have available when we first asked for it. They argue we misunderstood them. I could go on for days."

"And the length of the report?"

"We have to explain everything in the report so they have all the information they could possibly want so they don't ask any questions. But they still do. It is frustrating."

"I understand," John said encouragingly. "To solve these issues we need to become better focused, speed up our processes, shorten the audits, and communicate results faster. We're implementing Agile Auditing, so we're moving from talking and doubting, to believing and acting. Thanks for the background. Tony mentioned some of those issues a few weeks ago and I wanted to chat with you about it and discuss the connection between Agile Auditing and faster and shorter reports. Your thoughts help me understand the past situation better."

"You're welcome. Let me know how I can help."

"I will."

--------------------||--------------------

"Happy Monday everyone!"

"Happy Monday, John," came the reply.

"How was your birthday, Brian? Sunny and warm where you are I hope?"

"For the most part. San Francisco is always cold. The coldest winter I ever experienced…"

Before he could finish Carolina interrupted him: "Is a summer in San Francisco. You should come to London sometime if you want to experience cold in the summer. It is always overcast and drizzly here. We hardly ever see the sun."

"OK. You beat me."

"And if you think it is bad there or here, you should visit Norway or Iceland. Long days in the summer. Very nice, but cool, windy, and wet."

"What should you do if you get lost in a forest in Iceland?" asked Miriam.

"What?" came the response from Brian while Carolina smiled indicating she may already know the answer.

"I don't know. What should you do?" asked Brian.

"Stand up!" answered Miriam laughing loudly.

"I don't get it," said Brian with a confused face.

"Well, there are few forests in Iceland, and many are small due to the sweeping winds or just young plantings, so if you stand up you can see where you are and find your way out," she explained.

"OK folks, intervened John. If you haven't been to Iceland, I suggest you look into it. It is a spectacular country. A bit out of the way, but its uniqueness, waterfalls, rolling mountains, make it worthwhile. The country also benefits from tourism income if you want to consider it. Plus, their glaciers are melting due to climate change. Which is also a good segue for me because I want to talk to you about change and our titles and roles. We are a small unit, as you may have already noticed, so not much room to promote up. I just can't do it. There aren't enough positions to promote people up. But, what I can do is help you grow, which in a way is what promotions were supposed to do, but let me ask you a question, have you heard of staff who do the work of audit seniors in other organizations?"

They nodded in agreement.

"Have you seen senior auditors doing the work of managers in other audit organizations?"

They nodded again.

"You get my point. I've even seen VPs in some organizations who are senior auditors and managers at other organizations."

"VPs?" asked Brian.

"Yes, I've seen it, especially at banks. Almost everyone is an AVP or VP," said Rachel.

"OK, without criticizing banks, this helps me make my point, which is, one of my goals is to help you develop as professionals, so I'm looking at ways to broaden your skills set." As he said this, he noticed his team was listening attentively. This was a very important topic for them.

"I'll provide as best I can a variety of duties, so you learn on the job. Has anyone heard of job enlargement?"

The silence from the team indicated this was a new concept, so John proceeded to explain the term.

"Job enlargement is when the scope of the job increases by broadening the range of duties and responsibilities. This usually happens within the same level or title, so for example, someone who is staff would focus on more than just inventory or AP or AR for example, and always do that type of work. Instead, we would broaden the duties, of course, with appropriate training and coaching, so you can also audit treasury, construction, or manufacturing, for example."

"It sounds like growing the job horizontally," said Miriam.

"Exactly," replied John.

"So instead of creating specialists we become generalists?" asked Rachel.

"I wouldn't put it that way, but technically you could say that it contradicts the idea of specialization because instead of making you an expert in a few things, we would expose you to a wider variety of auditable areas. Doing the same thing all the time can be boring. For a while I was the inventory and warehousing guy at one of my previous employers. I liked being viewed as an expert in those areas, but after a while I started getting bored and wanted to learn to do other things," John explained by sharing his personal experience.

Brian, Rachel, and Carolina nodded in agreement as if indicating they might be experiencing that feeling presently.

John continued. "You would still learn and need to be good at auditing what you're assigned. Like I said, training and coaching would be provided."

"The Standards also require us to have the competency to do our jobs," Tony chimed in.

"Exactly. I agree. I won't send you to do audits unprepared. It does no one any good."

After a short pause to let this fact sink in, John continued.

"The other is job enrichment. Here you do more of the work vertically. You do more challenging tasks which require more skill. For example, as a staff you probably focused almost exclusively on fieldwork testing, right?"

Brian and Carolina replied in the affirmative by shaking their heads.

"OK. With job enrichment, you could start to work on preparing the risk assessment and develop audit programs. You are documenting observations now, but sometimes staff don't get to discuss them with the audit client or present them at the exit meeting."

"That's right," said Rachel. "I would like to present my work. We've had problems where someone presented my work and didn't explain it well, and I had to go back and explain the whole thing to the client. We would have avoided all of that if I had presented the findings in the first place."

Rachel did not realize that Tony's facial expression soured when she said that, clearly hitting a nerve. John did.

"Good example, Rachel. So that is an example of job enrichment. So, you, Brian and Carolina would learn new skills, and hopefully would be excited about the new things you would be doing."

John was about to say something positive to ease the concerns that Tony and Miriam may have about this, but Tony got ahead of him and asked.

"Would this affect our workload?"

"That is something we need to manage. I don't want this to be just add-on work, but rather some replacement. It would benefit everyone as collectively we learn to do more of the process from beginning to end, and people can also fill-in for others."

"How about our audit clients. Will they be OK with this?" Tony asked again.

"We will need to explain our roles and responsibilities when we send the engagement memo and when we do our kick-off meeting. We also need to follow-through during the audit, who does what needs to be aligned with this too, but in general, we'll build the team so everyone, over time, can do the majority of the entire process," John explained.

"That makes sense."

"You said we would be trained, right?" asked Rachel.

"Yes," replied John immediately.

"OK, because I worry about my performance going down if I need to do new things and I don't get training. We won't be as efficient at first, you know."

"I know. This is an investment in your career and our goal of upgrading our unit," said John acknowledging her comment and empathizing with her concern.

--------------------||--------------------

"Hi Tony and Miriam. You heard me talk about job enrichment and job enlargement at our last staff meeting. I want to talk with you about ways to do this, so we avoid stressing the rest of the team or demotivating them. You heard some of their questions, so they realize there is some risk to this. I realize there is some risk to this too, but risk-reward, right?"

"They nodded in agreement." Miriam added, "I was going to ask you about that. I'm glad you brought this up."

"Job enlargement means more horizontal tasks, so for example, Rachel has been reliable and strong when it comes to reviewing T&E. We have been giving her this audit for a while, and although we value the expertise she has on this, we should cross-train her so she can audit other areas too."

"We can't afford to. Who is going to audit T&E then?" asked Tony.

"We need to train someone else. Carolina," replied John.

"How much time will it take?"

"That is a good question. It could be quick, if we have a plan in place, make you a coach and provide some useful pointers, and we put Carolina on that project promptly after the training, so she doesn't have time to forget what she learned. On the other hand, if we go at it without a plan, it will likely create more problems than solutions."

"I see," said Tony. "When do you want this implemented?"

"I would like us to get started soon. We are already halfway through the year, and we want to bring some tangible changes to our department. So, we have the second half of the T&E audit coming up. The modified first phase was a success and Rachel did an awesome job. Let's start planning on it so Rachel can start training Carolina and at the same time, we need to make that T&E audit more robust. There are certain things about how we audit T&E that we need to improve."

"Now, in terms of job enrichment. This is where we add more tasks vertically to the role, so Rachel would then have more authority and can work more independently too."

John continued. "This is a lot of change, but Carolina and Rachel are smart and motivated. I believe we can upskill both of them to do this. In addition to Rachel helping Carolina, I also need you Tony to work with Rachel on the risk assessment, creating the work program and writing the report."

"That will take a lot of time!" said Tony in a concerned tone.

"Yes, very likely so, but risk reward, right? I'll work with you on this, so you're not doing this alone. The idea here is that we redesign what and who does the work. We're shaking things up, but I firmly believe we'll be much better off on the other side of this."

"Questions?" John asked.

Neither one of them said anything.

"OK. I understand. This is a lot to ask, but we'll work through this together. Tony, you'll be working with Rachel on this. We'll have weekly status meetings so there is ample communication. We'll have meaningful agendas for these meetings, so they are purposeful. Miriam, we haven't discussed your situation and your work with Brian. I need you to do the same. Same approach, weekly meetings to guide and assess progress with me."

"OK," they both said silently.

John wanted to impress on them the importance of moving forward and that he would support the process. While he wanted them to express any concerns, he wanted them to understand that status quo was not an option.

"Forward we go then! We're building a better internal audit department and we're all in the field. We're too small for anyone to be a spectator. We're all players! Have a great weekend," he said as he ended the meeting.

--------------------||--------------------

John often sent his team motivational messages. Since it was almost the weekend, and they had been talking about changes, he wanted to include a couple of messages. He chose a quote from Louis Pasteur, "Chance favors the prepared mind," with a note saying that as they prepared, good outcomes would follow.

He added another one that encouraged them to embrace bold initiatives. It was the Latin proverb "fortune favors the bold."

--------------------||--------------------

"Happy Tuesday everyone. Hope you had an enjoyable long weekend. BBQ, fireworks, beach anyone? Everyone?" asked John.

"Not me. We don't celebrate July 4th in the UK," said Carolina.

"I understand. Did you have nice weather over the weekend?"

"We did."

"OK. Perfect opportunity for an asado, then. Why not celebrate? What's your excuse?" he asked with a friendly smile.

"You're right. We had an asado two weeks ago at a friend's house but didn't think to have one this past weekend. Very unpatriotic of me!" she said with a smile.

"Yes, very unpatriotic. We'll see if we authorize a visitor's visa to the US next time you want to come," John said jokingly.

"How about you Tony. How was your weekend?"

"We went all in. Fireworks, lots of food and drinks at the beach. It was awesome!"

"Glad to hear that. Brian, Rachel, Miriam?"

All gave similar versions of fun activities with their friends and family members. Miriam complimented John on the quotes he sent the previous week.

"OK Carolina. 9 de julio is coming up so we expect you to celebrate Argentina's Independence Day big time and send us pictures. We won't have fun by ourselves, right folks?" said John rallying the group.

"You still have time to redeem yourself," said Rachel with a colorful red, white, and blue blouse, clearly still in a festive mood.

"Are you up to the challenge?" asked Miriam.

"Yes, I am."

"I voluntold Tony and Miriam to help me launch a new initiative where we are going to make your jobs a bit more interesting and challenging, but we believe, more rewarding and a push in terms of you learning new skills. I mentioned job enlargement and job enrichment some time ago, remember?" asked John pausing for a moment to give context to the plan he was announcing.

"Yes, came the reply from the team." Carolina asked, "can you give us a quick reminder of what the terms mean again?"

"Sure," replied John, appreciating the honesty of someone who didn't know, didn't remember, or was being an advocate for others too shy to ask for themselves. Either way, it made it possible to level-set knowledge.

"Job enlargement is where we broaden the range of duties and responsibilities. It usually happens horizontally within the same level or title."

He continued. "Job enrichment, on the other hand, involves vertical growth of the role. So instead of just knowing and doing one piece of the process, the person does more of the entire process."

"What this means is that we will help you learn new tasks so while you are an expert at certain things presently, you are now going to learn additional things. So, for example, Rachel you have been our resident T&E expert. You have done that audit several years in a row. We made some changes during the first phase of that review earlier in the year and are going to make additional changes to how we audit T&E, but also show you how to audit other areas too. You have been focusing on testing, which makes sense, but we have a small department, so the goal is to show you how to do more of the process from beginning to end, so rather than keep you testing, we're going to bring you in when we do our risk assessment, when we prepare the audit program, and when we write the audit report, which Tony has been doing up to now. Exciting, right?"

The reaction was not as enthusiastic as John was hoping for. He made note of the lukewarm reception and continued. "To help you along the way, Tony and I will be working with you to help you get the skills you need going forward. Same for Carolina. Rachel will help you learn more about the T&E process. We're learning together, so this is a team effort and I voluntold Tony and Miriam to help me with this."

"Sounds good?"

Again, the reaction was not particularly enthusiastic, which John interpreted as meaning they were nervous about the plan.

--------------------||--------------------

After the meeting John messaged Miriam.

"Hi Miriam, thanks for taking the call."

"Sure. No problem. What's up?"

"Did you notice that Rachel, Carolina, and Brian were lukewarm about the new idea? I thought they would be more excited."

"Yes, I noticed that. Are you asking me if I know why?"

"Yes. Do you know why?"

"I believe it's because they feel it is more work and they haven't heard anything about more money. They see this as more work without more pay."

"All of them?"

"Carolina and Rachel. Brian is new and he is generally upbeat. Or maybe he hasn't been tainted by past practices. But the other two, especially Rachel has a few grievances that I'm sure you know about, and one of them is about the size of the department. She has been asking why we don't do more robust work and grow the department. She was very excited about the changes to the T&E audit and was very proud of the success in front of Dan."

"Hmm. OK. I see. So, explaining the benefits career-wise and how the work would be more interesting is not what appeals to her."

"Right. I believe you explained the benefits, but I believe, she in particular, sees the costs as high. Carolina is in the middle, she's willing to try new things and wants to learn all she can. The problem is, and this goes back well before you got here, is that they have been asking for more staff and it hasn't come, so now they see this as a way to get them to do more work without hiring more people or paying them more."

"Yikes. OK. I need to explain this better. How do you feel about it?"

"I like the idea, but I'm also a bit concerned, quite honestly, about growing the jobs and trying to do too much too fast. I know we need to get better. I just want to make sure we do it right."

"I appreciate your honesty. Yes, we'll do it right. It is going to be better on the other side of this, but we need to prove to senior management and the board that we're up to the challenge and can deliver. They were not pleased with the performance of the unit before I arrived, so they want to see sustained results before they agree to put more resources into it."

"I understand."

"Thanks again. Anything else I'm missing? You are high on the emotional intelligence scale, so I value your opinion."

"No. That's all I know."

--------------------||--------------------

"Happy Thursday everyone. We're on the second half of the week and Friday is in sight!"

"Yeah!" said Carolina, showing her characteristic enthusiasm.

"Do you have big plans for the weekend?" asked Brian.

"Yes, F1 party at my place. We're getting several of my friends together and we're watching the race. Some of these people I haven't seen for a while and my cousin will be visiting. She lives in Mendoza and is backpacking through Europe."

"I remember doing that when I was in college and again right after graduation. Such a great experience," said Miriam.

"I second that," said John.

"I went all over on a student train pass. It was incredible. Wish I could do that again. Maybe someday, but with a rollaboard bag, first-class train tickets, and nightly hotel rooms," said Miriam.

"I'm not sure you can call that backpacking," corrected John.

"Miriam, take a backpack purse," offered Carolina. "That's how I do it," she said proudly.

"That and credit cards so I can go to nice restaurants," said Miriam again.

"Exactly. The food, the sights, a nice comfortable and quiet room at night," said Carolina. "She likes to do things her way; she's very independent-minded."

"Is this her first time traveling to Europe?" asked Miriam.

"No, she has traveled with her parents before, but she wanted to do this on her own."

John just smiled at the camaraderie between Miriam and Carolina. Funny how these conversations often provide a segue for the topic I want to introduce. I'm not sure how this happens, but I like it. "Your cousin is doing this, with a bit of discomfort, let's call it that judging by the 4 and 5-star hotel and 2 Michelin star ratings she could be aiming for, but she's let's say, roughing it through Europe so she has a different learning experience. And she gets to travel her way."

"She wants to experience how real people live."

"Travel is fatal to prejudice, bigotry, and narrow-mindedness, and many of our people need it sorely on these accounts," said Miriam.

"Mark Twain. Very good and very true," acknowledged John. "Hope your cousin has a wonderful trip, Carolina."

He continued, "I want to talk to you about our approach to implementing agile auditing. I have some ideas that I'll share with all of you. I'm going to share a presentation with you. Can you see it?"

He saw a combination of heads nodding, thumbs-up, and moving lips, with one or two audible "yesses."

"First of all," John began, "there is a need for a certain mindset to take hold. This means before we can *say* we are agile, we need to *think* we are agile, or at least going to become agile. It means we start to imagine us focusing on the key tenets of agile. Some of you are already familiar with this, others not, so let's review. For example: we need to focus on individuals and interactions rather than processes and tools. We'll talk more about tools later, but the focus is on our people, our clients and how we interact and work with them, and less about the methodology. There *is* a methodology, but that is a means to an end.

Second, we need to focus on communicating results to our clients and less about comprehensive documentation. This doesn't mean we don't document. We *must* document, it is integral to our role and evidence of our work is necessary." However,

John was deliberately emphasizing the word, "we need to make our narratives, e-mails and our reports shorter, clearer and to the point. We, and I mean us here at InSports and in the profession in general, tend to write a lot, much more than necessary in most cases. It is unnecessary and inconsistent with what agile calls for. People don't have time to read novels, as much as you may be proud of your literary prowess, they don't have the time, so we need to shorten our written product. In some cases, we will rely on recorded documentation, like video and audio, but I don't want to get into those details just yet. Remember, I'll talk about tools later.

Third, customer collaboration over contract negotiation. Now, that sounds very formal and you may be thinking 'well, we don't write contracts here, that probably came from the official agile mantra and more appropriate for IT environments' and while that may be somewhat true, we do contract with our clients. When we send an engagement letter; when we ask our clients to confirm they agree with the audit timeline and the rest of it, we are entering into a form of contract. The audit program that we sign-off on within audit before we start the work is also a form of internal contract. So, what I'm saying here is that collaboration is key. We work with our clients to determine what is most important to them, and we focus on that. For many years audit had its own ideas about what are the riskier topics and within that, what procedures we should be performing. This third item means we work collaboratively with them so no auditing in a vacuum.

And the fourth item here is responding to change as opposed to following a plan. This builds and relates to what I said for item number three above. Agile is flexible and it relies on collaboration, and trust, between the auditors and clients. We balance the high-level goals of performing the reviews, checking things off the audit plan for the year and writing audit reports, with a more fluid approach to getting things done. More conversation, more collaboration so we move *together* in terms of what is and should be in the audit plan, then at the project level, we are also more flexible during the audit, so the audit program is going to be reviewed constantly. We will have a process and visibility on what we're doing, so don't think this invites chaos. It doesn't. But we are not fixated on a premade audit program. A lot of auditors struggle with this, so we will pay close attention to this as we proceed.

Let me pause here. Questions? Comments?"

"Yes," said Rachel. "We made some changes to the T&E audit program. Are we going to change all audit programs?"

"Very likely. I've been reading the audit programs for past audits and they focused disproportionately on compliance and most of the procedures were controls-based, not risk-based, so we'll change them. Your T&E audit, phase one, was a success, wasn't it?"

"It was, that's one of the reasons I'm asking!"

"Very good! So the quick answer is yes, we're changing the methodology and that includes audit programs. Now, let's turn our attention to a few additional aspects of agile auditing.

Agile also uses the concept of a backlog. This backlog of audit risks within the project or areas to be audited are the main source of work items to be completed. This list must be prioritized continually. The key thing here is focusing on risk exposure and organizational needs. This is consistent with the Standards, which compels us to align our work with the business objectives of the area or process under review, as well as those of the organization.

Items on the backlog are removed if they no longer contribute to the goal of providing risk-based reasonable assurance and give us a useful conclusion. Items are added to the backlog when an essential task, risk or situation is known.

Before starting to review an item on the backlog, which will now serve as our audit program, explicit, clear, and agreed-upon acceptance criteria must be defined based on client requirements.

Communication is essential for success with agile. Instead of committing to a rigid audit program, now we can promptly add or remove new risks or auditable areas throughout the engagement. I will be applying agile to our audit plan too, so the same principle and practice applies, instead of committing to a rigid annual audit plan, now we can promptly add or remove new risks or auditable areas throughout the year. This requires collaboration with stakeholders during the planning and prioritization process.

When it comes to communication, we need to implement continuous feedback. A common Agile practice is a daily stand-up meeting of normally no more than 15 minutes. The team discusses each member's contributions and any obstacles. So, auditors regularly check in with each other and raise questions or issues as soon as they come up. Generally speaking, the agenda consists of what you did yesterday that helped to achieve the sprint goal, what will you do today and what impediments or constraints are you facing, if any.

Don't wait until the fieldwork is done, or even the report is published, to start supervisory and quality assurance reviews. These should be built into the daily audit activities.

Next, reporting. Short and sweet. If you have been communicating with the team and the client like I just explained, the report should be a summary of agreed-upon actions and the contents would be known by everyone. Early and frequent communication with stakeholders means the final report or presentation should simply reflect a visual summary of the insights already discussed. Often through dashboards and updates, rather than formal audit reports."

"What about the length of the reports?" asked Rachel.

"Yes, about that. Short. You probably want me to give you a page count. I don't want to commit to a number, but three pages should be enough at the end of every sprint. So let me explain sprints.

Sprints are iterations, which are a standard period of time, usually from two to three weeks. The team will deliver short, usable, and tested reports, or you can call them packets. We have a short audit program, or backlog, of a few questions or objectives to check. Priority should be results. We do that, we report on the results. Done! Questions for me?"

"You say short audit program that fits into the two-to-three-week cycle. How many items do you have in mind?" asked Tony.

"Generally, four to six events per sprint. All agreed-upon with the client so we get commitment for the work and the deliverables."

"What are some examples of the types of items on this new type of work program, or backlog?"

"Things like quality, risks of course, client needs. Things that have a direct impact and benefit to the business. We need to keep an eye on timeline and budget because we have to get things done, but they are no longer the most important thing. We manage for results!"

"What are the mechanics like? The general flow?"

"The specific mechanics of this is that items that move off the backlog are divided into sprints. This provides a structure and cadence for the work. So, fieldwork would consist of fixed-length activities that are appropriately sized to promote tight deadlines without stressing available resources. It eliminates unnecessary work and efforts within a sprint. You should like that, right Brian?" John said to engage the group and bring the team back into attention since they started to look a bit tired.

"What about GANTT charts? Do we still prepare those?" asked Tony.

"No. We avoid GANTT charts and other types of elaborate planning tools. We need to have an idea of what we are going to do, but don't over invest in instruments like those."

"How do we keep track then?"

"We focus on status updates – daily and weekly! We need to allow, but manage, variances, so it is not chaotic, it is just simplified. Whenever possible, you should gather evidence independently. I know we've had some issues with that, so we need to fix it. We won't get there on day one, but the goal is to make sure you know where data lives and how to extract it, so we don't have to rely so much on the client. We will work with them, but we also want to show some independence and initiative too."

"So, slow, methodical, lots and lots of documents, War and Peace type narratives?" asked Brian lightheartedly noticing the tension in the air.

"No, short and sweet! Now, this is important for everyone, especially the managers because you do QA on the workpapers; you need to remember that during these sprints you check and tweak your work every week because in two to three weeks the sprint is over. Since some projects will have multiple sprints, you don't wait until the end of the project either. QA happens in shorter intervals. Planning, fieldwork, and review are quick, so we streamline the work and documentation, so everyone focuses on insights, risks, and opportunities that stakeholders need. The whole thing is more adaptive.

Agile streamlines the process, so we reduce the requests for evidence that are too vague and get a better approach than sending emails back and forth when a phone call or in-person meeting would be more productive. We also reduce the practice of exhaustively explaining every audit step and procedure when concise documentation could be enough.

By now you should get a sense that the team is more empowered to work. This is also key to agile. I will let you do the job. We have to eliminate bureaucracy and focus on results. You are smart and with the training, you will be skilled and ready to do amazing things."

When John said this, there were smiles on everyone's faces. Tony not as much because his influence seemed to be waning, but the rest of the team felt an emotional boost; their boss believed in them and was willing to invest in them.

He continued. "There is this thing called retrospectives. After every sprint, review the process and outcomes before the next sprint planning meeting. Discuss processes, tools, people, and relationships. Review with key stakeholders to discuss results and get feedback. Also discuss internal audit perspectives and observations and review future sprint tasks."

"Is there a model or something like that for these retrospectives?" asked Carolina.

"Yes, there is, A simple way to think about it is, what should we keep doing, what should we start doing, what should we stop doing, what should we do less of, and what should we do more of. Those five elements make for a predictable model to follow during those sessions," John explained.

"And a simple and easy to remember one too!" added Rachel, who seemed more energized than ever.

"Exactly! We could also say intuitive, I guess. To summarize, the cycle is first, a sprint planning meeting followed by a succession of daily scrum or stand-up meetings. We say stand-up but Zoom or Teams would do the same. The name is a carry-forward from when work was done almost exclusively in the office. The key is short, as in 15 minutes or so. Then, the third item is at the end of the sprint we have the sprint review meeting and after the various sprints, we have a retrospective where we do the closing and feedback. How does this sound?"

"Very good. It is very different from what we're accustomed to, but I believe we can do it. It has been common in IT for a while," said Miriam with an even tone showing her realistic approach to things.

"Agree," said Rachel, again siding with Miriam as a tag team.

"I have a question."

"Yes, go ahead."

"I've heard people talk about Kanban. I know it has something to do with inventory management, but I've heard it mentioned in the context of agile too. How does it fit into all of this?"

"Yes, good question Carolina. Let me give you a little background. Kanban is a Japanese word that refers to a scheduling system for lean manufacturing. You may have heard of just-in-time manufacturing, or JIT. It was invented by an engineer at Toyota by the name of Taiichi Ohno, to improve manufacturing efficiency. The system uses cards that track production within a factory. Now, when it comes to agile, we use a similar flow. The cards can be post-it notes or in a software platform, they can be tiles or something like that. The board is divided into sections, generally starting with 'to do', which coincides with our 'backlog' as I explained earlier. The next phase is 'in progress', then 'testing' and lastly 'done'. The cards move from phase-to-phase as the work gets done. It provides visual management of the tasks."

"How do you keep track of who does what?"

"You can have each person assigned to a particular color. So, let's say you are red, Rachel is blue, Brian is yellow, and Tony is green. You can simply glance at the Kanban board, and you can tell if there is a large cluster of items on one phase or another, and whose tiles are getting backlogged or spread out, meaning, they are moving items along and towards 'done.'"

"Sounds complicated," said Tony.

"Maybe, but not necessarily. Then again, things that are new may appear so until you start doing it. In general, Kanban tells you what needs to be done, what activities are in progress and what activities have been completed. Imagine relying on your stand-up daily and weekly meetings, then just looking at the Kanban board without having to ask people how their work is coming along to know the status immediately!"

"That would help!" said Miriam.

"I think it would help. How much time do we now spend preparing status update memos. Between asking for and gathering the information, which might mean chasing people around for the information, then summarizing it, writing it down and finally sending it out. Anyone can look at the board and know what's going on. You can also split the board horizontally so items that are stuck can go below the line so the entire team can see that immediately and keep an eye on stuck items, so they are not forgotten and try to unfreeze them. Neat, eh?"

"I kind of like this idea! When do we implement this?" said Rachel.

"We're implementing some aspects of agile as we go, but should have all of it up and running by yearend. Rachel and Brian did some EHS work earlier in the year, and that was done in a few weeks. Rachel did some of that on the T&E audit too when we revised the audit program, split it into phases, and had what were two sprints during phase one. We'll introduce agile officially soon, but before we do, we need to do a gap analysis and provide some training. We'll have some training in two weeks and I'm bringing in an instructor for that. You will get more details soon."

With that John ended the meeting and thought to himself how excited Rachel seemed in learning and moving forward.

--------------------||--------------------

The team met in the New York City office, with Carolina joining remotely.

"Welcome everyone. Thank you for being on time for our training on Agile Auditing. We have brought in an instructor to help us with this. You have seen her profile and you can see that she is eminently qualified in terms of the concepts but more importantly, the practice of agile auditing. She worked in oil and gas for several years at several top companies in the world and she implemented agile there. She has also done consulting work and she is now here with us.

A few ground rules before we begin. Pay attention and take notes. Ask questions. Participate in the exercises. Think about how we will implement this in our organization; every organization is different, and we need to tailor our approach. I asked you to clear your calendars of any meetings, so now I need you to focus on the class and not get distracted with e-mails, messages, and other things. Maximize the time you have here with the instructor and remember that I will be asking for your feedback and lessons learned at our next staff meeting. Participate, discuss, maybe even debate, but do so professionally and respectfully. It will help the learning process and make it more productive and enjoyable.

I will be checking in periodically. If you need me, you can text me, but I will be back before lunch and before you're done at the end of the day. There is also a quiz that I asked our instructor to impart at the beginning and at the end of class, so answer to the best of your ability and I hope that your scores improve at the end of the day.

That's it. Learning can be fun, so have some fun."

And with that, John left the meeting and Lynn took over the class. She started by providing a brief history of agile as a system development methodology and how it differs from the waterfall and cyclical development methodologies. She then explained the Manifesto for Agile Software Development and went into detail about the 12 principles. "I worked with John adjusting the language on these principles to reflect the audit environment in which these will be applied and also to reflect the language commonly used at InSports. So, let's take a look and discuss each of these.

The first principle is 'the highest priority is to satisfy the customer through early and continuous delivery.' As you can see, we begin with what already looks like a departure from traditional internal auditing practice, she explained. Rather than waiting until the end to issue a draft and then a final report, agile auditing calls for continuous delivery. We'll define continuous a little later, and also what the delivery item or product looks like, but notice those two words, 'continuous' and 'delivery'. No longer relying on one big deliverable after months of work. By the way, what is the average time from kick-off until the report is issued?" she asked the group.

After a few seconds, when everyone was looking at each other hoping that someone else would answer for the team, Tony took the bait and replied with a question – arguably buying time.

"Which report? The draft or the final report?"

Picking up immediately on how they were using a technicality to avoid answering the question directly, Lynn returned a perfect volley of her own. "Let's talk about both. How long from audit kickoff to the issuance of the draft report, then how much time from the draft report to the publication of the final report?"

Miriam immediately realized the delay tactic might actually expose yet another flaw in their current practice, so her immediate reaction was to smile sheepishly and close her eyes momentarily. Tony, attempting to defend the team and its processes, adjusted nervously in his seat, then said, "well, it depends. Some audits take longer than others. There is a range, you see…"

"Ok, Mr. smarty pants," said Lynn, simultaneously frustrated by the antics yet amused by his attempt to be clever with her and her questions.

"How about an average, then a minimum and a maximum. We just need to get a sense of what that metric looks like. I'm not grading you on the accuracy of the answer, so roughly, what are we looking at for cycle time?"

Tony looked to his right at Miriam and answered with a tone that sounded more like a question: "what was it the last time we looked at that, average six or seven months, minimum around five and maximum, help me out here, how much was it again?" he asked hoping for what amounted to a life jacket.

"It depends," said Miriam attempting to help but providing a non-answer answer. Without providing a definitive number, she was already suggesting that the number was large. "We have published final reports a week after the draft and sometimes it takes several weeks, or maybe months, for the final report to go out."

Lynn decided to turn this into a teachable moment and not relent; it looks like the team likes to dance around bad news, so they should learn the importance of transparency going forward if they wanted to implement agile successfully, she thought. "I hear you," she said when they were done with the verbal squirming. "Minimum five or so, and maximum? Roughly?" she insisted.

"About a year and a half." "We have two reports, one we finished last March and the other around May, so that would make those well over twelve months old. The truth is we are trying to figure out how to publish the final now that so much time has gone by," he confessed.

Lynn had been looking directly at him while he explained the situation and when he was finished, she said, "Thanks Tony, I realize it was not easy saying that and I put you in a somewhat awkward position, but I wanted you to get to the datapoints as best you could now for a reason." Then she turned to the rest of the class, "we need to own our collective results. In a way it is this team or that team, this audit or that audit, this audit client or that audit client, but in the end, they are internal audit's metrics. Our metrics. Our timelines. Our cycle time. They may not be where we want to be in the future, and that is why we're all here today. The past, or even the present, doesn't have to shape our future. In fact, we're here to learn how to shape a better future." Then turning back to Tony, she said kindly and reassuringly, "agile auditing should help avoid having to have this awkward conversation in the future because, and she read aloud as she pointed at the words displayed on the large screen in front of the class 'early and continuous delivery'."

She then turned to the rest of the class as she walked toward the middle of the room while pointing at Tony and said "he should get a reward for his bravery. You get to go to lunch early today," making everyone in the room laugh good naturedly.

"Good. We covered Principle One, Phew! right?" Lynn said with a smile eliciting returned smiles from the class. "Number 2, 'Welcome changing requirements, even late in the process because the goal is to leverage change to improve the customer's competitive advantage'. Remember the definition of internal auditing. 'Internal auditing is an independent, objective assurance and advisory activity designed to add value and improve an organization's operations. It helps an organization accomplish its objectives' and it then goes on about the methodology, which is systematic and disciplined and in what areas, governance, risk management, and control processes. OK. We see here a parallel in terms of improving the customer's competitive advantage. I would say that is one of an organization's main objectives. The definition of internal auditing says we 'help an organization accomplish its objectives'.

Let's also relate this to another Standard. We must consider the strategies and objectives of the activity being reviewed, and the extent to which management has established adequate criteria to determine whether that activity has accomplished its objectives and goals. Basically, how they monitor and control its performance. So, we see once again, how agile auditing is aligned with the IIA Standards and how it supports our pursuit of best practices."

"What if the area we are auditing doesn't have objectives, or they haven't documented them yet?" asked Brian.

"That is a very good question and something that I have encountered in different ways at different organizations. If they haven't documented those objectives, that is a good observation to bring to management's attention so they can work on that. If they have them, but haven't communicated them; again, a good observation to bring to their attention. If they communicated them but are not monitoring performance and assessing the extent to which they are making progress towards their achievement, or hitting those objectives, then that can be an observation too. Note I didn't say 'finding'. We can talk about the label for these things separately, but let's call them observations for now. Oh, another thing, if the criteria for evaluation is inadequate, we must identify appropriate evaluation criteria through discussions with management."

"This sounds like you're applying a progression to this, kind of like the CMMI, not the part about observations or findings, but the part about if they have documented objectives, if they have been communicated, if they manage to them," remarked Rachel.

"Yes, that is true," replied Lynn. "I like to think about the progression of events and the quality of items, not just their presence. You can have a document or a procedure, but it could be of really low quality. The world of audit is not always binary and the Capability Maturity Model helps to show that."

"Is that something we should be talking to management about?" asked Rachel while looking at Tony, indicating there was some history to this question.

"I think so. Yes. It is important and, in my experience, management appreciates the conversation about the nuances because that's the world they live and work in. Things are not always black or white, but shades of gray and to the extent that we can show our ability to see that range of possibilities, process the underlying elements that define the context, and make a well-informed conclusion, they will respect the depth of your thought."

As Lynn spoke, Rachel was taking notes intently and when she was done, she looked at Miriam and winked at her with a smile.

Lynn noticed the exchange and reacted with a smile as an acknowledgment, "I believe there is a whole story behind this conversation with management. Maybe you can bring me up to speed later, but for now, let's take a look at Principle Three," turning her attention once again to the large projection of her presentation materials.

"The third principle is 'Deliver product frequently with a short timescale, ideally within two to three weeks.' So here is the general definition of continuous that we first touched upon in Principle One. We no longer rely on a final report after months of planning, fieldwork, and reporting. We provide results and conclusions right away."

No sooner was she done speaking than Tony interjected, "I am interpreting product to mean things like an audit report, so here is my question: How can we... No, does anyone really issue a report in two to three weeks? I think that's impossible!"

"When I was at another company we issued reports at the end of fieldwork," said Rachel defending the practice. "We did branch audits, and we had a report ready for review at the exit meeting. We started on a Monday and shortly after lunch on Friday we handed the branch manager a report. The District Manager got a copy too!"

"Those were cookie-cutter audits. Very narrow focus and specific...." replied Tony defending his question with skepticism, but was interrupted by Carolina.

"We did operational reviews, and we often issued a draft report at the end of fieldwork. Those were two and three weeks of fieldwork and the draft was prepared as we went along. It was hell for the senior, well, not really hell, I'm exaggerating, lots of work, but you got used to it. We got organized, kept good notes, moved things from fieldwork results to observation documentation as soon as we presented them to the client during fieldwork. You get used to it and develop a technique," explained Carolina.

"Maybe so," replied Tony still skeptical. "Maybe where you were, but I don't think we can do that here."

At this point Lynn joined the conversation to settle the argument. "I agree it can be difficult, and to Rachel and Carolina's point, it takes training, organization, and practice, but it can be done. I've done that too and those are the three key elements to get there. Once again, Agile Auditing calls for it and yes, Tony, companies are publishing reports every two to three weeks. But let's talk for a moment about the word 'report'. We need to communicate the results of our engagements and that communication can be in written form, as in a report, memos, slides, or meeting notes of presentations. This means we can find other ways of communicating that are shorter, to the point, and require less writing. We should still meet the criteria for high-quality communications. Remember? Those seven attributes? I believe that was, let's see AOCCCCT: accurate, objective, clear, concise, constructive, complete, and timely."

"The writing of audit communications is my nemesis," said Tony.

"Why is that?" Lynn asked.

"I don't know if you knew, but I'm primarily responsible for quality assurance, so they call me '13'."

"Affectionately," said Miriam.

"Not sure I follow," confessed Lynn, clearly confused.

"Yes affectionately," said Tony responding to both of them at once, "the joke started a while back with the IIA's 1300 Standard being the one related to the quality assurance and improvement program, so, drop the zeros and I'm the bad-luck guy, number 13 who has to enforce among other things the clarity of communications. I spend a lot of time with almost everyone here to make sure our communications meet high standards."

"So, you will love Agile," replied Lynn now understanding the situation better, "because chances are that as you adopt Agile, communications will be shorter. For a lot of companies, it is like a memo or even a PowerPoint presentation or something like that. Simple, clear, to the point. Tell them what they need to know and let's move onto the next value-added activity. Spending weeks writing lengthy and complex audit reports is not viewed as really adding a lot of value for a lot of people."

"Second that!" said Rachel.

"You just don't want to do any work Rachel," said Tony.

"Work smarter, not harder," replied Brian with a tone that implied "I'm pursuing that universal goal you must have heard of," rocking his head and raising his eyebrows to match his tone while diffusing what looked like a tense situation.

"OK, OK!" Lynn intervened good naturedly. "Yes, we are ALL going to work smarter when we implement Agile. And to your point, Brian, you are going to LOVE Principle 10!"

"Principle Number 4, who wants to read it for us?"

Carolina and Brian raised their hands and Lynn chose Carolina. "Please. Go ahead."

"Businesspeople and auditors must work together daily throughout the project."

"Thanks Carolina. How about that! We now have a good argument to tell management we don't want to be assigned to the little closet in the basement next to the boiler room when we audit. We should probably sit close to the businesspeople upstairs somewhere, what do you think about that Brian?"

"I like it. Maybe I can ditch the earplugs when I work now! He said returning a humorous statement of his own.

"Exactly. Some of this may be done via Zoom or Teams, but the point is made, work together. No more working in a vacuum or isolation. Gone are the days when auditors would request tons of reports, documents, and SOPs, then sequester themselves in a conference room during the entire audit, and only leave the room for water and food. We have been talking about collaboration in audit for a long time, so here we see this being highlighted again."

Lynn continued, "Number 5. 'Build projects around motivated individuals. Give them the support and the environment they need and trust them to get the job done.' Agile is great for everyone's career advancement because it broadens your skillset tremendously. But note it mentions 'motivated individuals.' There is a difference between will and skill. You can have the skill, but you must be willing to use it. Motivation is highly important here because you are working semi-autonomously. The team sets its working details, checks on each other's work, and moves along towards getting the work done very two to three weeks. You have to be motivated to succeed. Everyone helps everyone else, so you're never alone, but motivated we must be," she explained as she took a sip of water and called a 15-minute break.

When they returned, Lynn got things moving again. "The 6th principle please," as she gestured with her open hand at Miriam.

"The most efficient and effective method of conveying information to and within the audit team is face-to-face conversation."

"Has anyone heard of 'auditing by e-mail'?" Lynn asked the group.

"I have," said Rachel.

"Can you give us a brief summary of what it is, please?" Lynn inquired.

"Yes, it is when an auditor relies almost exclusively on e-mail to request information, provide updates, ask for information and in general, most communication and interactions are done using e-mail."

"Thanks, Rachel. So, what is wrong with that?" asked Lynn engaging with the group, but before they had a chance to answer she asked another question: "don't we need to document everything we do? Isn't e-mail a form of evidence so now you have it, what it is, in writing?" she concluded.

"We can call or meet with the client, then send an e-mail as confirmation of our understanding. That way we connect personally with them, and also get their agreement in writing," said Brian recalling the argument last winter involving Kate and Barry in IT.

"Very good, exactly," said Lynn agreeing with the answer provided.

"But what if they don't respond to the e-mail? They can say 'I never saw the e-mail; I didn't agree to this? Or I didn't say that'?" asked Tony.

Lynn reacted by biting her lips, squinting her eyes for a moment, then she smiled as if she had mentally processed the statement, envisioned a scenario, saw it play out in her mind and a solution had been produced in her mind all within four seconds, then she said, "I wonder if you are describing a situation where there is a lack of trust between the audit team and the people you are auditing."

Rachel started coughing because she choked on the water she was drinking at the moment. Tony's eyes bulged out as if they were about to fall out of their sockets, and

Carolina laughed instinctively, like people do sometimes when a secret has been revealed. Miriam then asked Lynn, "are you sure you don't work here? You hit the nail in the head!"

Rachel nodded as she gave a thumbs-up because she still couldn't talk; her face was red from nearly drowning a moment ago.

"Thanks for confirming my suspicions, everyone. Rachel, do you need a moment. I'd hate to lose anyone while the class was in session, John left you in my care," she said with a friendly smile that showed her keen ability to connect with her audience.

"Trust is an integral part of agile. Because there is less documentation, and so much of what happens is done verbally, there must be trust. Now, trust doesn't happen overnight. It takes time. You need to show them, not just tell them, that you value the relationship, that you have their best interest at heart, that you are there to help them achieve their objectives. You need to be honest. You have to honor your commitments. Say what you mean and mean what you say. Above all, focus on being helpful."

"Let's do this," Lynn said. "We're at the midpoint with our Principles and I was planning on having us do an exercise anyway, and our conversation further supports that idea. So, this is a good time. Let's break up into working groups and work on this for a while. Miriam and Brian, and Tony, Rachel and Carolina. What can we do? I just gave you several ideas. What can we do to help build trust, and trusting relationships with our clients? Write five detailed ideas and when we come back together, we'll debrief and compare notes. 20 minutes everyone!"

After the debrief session, Lynn continued her presentation.

"Principle number 7, 'Accurate results, insightful conclusions, and actionable recommendations are the primary measures of progress'."

"Let's dissect this a bit," said Lynn, elaborating on the quote she just read. "'Accurate results.' As auditors there is nothing surprising about that statement. Recall we just spoke about the attributes of effective communications, and the first one listed is 'accurate'. So, check," she said drawing a check mark in the air. "Now to the next. Insightful conclusions. Again, we must use appropriate techniques and tools to base our conclusions and results. That would make them insightful. So, check, again," Lynn said drawing another check mark in the air. "Actionable recommendations."

"The 8th principle 'Agile processes promote sustainable development. The sponsors, auditors and users should be able to maintain a constant pace indefinitely.'

"'Number 9: Continuous attention to excellence and good audit work enhances agility.'

"The 10th principle: 'Simplicity is essential. This means honing our skills in the art of maximizing the amount of work not done.' Sounds like you Brian?"

"It does. My favorite!"

"Glad you like it. In terms of gathering and documenting information, we must document relevant, reliable, and sufficient information. It doesn't mean exhaustive. It doesn't say voluminous. It doesn't say vast or ample or lots of it. Sufficient. While that can be seen as relative, and it is, we aim for enough. We do what we need to do and nothing more."

"But that is subjective!" said Tony.

"Yes, I agree." "A determination of when you have enough is not always easy to do, but that is our goal. I know, still not a precise answer and as auditors we love precision, but this is where audit earns the label that it is both a science and an art." Looking at the rest of the team so as not to insinuate the following statement was meant for Tony, she said, "You will learn that through practice and with the guidance of your managers. But that is the goal," taking a pause to let the words sink in.

"By the way," she started talking again, "this means we don't write very lengthy narratives and reports because we find it necessary to squelch management's objections or attempt to object to what we are communicating. Sometimes we write a lot as a defense mechanism just in case management thinks to question us, we are going to pre-empt that; stop them on their tracks," while holding her palms open and facing the class as a stop sign. "Quite often this is a reflection of our insecurities and, or our collective lack of trust. As we trust and get to know each other, we have less of a need to do these things. Remember Principle Four; the more we work together the more we get to know each other, trust each other, and document what we need to document."

"I worry someone is going to put a hand-written note in the workpapers and say 'I'm done'," objected Tony.

"Hmm. There is nothing inherently wrong with handwritten notes. In fact, I've drawn flowcharts by hand, neatly, and put them in the workpapers instead of spending the time drawing one using Visio, or something like that. Not that Visio is bad or anything like that. Just that the size, complexity, and time constraints I was dealing with suggested I needed to 'just do it quickly, neatly, and keep moving'. Notes are a little different because there is likely to be more words around and penmanship becomes a bigger issue. We don't document just because the Standards say we must, or a manager is going to be upset otherwise," she said smiling at Tony, acknowledging his role as the most senior manager and quality assurance reviewer. "We document because others need to be able to verify and maybe replicate our work. They need to know what we did, why we did it, who was involved and so on. If they can't read the notes, then what's the point? Plus is has to do with professionalism. You want your work to look good, right? Anyway, you can type it all. Just don't write War and Peace, someone did that already!"

"John used that same book as example of what not to do," said Rachel.

"Right. Don't write The Lord of the Rings or one of the Harry Potter books either. OK?"

"I have a question," interjected Brian putting an end to the joviality of the moment. "This may sound radical but hear me out. We do risk assessments, we develop audit programs, we write narratives, we write audit findings, and we write audit reports. Each is a different and separate type of document. If we are going to write so much less. Make it short and simple and to the point. Use bullets and so on. Could we consolidate all of these types of documents into one and document everything in an Excel spreadsheet?"

"What? Impossible!" said Tony. "No way we can put all of that in one document!"

"Not so fast," said Rachel. "Let's hear Brian out. Go on."

"Yes, the risk assessment we already do in Excel. The audit program we do in Excel. The narratives could be Excel if short and like bullets, or maybe stay in Word, but we make sure the risks, controls and weaknesses are referenced to the risk assessments. The findings we do in Word but there is no reason we couldn't fill out the CCCER elements and the risk rating in Excel. And the report, I haven't spoken about the report, but that could be PowerPoint. Visual. Simple. Bullets. Two maybe three documents. That's it," he explained.

"I like how you're thinking," Lynn intervened with some positive feedback. "I can't change your process and requirements, but this could be your way forward."

"Let's do this. Brian, since this is your idea, why don't you make it a formal proposal for John. I can review it before you send it to him, but I like this. It would save us a ton of administrative time," offered Miriam.

"I'll work on it and have something ready for you in a few days."

"We're getting close to the end of the principles," the group heard Lynn say. "Only two left. Principle number 11 states, 'The best design, requirements and results emerge from self-organizing teams.' You probably know that organizations can have a tall, or pyramid-like structure that is often characterized by a hierarchy of multiple layers with a top-down management style where instructions come from the top and in many cases, decisions go through multiple layers for review and approval."

She continued, "organizations can also have a flat structure with fewer layers and decision-making often happens closer to where the real action is. There is also a matrix style for organizational structure, but tall and flat structures are the most common. Well then, self-organizing teams have some of these flat organizational characteristics and they are generally quicker to act. But as you read this principle you notice that it refers to design and requirements, so this means that the best teams set their own rules and goals, right? This is very important. People, and teams that set their own goals, requirement, and definition of what 'good' means, fare better because they are personally invested in them. This is better than people or teams that are 'told' what to do and how."

"But if they don't have the skills they could fail too!"

"Yes. That's true," said Lynn turning to Rachel who made the remark. "They can have a spectacular failure and that's one of the reasons why no one should implement agile, or other major initiatives without providing those involved with training and even coaching."

She continued: "here is the last principle, number 12. Principle 12 states that 'At regular intervals, the team reflects on how to become more effective, then adjusts its behavior accordingly.' This is a nice complement to the previous one because we see that the team designed its goals, requirements, and results, so now it is going to reflect on how it performed. Accountability and ownership of the work is a big part of agile and resides with the team."

"Tony, didn't we use to do post-mortems a few years ago?" asked Rachel.

"Yes, we used to y e a r s ago" replied Miriam instead, dragging out the word "years" to indicate it was a long time ago.

"Why did we stop?" asked Rachel once again.

This time Tony answered. "I don't remember, but it was a good practice, and it would be good to bring it back," he responded reassuringly.

"We used to do post-audit debrief sessions at my old company and those were very, very helpful. We talked about what worked, what didn't work as well and what we should do differently going forward. Very focused agenda and everyone came prepared after a while. It became something we just expected to do," added Carolina.

"Sounds good, everyone. We are at time," said Lynn starting the process of ending the class. The group spent a few more minutes chatting with each other since face-to-face opportunities had become fairly rare since the pandemic.

--------------------||--------------------

"Hi Rachel, how are you today?"

"I'm OK."

"I'm meeting with everyone individually to see how the training on agile auditing went. I have the evaluations, but I also wanted to check in personally with each of you. And while we're at it, check in on how people are really doing. So, how are you doing today?" John insisted.

"I'm OK. I guess. I like the idea of agile auditing. I'm just a bit concerned that it is a lot of work and we're not talking about growing the department. Don't take this the wrong way, but more work and the same staff level and the same salary."

"I understand your concern and it is reasonable. I've been thinking about that too and the challenge we're dealing with is two-fold. One, the legacy of a relatively underperforming department. Not anyone's fault, but it is a history we have to own. Two, I've spoken with the audit committee about more resources, but because of item One, they want to wait before they agree to increase resources. They believe we are performing fewer audits and issuing fewer reports per year than we could or should. There is some truth to that, so we have to prove ourselves. I believe we can. I know we can. And Agile Auditing is one way we'll get that done. When that happens, we'll have evidence to show that we have the ability and willingness to up our game and ask for more resources."

"When would that be?"

"We're aiming for year-end. If we can show an increase in quality and quantity of work, I believe we have a very good chance of getting additional resources. We have an opportunity to really impress them, and I would like you to be part of that success story."

"OK. If you put it that way."

"You are bright and motivated. That's what I refer to as having the will and the skill for success. If you help the team out with this transformation, I believe we can learn a lot and find ways to reward the team for the results."

"Sounds good. Thanks."

"You're welcome. So how was the class?"

"It was great. I enjoyed it and learned a lot. Lynn was very attentive, knowledgeable, and engaging. She made Agile sound much better than so many of the dry presentations and articles I've read about before. I want to get involved."

"Excellent. I'm very happy to hear that."

"OK. Anything else you want to talk about while we're here?"

"No. Nothing at this time. I'm fine."

"Good. OK then. Have a good day, and if you ever have any questions, just let me know, OK?"

"Sounds good."

And with that they left the meeting, unbeknownst to each other, they sighed in relief simultaneously for the same reason, even though they were hundreds of miles away.

--------------------||--------------------

10 Providing Advisory Services

"… he said he was lucky he was wearing a helmet or who knows if he would have made it."

"I'm not sure what to make of the conversation I just walked into," said John.

"Oh, Brian was just telling us about his friend who was skiing in Chile. He went off the trail and ended up hugging a tree," explained Carolina.

"Is your friend, OK?" asked John. "Anything broken?"

"No. He said it happened so fast he can't remember all the details, but the helmet was scratched up, so his head hit some branches. He's bruised up a bit, but he skied down the mountain by himself."

"Did he go back up after that?"

"Yes, we have a rule. You have to get back on the horse right away," so he did. "He did it once. Then he spent the rest of the weekend by the fireplace."

"Get back on the horse right away. Good rule. I'm glad he was not hurt badly." The team had been talking about their weekend activities; who went surfing, who read what book, who did home repairs, and who worked on their hobbies and special interests. The group was quite surprised to find out that Tony spent Saturday afternoons at an Elder Care Center, helping residents with errands, reading, talking, or simply sitting with them.

"How is your cousin's trip coming along?" asked Miriam.

"She's enjoying it very much. She was with me in London for a while, and she then went to Paris, Bruges, Amsterdam, Berlin, Munich, Prague, Budapest, Bucharest, Venice, Rome and she's now back in Argentina."

"Awesome itinerary. Did she like it?"

Before Carolina could answer, Tony chimed in with a two-part comment that struck everyone as odd: "she was all over Europe. With so many nice places to visit, why go to Romania?"

"A good traveler has no fixed plans and is not intent on arriving," said Miriam.

"Lao Tzu," said John.

"She went where her spirit told her. She was wandering about," explained Carolina.

"Did she like it?" asked Rachel.

"Like it? Nooo," Carolina replied with a big smile on her face. "She loved it! She said as she tilted her head backwards for emphasis. She can't stop talking about the trip. What's interesting is that on top of all she did and saw, she surprised me with the maturity of some of her comments."

"Like what?"

"She told me that she always made it a point to see where students and artists lived, but also where working class people lived. She searched out those places to do

 DOI: 10.1201/9781003322870-12

what she refers to as her own social studies research. She kept a diary and is talking about writing a book."

"Nice. Good for her."

"Let's talk about the consulting project you are going to start soon," John directed the group so they would change the topic of conversation and get the weekly meeting started.

"Sure. The manager of the unit tells us that they could use some help because although he started just three weeks ago, he has seen and heard from his staff that their processes need to improve. He shared his financial and operational reports, and they show poor performance in several ways. It looks like there are many things to look at, and although I have some ideas, we feel a little stuck quite honestly."

"Have you heard of the 8 Forms of Waste? It is also often related to Lean."

"No."

"It's a relatively simple, yet very useful way of thinking about the common forms of waste within a program, process, or unit. They are Transportation, Over Production, Over Processing, Inventory, Defects, Waiting, Motion and Underutilized Skills," he said balancing enthusiasm with his professorial demeanor, taking advantage of the opportunity to turn this into a teachable moment. A quick look at their faces and he knew they were at attention, so he continued.

"Transportation relates to movement that doesn't directly support immediate production needs. When I say production, it doesn't have to be manufacturing. It can also apply to service environments where there is some type of production-type activity like invoicing or processing payments. Transportation becomes an issue when there is an improper facility layout, workplace organization, or poor production planning. Another way this manifests itself is through poor scheduling. Transportation waste is about unnecessary additional transport, usually of materials." "Makes sense?" he asked as he looked at each in turn asking for their feedback and they nodded their heads in agreement.

"OK. The second area of waste is Over Production. The concept seems quite simple, and it is, but there are three ways that this usually happens. One, producing more than is needed. Two, producing faster than needed, or three, producing before it is needed."

"Doesn't forecasting take care of that?" asked Rachel.

"Yes, it usually does, but you would be surprised at how many times forecasts get it wrong. Even then, forecasting usually help with number one, producing more than is needed and three, producing before it is needed. But condition two is producing faster than needed. This can happen due to automation in the wrong places that end up creating bottlenecks along the way, lack of communication between production units, and one that I remember encountering at one of my previous jobs where they had a just in case reward system that resulted in overproduction waste. The production group was rewarded for keeping unit costs as low as possible, so they produced in very large batches, which brought the unit costs beautifully low, but created stockpiles in the warehouse."

"Would a review of inventory balances tell us if that is happening?"

"Yes, it should," John responded while nodding. They were not merely listening but active participants in the conversation. These were the moments he enjoyed the most.

"Unless they are not paying enough attention to it. Sometimes people treat the growing inventory only as an asset and not the eventual liability it could become if it doesn't move. Another possibility is the forecasts continue to paint a positive outlook for growth that forecasters sell successfully to management, but the day when things turn for the better keeps getting pushed into the future," he explained.

"Who creates these forecasts, anyway?" asked Rachel. "We audited inventory so many times over the years, but it was always about the valuation. At one point we merely asked if forecasts were produced, but never really looked at them closely."

"We have a production planning unit out of New York that usually prepares forecasts, or review them. I only know this because last October during the 5K charity run I was talking to a guy who worked there," shared Brian. "Jack from Des Moines, I remember him well."

"Good," thought John. Now they were not only learning from him, but they were also learning from and sharing with each other. The lack of teamwork and information sharing had been brought up as an issue during a review of the exit interview notes from one of the now-departed internal auditors. The ex-employee grew frustrated by what was then described as some people hoarding important information that made it harder to get the work done and was sometimes used as a way to get ahead at their teammates' expense.

"You already brought up inventory. Interestingly, that is another area of waste. Well, excess inventory. It has to do with any supply above and beyond what the process needs to produce just in time. Inaccurate forecasting like we said earlier feeds into this. Inefficient processes or even suppliers can cause this too. Another reason is long changeover times and unbalanced production processes."

"The next area of waste is over processing," he continued. "It refers to redundant production efforts or communication that doesn't add value to one of our products or services. For example, getting into an endless cycle of refinement, too much information, process bottlenecks. Even unclear customer specifications from say Design, Manufacturing or Shipping. We are auditors so we should be careful that we don't contribute to this by encouraging management into redundant reviews and approvals," John said as he raised his eyebrows and tilted his head letting them know that if not careful, auditors could contribute to operational issues.

"We would never do that," said Carolina sarcastically, as she looked over at Rachel. She returned the gesture with a smile as she lowered her gaze sheepishly playing along. "Oh, of course not. We recommend more approvals? If one approval is good, more must be better," she said playing along.

"And if the manager is a good reviewer, the VP would be a better one," replied Carolina, saying it with such ease, confidence, speed, and humor that John figured this was an old joke among them.

"This sounds like you lived through this scenario in audit?" John finally chimed in, becoming part of their comic duo.

"Yes, we've had conversations about this in audit," she replied drawing air quotes when he said "in audit" to emphasize the internal philosophical divide they had been living through before John's arrival.

"I see. Well, all of us know better now and my plan is to free us from antiquated practices."

"You already have, John. You already have," said Rachel as she took a deep breath and sat up in her chair showing relief at the improvements already underway in the department. "It is refreshing."

John let this last comment sink in for a moment, then continued.

"OK. Thank you. Yes, where were we? Yes, over-processing," said John answering his own question. "You just highlighted one of the common reasons for overprocessing and it has to do with decision-making at inappropriate levels. It can also be caused by inefficient policies and procedures. Have you had anyone say 'we've always done it that way' to justify an outdated practice?" John asked in a way that most would interpret as hypothetically since so many organizations suffered from this issue, but he wanted to keep the meeting as a conversation.

"Yes, especially at some of our older facilities and among the people running some of our older computer systems. I believe culture can play a role too as some people just want to be told what to do and even if they have good ideas of their own to make improvements, they may defer to the manager for every instruction," said Miriam.

"Exactly," said John snapping his index finger acknowledging the remark, and showing both agreement and providing a verbal reward.

"We can also have this happen due to a lack of customer input concerning requirements or poor configuration control," said John as he paused, pressed his lips, and rubbed his chin and neck before letting it rest in his left hand; a sign they had learned meant John was going to bring up a troublesome topic everyone should listen carefully to.

"And made-up quality standards," he said with a pause for effect. "We need to work within our department on how we write audit reports. Over editing our reports is a form of over-processing and made-up quality standards in our unit come along by mixing up form over substance, preferences over material improvements to the communication. I'll talk more about this in our staff meeting."

John continued, "the next one is defects. As the name suggests it is about errors. As auditors we usually gravitate towards this one because we are usually looking for activities or transactions that don't meet requirements." Realizing that the meeting had been heavy with facts and concepts, he reminded himself to keep engaging his staff so they stayed alert. "How else do you think this would come about. How would we find defects?" he asked.

"Scrap?" said Carolina.

"Yes," acknowledged John. "Other ways to identify defects?"

They were silent unable to come up with another answer.

"How about repairs, or rework of a product that doesn't meet specs?" John said coaching them.

"Excessive variation in production processes sounds a bit technical, but defects or errors can often be summarized that way. Let me ask you what audit procedures, or root causes, might tell us that this is happening? Growing scrap would be one of them, right?" John said helping them get started.

They nodded in agreement.

"Maybe high inventory levels in returned inventory or warranty claims?" said Rachel as an answer but an upward inflection that made it sound like a question instead.

"You're right! That would tell us this is happening," said John in a congratulatory tone. "How about possible causes?" he pressed them on.

"Inadequate tools or equipment?" said Brian.

"Right again!"

"How about insufficient training, or items damaged during transport due to poor packaging, layouts or unnecessary handling?" said Miriam finally getting into this part of the conversation. "There is a code in the system they are supposed to use whenever an item is damaged. We could pull that information to see how many items this affected, when it happens, and why."

"Exactly Miriam," said John nodding in agreement. "So now we start to link concepts that highlight operational risks to audit steps and data analytics, and possible causes, or as I call them 'usual suspects'," he said making air quotes to emphasize "usual suspects."

"I think we're up to six or seven. Anyway, the next one is waiting and that can be a little tricky. It refers to idle time occurring when other events are not synchronized. For example, things like operators waiting for equipment or materials, or Production waiting for operators. What else do you think?" said John moving the conversation forward and sharing another possible area of waste.

"How about Production bottlenecks when somewhere in the cycle there is a pause for the next step to pick things up to move things further?" said Carolina.

"Yes, that's a good one. Does it happen often?" said John making both a statement and asking a question.

"Yes, fairly enough. Not all the time, but enough to be a routine problem," she replied.

"Ok. Let's remember that," said John. "A concern that is not merely hypothetical but occurs making it real and current. We would just have to quantify its prevalence and impact. I like where this is going!" John said enthusiastically.

"I have one," said Carolina again. "When I was in Operations we sometimes had unplanned equipment downtime like when there were long setup times and everything stopped until those got setup. We had that happen sometimes once a day on some lines."

"Would equipment maintenance fit in here too?" asked Tony.

"It could, especially if not scheduled appropriately or done poorly, so it takes longer than necessary forcing others to wait," answered John.

"On a few occasions we stopped to do equipment maintenance and they said it was done so we could resume work and they did it poorly, like a calibration miscalculation on a line, and we had to stop a second time. That also created some waste when the parts came out defective."

"Yikes, I'm sure some people were unhappy about that!" added John.

"Unhappy? There was some serious yelling because we were late delivering on some key orders. It was a mess."

"At another level, some factories have shutdowns to do major maintenance work. Often in the summer or winter. Do they do that in our factories?" asked John inquiring about procedures and thinking that might be some documentation Audit could review.

"Not sure. Not in Georgia. Maybe in some of the older factories like the ones in Latin America."

"All right. Thanks. Let's look into that another time. Moving on. Another one is motion," said John. "Don't confuse that with Transportation. Motion is usually what I call micro-motion, smaller movements, reaching for things. Imagine a workbench area and the operator is reaching for tools, parts, and supplies. The worker reaches for a part, puts it on one side of the workbench, turns left to grab another part, then swivels on the chair and grabs a tool, returns to the starting position, and reaches for a nut and bolt set, then proceeds to build that assembly. Turns, puts the assembly in a bin, and repeats the process. Things like reaching, bending, gathering tools and supplies more than necessary. Unnecessarily complicated procedures, so we look for inefficient and consequently ineffective workspace layouts and poor organization."

"A place for everything and everything in its place," said Carolina.

"Well, yes. That is related to this and helps reduce the likelihood of having to look around for what you need. Having things in their proper place is commonly related to Straighten, or Seiton in Japanese. One of the 5Ss of Lean. It has to do with orderliness or setting things in order in the workplace," explained John noticing the nodding heads agreeing with his explanation.

"What was the eighth?" said John forgetting the eighth item he wanted to explain to the pair. "Oh yes, underutilized skills or underutilized employees. It typically has to do with workers whose skillset is not being used as much as they could or should be. These are workers who may be in the wrong job, working on tasks that may not be leveraging their full potential. Note I didn't say beneath them, because we have to be careful not to create some kind of a classist dynamic. Sometimes you just have to jump in and help out, but how much of that jumping in and helping out is happening? Is that somewhat incidental or are workers habitually doing this rather than working at their level of competence. Since there is an hourly rate for everyone, how much are we paying for this person to do x? Maybe someone with fewer skills and at a lower payrate should be handling those other tasks. Another aspect of this is allowing employees to work in silos, which keeps them from sharing their knowledge and working collaboratively." John thought this was a good time to link the concepts with audit procedures and the improved methodology he was advocating. He asked them.

"With that explanation, and to avoid creating this waste ourselves, do you think you can build a work program that might help us look for those areas of waste?"

They nodded their heads indicating they could.

"Good! Let's practice one of them. Pick an area of waste and tell me what are some procedures you believe might help us find out if that is happening and to what degree?"

After a brief silence while they thought about the question, Carolina started.

"Inventory. It is an easy one but let me try that. OK. So, we look at the average amount of inventory to see if it is rising or falling. We also look at the valuation of the inventory, how long items have been in stock and inventory movements."

"Yes, that's a good start", encouraged John. "Go on."

"They said they sometimes run out of parts, so we also look at stockouts. How often they run out of parts and which parts they usually run out of. That's all I have." She concluded.

"That's good. What would you do for those items that they run out of?"

"Write them down for the report?"

"Yes, eventually. But we should do some root cause analysis on those. For example. Look at the lead time for those parts to see what patterns you see there. They may be ordering them too late or there may be an increase in their use of those parts, but they are still ordering same number of parts as before the surge in production, so that could be causing the stockouts."

"And if they are ordering too late? How can they fix that?"

"They should calculate an optimal replenishment point and timeframe, so the right quantity of needed parts arrives sooner."

"And if they are ordering the wrong amount. You know, not enough?" asked John again.

This time the pause was a bit longer as they thought about that question. They had never spent this much time thinking through an audit program because these were usually repeats of prior year audits. In this case, they had never looked at supply flows. Whenever they looked at inventory, the focus was always the amount and valuation of it, and John had not even mentioned looking at system-generated inventory reports.

"A forecasting issue, maybe?" replied Brian hesitantly.

"Exactly! The Purchasing group may be buying insufficient quantities based on the instructions they get from the forecasts. So yes, take a look to see how accurate forecasting is in relation to actual production. There could be a clue there." "What do you think about the vendors supplying those parts? Should we look at that as part of this?" asked John.

"No. That would be out of scope. We look at that during a Vendor Audit and that's not in our schedule," answered Tony.

"Well, you make a good point, and we need to avoid scope creep. In this case, however, vendors may be in scope to the extent that they are providing the inventory parts that we may be missing in our production process. What role might vendors play?"

"The vendors supplying parts to this process could be late?" said Carolina tentatively.

"Yes! You're right. And they could be doing that even if our lead times are correct. We order on time, but they deliver late."

"What else could vendors be doing that could throw off our supplies on hand for production?"

They looked at John with blank eyes. That was a lot of questions and a lot of thinking.

John gave them some time to think and then helped them out a bit.

"How about we ask for Part A, and we get Part B instead?"

They shook their heads as a sign that they understood the point he was making.

"Funny you say that John," said Rachel. "When I was talking to Dianne in supply chain, she mentioned they are having problems like that. She specifically mentioned the rollers on some of the treadmills. There is a vendor, she said, when they get a shipment, they scratch their heads twice. The first time when they get the shipment because they don't know if they are going to get what they need. Then again after they open the boxes because they have to figure out what to do with the wrong size, wrong quality, and wrong color parts they get with the shipment. Well, it isn't funny, but you know what I mean."

"So, you just illustrated my point. Vendor relationships can introduce a risk into the process, so they can be in scope for this engagement."

John noticed that Tony did not look pleased. He may be embarrassed after being proven wrong, so he wanted to reassure him.

"Are you OK with the process for drafting the audit program, Tony? What's on your mind?"

"I think if we do all that you say we will never finish that audit. I also believe some of those things you said should be done by management."

"I hear you. You raise some good points about the amount of work. Remember. You only focus on what we can connect to key objectives of the process and risks that could get in the way of achieving those objectives. Also, you don't have to do all the work. Work with the client. We ask for data beforehand so we can look for transactions that we want to look at more closely. We also ask them to do some of the work. We won't be there too long. We can't. Go ahead and work through the 8 Forms of Waste and prepare a work program like we just did. For now, I want you to practice thinking about audits and advisory projects like this. We'll review, add, or remove things together, but work on this together so you practice. OK?"

"OK," they replied in unison.

"When can you have a draft for us to review?"

"Four days."

"Focus on this and let's try for two days. Don't over think it. Think like a businessperson. Like you are managing that department and what questions you want answered. That should help you a bit. Also, it is better to find out if you are or not on track in two days, than give you four days and find out you are not on track. Sounds good?"

"Yes," said Tony with the tone of reluctance in his voice. Rachel on the other hand, sounded enthusiastic as if saying, "we are finally making audit work creative and fun!"

John waited in the waiting room for the meeting to start. He was wondering what Dan needed. The subject of the meeting was not very clear, and the agenda was equally unclear. Tony was already on the call too. So, after exchanging some pleasantries, they were individually checking their computers. John was reviewing some workpapers and some exit meeting notes.

"Hi gentlemen!" said Dan when he joined the meeting. "Sorry for being late. We should schedule meetings for 50 minutes instead of a full hour, that way people can take a bio break or attend to quick emails or messages. There needs to be a buffer in between meetings."

"Good idea, Dan. We started doing that a couple of months ago and it has been working quite well for us," said John.

"That's exactly why I wanted to talk with you John. And Tony; didn't mean to leave you out."

"No problem," said Tony, suspicious of Dan's intention since internal audit had audited them three years ago and there were some basic issues reported. In fact, they had pushed really hard on the finding about not having policies and procedures and stated repeatedly that the staff was familiar with the work, and none were needed. When the risk of staff turnover was mentioned, they again objected to the observation and claimed that their turnover figures were low and they could absorb some turnover.

"I need your help because this Great Resignation problem has hit us hard. We lost several employees and those coming in are not getting up to speed fast enough, so now we have a growing number of errors affecting client relations."

"I'm listening. How are you planning to upskill your staff?"

"Well, that's where you come in. Tony seems to have a lot of experience with policies and procedures so can you lend him for a few weeks to document our processes?"

Without much hesitation, John responded. "Our role as internal auditors requires us to be independent so we can review any process or unit without compromising our objectivity. We generally have to excuse ourselves from doing work like that because we subsequently could not review it; we would be evaluating our own work."

"Can you make an exception for us? We need to get this fixed and it was in your audit report."

"I understand. To be clear, we want to be helpful without creating long term complications for all involved, so when it comes to policies and procedures this is what we can do. I can have Tony work with one or two of your staff to document the process. He would be guiding and assisting, but the writing would be done by your team. You should also review it before implementation and sign off on it. Can you do that?"

"I guess. Yes, I can have Nancy work with Tony."

"How much time do you think this might take?"

"I'm thinking two weeks max four?"

"Tony, do you think it can be done in two to four weeks?"

"I think so."

"OK. We should have narratives and maybe flowcharts, right?" John asked.

"Narratives. No flowcharts," replied Tony.

"OK. You can build off those narratives to speed up the process. Draw some flowcharts too for additional documentation. When do you want to start Dan?"

"Juan is leaving in two weeks, so can you start sometime next week so you can ask Juan what he does? He is a key member of the team, and we need to document what he knows and what he does."

"OK. That works for you Tony?"

"Yes."

"Alright. I'll leave you to it. No more than four weeks, and I already explained the process. I'll put it in an e-mail so we're all clear. Dan, I need you to reply agreeing to that or listing any changes you want to this plan. OK?"

"You got it. Thanks John. Truly appreciate it. Thanks Tony, you're a life saver."

"Don't mention it," said Tony.

--------------------||--------------------

"We seem to be having some issues with our ethics training."

"I don't know why. We have been providing ethics training for years."

"How many years?"

"At least ten years."

"Is it done annually?"

"Yes, everyone has to take the class."

"Who provides the training?"

"Corporate compliance."

"What's in the training?"

"Mostly a review of company policies, but they handle it all."

"So, you don't have any strong memory of what's in the training?"

"Not really. It is kind of boring quite honestly."

"Do you remember the training content changing much or at all?"

"It has been pretty much the same all this time."

"You have been here for over ten years. You have taken the class many times. The contents don't seem to have changed much during that time, yet you don't remember much. Do you see the irony? You don't remember much of what's in the class."

"I guess so."

"What happens if someone doesn't take the training?"

"I don't know. Compliance handles that."

"Let's ask Miriam and Carolina if they remember," said John, typing quick messages in Teams as he spoke. A few seconds later they responded, and John rocked his head from side to side as he read indicating he was assessing their responses as he got them. A moment later, he provided his summary.

"OK. It looks like it is basically a review of company policies like you said. We have a staff meeting in a couple of hours. I have some ideas," said John seeing an opportunity.

--------------------||--------------------

"Good morning, everyone. Good afternoon, Carolina," John greeted his team.

"Happy Friday," he said in a cheerful tone.

"Happy Friday!" said Rachel enthusiastically with a cheerful flowery blouse to match.

"You're happy today," said Brian. "Big plans for the weekend?"

"Yes, my parents and my younger sister are coming over tonight and spending a couple of weeks with me. I'm really looking forward to seeing them," she explained.

"That's great," said Carolina. "So good to see your family. I miss mine being out here in London."

"I know. It is hard. What's funny is I used to fight with my little sister all the time and now I miss her terribly. We're really good friends now and she looks up to me, so she makes me behave," she said with a smile that oddly also tried unsuccessfully to hide her teary eyes.

"You don't choose your family. They are God's gift to you, as you are to them," said Miriam.

"Was it Desmond Tutu?" asked John with less confidence than usual about the source of the quote.

"Yes, Desmond Tutu," answered Miriam.

"Enjoy your time with your family," said John.

This was an unusual day for the staff meeting. They moved it to Friday to accommodate upcoming time off planned starting the following week. After discussing project updates, upcoming tasks, roadblocks, and sharing some news about some volunteer opportunities available on company time, he turned their attention to the topic of ethics.

"We just found out that we have some issues where some salespeople engaged in questionable practices. Without getting into the specifics, they did not disclose key features and limitations of some of our products. We had another incident where some warehouse employees sent refurbished product to customers instead of new product like they should have because they didn't have enough inventory. They should have escalated the issue and found other solutions, but instead they lied to customers. Then, we've had some managers treat their staff very poorly against our values and that in my mind is also an ethics-related issue. We must treat each other, employees, contractors, customers, vendors, everyone with respect, tell the truth and do what is right. If we can't, we need to escalate that to someone who can look into it and make a good decision about it. Some managers were terminated for creating a toxic work environment. In summary, we have some ethics-related issues at InSports.

I enquired about our ethics training. Miriam, Carolina, and Tony, you already had me ask some questions about this. Corporate Compliance is currently running the ethics training, but it looks like there are some practices and content that can be improved upon."

"Did you hear about the QA reports where some results were not released on time?" asked Tony.

"Yes, I heard about that too. Thanks for highlighting this, because sometimes people assume that QA, compliance, and even auditors are immune to ethics misconduct. For example, the SEC fined Ernst & Young, E&Y, $100 million, the largest penalty ever for an accounting firm for breaking accounting rules and hindering the agency's investigation by withholding information. The issue was that nearly fifty E&Y audit employees shared answers on the ethics section of the CPA exam between 2017-2021, and hundreds more who cheated on CPE courses. Many others knew their coworkers cheated and facilitated the cheating by not reporting the problem.

In 2019, KPMG agreed to pay $50 million to the SEC to settle allegations that former employees found out about plans by PCAOB regulators to review them, so they changed past audit work, and also because firm auditors cheated on training exams by sharing answers and manipulating test results.

Every ethics training should be more than a review of rules, policies, and procedures. It should be more than a compliance exercise so someone can 'check the box'," he said making air quotes. "Ethics training should be about reminding people of our company's values. It should be about instilling values of integrity and proper conduct, building capacity so people can make better decisions under predictable and unpredictable conditions. It should be about getting commitment to look out after each other so bad apples are removed, and the barrel doesn't rot. It should be about informing staff who to go to when they don't know what to do, and memorizing key rules and regulations so people don't make preventable mistakes."

John paused to let all of this information sink in. Without further prompting, Rachel asked,

"Are we going to do an audit of ethics and corporate culture?"

John's serious look immediately turned into a smile as he heard the question. His team was starting to appreciate the importance of auditing where the risks were.

"Yes, we are," he said nodding and with his typical smile, which the team understood meant that this was a priority.

"The things you mentioned sound like key objectives every ethics training program should pursue," added Rachel again.

"That's correct. Did anyone note where on the list is the objective about memorizing rules?"

"Last," replied Carolina.

"Exactly, it is last because knowing the rules doesn't mean people will follow them. We need more than memorization-type ethics training. We need capacity-to-make-better-decisions ethics training," said John.

"My experience is that most ethics training is about memorizing rules, policies, what not to do, and philosophical terms. I'm afraid we may be disappointed because the training may not be the second type you mentioned," said Rachel.

"Maybe so, but that is why we do these things. We go where the need for assurance is, and if there is a need for improvement, we'll gladly share our thoughts with our audit clients. It will be a different type of audit, but I believe it will be fun. Let's provide more, and better, ethics training," he said concluding the meeting.

--------------------||--------------------

The senior management meeting had been going on for 40 minutes already, and John was supposed to address the group 10 minutes earlier. He was running out of time because other officers were also on the agenda and had topics to bring up for discussion. When he got his chance to speak, he said.

"We are transforming internal audit to become a better service provider to the entire organization. The traditional view of internal audit was to focus on compliance and financial reviews. That was the case everywhere, not only at InSports. But the profession has shifted and even our governing body, the Institute of Internal Auditors, now defines internal auditing as an assurance and advisory activity. For some that may be a departure from tradition, but auditors in organizations worldwide are doing that already, so we are a bit late embracing that part of our role."

"What are the implications to your day-to-day work?" asked Nihal.

"We are going to balance out our audit plan. I have been working with my team because it is one thing to say we want to do something and another to have the people who can actually do the work. I've sent my team to training and I've been coaching them myself too. They are excited about this expansion of their role."

"That's good to know, but what does this mean in terms of the balance between assurance work and advisory work?" asked Nihal again clarifying his initial question.

"Yes, that is a gradual process to shift some of our time from assurance to advisory. There is no perfect ratio of one to the other, but in general, highly-regulated industries do more assurance as a percentage, but we're not heavily regulated, so I'm starting with 15 percent. We recognize the reliance you place on us to check things to make sure they are working like they should, so we won't ignore or neglect that ever, but the shift will result in my team supporting you," he said as he visually scanned the room and his hand created an imaginary orb indicating unity.

"When do you start?" asked Ron.

"We started already by clarifying and practicing this expanding role in the team. They've embraced this internally. We worked with Ken and with Kathleen and together found improvements to several operating areas. That was quite successful as proof of concepts go." As John said this, several heads nodded, and there were even some glances among participants because some of these issues were also present in their units.

"How many years of experience do your auditors have?"

"Our auditors have over twenty five years of collective experience. Most of it obtained here at InSports, so they are familiar with the organization."

"Are you going to lend them to us when we are short-staffed?" asked Nihal jokingly.

"John sensed the risk of misunderstanding the role of the internal auditors, so he carefully framed his answer. That's a good question. No, we're not providing staff augmentation. Consulting engagements, which are sometimes referred to as special projects or advisory services, should be viewed as an opportunity for audit to help you answer a nagging question, identify opportunities to save time, money, and effort so the work gets done faster, cheaper, and better. We cannot take on recurring, operational duties, and we cannot take on decision-making activities either. Those remain with you and your teams. We provide an outsider's perspective that is not influenced by working in the program or process daily. We come in, review, and analyze the situation, and share the results and opinions. Then we leave."

"This could save us a lot of money; instead of hiring outside consultants all the time," chimed Ron.

"Yes, that is another goal of this. Also remember, with outside consultants you have to provide a lot of background and context, which our auditors already possess. Collaboration should be easier, and results should be more appropriate to our needs."

"Thanks, John," interjected Ron acting once again as the task master keeping the meeting moving along. "We need to cover a few more topics on our agenda. Can you report back at future meetings on the progress you're making with this initiative?"

"Yes, absolutely. Glad to," said John, wrapping up his presentation and the official introduction of this new feature of his evolving team.

---------------------||---------------------

11 Empowering Employees

John started the weekly staff meeting without the typical chit chat.

"As you know, I've been making arrangements for training. I conducted some of those sessions and most recently, Lynn provided training on Agile Auditing. While I have some ideas on the type of training I would like to see some of you take going forward, it is not just for me to decide. I want each of you to take ownership, and responsibility, for your professional development. So, spend some time thinking about what training you would like to receive, and we'll talk about the best way to help you get it."

"Training has changed over the years and while many of you, like me, have been accustomed to attending a classroom-type event, with an instructor and you sitting in a classroom, or hotel meeting room, that has changed lately. It started before the pandemic, but since then, there are far more options for online training, both live and self-paced. So, I went ahead and bought our department several subscriptions to self-paced training on internal audit, IT, cybersecurity, and soft skills training. I'll post the access information in the shared drive, so take a look and let me know if there is anything you need that is not already there. Question: Has anyone used the HR training resources available?"

With that introduction, John empowered his team to take ownership of their training, he set expectations for himself and the team, and offered support in their overall development. The team looked on silently as the leap forward settled in their minds; their experience had been one characterized by the management driving decisions, steering training based on their own perspective, priorities, and budgets, and relegating the team to one of mostly passive participants. They were now in the driver seat!

Then John steered the meeting toward their weekly agenda of what did you accomplish last week, what are you working on this week, what obstacles are in your way, and how he could help them continue moving forward; an outcome-driven routine.

---------------------||---------------------

John was in Kathleen's office with Terry. The agenda was to discuss an audit of corporate ethics and culture.

"Auditing ethics and culture is a relatively new field in internal auditing. The profession has recognized its importance for years, but the focus has historically been accounting, finance, financial reporting, which relates to the other two, and compliance. Increasingly IT and cybersecurity, and governance. I realize I'm giving everyone a long list, but my point is, ethics and culture were considered important, but not quite central. They were viewed as very subjective and intangible topics, and unfortunately, treated as somewhat tangential. But that is changing. Auditors have been paying attention and noticed a while ago that when ethics and the culture are compromised, many of the other topics I mentioned previously, are also compromised. An unscrupulous accountant may forge report numbers and now the financial statements

DOI: 10.1201/9781003322870-13

are compromised too. An unscrupulous salesperson may lie to a prospect and misrepresent the features, price, or warranty on our products, and now our reputation is compromised too. A culture of sloppy work and a generalized lack of accountability for one's work results in poor quality and poor customer service. Ethics and culture in many ways drive the quality of internal controls and management practices, in some cases even overriding system controls."

"How can that be?"

"Some of our systems allow management override, so a manager can sometimes authorize a change in procedure and related recording of a transaction."

"Why is that allowed? Is that OK?"

"We need to be responsive to customer needs, so sometimes exceptions are made to rules. So, while this may be OK as a general rule, the type and frequency of these changes can turn into an issue. I'll give you some examples. If an employee doesn't want the payroll payments made to a bank account, we may produce physical checks. If an employee doesn't have a credit card or insists on not using their own to pay travel expenses, we may issue that person a travel card or give them a travel advance. Here's another example now more problematic. A manager tells their staff not to perform the monthly bank reconciliations and to focus instead on other activities deemed more pressing. That's not what we would like to see. Similarly, a manager who tells the staff not to research reconciling items and discrepancies may also be working against best practices."

"I read somewhere about journal entries and how critical those can be. Some companies have gone bankrupt due to manipulation of those, right?"

"Yes, those can be troublesome too. If a manager reverses transactions and through journal entries reclassifies transactions, can be creating a significant issue for the organization. Then there are things like harassment, ignoring laws and regulations and the list goes on. So, given the many risky dynamics associated with people's behavior, we are launching a review of our ethics training as the first phase of an ethics and culture review. The culture portion we will do later."

"But ethics training has been in place for years! Compliance runs that."

"Yes, that is true. The review will be a collaborative effort between internal audit and corporate compliance."

"What does the review entail?"

"We did a review of our cybersecurity training some time ago. Several of those procedures are applicable here too. Things like did employees attend training, but also how long after the date of hire? Did they do the refresher trainings annually after that? but there are other things even more important than attendance."

"Yes, did they learn anything?" said Kathleen.

"Exactly, that is a key objective that should be pursued with training, but not always checked upon."

"How can we assess whether participants learned anything?"

"One way is to have them take a test at the end."

"How about can they make good decisions? How can we assess that?"

"Have them make decisions during class!"

"What else. We spend a lot of money on training and this one, like cybersecurity, are some of the most important."

"Well, participants should have some scenarios in the training that they read, analyze then indicate what they believe the person in the scenario should do."

"Well," Terry jumped in after listening to the conversation for a while, "we don't do any of those things."

"What do you mean?" asked Kathleen.

"The training was designed to show participants our Code of Ethics, Code of Conduct, some of the key requirements indicated there, the phone number for our Ethics Hotline, but not much more."

"I understand, but we are now looking at our programs and processes from the perspective of business objectives. Recalling the Ethics Hotline number and some of the key provisions in our policies is important, but some other goals include being able to make ethical decisions."

"A more important objective," said John.

The conversation continued as they brainstormed objectives and ways of testing them. As the conversation progressed, Kathleen's mood went from surprised, to annoyed, and to almost embarrassed by the number of shortcomings of the training program that they had identified in a half hour. She was now delighted, because she felt that the result would be a much better training program and perhaps fewer complaints from participants. Recent class evaluations had criticized the class for being boring and repetitive.

"Will this audit result in recommendations?"

"Very likely. That is common practice to provide ideas for corrective action, but these will be discussed with you first."

"It looks like there won't be too many things to test here," said Terry.

"Is that good or bad?" asked Kathleen nervous about what that statement might mean.

"We test to verify our understanding of things and prove or disprove whether objectives are being achieved, risks are occurring and if controls are operating as intended. When our review of the program or process shows that objectives are unclear and controls are missing, we may decide early on that testing is best left for later. We can indicate in our communication if that is the case, but it looks like we can provide an outsider's perspective on the training program and give you some useful recommendations."

"OK then. Let me know when this will start and who we need to inform. I suppose Compliance since they run the training."

"Yes, I'll draft an announcement letter when we'll proceed."

--------------------||--------------------

After the staff meeting where the team discussed job enrichment and job enlargement, and consistent with John's goal of looking at more than accounting risks, he instructed Rachel to contact EHS and include workplace safety in her audit procedures when she visited the plant.

"Why do you want to go there?" asked the plant manager who at this time was also acting as a tour guide.

"I just want to take a look, if you don't mind," replied Rachel calmly as they stood facing a door.

"You are awfully curious. I have never had an auditor ask so many questions and want to veer off the tour we prepared for them. The work is being done in here and that's what I'm showing you."

"I understand. I just want to take a look because workplace safety is also a risk we consider in our work."

"But we have the EHS group for that!" he said exasperated.

"Yes, you're right. I've spoken with several of the inspectors in EHS, in fact, some of them are on the company's chess club with me, and I play volleyball with some of them too. Anyway, internal audit focuses on risk; all types of risk, and while we're here we are making sure we understand how the work gets done, who, when, where, and how workers do their jobs, and we also need to verify they are safe. So, I want to understand how employees enter and exit the buildings for work, and how they would exit if there were any emergencies," Rachel explained.

"Come with me, let's take a look," Rachel said in both a friendly and a commanding way as she took a leadership role in the process. When they opened the door, it quickly hit an object on the other side. As they walked around the obstructed door, they noticed the landing was filled with at least six stacked boxes, two broken chairs, and a three-legged table on its side. Next to the table, there were two mop buckets, and a third was in the corner almost full of brown water and a mop sticking out of it.

Rachel looked at the accumulated debris, looked at the speechless plant manager, and retuned her gaze to the haphazard assortment of items obstructing the means of egress.

In front of them was a dark hallway with chipped and discolored tiles, a left wall that could use a coat of paint, and lighting that would be much improved if they replaced the missing lightbulbs. And for those light bulbs still there, replace them with brighter ones. As she stepped aside to avoid a water puddle, she noted there were several doors on the right side. When she came upon them, she realized those were doors to the restrooms.

"So, employees would be walking this hallway throughout their work shifts whenever they need to use the bathrooms?" she asked rhetorically. "Kind of a tough image every time they go there, eh?"

At the end of the hallway was the outside door and as Rachel was about to raise her hand to push the door open the plant manager confessed, "that door is always locked."

"Good. Yes. Outside doors should be locked to prevent unauthorized people from entering the building through doors like this one." As she pushed the door, she realized what the plant manager meant because the door wouldn't open.

Perplexed, she pushed it again with the same result. The door wouldn't open. "Oh, so the door doesn't open at all?"

"We locked it because employees would sneak out when they were not supposed to or they would prop it open when they were going out to smoke or for lunch, so we decided to lock it permanently," he explained.

"But this is a fire hazard," said Rachel.

"There are other doors they can use if they needed to evacuate."

Without saying a word, Rachel looked up toward the ceiling and fixed her eyes on the illuminated red "Exit" sign. She looked back down at the plant manager's ashen face.

"Let's return to the shop floor," said Rachel as she started walking back the way they came with a speechless plant manager in tow.

--------------------||--------------------

"Welcome to New York. Hope your travel was relatively hassle free and you enjoyed yourself yesterday. You arrived Saturday, right?"

"Yes, it was awesome," Carolina jumped at the question. "I rented a bicycle and rode probably 100 miles all around Manhattan."

"Where did you go?"

"Central Park, then headed South down the West side. I believe it is called the Hudson River Greenway. Took pictures of the Statue of Liberty at Battery Park, then up the East side. It was amazing!" she said relishing the memory of the Sunday spent riding around the city.

"I ran close to 10 miles," shared Brian. "Didn't see all that you saw, but it was great meandering around the city with such great weather."

John had an idea. "All of this talk about exercising has me thinking. Would you like to set up a... let's call it an exercise club? We can keep track of walking, running, rowing, etc. maybe convert it to steps, and see what we're doing as a team. Do what you're comfortable with, but it would be a fun. Exercising together kind of a thing."

"I like it," said Brian. "I'll keep track of it if everyone sends me their totals every Friday."

"Which reminds me," said John. "How is our book club coming along? We don't cover that for another couple of weeks, but are you making progress on that?"

Heads bopping in agreement, then Miriam spoke: "It's my turn to lead the group, so I hope everyone is reading up on this. I think we have a real winner this month. Great choice. Who recommended this one? Oh, it was me!" she said jokingly.

"Good, good. OK. So. let's turn now to our training session since the goal was to vacation in New York and maybe do some training if time permits, right?" said John jokingly to bring the meeting to order.

"First thing is root cause analysis. We have been talking about this in our profession for decades, but lots of auditors still struggle with this, so let's talk about it, what it is, what holds us back from doing root cause analysis well, and ways to make it a standard part of our audit and consulting engagements."

"So, let's start with: What is root cause analysis?" said John promptly engaging with his team.

"I honestly don't know if I can define it scientifically, but in simple terms it has to do with getting to the root of the problem," said Brian.

"You can't use the word in the definition of a word," said Rachel in a tone that sounded as if she were chastising him.

"I know that," he said with a sarcastic tone, "at least I'm trying," followed by a headshake and eyes rolling. "You define it."

"Well, root cause analysis, or RCA, is defined as a collective term that describes a wide range of approaches, tools, and techniques used to uncover causes of…" said Rachel reading the definition from her phone.

"Clever, very clever. So, you looked it up. I could have looked it up myself too," said Brian still justling with her.

"But you didn't."

"OK you too. Nice to see you getting along so well. The point is not just to memorize, recite or lookup and read a definition, what I was getting at is the meaning of it. What is it in practical terms?" "Rachel, you just read it. Can you give us an example of root cause analysis?"

"BAM! Big mouth got busted!" said Brian.

Rachel closed her eyes and while shaking her head showing mock disbelief said, "the 5 Whys is a technique to perform root cause analysis. It consists of asking 'why' five times to dig, or probe deeper at the source of the problem. Each answer becomes the basis for the next question until you exhaust the answers, at that point, you are likely at the source of the issue. It could be five, could be three, maybe four, but five is the number used."

"Is this something we should do individually, within the team or with our clients?" asked Tony.

"All of the above," replied John. "It can be used in all of those scenarios. Remember 'the Cause and Effect Diagram' that we spoke about a few months ago? So all of these are tools we can use so our audit observations are not just superficial narratives of issues, but rather, they include, as best we can discern, the source of the problem. It is also an important component of our documentation. We need that when completing the CCCER model."

The team spent the day learning about root cause analysis. In addition to The Five Whys, the Cause and Effect Diagram, Failure Mode and Effects Analysis, and Regression Analysis, John led the team through discussions and exercises relating the concepts to dynamics and issues at InSports.

--------------------||--------------------

John let the team work on their own on a case study the next morning. He wanted them to bond together without him always being around. Instead, he had a presentation to deliver.

The orientation that John delivered during the winter received great feedback, so now internal audit was conducting monthly presentations on various topics. Sometimes it was welcoming new hires, sometimes it was speaking at the Controllers' Conference, and sometimes it was a lunch and learn event. John was still delivering most of these, but he recruited others in the team to do the same. This was an opportunity to put internal audit's best foot forward, but also to help develop his staff. By speaking at these events, they would act as advocates for the department, but also acquire presentation and group management skills. He still attended these events as an observer when others presented, so he could show support. Today, he was the main speaker for internal audit.

As the orientation session started, John thought about the audience. This was a large group, and while some appeared eager to learn, others not so. Some of them looked like they would rather be somewhere else.

He began the session with a question, "is legal always ethical?" While the audience perked up as they processed the question in their heads, he took advantage of their newfound attention to start his presentation.

"A common misconception is to equate what is legal with ethical and conversely, what is illegal with unethical. Yes, many things that are legal are ethical, but some things can be legal yet unethical.

For example, is paying the minimum wage at the federal rate of $7.25 per hour ethical when the cost of living is so much higher just about everywhere in the US?

Other examples; paying bribes to government officials, redlining neighborhoods, forbidding women from voting or even getting a credit card, laws that forbid adults of mixed race from marrying who they choose, or apartheid-like laws that kept members of minority groups from eating at a diner or drinking from a water fountain. Those actions were legal at one point but unethical.

The absence of a law forbidding the pollution of rivers does not make it ethical to pollute the river. If we have a factory in a country, and there is no law in that country saying you can't dump chemical waste in the river, is it OK to dump the waste in the river?

The absence of a law forbidding the payment of bribes does not make it ethical to pay bribes. So, no law does not mean ethical!

Even when there is a law, some take the lack of enforcement or miniscule penalties as an implicit authorization to break the law. For example, that country where they didn't have a law against dumping waste in the river passed such a law, but the fine is $1,000. The cost to properly dispose of the waste is higher than that. Is it OK then to dump the waste in the river since we save money doing so? Of course not. Again, not ethical, and not legal either!

Can illegal be ethical? Consider the need to drive above the speed limit to get a seriously injured person to the hospital? Or consider a homeless and hungry child who steals bread. This child is doing something illegal; theft, but we could argue ethical due to the need to survive. Driving over the speed limit to take an injured person to the hospital. Stopping traffic so an elderly or disabled person can cross the street. A controversial one is assisted suicide for terminally-ill people. Jaywalking to help someone who has fallen and needs help. These are all examples of actions that may be considered illegal, but we could argue, ethical."

By now the group was very focused on every word John said. He spoke about InSports' legal, compliance, EHS, human resources, and internal audit departments, and how these units, in addition to the existing policies, statement of values, code of ethics, and the whistleblowing hotline, provided multiple avenues to educate and assist new hires if they encountered situations that challenged ethical norms.

The session concluded with John sharing a link to the online evaluation and a request for feedback.

He rejoined his team in the afternoon as they learned about "Is Is-Not analysis" and applied its principles to problem-solving. He then engaged the group on a lengthy discussion about empowering auditors to think and act like consultants, engaging their clients and how this approach differed from the traditional auditing approach of acting in relative isolation from audit clients. They discussed the importance of helping the organization succeed and balancing that goal with the requirement to preserve independence and objectivity.

--------------------||--------------------

"OK Carolina, tell us about the 200 miles you rode around New York City yesterday," said John redirecting the group from the multiple side conversations already underway.

"200? I rode 300 yesterday!" she said jokingly.

"All after we left yesterday at 5:00 PM. You're amazing," said John playing along.

The team had not gone out together the night before, so he asked each person what they did to give everyone a chance to share. After a few minutes, he redirected the group.

"I like to start multi-day training sessions like this one by spending a few minutes reviewing what we learned the previous day. A summary of what you learned, key takeaways, action plan items, and of course, answer any questions you may have, before moving to new topics." Who wants to start?"

After giving everyone a chance again to summarize the experiences and lessons learned from the previous day, John thanked them and redirected the team to the agenda items for the day.

"Very good. We start today with some soft skills, and the first item is emotional intelligence. You may know that this concept was popularized in the 1990s by Daniel Goleman as a set of skills, characteristics, and actions that lead to better leadership, higher performance, and general success. In general, self-awareness, self-regulation, social skills to work collaboratively with others and manage relationships. What else?"

"It has a lot to do with empathy," said Miriam.

"Very good! yes. Empathy is arguably a common denominator within EI. Why does this matter?"

"Because we should try to understand our colleagues and auditees," Brian replied.

"Clients, not auditees," replied Tony.

"Thanks, yes, clients. I almost forgot the grammar police was in the room," Brian said jokingly.

Tony replied jovially by rolling his eyes and turning his hands up toward the sky in a sign of mocked frustration.

"Yeah, you're frustrated," joined Carolina. "You know you like being the corporate cop!" she said joining in the lighthearted humor.

Sensing the change after trying for so long to get Tony to stop calling them auditees, John wanted to reinforce the breakthrough.

"You're right, Tony, it makes a difference. We have been trying to stop using the word 'auditee' but it is very sticky. We should think of and refer to them as clients. My point is that we should try to understand our clients so we audit what matters most to them and provide assurance on the topics that matter most to them and the business, not just what audit likes to review or thinks we should review in a vacuum. Empathy goes even a bit deeper, because when we communicate with them, at the beginning of the engagement, during, and at the end, we should empathize with their resource constraints, their information needs, and how best to present the message given their situation. We don't water down or change the message; we just have to be mindful and understanding so it resonates with them."

"Walk a mile in their shoes," chimed Miriam.

"Exactly. That's a good way to think of it. Walk a mile in their shoes. Never lose your independence or objectivity, but seek to understand before you try to be understood," said John.

"Stephen Covey," said Miriam.

"Exactly. Today we are going to cover EI, teamwork, conflict resolution, and negotiation techniques," said John as he stood. "We already started with EI, let's continue there."

--------------------||--------------------

Two days after the training, Tony met with Rachel to go over an audit report she was writing. The process of job enrichment was underway.

"How are things Rachel. Did you have a nice time off?"

"Yes, it was good. We went to Martha's Vineyard. Beautiful place, oh my. Have you been?"

"Yes, it has been a few years, but I still remember it like it was yesterday. Edgartown, Oak Bluffs, and of course Vineyard Haven."

"Yes, great shopping, great restaurants and then you have the beaches. Wow! This was my first time there and I want to retire there. So nice. What did you think about my report?"

"It looks good. The observations were well written and if this doesn't make them take corrective action, I don't know what would. You saw my notes and I mentioned this there; just a couple of minor things."

"Sure. Tell me."

"When you wrote the condition, you mentioned the percentages, but not the actual amounts involved. I like that you quantified things, and that is very helpful. Adding the actual monetary figures would provide a better reference point for the readers because they would see that we're talking about tens of thousands of dollars and many inventory items."

"That makes sense."

"The diagrams."

"What about the diagrams? You asked me to change some colors, but I don't understand why."

"Oh yes. Those were good. Visuals help, and change the colors so you don't use green, yellow, or red because those are typically challenging for people with color blindness. When contrasting information, use red and blue, or yellow and blue. This helps minimize the chances that someone can't fully perceive the differences, but it also avoids the image of red means bad and green means good. Even if the person can't fully see one of the colors, the contrast will help draw the difference. You can also add texture to the bar charts and the pie chart."

"I had not thought about that. Good point. We should tell the rest of the team now that we are including charts in our audit reports."

"Yes. I'll do that. Thanks for the reminder."

"Grammar was good?"

"Yes. It flows well and this being a sensitive topic with a tough client, I believe this will go well."

"OK. I'll change the colors on the chart."

As Rachel left the meeting, Tony was pleased at the way the relationship with her had improved. Conversations were easier, and they were producing better reports faster. It took a while, but interacting with her was much more enjoyable now that they were getting along.

--------------------||--------------------

"So I'm looking out my window and I see students coming back for the fall semester, right?"

"Right."

"And I'm about to lose my mind. There is a constant parade of kids throwing boxes into the trash, which is a no-no. There are recycling dumpsters next to the trash dumpsters. But that's not all. They don't even bother to collapse the boxes!"

"I hate that!"

"Me too. It takes so much less space, right?"

"Of course. So, at one point I see this guy walk up with these monster boxes. He nested a few of them, but there were two stacks, so even with smaller boxes inside bigger ones, the whole thing would take up like half the space in the dumpster. I was about to yell at him from my window to crush them first. Don't they teach people that?"

"They're young. They don't think about those things."

"I guess. Well, I felt better when a young woman and an older man, I'm assuming the father came out and they had stacks of neatly collapsed boxes. Edges lining up. Largest to smallest. Oh my, I almost ran downstairs to congratulate them!"

"You should have."

"I should, I was about to yell at them 'thank you, thank you' but they would have thought I was crazy."

At that moment, John's image came up on the screen and he smiled immediately. "Not sure what I'm walking into, but the first thing I hear is 'they would have thought I was crazy'. Should I ask?"

"Tony was about to go ballistic because college students don't know to collapse moving boxes before throwing them into the dumpster," said Rachel bringing John up-to-date with the topic of the conversation.

"If it were up to Tony, they would place them, according to size, color and thickness, neatly, into the dumpster," joked Brian.

"Yes, see? Brian gets me. Would that hurt?"

"You are meticulous."

"I am. Yes. And proudly so."

"We appreciate you, Tony." On that note, the weekly staff meeting started where they reviewed what they did the previous week. Since they were in training together, they recapped the lessons learned. They then talked about what three things they were focusing on that week, what resources were needed to accomplish those goals, and what blockers were anticipated.

--------------------||--------------------

"Hi Rachel, how are things?" asked John as her camera turned on.

"Good," she replied with a very business-like tone on her voice as if he might be interrupting her.

"I want to congratulate you on your creativity and resourcefulness during the audit. I spoke with the client and they were happy about the way you honed in on the error rate. Catching the trigger point where error rates shift was great so now they can put in a procedure to prevent errors and lower the curve. Nicely done! Everything else is good?"

"Thanks for the feedback. Yes, doing fine."

"I need to ask Carolina a question. I hope it's not too late to ping her."

"No, not at all. We're working together right now."

"What do you mean?"

"Carolina and I sometimes log onto Teams and work together. Not always on the same project, but like we're in the same room, just keeping each other's company."

"Hmm. That's interesting. I like that. Do you do this often?"

"Yes, every week at least twice a week. Working from home can be lonely so this way we keep each other company and if we have a question, we just ask it. Sometimes we chit chat a bit, like we would if we were in cubicles next to each other. Since we're not together physically, we do it virtually."

"I love that idea. I really like it. Anyone else does this in our team?"

"I don't know. Maybe, but I don't know."

"How long have you been doing this?"

"Three months maybe? I don't remember exactly."

"Do you mind if I bring this up in our next staff meeting? No. Do *you* mind telling the rest of the team what you and Carolina have been doing? This is your thing, and I don't want to steal the spotlight."

"Not at all. Thanks. Sure. I can talk about it."

"Thanks for looking after each other. Well done."

"Thank you."

As John hit the Leave button, he thought to himself about this practice and how pleasantly surprised the news made him feel. Team members checking in with and keeping each other company virtually. Nicely done he thought to himself. Nicely done.

--------------------||--------------------

"Hi Carolina. Working a little late?" John asked as Carolina's camera turned on and she came into view.

"Not really. It is only 6 PM. I live alone and I started working late today anyway, so I'm just making up my hours."

"I appreciate that. Like I said, I manage to results, and while I need people available during certain hours, the focus is on outcomes. So, if starting a little late and finishing a little late in the day is what you need to do, go ahead."

"Thanks." While she sounded a bit short in her response, it also felt like she was happy to hear from him.

"So, I'm taking a look at the audit workpapers from the audit that you and Tony worked on. I have a question for you."

"Oh, oh. Am I in trouble?"

"No. Not at all. Quite to the contrary. I noticed that you worked with the client and created an Is Is-Not Diagram, then you also did an Affinity Diagram all online. That was some really good work."

"Gee thanks. I didn't think you would notice."

"Did Tony notice?" he asked without responding to her statement.

"He must have because he signed off on the workpapers."

"I know he signed off. I can see it in the notes to the workpapers, but did he say anything?"

"No. Not really."

"OK. I am," choosing this moment to reply to her statement. "Thanks for all you do. I appreciate your creativity and for going above and beyond."

"You're welcome. I appreciate you telling me."

"Sure thing. That's all for now. I'll let you get back to what you were doing. Have a nice weekend."

"Thanks, you too."

As John clicked the Leave button, he opened the notes file he kept for Tony and made an entry: "Coach Tony to acknowledge work above and beyond what's expected." As he closed Tony's file, he immediately opened another file where he kept general manager notes and made a similar entry, this time; rather than just "Tony," he included Miriam to make sure she was also coached accordingly, and this would become common practice in the unit.

--------------------||--------------------

"English is a crazy language," said Carolina to Tony. "All these words with silent sounds. Why does psychology have a 'p' in front of it if you are not supposed to pronounce it?"

"I don't know. It is at the beginning of the word, so it should be easy to remember that words starting with 'psych' don't pronounce the 'p'. Maybe something about the Greek origin of the word."

"OK, that's fine for the beginning, how about raspberry. The p is in the middle. Explain that to me."

"I can't."

"Hah! Riddle me this Mr. Grammar King. 'Knife'. Did you hear me pronounce the K in king. Why not the k in knife. Or the k in knight."

"Sorry Carolina. English is a little different from Spanish."

"A lot different. Anyway, I just had to get that off my chest. How is my narrative?"

"Phew. You write nicely, which doesn't require you to figure out all those silent sounds."

"Thankfully."

"OK. A couple of things I believe we can improve upon on the narrative. You write beautifully, but for some things you can use bullets that would allow you to skip the need to write long sentences and transitions. By the way, if the order matters, use numbered and outline bullets rather than just a little dot or square, or whatever bullet you want to use. It helps the reader track things better."

"That makes sense."

"You explained several relationships and their amounts, but I think you could have created a graph for some of those. You would have to write a lot less and it might convey your message better."

"That should work."

"Didn't you take a lot of pictures during the visit?"

"I did. I included several in the narratives."

"Yes, I see a few, but then you spent a lot of time describing what you saw, and the pictures are in the shared folder but not in the narrative, referenced or even mentioned. I think that would help a lot to explain what you saw. All of that is evidence and helpful for the reader to appreciate all you saw and did."

"OK, I will."

"How much more testing do you have to do? The program says it isn't much."

"That's right. I'm almost done. Another couple of days and we should be able to wrap up the testing before the exit meeting Thursday afternoon."

"Good. Do you need anything else from me now?"

"I don't know. See what I did there?"

"I get it, now and know; silent k. You are good!"

"Tony, you are good with grammar. That's why I mess with you about these things."

"Thanks!"

"You are welcome. Bye!"

"Bye."

--------------------||--------------------

12 Remove Barriers to Action

John walked out into his garden and sat comfortably in his Adirondack chair. It was a warm summer afternoon, and he was taking a break surrounded by trees, flowers, and a few singing birds. The gentle breeze was relaxing, which is exactly what he was looking for. Lemonade on the side table, feet up on the footrest, and dog by his side. He called his friend.

"Hi Frank. How is the summer treating you?"

"Very good. We're on Florida's West coast. It is very hot, and the beaches are amazing. The sand is like white powder. Have you seen it? I'm in a café on St. Armands Circle in Sarasota. Siesta Key on one side, and Longboat Key down the road the other way. Sunsets have been spectacular. Did I say how amazing the sand is? Anyway, right now I'm sitting waiting for the food to arrive in a cool room and enjoying a refreshing drink. Wish you were here."

"Sounds amazing," he said wondering if he would trade his quiet, nature-filled backyard for the constant activity of one of the most popular Florida West Coast locations. Then again, the thought of the beach was quite appealing.

"It is amazing. What's on your mind?"

"Two things I could use your opinion on. As you know I've been working on promoting change here and so far, it is going well. But I have a staff member who has been slow to change. Making progress, but it has been a long process. Some of it is probably due to deeply set habits, but it is tiring trying to get this person on board with the rest of the team."

"That is a common issue, John. There are reasons people object to change."

"For example?"

"Fear of failure comes to mind. The individuals have done well doing what they've been doing, and they may be afraid of the unknown or of failing at whatever 'new' means."

"I can see that."

"Here's another one. How about loss of power or status. They may have reached a place where they've earned, let's call it, a place of privilege, or comfort. They have been rewarded. Now change will force them to a place where they may not have the same power or status. Sometimes because of different access to information or resources. They may be moved down the chain of command during a reorg, perhaps."

"I can see that too."

"Mistrust is a big one. When there hasn't been enough communication, the person may feel that what they are being told is not true and things will be much more different, or simply different in a bad way."

DOI: 10.1201/9781003322870-14

"I believe I've done a good job presenting the shortcoming of our current practices and painting a positive outlook for the new state in honest terms."

"That's good. I'm not saying you're doing any of these things, or that your staff members fall into any of these categories. They are examples, or possibilities."

"I understand. How about habit or inertia?"

"Yes, that's a big one. People being too accustomed to the way things have always been. This can be true for those who have been in the company for a long time, in their current job for a long time, or in their line of work for a long time."

"Interesting point there, Frank. The person I have in mind meets all three of those as the one with the longest tenure and most experience."

"OK. That could explain it. There is another one I haven't … yes, that's mine… no, over there, please. Excuse me, before you go, could you bring some mayonnaise… and ketchup. Yes, and water for everyone on the table please. Thanks" were the last things John heard as Frank was undoubtedly talking to someone else who had just arrived at their table.

"Sounds like your food just arrived."

"Yes, it looks good, and it smells good. The portions are going to do a job on my waistline, but I'll walk it off later. No counting calories when you're on vacation."

"You're always on vacation Frank. You're retired!"

"Ha, my point" said Frank with a loud laugh. "I don't count calories. I focus on balanced meals, lots of exercise, and staying hydrated."

"I'll leave you to it Frank. Enjoy your lunch."

"Thanks. Be well John."

"Thanks. Bye."

--------------------||--------------------

As John went for a walk after dinner later that day thinking about the nice weather, he was enjoying he thought to himself, "at least it is not as hot and humid as it is in Florida. I feel bad for Frank." A few moments later, he thought further about it. "Sour grapes, that's what that was. Feel bad for Frank! Ha! He's enjoying himself just fine." As he continued walking in the woods, he kept thinking about all the reasons Frank gave for why people object to change and he couldn't pin any of them on Tony. "I wonder what is making him so reluctant to embrace the change. As my most senior staff person, he is poised to benefit most from all of this," he thought.

Then again, Frank said at the end of the call there was another reason, but he didn't get to it because the food arrived. What might it have been?

Apathy? I don't think so. Tony is engaged otherwise, just not to change. He has the most experience, just differently. As he thought about this, he remembered how he was the inventory expert early in his own career. He was the go-to person. He liked the recognition and comfort of knowing that he mastered that aspect of the work. Later, when he was getting bored, his manager suggested he review other aspects of the organization. He was excited but also apprehensive. It took a lot of will to move onto other topics because he was afraid of failure.

Then it hit him. Beyond the fear of failure, which Frank mentioned, how about the change threatening Tony's expertise?

That's it! Change threatens Tony's expertise. He knows the most about the current methodology and by changing things significantly, he may fear these changes will threaten his expertise.

--------------------||--------------------

The next morning, John contacted Tony.

"Hi Tony. How are you today?"

"I'm fine. The audit is coming along well and we're on track to meet all our deadlines."

"That's good. I'm glad to hear that we're on track. I wanted to meet with you to discuss the changes we're making in our department and get your reaction. You know, your impression about things. So, how do you see these changes?"

After a moment to gather his thoughts, Tony replied.

"Well, the changes make sense, and we were having problems with auditees, so I'm glad you're correcting that. We need to regain our credibility and we need to be listened to."

"Yes, we needed to rebuild bridges with our clients. Remember we're trying to get away from calling them auditees."

"That's right. Clients. Anyway, so all of these changes seem to be coming too fast. Agile Auditing, changes to the way we write reports, how we interact with our clients, our methodology. It's too much!" he said sounding worried.

"I know it is a lot, and you have every right to feel overwhelmed. We are doing a lot. These changes are necessary and will take us to a really good place. Do you agree with that?" asked John trying to get Tony engaged and participating in the conversation rather than merely listening to a lecture from his manager. Getting others to agree early on had also been effective many times in the past, so he tried that.

"Yes."

"We have to move quickly because the company needs it, the audit committee wants it, and our clients deserve it. They have not been getting what audit can offer for a while. Would you agree with that?" John asked again.

"Yes."

"I believe you are a very knowledgeable, talented, and important member of our team," John said personalizing the conversation.

"Thanks," said Tony feeling a bit flattered.

"You are our most experienced auditor. You have deep institutional knowledge. Virtually everyone in the company knows you. You are one of my key ambassadors at InSports," said John highlighting key aspects of Tony's qualities further.

"I appreciate it," he replied.

"Sure. You're welcome. Now, given all that wealth of talent and potential, one thing that is concerning me a bit is that I don't see my top manager leading the rest of the team and championing some of these initiatives. Is there anything about these initiatives that worry you?" he asked now wanting to hear what was holding Tony back.

"Too many changes, too fast," he said almost apologetically after his boss made such positive remarks about him.

"Do you agree that we are all going to be better off in the end?" repeating a previously asked question again.

"Yes, definitely," Tony heard himself agreeing again.

"Do you see your role as the same, better or worse as we implement these changes?"

"I don't know," said Tony winking extensively as he frowned his eyebrows, showing in his body language that John had uncovered an important feeling. As he lowered his voice and shrugged his shoulders, he said, "maybe all of my expertise won't matter as much, especially after auditees, I mean, clients, start driving so much of the audit plan and audit programs. So many of the tools you are asking us to use. The new writing approach. The data analytics and IT focus. I started in audit when none of these things were the norm, you know?"

"I know. They weren't the norm when I started either, but I learned them, practiced them, and now show others how to use them," said John sharing his personal experience. "I learned and you can too. Your expertise is an important building block for what we want to build here."

"Does my knowledge matter with all the new things replacing our old approach?"

"Absolutely. Some things are essential for success. I'll give you an example. Knowing the history about many of our relationships at InSports, that way we know how to re-create those relationships. Your knowledge about our computer systems and processes; you just need to learn to change the audit approach, but you know the systems, processes, and the people working there." John took a pause to think about another example, but before he could say it, Tony asked another question.

"If all of these things are documented in flowcharts, narratives, SIPOC diagrams and everything else, what will I be doing?"

"You can lead the team, so we know more about the company, learn how to audit what matters most, present our observations faster and better, and grow with the company. Every day will be different given the changing risk environment and company expansion plans. Knowing where we came from is important so we don't go backwards. Want to lead our forward movement, Tony? You could continue to be that respected presence who was here when we were X, and now when we are Y and, in the future, when we become Z. Your expertise would evolve, grow, and could lead the growing department. Are you in?"

Tony bit his lips. Smiled and said while nodding in agreement. "Yes. I'm in."

John saw a little sparkle in Tony's eyes, then he said. "Good. Tony, you're one of my two lieutenants. I need you like I need Miriam and the rest of the team. I'm glad you're in. If you ever have concerns about what we're doing, or how, reach out and let's talk about it. We're building something great and you're part of it. OK?"

"OK."

"Take care."

"Yes. Bye."

As John said, "bye," he clicked the Leave button and felt like he and Tony just had a breakthrough moment.

--------------------||--------------------

13 Determining Future Resource Needs

"Hi Frank, how are you today?"

"Good. Enjoying the time off."

"Time off? You're retired!"

"Ever heard of Abe Lemons?"

"No, who is that?"

He was a college basketball coach from Oklahoma and Texas. He said, and with that he started laughing before he even started telling the quote, "the trouble with retirement," and he had to catch his breath because he was laughing so hard "is that you never get a day off." "Get it, John?"

"I get it, Frank. You like to rub this retirement thing in my face don't you."

"Of course, I do. I want you to come join me on the golf course, play some tennis, eat lunch by the water. But after you get your job done. You are on a very important mission, so don't mind me. Do what you need to do, turn that ship around, but remember, when you're ready to leave the northern cold and retire, I'll introduce you to my friends down here. In fact, we're having lunch right now by the pool."

"I'll keep it in mind."

"Good. So, what's on your mind this fine Wednesday?" asked Frank.

Before John could answer, he heard other people talking and laughing nearby. Probably his friends, thought John. "Well, the last time we spoke you didn't get to share your last thought. As I thought about other reasons why my most experienced person has been reluctant to embrace change and is a late adopter"

"Wait a minute. Sorry. Your most experienced person? Why didn't you say that at the beginning. People like that are often reluctant to embrace change because change threatens their expertise."

"Exactly. That's exactly what I thought!"

"Good. We agree then."

"Yes. So, I'm working on turning him around and otherwise, we're on track moving at a good speed, but I can't do much more with this group."

"What do you need?" asked Frank followed by him saying, "no thank you, that's Ok, thanks."

"I need more resources. Money and people."

"Of course. Once you've maxed out on the resources you have and gotten as much efficiency as you can from them, the only way to do more is to increase resources. Well, you can start asking for more resources, but one of two things will happen. One, they go ahead and give them to you because you've convinced them that you're the real deal. Two, they say 'no' because they have not been convinced yet. Do you fall into scenario one or two?"

As John was thinking about the question, he suddenly heard Frank start coughing.

 DOI: 10.1201/9781003322870-15

"Frank, are you OK?"

In between coughs he said, "yes, I'm… OK… should remember to"… cough… "chew before" …. cough… "trying to swallow…steak tip…" and John heard at least two more voices also asking Frank if he was OK.

"Yes, I'm Ok, but I should probably go. I'm OK, John. Good food will either nourish or kill you," he said again laughing at his own joke.

John shook his head in amazement. His friend was obviously having a good time, and even when he was choking, he still found humor to carry him through.

--------------------||--------------------

That evening, while cooking dinner, John kept pondering Frank's question, which was also a statement of sorts about getting additional resources. "One, they go ahead and give them to you because you've convinced them that you're the real deal. Two, they say 'no' because they have yet to be convinced."

"What does the audit committee think about our progress so far? Scenario one or two?"

--------------------||--------------------

As the meeting with his team started, John said, "variety is the spice of life," then paused to let the words sink in.

"William Cowper. The Task."

"Thanks Miriam, I love the proverb. I never knew the source. Now we know. On that note, let's mix up the meeting a bit. We usually start with the agenda that's in the Teams invitation. As you know, that is a standard agenda and we have been covering that consistently for months, and that's good. Today, however, I would like to turn the process upside down, instead of me leading the meeting throughout, following the agenda, and finishing with 'Other', let's begin with 'Other' and you tell me what You would like to talk about."

This reversal in the standard procedure surprised everyone because they weren't expecting it, but after a few seconds Rachel embraced the offer and started.

"We have been using Excel for most of our data analytics work, and it has served us well, but there are other tools that we may want to consider using that are more powerful."

"Like?" asked John.

"There's ACL, which later became Galvanized and now is Diligent. We used it for many years at other companies where I worked, and we could use that here too. It is a very powerful DA tool," she replied.

"Ok. Is that the best tool for our data analytics needs?" asked John.

"It is an improvement!" she said enthusiastically.

"I understand, but that doesn't quite answer my question. Would it meet our needs, or should we consider others?" he explained.

"Well, there's PowerBI," for example, said Miriam.

"In general, would PowerBI be better or worse than ACL/Diligent?" asked John.

"Probably better because around InSports several groups use PowerBI. I know that Internal Consulting, Quality Assurance and even EHS uses PowerBI," said Brian.

"I know the financial reporting group also uses it," shared Miriam.

"Good. That is something to consider then," said John.

"What about Tableau?" asked Carolina.

"Also a good tool to consider. It would help us improve our presentations to management tremendously," said Rachel.

"Anyone else within the company has it so we can avoid bringing in something totally new and lower our overall costs?" asked John.

"Yes, Marketing and the R&D group use Tableau. I used it and it would be great to have that here in our toolbox," said Rachel again.

"Should there be others on our list of candidates?" asked John noticing how engaged the group had become on this topic and the entire upside-down-meeting agenda approach he launched.

"There's Symsure and KNIME," said Brian.

"This is quite interesting. Let's do this," said John. "Miriam, why don't you take the lead on this and enquire about costs. We want to get the tools that would work best in our corporate ecosystem and so far, we're starting this off well if others in the company are already using them. It should make it easier with licenses and all. Can you get back to us at our staff meeting in two weeks, I believe that's a good amount of time to do some research on this, and tell us what you found? I think this is a good idea, Rachel. We'll look into this as part of our budget and planning for next year. Ok?"

"Thanks," said Rachel.

"What else?" asked John, encouraging more conversation from his team.

"Well, I was wondering if there is a way to do some volunteer work as a team during Volunteer Day," asked Rachel.

"When it that again?" said John asking for clarification.

"That's in September, right?" said Miriam.

"Yes, and we only have two weeks to get organized," commented Rachel.

"OK. That should build team spirit and get us doing something good together. Also, it would give us some visibility. Sounds like a win-win-win to me. Any specific thoughts on that?" asked John.

"Yes, there are several locations where we can get together and vote on a volunteer activity to work on," said Rachel.

"And what about those working alone or too far from an office?" asked Carolina.

"Good questions," said John suddenly realizing he should have thought about that sooner since some staff members had unusual circumstances.

"Well, maybe they can do something in their local community, like help at a library, join a group cleaning a beach or trails, or something like that," said Rachel. "Would you be able to do that Carolina? The Volunteer Day guidelines say you can do it locally. They also said they would appreciate you sharing pictures of what you are doing to build team spirit and to get support."

"That's true. She can do that. How about something people can do online?" asked Brian.

"Online?"

"Yes, don't take me wrong. I'm all for outdoor activities or going somewhere indoors, like painting the inside of a school, and that's fine. But maybe we should think of some volunteer activities people can do from home if they are concerned about health issues, can't or don't want to travel anywhere, even in their nearby communities. For example, some auditors are multi-lingual, they could do translation. Or visiting a classroom virtually to talk about careers," he explained.

"Exactly. Maybe we should think of a couple more ideas and provide a list to the rest of the team. This is good," said John acknowledging Brian's idea.

"Who wants to take ownership of our Volunteer Day participation and collect ideas?" asked John.

"I will," said Rachel.

"Thanks. This is great. Anything else?" asked John.

After a few seconds with no one commenting, John spoke again.

"Very good. Let's go back to our agenda. We'll continue working from the bottom up," and with that John addressed the agenda items and along the way introducing his team to another example of innovative thinking and staff engagement.

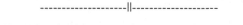

John sat at his desk with a freshly brewed cup of coffee thinking about his department. He was very pensive this morning as he took great pleasure in the aroma, the colorful garden outside his window, and the bright sunshine. He thought about what they were doing in internal audit and how things had improved. He basked in the knowledge of much improvement, and as he enumerated some of those accomplishments, he thought about the importance of getting validation from an external party.

"I need someone to confirm that we're making progress. My word is not enough. I need an external validation to get the resources we need and solidify our credibility. One, they go ahead and give us the resources we need because they're convinced that we are the real deal. Two, they say 'no' because they have yet to be convinced. Unfortunately, or fortunately, an external expert's word carries a lot of weight."

As he was creating a list of consultants, he knew that did this type of work, he considered the names of individual contractors and small audit shops. Large providers would cost too much. "We need an opinion on what we're doing and hopefully some mention of the progress we have made this year."

Not wanting to waste time, he wrote a list of work requirements and sent notices to half a dozen service providers requesting proposals indicating he would like the work done before Thanksgiving.

14 Setback and Generating Short-Term Wins

"John, we have a problem."

"What's the problem. What's going on?"

"We have a whistleblower alleging there is a ring operating in Buenos Aires that is stealing our equipment. The whistleblower doesn't even work for InSports, it's a gym owner! He claims he was solicited for some items, so he called our local customer service line. That's the only number he could find on our website and they relayed it to the local controller, who then contacted me. See what you can find out."

"I will."

"John."

"Yes?"

"I'm not happy. In fact, this is quite disappointing. You've been to Argentina twice and although you found problems, you seem to have missed a big one here. We can't keep drip-drip-dripping problems out of that place. We have staff and external auditors supposedly looking at inventory and now this. I would hate to add you to the list of people I trusted and failed to find a problem that was staring us in the face. We've been losing merchandise for months and no one can tell me where it is. Find out what is happening."

As John hung up the phone, he was wondering how many issues would originate in that location and if this was also connected to what Randy told him. He had looked into quality-related issues from the perspective of returns and found process issues that resulted in wrong shipments and excessive returns. A mess, as the local staff described it. Along the way, he had found the salespeople stealing samples and later the returns and refurbishment fraud. Now this. His reputation was on the line, and even though internal audit is not supposed to be the ones answering when there is fraud, it often turns that way.

He would call on Brian to do some work for him on this one. "I wish I had dug even deeper into this."

--------------------||--------------------

"Brian, I need you to do me a big favor. Contact Pablo in Buenos Aires and ask him for sales and inventory data. We decided during our earlier trip not to look at inventory because previous internal audit teams had done some reviews of inventory totals and found nothing, and external auditors looked at that quarterly too. We may have missed something. Check the aging of inventory, write-offs, and the reasons for it. Also ask for info on the complaints system; a list of allegations, dates, descriptions and the disposition on those. By the way, do you remember if the Returns and Refurbishment area is co-located with the general inventory, or separate?"

DOI: 10.1201/9781003322870-16

"I'll ask for the data right away. In terms of Returns and Refurbishment, that is a totally separate area, in fact it is a separate building."

"That's what I thought so we have the same understanding."

--------------------||--------------------

"Hi John."

"Hi Brian. So, what did you find out?"

"You were correct. I looked through the complaints system and found what you suspected."

"How bad is it?"

"Pretty bad. This reminds me of the conversation we had in San Francisco a few months ago. It has all come full circle."

"San Francisco? Oh yes, the access and application controls review. I remember. What do you have for me?"

"Excessive access rights into the complaints system, so some people can change the priority, or even remove complaints. Found several of those from the system audit trail."

"Tell me more."

"Four employees in the warehouse, who should not have had access to this module, removed complaints about shipments with fewer items than stated."

"These are customer complaints, right? Outbound shipments to customers?"

"Yes."

"How big is the problem?"

"The missing merchandise and edits started about fifteen months ago, lots of stuff but mostly smaller equipment like iPads, portable elliptical trainers, medicine balls, even climbing ropes, and rock-climbing gear. Even some freestanding kick-boxing punching bags."

"All new stuff?"

"No. Maybe two thirds, one third. Two thirds of it was new; things we bought and were supposed to send to gyms, hospitals, hotels and so on. The remainder were returns that were supposed to be refurbished and were subsequently sold, or so the record stated. But the items apparently didn't make it to the customer, hence the complaint, refund, or re-shipment."

"I would imagine it is hard for someone buying ten of something to not notice they're missing a few."

"I thought about that, so I looked at the reason codes, and it turns out they stated items, sometimes entire shipments, were damaged, lost, or stolen in transit. Argentina isn't all that dangerous, is it?"

"Well, there are crime-related issues there. Highway robbery affecting commercial vehicles happens sometimes and they rob trucks. They are often referred to as piratas del asfalto, or asphalt pirates."

"Oh, I didn't know."

"We still have to find out if the losses were from highway thieves, innocent mistakes, or employee fraud. "Thanks for the work, Brian. Really appreciate it. I'll need you to give me the details; SKUs, descriptions, quantities, key dates like when bought, entered into stock, sold, shipped, lost or whatever, and so on. We'll meet so you can tell me all you have in the data set so we can build a story about this issue."

"You got it."

As Brian left the Teams meeting, John sighed; "Maybe Randy was right."

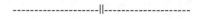

John and Brian arrived in Buenos Aires the following Monday morning and went straight to work. The last three days Brian spent doing analysis of the sales and inventory data with John's guidance. They found popular items with strong sales being written off. They found some popular items also sitting in the warehouse for long periods of time, and instead of selling those, they bought more leaving the old items in stock ignoring FIFO rules. Inventory always reconciled. Strange.

As John, Brian, Pablo, Eduardo and Carlos, the warehouse manager, toured the facility, John asked Carlos where they stored the medicine balls and punching bags. He thought they would be close to each other and they were, so he asked to go there. Upon arrival in that location, John asked for some boxes to be opened and Carlos reached for a box on the front row.

"No. Por favor abra una caja atrás," he said asking Carlos to open a box in the back. Carlos was surprised and was about to protest, but decided not to and proceeded to open a box from the back row as requested. The box was empty. The gasps from everyone present were audible, but John didn't seem all that surprised, as if he was expecting that result.

He asked Carlos, "Abra cuatro cajas más, por favor. De las de atrás," asking for another four boxes from the rear to be opened. Same result; all empty.

Even though there were five people present, he asked Brian to take pictures of the empty boxes and asked to be taken to where the climbing equipment was located. Upon arrival he asked for several boxes, in the rear and distant corners, to be opened. They found empty boxes where rope, harnesses, camming, shoes, and helmets should have been.

They moved to the portable elliptical trainers. Same result.

They looked at the iPads. There were no empty boxes, but the contents were not what they expected; the iPads had been replaced with cheap books of similar weight.

By now Carlos was sweating profusely, stammering, and his walking had become laborious. John asked him if he had anything to say about the missing items and he promptly confessed. Later, as he spoke at length about the scheme; he implicated three colleagues in Eduardo's and Pablo's presence.

John was in a meeting with the executive team. They were reviewing the status of company initiatives, some key challenges and obstacles they were working on, and getting some initial ideas out as they began planning for next year. Each C-level executive had ten minutes on the agenda. When it was John's turn, he said.

"Hello everyone. Internal Audit is introducing a new methodology that has proven quite successful for years at many organizations around the world."

Participants were busy people, and during the meeting it was evident they were multitasking. Eyes darting back and forth across the screen; a clear sign there were multiple screens open simultaneously. Some looked away and to the sides; possibly monitoring multiple computer screens. Others were looking down while their shoulders and hands made subtly movements, all indicative of texting. They weren't indifferent, just distracted.

John explained the origins of the name in IT DevOps. He compared and contrasted Agile Auditing with Traditional Auditing and explained the benefits of Agile Auditing.

"…and we issue shorter reports every two to three weeks, so you know what the results are of the work sooner. We are talking only a few pages, to the point, what are the results and what the team recommends. In fact, we would like to move beyond recommendations and have the team work on an action plan, so it is clear what is going to be done, by whom and when for each of those items so the report is an action plan that everyone agrees on."

That got everyone's attention.

John was feeling good as things were going smoothly until he started explaining roles and responsibilities. Nihal's body language was the most telling of them all as the reversal became evident. He blurted out.

"It sounds like those being audited are effectively part of the audit team. We would be helping the auditors audit us!" he said.

"That's fairly accurate," replied John, "the reason for that is," he started to say when he was interrupted.

"Why would we want to help audit ourselves?" Nihal asked again.

"That's a very good question and one people ask often about this methodology," John began as he explained the benefits of better collaboration, auditing what both agree is most important to the organization, an approach that is flexible, keeps communication channels open, and allows adjustment to the program as the entire team proceeded together.

Nihal moved his body away from the camera as he rested once again on the back of his chair and clasped his hands under his chin in attention. His stance had softened in reaction to the answer and his eyebrows were separating ever so slightly. He rubbed his chin signaling that he was processing the answer and perhaps telling himself that this sounded like a better approach if you are being audited.

"Also, recall what I said earlier," John continued taking advantage of the attention the question generated, "we close review segments from each sprint so we, not just audit, issue a short report or memo every two to three weeks. You are part of the process as we plan, execute, and close out each segment. No more waiting months for a report."

"We don't have to wait nine months for an outdated report that covers irrelevant topics? Shucks! I love waiting for those and now you ruined it for me," he said jokingly.

He's back on board, thought John.

"Sorry I ruined it for you!" John joked back.

Agile Auditing was now officially accepted by management.

--------------------||--------------------

Another rainy morning in London.

John arrived on the red-eye flight from New York. Rather than go home, he flew directly to London after the executive meetings the day before. He was tired. Sometimes he was able to sleep on overnight flights. Sometimes he could not. Last night's flight was one of those where he could not.

First, he was rattled by getting late to the airport. Traffic getting to JFK was particularly bad because it was raining. Then, getting through the security protocols had taken longer in part due to the large crowds, but also because it seemed everyone in line in front of him forgot they had forbidden items in their carryon: The woman with the oversized shampoo bottle – who needs to carry that much shampoo? Get a smaller one or buy shampoo when you arrive! They sell shampoo worldwide! The ever-so-thirsty guy with the jug of water – How could you not remember you have a gallon of water in the bag? The parents with the three children and their apple sauce, freeze packs, and juice boxes – OK, so he cut them some slack, but the three kids thought they were at a park and the security checkpoints were a jungle gym; they moved, individually, in every direction except straightforward.

He flew Economy class. He preferred window seats so he could lean to the side, keep his earphones in, eyes covered, and shut out the rest of the passengers. Instead, he was in the aisle. And the whole flight was one of being bumped on his left by passersby and the obviously new flight attendants with the cart that veered apparently straight to him every time they came around. From the right, he got encroached by a greedy elbow and tapped a hundred times by his unknown companion who kept getting up. In front, the man with the hot dog size fingers kept stretching his arms and hands over his head and hitting the TV monitor. And behind, he got kicked so many times he eventually turned around to see if the child's parents could save him, only to come face-to-face with the highly active children from the security line sitting next to their distraught parents who were at their wits ends.

Sunday mornings are quiet in Central London. After such a tiring flight, he knew his luck had turned for the better when the hotel staff surprised him with the news that his room was ready at 8:15 AM rather than the customary 3:00 PM, or 15:00 as Europeans refer to it.

He unpacked, grabbed his hat, his coat, and headed downstairs to the hotel lobby. He was going for a walk because "keep moving and looking for sunlight" was his mantra whenever he traveled across multiple time zones and needed to acclimate to the new environs. A well-placed nap would have been good, but he was stubborn in his belief that "If I nap now I may never shake off the jet lag"; so he stepped outside into a cold and drizzly day.

Soon he was in Hyde Park where only a few people were brave enough to get up that early in such weather. It was the weekend after all, and most people would be sleeping in, so he meandered through the many paths for a while and watched a few joggers and dog walkers enjoy the early morning quiet like he was. As he headed South, he arrived at Wellington Arch and thought how impressive the monument looked amid the overall park and other relics, yet its position in the middle of a large traffic island with cars driving on the left side of the road required extra care not to step into oncoming traffic. "At least they built pedestrian access to it," so he walked over hoping to see the enclosed exhibit and climb up to view the surrounding area only to find a sign informing him he had arrived too early.

He turned around trying to decide if he wanted to reverse direction and head toward Knightsbridge and Sloan Street; go Southeast on Grosvenor Place toward Victoria, or go Northeast on Piccadilly. He chose to go East toward Constitution Hill so he could see Buckingham Palace. After a few minutes enjoying the Victoria Memorial and the palace, and taking the requisite pictures, he thought to himself he had made a good decision walking this way because on the other side of Buckingham Palace is St. James's Park and the lagoon where he could sit, stretch, relax, enjoy the views while the crowds grew, and people watch for a while. With this in mind, he walked South and around the westernmost part of the lagoon and went to the Playground Kiosk where he sat to enjoy some food.

It is always interesting watching parents and their children, and what seemed like a higher number of families together than he often saw in the United States. "Europeans and their family time," he thought while shaking his head in agreement with his own pronouncement. "A better work-life balance during the week and time to relax with your family on weekends. They may be onto something around here," he said to himself as he thought about what he would like his own family life to be like once he found someone to settle down with. "Someday," he reassured himself.

As the day advanced, he decided to head back to his hotel by walking through Green Park. By now the crowds had gathered, the clouds had mostly cleared ushering in a sunny and warm day. Rather than take the direct route on Park Lane, he chose to meander through the side streets and the residential area, and after a while he stumbled upon Grosvenor Square, where he spent a few moments at the September 11 Memorial Garden. He walked North on Duke Street and turned left onto Oxford Street as he headed back to his hotel near Marble Arch.

--------------------||--------------------

"Hey John, how are you?"

"I'm well. I meant to contact you for our monthly coffee chat, but I've been on the road the last couple of weeks."

"I understand. I've been very busy myself. Listen, it's Sunday, I'm home reading reports and prepping for a long and busy week, but I just want to let you know that I just finished reading your team's audit report. Tony, Rachel, and Carolina were the auditors on this one."

"Yes, that right. Everything OK?"

"Yes. I haven't had a need to say this in a while, and you know that when you started things were a bit shaky with internal audit, so I want to let you know that I appreciate all you have done with the team and the quality reports I've been getting lately. This one has some good findings and useful recommendations, so kudos to you."

"Thanks. Kudos to the team. They have stepped up."

"Yes, they have. I'll call a few people this week to make sure they get moving on these observations, but just wanted to let you know. Anyway, you said you've been on the road. Where are you?"

"I'm in London this week."

"Good. Stay dry and try to get to the theater if you can. You might as well, you're a tourist and should reward yourself too."

"I will. Thanks Ken."
"Bye."

--------------------||--------------------

Hi John,

I hope you are well, and your change initiatives are progressing as planned.

I just want to let you know that after several months the search is over. Jennifer Collins will be joining the AC this month. She brings extensive manufacturing and public accounting experience to the team, and we look forward to you meeting her.

These are great news, and we hope you have as productive a relationship with her as you do with Sanjay and me. You will meet her at our next AC meeting later this month.

Her CV is attached for your perusal.

Best regards,
Jim.

"Interesting. Manufacturing and public accounting," said John to himself as he opened the file attached. He noticed she had over 20 years of experience in manufacturing accounting, some of it in companies engaged in construction parts and equipment, and consumer goods. All of them B2B goods; nothing in B2C. She worked in public accounting for five years making it to manager, which was typical and had a CPA, but no internal audit experience or certifications.

John looked through the department's shared folders and couldn't find any information on board member onboarding packages. "I don't believe there is one," he thought to himself.

--------------------||--------------------

"Right now, the whistleblowing hotline is run by the HR department. While a lot of organizations have someone internal handling it, we don't believe that's the best approach," said John kicking off the meeting.

Tony sat to his right, and both Terry and Kathleen sat across the table looking a bit worried at the moment. The whistleblowing hotline had been under the oversight of the HR department for years and it was viewed as an HR hotline. Employees used it to complain about all sort of things; people who parked poorly and took two parking spaces for their precious vehicle, burnt or cold coffee in the breakroom, expired food in the refrigerator, and office space too cold for comfort or too noisy because a coworker used their computer's speakers rather than headphones or talked loudly on the phone. A recent call had caused both laughter and indignation when someone complained that the kitchen sink was not being cleaned often enough while dirty dishes and food scraps languished for days in plain view.

John listened attentively and offered a solution.

"Increasingly organizations are outsourcing the whistleblowing hotline so there is 24/7 coverage by a multilingual staff. But to your point about the random and let's say, inappropriate calls, it is both good and bad that they are calling. Good, because they know about the hotline, know how to reach it and are communicating issues they are concerned about. Not so good because it sounds like it is being misused. That's not the intended purpose of a whistleblowing hotline. Perhaps we should also think about an awareness campaign, explain what this is for, and direct employees to other avenues for housekeeping topics."

"Yes, that would help," agreed Kathleen. "How about the cost. We set this up internally years ago because we thought it would be best to have it handled internally and would cost less. Employees would know we cared and would trust us by calling us and telling us if there were issues their managers weren't addressing like they should."

"Yes, there is a cost," replied John. "Done internally is viewed as being free; just someone's job to monitor and respond to calls, but nothing is really free. Right now Terry is handling these calls and it sounds like it is a distraction from other more serious issues, or things managers in the field should be handling. From what I've been told we're not really getting ethics-related questions or allegations on this line, so that makes you wonder a bit."

"Don't we call it The Employee Hotline?" asked Tony getting into the conversation.

"Yes, that's the name we gave it. We didn't want to say 'ethics', 'fraud' or 'whistleblowing' because we thought it would prejudice employees or make it appear like we expected misconduct," Kathleen explained the rationale used when deploying the hotline.

"I agree those words may be a bit sensitive, and we can come up with a better name for it, but in general, it looks like it is being misunderstood and misused. Maybe an awareness campaign would help," suggested John.

"Agree," said Terry, who was frustrated by the way the hotline had evolved and how much time it was taking to handle what were often frivolous issues.

"Do calls go into an answering machine after hours?" asked John.

"Yes, they do. After 5 PM Eastern," answered Terry.

"I'm assuming no weekend or holiday coverage, so any calls go to voicemail too," John said, now correcting himself after realizing that "answering machine" is a relatively antiquated term.

"That's right. No weekends and no official company holidays either," explained Kathleen.

"What about our foreign locations?"

"No foreign locations except Canada, this service is for the US and Canada only," said Terry.

"Mexico?"

"Kind of. Silvia speaks Spanish, so at times we have asked her to translate calls for us, but that is hit or miss if she is in the office, if she is available, if the person wants to wait on the phone and so on. We received a few calls over the last four months or so and the audio quality was terrible so she only got bits and pieces, but we couldn't figure it out and since the person didn't leave contact information, we couldn't do anything," explained Terry describing a common problem with non-English speakers.

"It looks like we have some limitations with the current arrangement and an opportunity at the same time. How about we work together to do some research on this and get some quotes. Let's look for live 24/7 coverage, no voicemail, multi-lingual support, local free phone numbers, and see if we can enhance the features of the hotline with a portal for people to submit concerns; like a website they can go to. It would free some of your resources and help us focus on more significant issues."

"This portal," asked Kathleen seeking details about this feature. "How does it typically work?"

"In general, it is a website where the individual provides details by typing the information in. The system uses prompts to encourage and remind people, but one of the most valuable features is the assignment of a case number and login functionality so if later we are doing an investigation and run into issues, like we can't find supporting documentation because it has been lost or destroyed, we can post a request for the person to help us if they can, and submit it through this platform," explained John.

"That's really interesting," said Terry.

"And extremely useful during an investigation that has run against a wall."

"Can we leave status updates there too?" inquired Kathleen. "I ask because we recently had an issue where someone alerted us to a problem and then escalated it to Ron, telling him that the people working here didn't care about the company, didn't care about employees, we were all corrupt, and our values statement were a sham. It was a mess; all because we didn't implement a fix visibly enough and the person thought we ignored the problem," explained Kathleen shaking her head as she spoke making it clear to everyone that the situation escalated into an unfortunate and ugly scene due to a misunderstanding.

"Yes, that is a good point you raise. Yes, we would not leave too many details due to privacy and security reasons, but we can provide some status indicators. There have been cases where the person escalates their grievance outside the organization to regulators or the media, then the concern or complaint that could have been addressed internally tuns into a crisis that must be addressed with external parties too. I agree; the portal can help with that too."

"So, in terms of reporting, I would imagine they would provide status reports too."

"Yes, that is usually included and good for us to monitor trends and cycle times," replied John.

"We would need to develop an awareness campaign too to educate employees," said Terry.

"And managers. They need to understand their role in this too. How to counsel their staff, who to contact given different scenarios, how to make referrals to HR or the hotline, and so on."

"Very good. Looks like we have a fairly good understanding of what we need. I'm going to suggest we also conduct a survey to get a better perspective on the views of employees, baseline things for us before we build something new, then conduct surveys periodically after that. Everyone agrees?" asked John.

"Yes, sounds reasonable to me," agreed Kathleen.

"Me too," seconded Terry.

"We'll treat this as a consulting engagement, or a special project for internal audit. I'll have someone be our point person and we'll need to build a team with a representative from HR, explained John. "We will also use an agile approach, which everyone is familiar with by now so you will get frequent updates and official communications at least every three weeks. I'm excited about this."

"Thanks John. Keep us updated and let us know if you need anything from us," concluded Kathleen.

As Tony and John stayed on the call after Kathleen and Terry left the Teams call, Tony shared his impression of the call. John reiterated the importance to InSports of internal audit doing this type of advisory work and how it could yield dividends long into the future in the form of better governance, a stronger culture, and fewer audit and fraud findings later. Tony shared his concerns about doing noncompliance work, but admitted that this engagement was pretty straightforward and the necessary tasks were things he could do.

The last thing Tony said before he left the call was "there are so many issues at InSports that need to be fixed. Identifying the issues is less about the eyes seeing the problems and more about the mind perceiving the opportunities."

John was speechless.

--------------------||--------------------

"Hi Miriam. Hi Tony. How are you doing?"

"I'm well. Projects are moving along nicely. No major problems to report."

"Same here."

"Good news. Thank you for moving the whistleblowing and ethics training phase of the larger ethics and corporate culture planning process along. I also appreciate you addressing the day-to-day issues that I'm sure surface, but you handle so they don't have to escalate to me. As always, if I need to know so I'm not surprised by my boss or another leadership team member, let me know."

"OK," came the reply from both of them.

"Well then, that takes care of updates. Now, for the development part of our agenda, I want to share an important practice that I believe both of you should consider adopting. We have a feedback process where we have the retrospective meeting at the end of every spring, the post audit reviews and semi-annual performance evaluations from HR. Those are all formal feedback opportunities. Over the years I've found informal feedback to be as important, or even more important than those formal events. I like to provide feedback on the fly," John said alluding to his own practice as an example of modeling the desired behavior.

"Like when you called me out of the blue to mention how Rachel and I used the Ishikawa Diagram during the audit?"

"Ah, yes!" said John remembering he had done that a couple of weeks ago. "Exactly."

"I was surprised when you told me about it and later Rachel texted me too. She was also surprised because that was never done around here before."

"It is called behavior modeling. Do as you say. I believe the boss, manager, leader should demonstrate the desired behavior and not ask people to do things they are not willing to do themselves."

"I respect that," said Miriam.

"How often should we do this?" asked Tony showing his penchant for rules, policies, and procedures.

"There is no clear rule. Don't overdo it, but make sure it happens periodically. It needs to be intermittent so it is special and not replace typical day-to-day work practices, but the spacing should not be so long that it falls back into the formal schedule we have or be forgotten altogether."

"What's wrong with the formal schedule?"

"Nothing really, but in some cases the gap could be long, and people like to hear they're doing a good job, so look for positive things when you can. You don't want those reporting to you to feel that you are only complimenting them because it is time to do so. It needs to feel spontaneous and genuine."

"Sounds like extra work," mused Tony audibly enough that it was picked up by the microphone.

"It is part of your regular job as a manager and leader, Tony," replied John trying not to sound annoyed by the response. "It doesn't have to take a lot of time. We're talking a minute or two. In fact, there is a great book written by Ken Blanchard called The One Minute Manager. I'll get each of you a copy. The original book was written decades ago, and I believe it is still relevant today. There's an updated book now called New One Minute Manager and there are books on leadership too. We'll read it together as a one-off manager book club. It is a quick read, so you can read that and our regular book club book. Anyway. One of the rules is praise your staff because it gives them confidence. It boosts their morale, so they continue to do well and achieve goals. With that, there is also the concept of one minute praise, which means providing feedback to people immediately. Immediately, as you can imagine, means the minute you see them doing what you asked them to do."

"Is there a technique? I ask because some people are fake when it comes to giving praise or feedback."

"Yes. It is important to be genuine, first of all. Then, be specific about what the person did well, how you feel about it and encourage the person to do more of that. The idea is that as they see their actions resulting in praise and recognition by the manager, that they will want to continue doing that. But don't rush the praise, let it sink in for effect."

"This creates a successful cycle."

"Exactly."

John paused for a moment to allow Tony and Miriam, especially Tony, to assimilate the new information and ask any questions.

"How do we make this part of our natural routine?" asked Miriam breaking the brief silence that had fallen on the meeting.

"Good question. Some say it takes 28 days for a practice to become a habit. Others say it can be anywhere between 18 days and 8 months. I don't know and I'm not going to worry about the details too much because everyone is different, and situations are different. My viewpoint is, it takes a while. That said, use reminders to help you; schedule it, put reminders on your phone, your calendar and so on until you no longer need it. I will make it a note for our 1:1 meetings so I'll help you too. Does all of this make sense?" John asked giving them a chance to react to what he said.

"Works for me," said Miriam readily. "Those are great ways to remember to do it."

"OK," said Tony less enthusiastically, but he agreed nonetheless.

"Good. Our success as managers depends on our ability to mobilize our staff. We do what we need to do so they are focused, motivated, effective, and efficient in their work. This includes providing meaningful feedback periodically."

"When can we get the book?" asked Tony, showing a glimmer of interest in reading the book.

"I'll order it today or tomorrow and you should be getting it shortly after that."

"Thanks, John," said Miriam.

"Thanks," added Tony.

"You're welcome. We're getting close to quarter end, so make sure to update your status reports and we'll review them early next week. The audit committee meeting is coming up and I need to make sure we tell them all the things we're accomplishing."

"Bye," said John as he closed the meeting.

--------------------||--------------------

"John. I saw your e-mail and I figured it would be best to talk with you rather than try to explain it all in writing."

"Thanks. I appreciate that Miriam. If it is going to be faster and better to do verbally, let's do that and use e-mail for confirmation of the agreement. I couldn't avoid the teachable moment, which by the way, you exemplified perfectly! So, tell me."

"Yes, we talked about having a QAIP done, well, the external assessment, but we didn't think we were ready, so we skipped it. I don't believe the audit committee knows it is a requirement, so it has never been done."

"Got it. I know what I've seen about our internal QA process. How would you summarize it?"

"Hit or miss. Mostly hit. I mean, we do a risk assessment even though it was skewed towards compliance, we plan our engagements, identify controls, do testing, review workpapers before the draft report goes out so we make sure there are no mistakes, but we could do more."

"Go on."

"We need to do more extensive risk-based testing, more consulting, better review of workpapers."

"Agree. Well, this is what I think we should do. We should improve our internal processes and make sure we document things better. Not more; better. We also need to find out what our clients think of us. The QAIP is about better service and without our clients' input, we could be missing the mark. Then the external assessment. Beyond reviewing workpapers, what other things should we do in your opinion?"

"You just said what I believe should be a high priority; ask our clients what they think about our work."

"How?"

"A post-audit survey."

"Yes, but let's make sure we don't make the same mistake made in the past and allow a low response rate to slow our momentum or outright stop our forward movement."

"Yes, that was our problem the last time. What if we followed up with non-respondents and ask them directly for their input?"

"I like it. Also, if they give us a low evaluation; we should follow up on those too to get more detailed information."

"What else?"

"Training. We should have a better way of tracking training. We do OK, but there are gaps that we should be closing there. You implemented more training than we have had in years, so that's visible progress."

"Thanks. We'll get a more scientific answer when we have the data from the Talent+ project, but what gaps come to mind?"

"Soft skills. Data mining and analytics. Collaboration and customer service. Problem resolution and root cause analysis. Our risk assessment can be improved too, we keep auditing the same familiar areas even though I believe there are more important risks elsewhere."

"You didn't have to think for long on that question. Sounds like you had been thinking about this for a while."

"I have been, and it has been bothering me, but no one asked. Well, I probably shouldn't say no one asked. Several people asked but they didn't do anything, so I stopped talking about it. I t looks like you are serious about changing these things."

"I am. You can always tell me what's on your mind and what you think we should improve."

"Thanks. That's a refreshing change."

"Good. How about you prepare a roadmap to help us tighten our QAIP and help us prepare for an external review. When can you have it ready for me to review?"

"Give me a couple of weeks. I believe that would be enough time to go over things."

"Sure thing. Thanks, Miriam. Let me know how things are coming along and if you have any issues."

"I will."

"Bye."

--------------------||--------------------

John entered the Underground at Marble Arch and promptly got on a Central Line train heading East. He got off at Tottenham Court Road, left the busy intersection, and walked South on Charring Cross. As he crossed Cranbourn Street and took the narrow streets, he noticed the growing crowd in the near distance, the smells, sounds, and rising energy; he knew he had found Covent Garden.

He saw her standing in the corner wearing a classy white jacket and a baseball cap. She was looking at her phone while holding a gold-colored gift bag from Godiva.

"Hi, how are you? So good to see you," John greeted Carolina who reacted with surprise.

"Oh, hi. Nice to see you too." I got distracted for a moment and didn't see you coming."

As they talked about the experience of working from home rather than in an office, the decision to meet rather than use Teams was an easy one so they could see each other in person. They joked that now the office was anywhere you wanted it to be.

They walked into a café, found a table in a quiet corner, and held their meeting there. They talked about Carolina's sales audit and how she was doing implementing

Agile. They had spoken frequently about the audit via video call, but it was a good time to talk face-to-face about it.

She described the sales processes in the EMEA region and the items in the backlog for this, the third and last, sprint. The first sprint covered bonus calculations and payments. No significant issues were identified there; just the need for slightly better documentation. The second sprint covered contracts and how they were drafted and executed. There were two significant issues there because some of the modifications in the language didn't get communicated to others who needed to know in Production or Shipping. Legal was aware of the changes and signed off on them, but the communication of unique requirements sometimes fell short of expectations impacting client relationships and ultimately reducing sales and increasing returns.

The third sprint was about training. This topic was chosen because there were complaints from different camps: production, shipping, customers, and even salespeople themselves felt they weren't getting all the training and support they needed.

"Training records are in the HRIS system. Did you get a chance to pull the data?"

"I have access and reviewed what's there. Most of the training information is there, but not all of it. I'm already seeing some issues with when they receive the training because some get it too late. For example, Sales Techniques training, which also includes compliance and FCPA, is only offered in January and June. So, anyone hired after the class runs in January has to wait until the next session in June. But given the sensitivity of the topic, that gap is problematic."

"Is the training given in person?"

"Yes. They have a five-year contract with an outside provider and they're in year two."

"Maybe we should look to see if it is feasible to offer the training monthly or change the delivery modality to computer-based so new hires can get the training immediately. Let's look at the cost and logistics of something like that. What else?"

"We looked at attendance and other than what I just explained, it looks good."

"What about the contents of the training?"

"What do you mean?"

"Does the training cover the relevant content and addresses the learning objectives? Some training just doesn't hit the mark because it doesn't deliver the knowledge participants need."

"How do we audit THAT?" she asked perplexed.

"There are several things we can look at. First, did they list learning objectives for the training. If they did, do they make sense and how do they verify those were achieved? If they didn't list learning objectives, they should."

"I'm not familiar with learning objectives."

"There's a famous methodology called Bloom's Taxonomy's Levels of Learning that is often referenced in learning and instructional design. It is progressive and begins with recalling knowledge, like defining terms and memorizing facts. Then it moves to comprehension, where learners understand what a message means so they can explain it to someone else. The next level is application, where learners develop the ability to apply what they learned to solve problems. The fourth is analysis and this involves the ability to break down the acquired knowledge into parts to effectively analyze a given situation and solve problems. Synthesis is the next and here learners bring ideas together to form new solutions. They get to organize, plan and create new solutions. The last one is evaluation. For this last level, learners get to assess or judge the value or quality of ideas based on established criteria, so they are able to critique proposals, judge the merit of ideas and recommend solutions."

"Wow," she said as she shook her head. "Sounds like the higher you go, the deeper the knowledge and the ability to do something with it."

"Exactly, so in the case of ethics training for example, we don't want employees to simply memorize facts, rules, and policies. We hope they can learn to make ethical decisions and judge situations effectively. And if they can't, then find someone who can help them rather than make a bad decision and get themselves and InSports in trouble. For sales techniques, compliance and FCPA, the same applies."

"What are some ways to achieve this?"

"It varies, but those developing the training materials need to understand the goal of the training and include activities appropriate for adult learners that will help them achieve these objectives. It could include quizzes, case studies, examples, discussions, presentations, and exams at the end of class."

"I'll check. This lines up nicely with the idea of business objectives, which is central to internal auditing anyway, right?"

"Yes, that's right."

With that they continued talking about audit procedures, communication, and collaboration with the client. When they were done, they had some gelato nearby and walked to the Covent Garden Tube train station, where they went their separate ways.

--------------------||--------------------

The whistleblowing and ethics phases of the larger corporate culture audit with HR was underway. The team gathered to report the results of the first sprint.

"We finished our first sprint on the Whistleblowing and Ethics Hotline project, which is part one of an ethics and corporate culture audit. The corporate culture portion will be done next year. For the Whistleblowing and Ethics Hotline portion, there were two main objectives: One, conduct a survey to collect opinions and concerns from our co-workers worldwide, and Two, develop an awareness campaign."

Tony continued, "as you know this has been a collaborative effort with great results! We developed a 12-question survey, each with a 5-point Likert scale. We didn't want just 'Yes/No' or 'True/False' responses as they tend not to show enough nuance. We also added 'Comment' fields to each question in case respondents wanted to add additional detail to their response. Lastly, it was done worldwide and while there is a general expectation that everyone is fluent in English, we decided to offer the survey in English and Spanish, since these represent our largest linguistic groups within the organization. That determination was made with HR's input and from data they have."

"So, I'll share my screen so you can see the results, and as I do that, I believe everyone is going to be pleased with the results and how much we learned in three weeks. Very good. Here…we…go, good! Is my screen showing?"

"Yes," was the collective response with a few heads similarly agreeing and a couple of thumbs up as well.

With that, Tony shared the survey questions, individual responses, salient comments, and some commentary developed jointly with HR on the interpretation of the survey results. After a few questions, the focus moved to the next item on the agenda.

"As I indicated at the beginning, there were two objectives for this sprint, so let's take a look at the second objective, which was to develop an awareness campaign. Proud to say that we did. We worked together and based on the input from the survey, we will be working with our instructional design team to develop a 1-hour in-person program and a 1-hour self-paced recorded program. The agenda is as shown on your screen."

Then Tony showed the group assembled a 7-item awareness program agenda. He and Terry alternated the reading and description of the items. Terry started with item 1, an overview of ethics in business conduct. Tony explained the second, which consisted of InSports' values statement and principles of conduct. Terry described the third item: an overview of fraud and examples of its negative impact on organizations. They continued down the list; item four, a description of the whistleblowing program, the use of a third-party provider and the benefits, and different ways the hotline could be contacted. Item five related to the process of handling allegations and how each case was handled. The sixth item was about the role of the Legal, Corporate Compliance, HR, Loss Prevention, and IT departments as a team to work collaboratively to investigate all allegations and inform senior management of the results, while internal audit played a consultative role. The seventh item explained the role of internal audit as the Third Line making sure that all allegations were handled promptly and addressed within a reasonable amount of time, verifying that performance reports were reviewed, and other improvement opportunities were investigated.

John thanked the group for their report, and as he was about to turn the floor back to Tony so he could explain the next sprint, Kathleen said. "I believe I speak for the HR team when I say thanks everyone who worked on this project. It is not done yet, I know, but three weeks! This is quite a departure from the internal audit department I knew. That's Number 1. Number 2, this is quite a departure from accounting and finance reviews. John, I was talking to Rachel a few days ago and somehow we started talking about the Standards and she mentioned that Internal Audit is expected to audit ethics. I knew auditors looked at accounting and financial reporting. I also knew they investigated fraud, but ethics is at the beginning of the process. Before someone starts the slide towards fraud. She explained the link between fraud and ethics, which I thought was very helpful, but then she mentioned one of your Standards, which one was it again Terry, Tony, John?"

Tony replied, "maybe the one stating we must assess and make recommendations to improve the organization's objectives, policies, and processes for promoting appropriate ethics and values."

"Yes, thanks. We need to tell employees about that. If I was surprised, I can only imagine how many employees have no clue this is what internal auditors do these days. We need to include that in the program!"

"Thanks Kathleen. We will. Yes, internal audit has come a long way and raising awareness is an important part of what would truly help InSports. Let's make sure that is included."

"Thanks you for thinking ahead and pointing out the expanded scope of work, and support, internal audit can provide organizations. This is a teachable moment at InSports and we would like to take advantage of that opportunity," Kathleen said as the meeting ended.

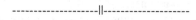

"John. Thanks for lending me Tony for those three weeks. He did a great job documenting the process for us. Sorry, *with* us. Nancy told me that they had to work really hard and fast to get all the AR information needed, especially the part that involved Juan."

"Glad it worked out. We'll do what we can to help within the limits I described."

"I appreciate it."

"Tony told me the work was done and you signed off on it. He also said the observations from two years ago were also addressed, so I updated our database to show that those observations have now been remediated."

"Oh, yes. That was part of the audit report and they rolled the resolution into this project since they were related."

"That's right. Back to the P&Ps. Are you making arrangements to train the staff on those procedures? Documenting them does not mean the staff is ready to follow them."

"You're right. Hmm. I'll talk to Nancy about that."

"Tony told me he's willing to help with the training, but again, he'll only do it as an assistant, so there's a need to coordinate the staff's availability with Nancy and Tony."

"Ok. Yes. I'll get on that."

"As you saw from the P&Ps project, our observations can help your results. When we spoke before, about three weeks ago, you mentioned having some client relations issues. The report from two years ago also indicated that shipping information was not always captured accurately so there were discrepancies in terms of the specific items, the quantity that should be shipped, and the exact destination. Since those have been addressed and you have newly printed P&Ps, I'm hoping things become more predictable in AR so customers pay the bills fully and on time."

"John, thank you very much for helping me, us, through this. This project was really helpful and Tony really got into it after a while. Nancy said that he found a consultant's hat somewhere. Oh, and just in time because Juan is leaving Friday."

"Glad we could help."

--------------------||--------------------

"Hello everyone.

We're getting close to the end of the summer and soon the green foliage around us will start to turn yellow, orange, red and brown as the leaves turn and fall in preparation for the cold winter.

We have been working really hard all year and through the summer. We have taken vacation and enjoyed the sun and long days, but we have also worked really hard to accomplish a great deal to benefit InSports.

We worked on some very challenging projects this year, this quarter, and this month. You should be proud of yourselves and your accomplishments. I am. Senior management has been impressed by the things you have been doing. The audit committee is too. So, thank you.

Enjoy the weekend. Rest, relax, have fun, sleep, cook, spend time with your loved ones, do what makes you happy. You deserve it."

With that, John stopped the recording and sent the video message to his team.

He then sat back in his chair and felt a little tingling feeling down his back. He was proud of his team and how far they had come. They needed to hear how proud he was of their accomplishments.

--------------------||--------------------

Summary
Summer

"Hello John. Before we begin, I want to introduce you to Jennifer Collins. She is joining the board starting today, so this is her inaugural meeting. She brings 22 years of experience in manufacturing and five years in public accounting."

"Hi Jennifer. Nice to meet you," replied John.

"Nice to meet you too," said Jennifer. "I've heard some very positive things about you and your team."

"Thanks. Yes, we have been making significant, and meaningful changes within the department. I believe you will like where we are going."

"Not only where they are going, but where they came from. Thanks John. Please give us an update," said Jim abruptly congratulating John as he checked an item on a printed sheet of paper and moving the meeting to the second item on the agenda.

"Yes, thanks Jim. You will notice a new look to my quarterly report. I also added a few new metrics in terms of audits closed, and by that I mean the final report was issued. We are moving faster as you can see the month-over-month totals, the year-to-date, and the comparison to last year. It is not just a matter of more audits; we are executing better and getting positive feedback on the results. These numbers basically show the wins the team is achieving. We had another fraud in Argentina; the amount was large but not material and we're pursuing criminal charges against them. There are several improvement opportunities there, which we have already shared with management. They were received very well. In terms of our aggregate yearly results, I found out that Internal Audit has not produced an annual report," said John.

"Yes, they did," said Jim attempting to answer the question. "We can send you the last couple of them for your review."

"I should re-phrase that because yes, I've seen them. I actually have a different image of an annual report. The ones produced so far summarize the number of audits completed, the number of findings, hours worked and how much of the audit plan was completed. Those are useful metrics, but I want to include more operational information, like waste identified and reduced, processes accelerated in terms of days whenever possible, but also the improvement opportunities, which to some extend fall into this category too, but how many operational improvements has internal audit and our clients identified and implemented."

"I like that! Yes, do that. Would it be published at year-end?" asked Sanjay.

"At the start of the new year so we include everything for this year."

"And I would like some infographics available for the entire organization," added Jim.

"That sounds like you're trying to sell internal audit to InSports!," remarked Sanjay.

"Yes, I intend to do that. It would help raise the image of internal audit and help us get more collaboration from operating units," explained John.

"I can't believe we hadn't thought about that until now," remarked Jim.

"There wasn't much to talk about or be particularly proud about until now," said Sanjay.

"With all the changes, let's tell, and show, where internal audit is adding value!" remarked Jim.

Suddenly Jennifer asked a question that caught everyone off guard since they had grown accustomed to talking among the three of them. "I have a question for you, John. How is internal audit identifying and going to address new and emerging risks? I understand we've had some fraud problems, so how can we reduce the likelihood of this happening again?"

Sanjay's eyes opened wide as he slowly turned his head to look at Jennifer. He considered himself the one asking the tough questions in the meetings, and he suddenly felt his role being threatened by the new committee member he recruited.

John, for his part, was delighted that the new person was already speaking up and would counterbalance Sanjay's frequent, yet well-intentioned, daggers.

John noticed the body language in the room and without missing a beat answered: "good question. It is part of our overall strategy and the direction we are headed. As the organization, and you the audit committee are confident that internal audit understands the needs for professionalism and how we will follow the Standards and add value in everything we do, what comes next is to focus consistently and uniquely on the most important, the most critical, risks to InSports. How do we do this?" John asked rhetorically and without much of a pause he continued, "key to this is the need to establish an effective mechanism to identify new and emerging risks. Otherwise, it is just words. There are many risks and internal audit now operates in a world where the number of risks is large and continues to grow. Three concepts related to risk I don't believe we have discussed are velocity, persistence, and volatility. We have spoken about, the enterprise risk assessment and even the audit plan are generally based on likelihood and impact, but these other three elements are important to consider."

"Mind going over them briefly?" asked Jennifer.

"Sure. Velocity is the speed at which the risk may occur. Some risks come at you slowly, like climate change, hurricanes, and demographic changes. Other risks occur faster, like an earthquake, a cyberattack, or a fire."

John paused in case the audit committee wanted to ask a question or add anything. He knew they would anyway, but he did so out of courtesy and habit.

"Then there's persistence," he continued. "This has to do with how long would the effects of the risk linger for. For example, if we were in the liquids transportation business and one of our trucks had a roadside accident resulting in spilled contents, it would be one thing if the tanker truck were carrying milk, and quite another if it were carrying gasoline or ammonia. Closer to home, we have the risk of a defective product getting to a customer. Since we have QA and QC in place, and customers that use our products almost immediately upon receipt, any defects should be caught rather quickly. Fraud, on the other hand, can unfortunately persist for over a year. In fact, there is an authoritative report issued every two years…"

"By the ACFE," said Sanjay, attempting to assert his position in the conversation.

"Yes, by the ACFE, stating that the mean time to detect fraud is, and I'm giving you a range because I've been watching this statistic and it varies a bit each time, but recent reports show occupational fraud lasts approximately 14 months to detection, or discovery. Then there's the investigation, pursuit of recoveries, litigation and the rest, the whole thing can go on for years."

He paused again. This time for a shorter amount of time hoping that the AC wouldn't ask about financial statement fraud because that detour could raise all sorts of issues he preferred not to address until he had had more time to strengthen his team and work more closely with the external auditors.

"Then there's volatility. How much could the risk swing in terms of likelihood or probability from one moment to the next. I'll use cybersecurity for this one because a hacker obtaining and releasing personal information, a DDoS, or ransomware attack can cause serious damage to our IT infrastructure and our ability to deliver services. If it spooks our clients who are sharing personal information, or our cloud services are shut down the impact could range significantly. This is not the impact we have spoken about before; I mean, each attack could cost us anything from nuisance to massive customer abandonment and a long uphill road to regain our reputation and customer confidence."

"DD what S attack?" asked Sanjay.

"Distributed denial of service," said Jennifer answering for John.

"How do you intend to monitor these new and emerging risks?" asked Jim.

"The one word that best summarizes the approach is scanning. It has multiple layers. Talking with senior and operational management to stay on top of what they hear, see, and know. Another part of this is scanning organizational, or internal, and external data. We have MORs, management operational reports, that provide quite a bit of information. They are good, but they focus on KPIs, which is understandable. I believe management would benefit from adding some KRIs to it."

"KPI or KRI, I don't know, but is there a reliable process to monitor our network traffic?" asked Jennifer.

"Good question. I've spoken with our cybersecurity team, and they indicated they monitor network traffic constantly. Additionally, they have a response plan, and periodically review and scale up InSports' bandwidth to make sure it has enough capacity for some surges in activity. We have the ability to add capacity promptly if needed, but that may never catch up against a well-orchestrated volumetric attack. We need to do a proper review."

"We have disaster recovery sites. Ron spoke to the committee about those a while ago," said Jim.

"Yes, but later Nihal said we should re-evaluate the sites," added Sanjay.

"That is consistent with what Nihal told me. We should revisit the operations in each type of DR site because that was determined a while ago."

"Let us know what you need."

"Thanks Jim, I will."

"What else is going on that we should know about?" asked Jim.

"We implemented agile auditing and ran our first projects. They have been consulting engagements related to our ethics hotline, which was underutilized as relates to its intended purpose. There was a reasonable number of calls, but most of them reflected concerns that should be addressed through the traditional chain of command. There is widespread support for the way the team performed, and we have another sprint in progress in Sales so they're off and running."

"You explained the importance of Agile Auditing in terms of efficiency and improved performance, which of course are priorities for this committee. Can you tell us some of the other key selling points for Agile Auditing?" asked Sanjay.

"Yes, sure. Some key selling points for Agile Auditing include problem-solving, critical thinking, innovation, and creativity; the ability to prioritize and deal with complexity and ambiguity, and one that is very important to me as we upskill the team is learning as you go. Also, communication because it focuses on the right information provided clearly, to the right people, at the right time. There is also data analysis and for that, the need for business acumen, so that's there. Due to short cycles, the team has to practice effective project management, operate with diversity and flexibility in mind, and deal with adversity effectively, or they'll fall behind. There is relationship management, which we have worked very hard this year to rebuild. Long list, I know. The last ones are probably presentation and presence as everyone on the team must speak up and do so promptly and clearly, focusing on outcomes."

"Thank you, John. What else do you have for us?" asked Jim enjoying the conversation because it had been a while since they had a knowledgeable CAE in their midst.

"One of the Standards calls for a quality assurance and improvement program, often referred to as a QAIP. It has two components, an internal one requiring ongoing monitoring of the performance of the internal audit activity and periodic self-assessments or assessments by other persons within the organization with sufficient knowledge of internal audit practices. The second component is an external assessment done at least once every five years by a qualified independent assessor or assessment team from outside the organization. We currently don't have either in place and I want to get that moving ASAP."

"Please elaborate," asked Jennifer.

"We have ongoing monitoring, but we need a periodic self-assessment or an assessment by someone else within InSports with knowledge of internal audit practices. I want to do the self-assessment. So, I will assign workpapers myself for review to make sure no one is reviewing their own work. I'll implement that later this year or next year. The big project I want to alert you to is the second type, an external assessment. Given where we started from and how much we have done ourselves, I believe it would be good for all of us to have an external assessment done and get an outsider's perspective on things, but since that would go on the record, I want to do a pre-assessment review first. That would happen later this year and the, let's call it official assessment, would then happen sometime next year. I'm thinking by mid-year."

"That puts you on record and the entire department too. Are you sure you want to do that?" asked Jim.

"I agree it is a big step for all of us in internal audit, but I believe it is worth it. I want validation for my benefit and yours of what we are doing and what are some additional things we should focus on."

"OK. Get that moving and let us know when the review will be."

"I will."

"OK. Let's call it a day. Good meeting everyone. Thanks John. Let's take a 15-minute break before we ask Margaret to come in. She is next on the agenda."

John was relieved because this had been a difficult quarter, but it was also rewarding. As he stepped onto the street, he noticed how warm it was for early October. There was little breeze in midtown, but he knew where it would be cool and scenic. He hurried to the subway station, took the train, changed immediately when he got to his hotel room, and went for one of his favorite walks in NYC. The views were majestic the entire time, with lights and sounds underscoring the endless energy characteristic of the city. Walking cleared his mind when he needed time to think, invigorated him when he needed an energy boost, and in moments like this one, it was also a way to celebrate feel-good moments privately.

Building bridges is an amazing thing and the Brooklyn Bridge is a great example of that!

A week after the audit committee meeting, John flew to San Francisco for the quarterly team meeting. As was customary, they had dinner together; this time it was seafood at Fisherman's Wharf. After dinner they walked back to their hotel along the Embarcadero. John walked with them and noticed how they seemed to enjoy the time together. They were talkative, shared personal stories, and there was almost an equal amount of laughter as words. John thought of this as bonding time, but also a good way to build some unspoken exercise into their collective routine.

As Day One began, John called the meeting to order by focusing their attention on the accomplishments of the quarter.

"Hello everyone. Nice to see all of you again. Summer warmth is fading and the long days are starting to shorten, but the vibrant colors are still with us; Rachel, you are our colorful fashionista and now it looks like the team is joining in. I like the brightness folks, in the clothing and in your attitudes. Now, clearly the summer is almost over and what a year we've had so far. Wow, lots of work but also lots to be proud of. We have a long list of things we accomplished this quarter. Let's take a walk down memory lane and recall some of those things. I'll go first. We took a close look at our performance metrics and noticed that we were, to a large extent, tracking output and not outcomes. More specifically, we were capturing and reporting on hours worked, but that does not necessarily show what we accomplished, or the quality of what we accomplished. So, we have better metrics now. Agree?"

"Yes," said Tony. "Agree. Can I share a success story?" he asked.

"Sure. Please."

"We had been talking about providing consulting or advisory services in internal audit, and I'll admit I was a bit on the fence about it, but I came to better understand not only why, but how, and now we have expanded our selection of services offered. We did some last quarter, and this quarter we reviewed the whistleblowing hotline, ethics and sales training, which were interesting. Now we are doing both assurance and advisory work."

"Which is consistent with the Standards."

"Yes. We took a step forward and our work is more consistent with the Standards."

"My turn," said Miriam. "We are doing a better job identifying what resources we need. My focus has been IT and I had been asking for more coverage of IT and to look at cybersecurity. We kicked the can down the road for a while, but now we're working with third parties to help us look at that until we have our own staff to help narrow the gap further. That was a huge win for me."

"Thanks. Yes, we took some huge strides there. Anyone else?"

Carolina spoke next, "I never felt totally ignored being the rookie here, but now I feel that I'm listened to much more. I guess making us feel more empowered is the best way to summarize it."

John wanted to acknowledge that right away even as Miriam was about to speak, he jumped in "I'm glad you feel that way Carolina. My goal from the beginning has been to let everyone share their thoughts and feelings because together we can get a lot more done. Everyone deserves to be heard, so I'm glad we accomplished that. Miriam, you were about to say?"

"Yes. I didn't know you felt that way Carolina. I'm glad we are fixing that. If you ever feel like we are not including you, or outright ignoring you, let us know right away. Inclusion is not just a buzzword; it is how great ideas come forward," she said. Then John continued.

"I didn't hire you, but I knew from your profile and talking with Tony and Miriam that we had a great team, and you're part of our team."

"Come on guys. You're going to make me blush. I didn't mean to turn this into a group hug," she said as she in fact blushed.

"OK, let's move on. Don't want to make you uncomfortable. Rachel? Anything comes to mind?" said John trying to shift the focus away from Carolina.

"Yes. Carolina, we have your back," Rachel said with a serious tone and expression on her face to emphasize her support. She then took a deep breath and said, "we are looking at data analytics tools. It was long overdue. So, I'm glad we're committed to making that transition and better able to show our clients things they didn't know."

"Very good. Thanks Rachel. OK Brian, bring it in. What did we accomplish this quarter?"

"We implemented Agile Auditing more fully and it is a success. It really impresses our clients. I'm going to be a little selfish here and say that I've been curious about Agile Auditing for a while since it has been talked about so much in the profession and was wondering what it was really like. I like it. It is very dynamic, the client is more in the loop, they have to step up and work with us more, and I get to interact with more people than before. I learned a lot from it."

"Good summary there, Brian. We almost forgot about surveys. We are now sending surveys after every engagement to get client feedback on our performance. We are producing some small wins that will continue to build and become even bigger wins."

"We almost forgot, Rachel and Carolina passed Part 1 of the CIA exam!" said Miriam announcing the news. The team joined in celebrating their accomplishment, which made Carolina blush again.

"Thanks everyone. You know I enjoy these conversational meetings. A lot more fun than hearing me preach for a full hour, isn't it?" He took a short pause then said abruptly, "and don't answer that!"

Next, John led the team reviewing key company performance metrics and news. He then shifted to internal matters, and they talked about what they were working on. They discussed their projects in progress and the communications sent to the clients. They discussed what was coming up next and timelines for closing out those audits. The conversation about challenges and potential obstacles was brief, since Agile Auditing had now created an environment where issues were discussed and resolved promptly within the team, which now included the client, and the language now used the word "team" to refer to the integrated whole.

Lunch was delivered to the room as had become customary for their quarterly meetings, and for about an hour after that they worked side by side on their projects. Then they dispersed as they went to meet and greet audit clients. Since the previous quarterly meetings had been in New York, this was the first time some of them had met clients in person in the San Francisco office.

Dinner was at a restaurant on the top floor of a building downtown. It was an unusually clear day so they could see Alcatraz, Coit Tower, Oakland, and the many buildings in the peninsula. As they talked, took pictures, and lingered so long the waiter started to look restless, John couldn't help but relish in the positive energy from the team, which made him enjoy the scenery even more.

Day Two started with what had become a tradition during the quarterly meetings; the training component. The first session was delivered by a senior manager in the R&D group. She had been with the company for several years, so she explained the progression in complexity and technological innovation in the product line and how ideas progressed through commercialization.

The second session was from a project manager whose presentation built on the R&D topic and focused on how projects were managed. The focus on objectives, risks, and controls was engaging as the speaker was able to connect what they did with the focus of internal audit. The third session was a video conference presentation from a sales manager who described the pricing and discounting practices as they applied, differently, around the world.

They chose to go out to lunch since no one was catching afternoon flights; going home was on red-eye flights this time around.

The afternoon was spent working together, even if on different projects, and meeting audit clients. John, Tony, and Carolina went to meet an audit client in R&D, while Miriam and Brian spent time with the IT group onsite.

--------------------||--------------------

15 Build on the Change and Consolidate Gains

"Hello everyone. Hope your flights home were enjoyable. Quite hot where I live, in fact, we had a severe drought as you probably know already," said John starting the meeting.

Brian joined immediately: "There were similar issues in California. Pretty bad in Australia and the UK too, right, Carolina?"

"Yes, we had some extreme temperatures too. Very surprising. It eventually got cool again, but very strange. Then again, the Continent also had severe weather with forest fires in several places like Spain, Portugal, and Italy."

"Crazy. Weren't there forest fires in Siberia too?" asked Rachel, getting into the conversation.

"Yes. That one baffles me. I thought Siberia would be cool and damp, yet they are having forest fires too. I don't get that," said Carolina shaking her head. "There is a serious drought in East Africa too."

Brian added, "the Hoover Dam is really low. You can see the lines on the side of the rocks!"

Rachel replied, "Yes, I saw that. Are you watching the Mississippi river and how low it is? They're worried about barges going down the river now."

John listened to the conversation as the team talked about the environmental changes worldwide and saw a teachable moment emerge. He joined the conversation.

"On that note, folks, let's think about that for a moment because there is a lesson here. This has a huge human cost, so let's acknowledge that first of all. Now, what we see in our world impacts InSports too. The drought and to Rachel's point, the difficulty moving cargo down the Mississippi affects supply chains. Forest fires can impact our supply chain and general commerce too, by, for example, delaying flights. That happened in Seattle, Denver, and San Francisco recently. It affects workers' ability to do their jobs. These things can raise inflation and impact our costs and sale prices. Storms also affect our ability to work, like this summer's hurricane. And as you are well aware, the pandemic transformed our workplace, so our colleagues usually work from home."

"Or Hawaii or Costa Rica," said Brian.

"That's right," John said smiling as he acknowledged Brian's contribution.

"Remote work programs and arrangements are common, even if that means working from a surfer village. All you need is a reliable and fast internet connection. But let's look at that too. All of these things carry some risk. I started talking about supply chains, costs, and pricing, but to Brian's point, what do you see as some of the risks of remote work?" he asked.

DOI: 10.1201/9781003322870-18

"Cybersecurity," said Rachel immediately.

"Yes, exactly. That is a big one. Things like?" said John encouraging the team to elaborate.

"Intercepted transmission through some kind of hacking, ransomware, data loss caused by bad actors or accidentally, things like that," said Brian as Rachel and Miriam looked on nodding approvingly.

"Good. What else comes to mind?" John asked again.

"Operationally it can make team dynamics more difficult and stymy creativity," said Brian as Rachel continued nodding in agreement.

"It can also cause conflict because people don't understand each other as well," said Carolina.

"And tracking project progress and connecting with people when you need them can also be difficult," said Miriam.

"Working remotely can limit communication frequency and quality," said Tony, surprising the team since his perspective was typically on project progress and his comment spoke to soft skills, communication, and people interactions.

"All of these are correct. So, do we need to audit that?" asked John.

"Yes, I think we should," replied Brian.

"Everyone agree?"

The answer came in the form of head nodding and audible "yesses" from the team.

"Good. That is part of what I wanted to highlight for today's meeting. The fact that our risk assessment, and the resulting audit plan, will be more diverse and flexible going forward because we need to review these topics. As you, as a team, indicated, there are IT, cybersecurity, workforce productivity and cultural adaptation issues involved. There are human resources implications too in terms of compensation, taxation, and time off that we need to check with HR because we want to recruit, retain, and maintain associates motivated regardless of where they live and work."

John continued. "Another thing. Creativity. So far this year we have incorporated several tools into our methodology. Facilitation tools like Miro, Creately, and Lucidspark. There is also Lucidchart, by the way one is a whiteboard the other is a diagramming tool. Anyway, we expanded our use of flowcharts and their content by adding value added and non-value-added data points to them."

"And backflows," remarked Brian.

"Exactly. Backflows. You found some interesting issues there with that, Brian during your audit. We also started using Z-Scores and SIPOC Maps. Cause and Effect diagrams."

"Thanks Ishikawa!" said Brian again.

John nodded agreeing with the other name for Cause and Effect Diagrams, but also enjoying the engagement from his team, especially Brian who was the most junior auditor and he was becoming more comfortable with his knowledge and the internal audit methodology. While some people may treat it as disruptive, John preferred the indications of engagement he was receiving and how the conversation had expanded into a form of review.

"RACI Charts anyone?"

"CAIRO," added Carolina.

"RASCI," said Brian.

"Exactly, all names of variants of the tool. We helped management implement a Responsibility Assignment Matrix and later on I spoke with one of their directors and she told me that workflows are much improved since they implemented the tool in their department. That was a big win for us."

"I'm mentioning all of these things because I want us to think back at all the things we have accomplished so far this year. We are making a difference, not just by introducing tools into our methodology, but showing how the tools help us help our clients improve their processes," said John.

"And achieve their goals," added Tony.

"And achieve their goals. That's the most important part about all of this, so thanks Tony for the reminder." John immediately thought how far Tony had come. The year started with him focusing on compliance controls and repeating the same audits year over year, and now he was adapting quite well to a flexible risk-based agile approach that was winning adepts throughout the organization.

"We need to update our policies and procedures to officially make these tools part of our toolbox. With that, I need one of you to take the lead updating our SOPs. Do I have a volunteer?"

"I'll do it," replied Tony to the surprise of the group and John, who simply smiled in agreement.

--------------------||--------------------

"Hi John. Do you have a moment?"

"Yes Ken. How can I help you?"

"I have a strange feeling that the contract manager, Giancarlo Fiori, and maybe the project manager, Javier Gonzalez, are engaged in some foul play at our construction project in Costa Rica."

"What makes you think things are not right?"

"The work had what would be considered red flags. I met with them to go over the work and the vendors chosen, one in particular, seemed dubious. Very little documentation. The work was delivered just in time, I mean, to the week. The budget and contingency amounts were spent to within $400 each on a multi-million-dollar budget. The progress reports were all perfect, which at the time made us happy, but in retrospect we should have been wondering how they could do everything so perfectly."

"What made you take notice of all of these things now?"

"We have another phase of the project starting in a few months and they are insisting we use the same vendor. I just thought it was suspicious that they insisted on granting the contract to them again rather than putting it out to bid."

"You said there was very little documentation. What was in the file?"

"Mostly nothing. Just a few notes saying they tried but couldn't find qualified vendors, so the business was granted to them and entered as a main provider. We have given 80 percent of the work to that one vendor."

John replied, "we could take a look, but it may be best to hire an outside auditor given the many suspicions you have and our small team here. It might protect the organization to do it that way."

"That's what I was thinking but I wanted you involved in the process."

"Ok. Let me get on that and search for a firm to do the work. I'll put something on the calendar as soon as we have something concrete in place. Shouldn't take too long."

"Thanks. You know we have several projects in progress and we have never had an audit. You said you have a small team, but is there a way for you to do a high-level review since we don't have a PMO? I've wondered for a while if everything we get from our project managers is accurate and complete, but since we didn't know of any real problems, we just kept things the same. Now with this I worry we may have problems lurking."

"We can do a quick review, let's call it a diagnostic, where we kick the tires for you. Then based on the results we can see what options we have. Would that work for you?"

"Yes. Sounds good to me."

"I'll schedule a meeting for the two of us to talk early next week. Anyone else who is knowledgeable of project management processes and metrics that you would like invited?"

"Yes, Michael O'Malley."

"OK. I'll add him to the meeting. I'll send the invitation today or tomorrow and we'll get together next week."

"Thanks again. Really appreciate it."

"You're welcome."

As the call ended, John thought to himself what a turnaround story he just witnessed. This was the same executive who at the beginning of the year wanted little to do with audit, and had now requested an investigation, which was not unusual in and of itself, since when there are problems management often asks audit to step in. They did the EHS review and that went well and Ken had been warming up to audit since. The second request was the real showstopper! He wanted a risk assessment to help identify trouble spots. "We're winning," John said to himself.

--------------------||--------------------

After a brief introduction since John had never met Michael O'Malley before, the meeting got underway and Ken, Michael, and John performed a risk assessment of the project management process. They discussed project selection criteria based on budget, scope, company strategic impact, and need for regulatory compliance.

When finished reviewing the list of open and upcoming projects, they ranked them based on criticality and urgency, with the size of the intersecting node reflecting the budgetary amount. They identified four capital projects, and the Costa Rica construction project was at the top of the list.

--------------------||--------------------

"Hi Rachel, Hi Brian, I have an assignment for you. I met with Ken and one of his directors, Michael O'Malley, and we performed a risk assessment of our projects. There are four capital projects and others not quite as large, but still important to InSports. We did a risk assessment, and identified a construction project we want to review. I want you to do some research for me. Do you accept this mission?" he said making a James Bond reference.

"Yes," said Brian nodding and with an expression that seemed to emulate one of the James Bond actors' signature looks.

"OK. Let's think things through a bit before I send both of you off to do the work. What aspects of the project might you look at from a risk perspective?"

After a moment as Rachel and Brian thought about the question, Rachel answered first, "cost?"

"Yes, how much will it cost InSports. Short term or long term?"

"All in. Full cost and perhaps even do a net present value if it will be going on for a very long time."

"Yes, Good. What else?"

"Scope," she said again.

"Yes. Good. Go on."

"Timeline. How long will it take. If soon, it is a bit more important than longer term when we might have time to fix issues. Right?" said Brian.

"That's good too. Timeline. Others."

"Criticality. How significant is it to our success as a company," said Rachel again.

"Yes, I like that."

"Safety implications. Whether physical safety like EHS or data, IT, cybersecurity," said Brian including some technical elements to the list of criteria elements.

"I like it. These are good. Good job. Now, how about tests, which is a big part of what I want both of you to work on. What will you look at to find potential concerns?"

After a pause to think about this new question, Brian spoke first this time. "How about over budget expenses?"

"Yes, budget and cost were a criterial element, so over budget at a set point in time and by how much. Percentage and amount. I like it."

Rachel spoke next, "we identified timeline, that was Brian, so activities behind schedule and missed milestones."

"Good, yes. Test of progress towards achievement of success criteria. What would you measure?"

Rachel replied, "number of days plan vs. actual."

She continued, "when we were building an addition to my house the contractor wanted to make changes to our original plan and we kept debating and having to rein him in because he was going to run up the cost on us. Is that something we can look at here?"

"Absolutely! Yes, those are called change orders in project management. They should be recorded so check the number of change orders, the type, the amount, the impact on the timeline in days, the name of the vendor requesting it and the person approving them," said John guiding his staff.

John continued, "good job. Ask Michael for the data. He will be your go-to person. This is an agile consulting project, so don't just ask him for stuff then go work by yourselves. Include him in the work. Check the validity of the data against AP, budgets, project management reports and so on. You're also showing him, and he showing you, how we check controls. Then do the data analytics and let's see what you find. Sounds good?"

"Sounds good."

"Call me if you have any questions or issues."

--------------------||--------------------

"Hi Carolina. How are you today?"

"I'm well. I spent a good part of my weekend taking out my sweaters. It is starting to get cold here!"

"Yes, indeed. Fall comes early to you with the shorter days and lower temperatures. I wanted to meet with you to review your narrative. Nicely done. Very clear, concise writing."

"Typos?"

"Just a couple of 'there' vs. 'their', some 'principal' vs 'principle' and one 'either' vs. 'neither'." As Tony explained the different usages to Carolina, they joked about the vagaries of the English language.

"Why do you write 'theater' in the US while Brits write 'theatre'?"

"I don't know."

"But they're pronounced the same. Right?"

"Yes."

"Ok. Ok. How about 'hour' and 'our'."

"Well, the 'h' is silent in English."

"No, it is not. What do you say when something belongs to a man?"

"His?"

"Say it again."

"His."

"You don't hear the 'h'?"

"I guess so."

"'Her', 'hers', 'heresy', 'hair' you pronounce the 'h'. You pronounce the 'h' in all of these words."

"Ok. You win."

"I'm not done yet. How about 'heir', you know, someone who is going to inherit stuff."

"I know the word and its meaning, Carolina."

"Good. Now you don't pronounce the 'h'. How am I supposed to know when they mean 'her', 'hair', 'here', 'heir', and 'ear'?"

At this point, Tony put his hands over his ears while laughing, which was unusual for him. "You're killing me, you know that?"

Carolina had now replaced her serious facial expression with a winning smile. "You can't explain that, can you?" she said with a mock angry expression that was really a playful gesture.

"No, you win. You win. I give up. Can I go now?"

"Yes, you may go," as she started singing and dancing on camera her adaptation of Gloria Gaynor's song "Go on now, walk out the door, just turn around now, you can't answer anymore."

--------------------||--------------------

16 Quality Assurance and Improvement Program (QAIP)

"One of the Standards calls for the development and maintenance of a quality assurance and improvement program. It needs to cover all aspects of the internal audit activity. While we have been conducting internal reviews of our work, we haven't conducted an external assessment yet. Regarding the internal review, we will be making it more robust in the future. We will also do what I'm calling a preparedness review to see how far we are from being prepared for a full-blown external assessment, which we are due for. So, we are updating our policies and procedures and we'll be reviewing our methodology to make sure it is risk-based and addresses the needs of our clients. Then we're going to hire someone to conduct an external assessment."

"Sounds like a lot of work," said Brian.

John replied, "quality is never an accident. It is always the result of high intention, sincere effort, intelligent direction, and skillful execution."

"Will A. Foster," said Miriam.

"Exactly," John replied.

"What's the timeframe?" Brian asked.

"For the internal or the external assessment?"

"Both."

"The update to our SOPs has already begun. The internal assessment ramp-up, I would like to see in two to three weeks, and the external assessment by midyear next year."

"That is a very aggressive timeline."

"Yes, it is, and I believe we can do this. We have already updated our practices quite a bit, so we need to formalize some things. Let's talk about the components of this. I already mentioned workpapers, better than before?" asked John.

"Yes," everyone agreed.

"More focus on client needs and flexibility doing so?"

"Yes."

"More of a risk-based approach at the project selection and project management levels?"

"Yes."

"Better relations with our clients?"

"For the most part," said Tony above the "yeses" from the rest of the team. This made John pause for a moment, and he acknowledged that some work was still necessary to improve relations with most clients. "You are right Tony, 'for the most part'

DOI: 10.1201/9781003322870-19

is a good way to summarize it, but have we made, and continue to make, improvements?" he asked.

"Yes," said Tony with a pensive look on his face.

"How about post-audit surveys? Those are back and scores are getting better. Right?" John inquired of his team.

"Yes, that is correct," said Miriam.

"Good. I'm going to have a consultant come in and do a preparedness review. I've been screening candidates and I'm ready to have a contract signed. I'll let everyone know when that is confirmed and the corresponding dates."

--------------------||--------------------

"Hello everyone. As I mentioned last week, we have confirmed the QAIP review. We have a consultant starting in three weeks and we need to work together and make this a priority so it can be done well and quickly. So, I need to retrieve some workpapers and I'm asking Rachel to be the point person for that. Miriam and Tony will be interviewed and will answer the majority of questions and facilitate the process. I'm available if you need me."

"What should we expect from the reviewer?" asked Rachel.

"Initially and primarily workpapers. The consultant will tell you which ones he wants, so provide those as quickly as possible. He will also ask for our risk assessment, audit plan, budget, and training records, so I will provide those. In terms of interviews, he may want to talk to each of you. I have an idea of what he wants to talk about, but I don't want to prejudice the process commenting on that. When asked, answer truthfully and completely. OK?"

"OK," responded Rachel.

"Don't worry about it. We want to know what is really going on, so we prepare and have an honest assessment of what we need to improve on. Next year is the real test, so let's do everything we can to prepare. You can think of this as a practice run, but it is still very important to me and should be to you also. Sounds good?"

"How long will this review last?"

"One week."

"Oh, that's quick!" said Miriam.

"Yes, this is a pre-QAIP assessment. I think of it as a diagnostic, so one week should be enough."

"What if we don't pass?" asked Tony.

"When it comes to the QAIP and the related assessments, it is not a matter of pass or fail. The main goal is to determine if we conform or adhere to the Standards. Along the way we will get some recommendations for improvement, but the assessment will result in an opinion that we either fully conform, generally conform, or do not conform. We hope to at least get generally conform to the Standards."

--------------------||--------------------

17 Institutionalize and Produce Even More Change

"Good afternoon and thank you very much for joining us today. Special thanks to the staff for the great support they provided us during the review. This year internal audit implemented Agile Auditing, and your team, as audit clients, embraced the new methodology immediately and effectively. This allowed us to focus on what matters most to you and InSports, and to move through the audit quickly."

"Consistent with Agile methodology, we issued communications at the end of every sprint, so every two weeks. In those communications we indicated what was working well and what opportunities were identified for improvement. We're pleased to say that in most instances changes have already been made addressing the issues noted, and that is exactly what we hoped would happen. This way HR can benefit from our collective work immediately, and by extension, the process improvements benefit all InSports associates."

"We have a short presentation to share with you. It provides key talking points and helps us cover the items we want to share with you. The report you received via e-mail is mainly the sum of those shorter communications we shared with you at the end of every sprint. New things you will notice now are an executive summary, the engagement's objectives, the scope of the review, and our conclusion. We also list all recommendations, and the corresponding action plans. Any questions so far?"

There was a brief pause, and when everyone thought Tony was going to continue his presentation, Kathleen spoke.

"Thanks for the overview, Tony. Yes, we received the previous communications, and we're OK with the results. In the past, internal audit reviewed payroll and employee files. In fact, you did some of those reviews. This time you, and the team, looked at different things. Some of us were audited in the past, and in general we were a bit surprised by what audit looked at this time. Can you explain again, what you covered, what you didn't, and why?"

"Yes, sure. Our past approach was focused on compliance. We recalculated payroll to check the accuracy of payments, made sure the payments went to the right person, and we verified that payments were not made past the termination date. For employee files, it was also mostly about compliance focusing on whether employees had a personnel file, if those files were up to date, if documents were being stored safely and for the required duration, and if all confidential information was protected from unauthorized access. The procedures were mostly manual and based on sampling."

DOI: 10.1201/9781003322870-20

"And now?"

"I'll start with the methodology. Instead of sampling, we now do 100 percent testing using data analytics, so we looked at all records with workable data. We identified a few incomplete data, so that was an observation for data quality improvement. By cleaning up the data, your reports will be more reliable without having to do a lot of monthly data cleanup and reconciliations. Basically, better and faster reporting. Also, instead of focusing on and testing controls, we identified the biggest risks and looked at the data to see if those risks had occurred, were occurring, or were likely to occur based on the existing process. There were no major anomalies and did not identify any fraud, but the process had several manual and redundant activities that resulted in frequent back-and-forth between staff every pay period and when preparing monthly and quarterly reports. We found some efficiencies and the staff are already happy by the changes because it saved them time and frustration when they did last month's closing."

"Yes, I saw that, and they told me about it; several times I might add. Anything else?"

"Since our new approach is more efficient and focused, we spent the extra time looking at key strategic initiatives and priorities. We looked at knowledge management, recruitment, and employee engagement because the team concluded that success for HR as a key support function within InSports depends on having the right people, with the right knowledge, working with motivation."

"Who do you mean by the team?"

"Two of us from internal audit and four from HR. It was a joint team."

"How about turnover. Did you look at that?"

"Yes, but not as a separate topic, but rather in the context of employee engagement."

"How so?"

"Because for the most part, employees that are motivated, learning, feeling like they belong, and succeeding are less likely to leave, so by focusing on the front end, turnover takes care of itself. Oh, we also asked and reviewed the latest market compensation study that was done showing that our compensation package is competitive, and the employee engagement survey results and action items."

At that point, Tony stopped talking to refill his water mug from the pitcher and the room fell silent. While he focused on not spilling water publicly, everyone in the room was exchanging glances at each other and shaking their heads as a sign of approval. When Tony raised his head, he saw people smiling so he asked, "did I miss something?"

Kathleen answered on behalf of the HR contingent. "Tony, we are smiling because we feel like audit has finally connected the dots. What you just described is an amazing audit that sounds more like a consulting engagement. The results make us happy because," and she made air quotes when she said, "we passed the audit." "Over the last ten years we have paid a lot of money for external consultants to come here and look at these things and the team did that for us. Thank you!"

"You're welcome. Thanks. It was a team effort."

John looked very pleased and asked, "anything else left to discuss Tony?"

"No, that was actually what was in the presentation. I guess we don't need to look at the slides after all."

"Thanks everyone," said Tony. "If there are no questions, and since we already have action plans for all items, the final report will be in your inboxes tomorrow."

--------------------||--------------------

"OK folks let's get the meeting started. We have a new addition to the department. Sandy Morris will be joining internal audit on a two-year rotation. She will start January first and helping us with our construction audits as she has some valuable, and needed, expertise in that field. I'll send an official announcement later today, so please welcome Sandy and make her feel at home."

The team thought about the significance of construction audit expertise and a rotation program, which was new to the department.

"Other news, as we build a stronger team, we're introducing a 360-degree review process. We're still a relatively small team, but that should not hold us back from implementing what I believe is a great mechanism," John said to a quiet team. "I know that 360 reviews sometimes work and sometimes don't and the determining factor is usually how safe it is to share honest feedback, so let's address that right away. We grow in the light, and everyone can get better. I'm not perfect, but I try to get a little better every day. It has served me well embracing this concept of Kaizen on a personal level and I invite you to do the same. I ask for feedback, and I would like to see everyone in internal audit do the same. Ground rules include, do it professionally, do it respectfully, use examples, focus on actions and results not personalities. If the personality is what you need to talk about, think it through so you are not hurtful. We'll work on a few additional ground rules, but that should cover a good 80 percent or so of the success factors. Thoughts?"

"Will we do this in person or over video?"

"Good question. Whenever possible, in person, but it is hard since we're a decentralized team, so video call is OK. That being the case, another ground rule is that we don't rush through the feedback. Give yourselves enough time to talk about the feedback and hear each other out. Also prepare beforehand so you are fair, as complete, and as eloquent as you can reasonably be. This is important. We'll schedule a session to go over the ground rules I just mentioned and others you think are important so we're all together on this. Another thing, I realize it is a delicate topic and you may feel uneasy about it especially if you have never done this before. So, I'm going to post some articles in our shared drive that you can also read."

Everyone nodded in agreement.

"In terms of our productivity numbers, here are some interesting statistics. When I joined the team, we were averaging far fewer audits per year than we did this year. After implementing some changes like Agile Auditing, over the last two quarters we have increased our individual and collective productivity. Here are the figures for you to see. There are a couple of reports in the works that should be done and published in the next few weeks, so I counted them in already. We should be proud of this. You should be proud of this. I am proud of this. It is also important to note that there is a difference between output and outcome. Performing more audits is not important if they are done poorly, so let's look at other measures. On a qualitative level, the verbal feedback I have received has been outstanding and the feedback on our post audit surveys have also been remarkable. I'll share this because you should see this for yourselves," said John as his gaze moved to select the correct file to share with his team during the Teams call.

"Can everyone see the charts?"

Everyone nodded in agreement with a few additionally giving the thumbs-up sign.

"OK. Recall we re-introduced the surveys during the summer. At that time, we had already started doing some outreach, but the numbers were still a little soft. Let's review the questions."

As John read survey questions about professionalism, verbal and written communications with audit clients, focusing on the key priorities of the client and what mattered most to them, and cycle time, he pointed at the scores which were 85 percent or above in all categories.

"Now here are the numbers for this quarter. Notice the numerical and the percent increase in the scores. This ... is ... awesome!" He said with emphasis as he pointed with his finger at the screen. "This is not one person's score. This is our department's score. But I should say, these are your scores. You're crushing it! and our clients are recognizing it!"

"By the way, some of you have received e-mails and Teams messages from some of our clients, so you knew the tide was changing. I also received calls and I've spoken with several of our clients, and I've heard the positive feedback firsthand. There is a lot to be proud of here."

"OK, my friends. Let's turn to the next topic on the agenda. Lessons Learned. This is an open forum topic where we talk about what you learned recently. Who wants to start?" said John with a smile as he held his open hands facing upward inviting the team to share.

--------------------||--------------------

"What's the name of the guy from FTX? Lived in the Bahamas? Crashed the company?"

"Sam Bankman-Fried," replied Tony.

"How do you pronounce the last name again?" asked Carolina.

"Freed, like 'free' and a 'd' at the end," he repeated the name, then Tony started to smile.

"As opposed to Fried as in Kentucky Fried Chicken, remember? KFC?" said Carolina nodding as she led Tony to a trap that he now realized he walked into.

"I know what you're doing," he said.

"What am I doing?" she said with a smile.

"Go ahead. Say it. You're dying inside," said Tony closing his eyes and shaking his head.

"You say it!" said Carolina with clear delight.

"Why pronounced 'freed' for his name, but 'fried' for the fast-food company?" he said.

"Exactly!" she said as animated as if she had won the lottery.

"What am I walking into?" asked John as he joined the Teams meeting.

"She has been giving me a hard time about the inconsistencies of the English language for months. She traps me with these impossible questions," Tony explained smiling.

"He used to get upset because he must have an answer for everything, but he doesn't get upset anymore. He is no fun now!" said Carolina with a frown.

"It looks like he is having fun, and is that a frown hiding a smile I see on your face Carolina? It looks like both of you are enjoying this game you have going on," said John enjoying the lighthearted exchange among his staff.

As both Tony and Carolina smiled to no one in particular but their own shared camaraderie, Brian decided to share a story of his own.

"Since we're sharing fun stories, I'll tell you what happened to me Saturday. I was sailing and it was a beautiful, sunny day with cool crisp air. Small waves so it is a fun day to be out and a nice wind in the sails. I'm feeling good then I have this idea to go into a beautiful cove thinking I would do a little turnaround for fun. Got there and the wind shifted on me, forcing me to try to zig zag to get back out. No luck. After a while the wind died. Stopped. In irons. Couldn't get it moving. Then I started drifting in the current and I was headed for the shore."

"Did you get out?" asked Tony with a concerned tone.

"Yes, eventually, but not before kicking myself for getting into that predicament. I was hoping I wouldn't get stuck in the sand. There were some people on the beach and a picnic area full of people nearby. It looked like I interrupted their party. With nothing happening on the boat I could see them pointing at me and the kids waving and shouting. They thought it was hilarious. I could tell they were watching me and wondering why I was in there. So embarrassing."

"Colorful sail?" asked Carolina with a big smile on her face.

Brian closed his eyes and was shaking his head side to side as if seeing the boat in his mind. "Yes, orange, red, and blue. Very bright colors if you must know," he replied.

"There are probably pictures of you on social media, Brian," Rachel said. "Should I look?"

"Please don't."

John, noticing that while Brian was resilient and good-natured, he was going to get uncomfortable soon. He saw a teachable moment. "I had a few mishaps. Even capsized a few sailboats when I was learning to sail."

"You did?" asked Brian incredulously as he opened his eyes widely.

"Yes. When I was younger, like you, I tried a few things, stopped paying attention or tried to sail when the wind or waves were a bit much for my experience level. I made it OK, thankfully, but learned to be careful. What type of boat was it?"

"A Widgeon."

"12 feet? 14? 16?"

"14."

"Centerboard or keel?"

At that moment Brian closed his eyes, and slapped his forehead with his hand without saying a word.

"What does that mean?" asked Rachel.

Brian chose to answer the question himself. "The boat had a centerboard. If you get stuck in the sand, you can just raise it, get off the boat, and push it back."

"Oh," said Rachel understanding the implication but not saying anything else to avoid embarrassing Brian anymore.

"What size boat did you learn in?" asked Brian shifting the attention away from himself and also curious about one of John's out-of-the-office experiences.

"Laser 12, then moved up to Cape Cod Mercury and Rhodes 19. Fun little boats."

With that John shifted the conversation further to move onto business topics while in the back of his mind he was thinking what this conversation represented. Sharing. Adventure. Pastimes. Common experiences. Everyone, including the boss, makes mistakes and we should learn from them. We can laugh at adversity; stand back up when we fall and continue our life journey.

He made some announcements about things the department was implementing, including improvements to the QA process, and streamlining the workpaper review process.

--------------------||--------------------

"It is so good to see everyone. As you know, we have been making some changes in our department. We embraced data mining and data analytics and a few other things. This is our first official brainstorming session where we start to envision what we can do going forward into next year. I have to do that when developing the audit plan and managing the department, but one of my goals when I joined InSports last winter was to bring changes to the department. I told you then we would. And we have." He paused again to let the words sink in so his staff would appreciate the significance of his words.

"Are you happy and proud of what we have accomplished?" said John and paused again. He knew his statement could be interpreted as a rhetorical question, and that was his goal – to make a point and create dramatic effect. He now wanted to change the tone to open discussion.

"What are some of the changes we made?" he asked the group inviting conversation.

"We implemented Agile, updated our reporting by introducing different templates. We also changed our planning process to be more flexible," said Rachel excitedly. She had been hopeful for changes in the department for years, and they were happening now.

"Yes, we made those changes quite successfully I might add," said John proudly. "What else?"

"We re-introduced the post-audit survey, which I think was very helpful to see how we performed," added Tony.

"Yes, we're now getting some great feedback from our clients," added John.

"We introduced the auditor rotation program," said Brian.

"Do you think that will work?" asked John knowing that this was a new initiative that had not had time yet to show results. However, John thought this as an opportunity and asked to continue the practice of encouraging the team to think beyond actions and outputs, but outcomes.

"Yes, definitely. We will have more help which we didn't before," replied Miriam.

"We started doing consulting. That was interesting!" said Carolina.

"And we didn't get excommunicated for doing it," said Tony adding some humor to the conversation.

"That's right," acknowledged John with a smile.

"Very good everyone. This is a good and long list. Earlier in the year we embarked on this journey to improve our department. We set a vision, and remember, a vision without action is merely a dream," he paused thinking that perhaps Miriam would add the author.

She did. "Joel Barker"

John nodded and smiled at Miriam, then continued. "You show how action is turning our vision into reality. Another important thing here, one, I couldn't have done it myself. 'We' did it together, so you should be proud of the work you did. Two, our changes are not self-serving; these changes helped us deliver a better service to our clients. We are here to serve our clients. And three, success begets success, so we should keep innovating and using our creativity to continue to make positive change. With that in mind, one of our accomplishments was the introduction of the rotation program." As he said this he turned to Brian, "thanks for mentioning it so we could add it to the list just now," acknowledging the contribution.

"What do you think about a reverse rotation, where someone on the team can rotate out into the business to get some operational experience?" asked Carolina.

"That would be great," seconded Brian. "We would learn a lot doing something like that."

"Yes," chimed in Rachel. "We would get a much better understanding of how they do their work and that would help with our audits and advisory work."

"All good points. Yes," said John.

"How long would those rotations be for?" asked Caroline.

"We would need to coordinate with the departments you go to, but in general, I'm thinking three months to a year; at least that is what I would propose."

"Internationally?" asked Carolina.

"I don't see why not," replied John.

"I vote for Hawaii or French Polynesia; Tahiti works too," said Brian.

"Let's not go crazy here, folks. We should probably have operations there if we're going to call it a rotation program," admonished John.

"You know what?" said Tony, then pausing without elaborating.

"We don't know, Tony, help us out. What?" said Rachel.

"With people working remotely, couldn't we do that?" Tony explained. John thought Tony's insistence on the topic was interesting. He could have felt threatened by what seemed like his most senior manager's persistence, but after the heart-to-heart they had and the conversation about different ways and places people work, and how performance was measured in a modern workplace, he treated this as a reflection of Tony's newfound awareness. Before he could answer, Miriam commented.

"They're called digital nomads."

"Generally speaking, yes," replied John. "We are already working remotely, and a good amount of our work is already being done remotely. To your point Miriam, some countries like Barbados, Bermuda, Costa Rica, Germany, Mexico have some kind of visa that allows that."

"And Portugal," said Carolina jumping into the conversation.

"OK. Yes, and Portugal. My point is, you can do that now if you wanted to. The idea of a rotation program would be an organized program and rotation within InSports. If you go to live in one of these countries, that would be like you deciding to move to Kansas because you like it there. Not much more different except that now you would need to take care of your own, I mean private, visa application and foreign taxes, get fast and reliable internet access. By the way, I believe Bali has a nomad visa program, but that is in Indonesia. I don't know about Tahiti."

"It sounds like you have given this some thought, John," said Brian with a sly tone.

"I'm a Renaissance Man. I just happen to know a little about a lot of things," he said playing along with a wink and a smile. "Back to our list. Other ideas?"

"Can we issue reports verbally or create a video instead of text?" asked Carolina leaving the team dumbfounded.

After a short pause, John broke the silence, "that's an interesting idea and I had not thought about that." While rocking his head from side to side and pursing his lips in a thoughtful manner. "The Standards just say we have to communicate the results of our work. They don't say 'how'."

"That would be a modern, if not a bit revolutionary, to say the least," said Tony.

"Well, let's add it to the list. I asked and my team delivers creative ideas. We'll look into that for next year," said John as he wrote down the suggestion. "Other ideas?"

"Can we get a drone?" asked Miriam.

John smiled immediately. "Interesting way to put it, Miriam. Before I respond, what would you do with it?"

"Well, let's see. Inventory counts or inspecting our buildings?" she said.

"Is that an answer or a question? It sounded like a question."

"I'm not sure," she said.

"In general, I don't like to question suggestions during a brainstorming session. We've done brainstorming sessions before and you know I follow the approach of letting ideas flow without judgment then evaluating them later. In this case, I'm asking because this topic came up earlier in the year and we couldn't come up with enough viable uses of them to justify their introduction. I was just wondering if you had specific ideas now that we had not thought about before. To your point about inventory counts, at the time we determined that our inventory was inside warehouses where flying drones would not be practical, or safe. In terms of inspecting buildings, they are not very spread out, in had to reach locations, or large enough that walking around became impractical. We do, however, have some construction projects... So, I'm not shutting down your thinking, just wanted to explain."

"I'll put it on the list for now because other uses may surface, but your ideas on ways to incorporate them are helpful."

"How about AI?" asked Miriam.

"There is a lot going on there. I'll add it to the list to research."

With that, John transitioned the meeting to projects in progress, upcoming activities, and anticipated roadblocks. They also spoke about the upcoming holidays and team members' travel plans.

--------------------||--------------------

"Good morning, everyone. Thank you for joining us as we provide an update on our whistleblowing program special project and report on the result of our most recent sprint," said Rachel kicking off the meeting.

"For this sprint we had two objectives: One, deliver an awareness program to the entire organization and two, review the results of a post-training test and post-training survey with accompanying recommendations. For our first objective we are pleased to report that the training was successfully delivered to employees and included contractors of InSports worldwide. This was done live for many of the employees who work at, near to, and were willing to come in for the live sessions. Meeting colleagues onsite was chosen by more people than we thought would and the reasons for that I will explain when we get to our second objective. Questions?"

"Yes, said Ron raising his hand. Did you say contractors? Why were contractors included?"

"Good question. Yes, we included contractors because after talking with HR and Accounts Payable we found out that we had almost a hundred individuals working as contractors for our company and many of them were working with us for months, sometimes years. And many of them worked onsite too so the thinking was, could they see, hear, or otherwise find out about ethical issues that we don't know about? So, we decided to include any contractor working with us for more than two months."

"You know what's interesting?" said Ken. He had cupped his hands under his chin while looking at the ceiling verbalizing his thoughts. "We had an incident where a contractor was solicited to get involved in the theft of merchandise and declined the offer, but the employee kept looking and found someone else who agreed to the scheme. They stole thousands of dollars. The first contractor knew about the scheme as it evolved but still didn't say anything. When we finally caught up with the fraud and interviewed him, he said, 'I wasn't sure who to tell, I didn't want to be blamed or punished because I needed the work, so I kept quiet'. Great guy, but we had to terminate the contract nonetheless. Good thinking folks!"

"Thanks for sharing that story, Ken. Do you mind if we include it in the next round of training sessions? It illustrates the importance of what we're doing here."

"Sure. Go ahead. No names of course."

"Of course. Just like you told the story. What happened with limited boundaries around location, actors, and amounts, but a true story to show the relevance of our approach."

He nodded in agreement and winked at John showing his admiration for the renewed professionalism of the auditors. He was, after all, skeptical of audit's work earlier in the year.

Rachel continued. "The second objective was twofold, 2-a, post-training test. For this one we were working off a larger objective which we mentioned during a previous sprint. Namely, the training is conducted to help build capacity within InSports so those trained are better equipped to make ethical decisions."

"What happened to just check the box?" Ken said with a flourish in the air and checking an imaginary box in the air, "we delivered the training," he asked again.

"We don't do that anymore," said Rachel very seriously and instinctively while turning to look at Ken, at which point she realized he was joking. "Oh, I get it, she said smiling. But still, we don't do that anymore in a more congenial tone acknowledging the pleasant tone in the room."

Rachel continued. "At the end of the training everyone took a 12-question quiz that included 6 short vignettes. Eighty five percent of participants passed on the first try.

98 percent on the second try and the remaining 2 percent on the third. This is globally. We reviewed the results to better understand the reasons for failing and they all look like design issues. A few due to possible language reasons because they were all non-English speaking countries. Some in Latin America and others in countries where the language dynamics are even more significant, like a different alphabet as is the case in China and the Middle East. We made a note to examine that for the next go-around next year."

"As far as objective 2-b, it was a training satisfaction survey. Again, very positive results. It was a fifteen-question survey, and that includes three demographics questions. Overall satisfaction with the training 4.5 out of 5. Specific to the individual questions," she said as a chart appeared on the screen with several bars and a red line bifurcating the data points. She pointed at the one item below the red line, which had a 70 percent written at the intersecting point with the y-axis.

"The lowest rating was 3.2 and that had to do with 'examples that relate to my line of work'. We included five scenarios, and the test included those five plus a sixth one as I indicated previously. InSports is a large and complex organization and although we included scenarios about sales, marketing, manufacturing, accounting, human resources, which by the way, was about hiring decisions so it applies to more than just HR, and shipping, we had participants indicate they would like more examples."

She continued, "In the 'Comments' box there were, and I kid you not, eighteen suggested lines of work!" She said using her hands for emphasis.

"Do we have eighteen lines of work at InSports?" asked Ken incredulously.

"I guess so," said John feigning surprise since he had seen the report and asked the same question two days previously while reviewing the team's work.

"Yes," answered Rachel, happy for the positive reception their work was getting and how the adage "tell them something they don't know" was happening before her eyes. "Participants mentioned things like 'transportation', 'trainer operations', 'bidding', 'contracting', 'supply chain', 'reverse supply chain', 'retail,'" she read from her notes, "oh, here's one that really surprised me, 'artificial intelligence'."

"Artificial intelligence?" asked Ken, now turning his previous jovial tone into a very serious and surprised, tone.

"Yes. I know. I was surprised too but goes to show they were paying attention. They were thinking or had thought about this beforehand and were waiting for an opportunity to share their thoughts. Either way, it makes sense because we are working on some products that will generate training regiments for subscribers based on personal information like age, gender, BMI, past exercise metrics and so on" Rachel said while looking around the room and making eye contact with everyone present for emphasis. "With AI there is a question about gender and age bias, for example, and with all the medical information we are collecting and having our AI process it, we should be careful not to cross ethical lines."

"Are we collecting addresses, along with things like blood pressure and heart rates too?" asked Ron.

"That's what I've been told," replied John.

Ron nodded indicating both agreement and that he was processing this information further in his head. No doubt this was not the last time ethics and AI would be discussed as related items.

"So, 3.2 was the lowest. What is that one over there about two bars to the right of 3.2? The next lowest one," he said pointing at another bar on the chart slightly taller than the one just discussed.

"That's 'cultural appropriateness at 3.5'," she said pointing to the bar only tall enough to touch the red bisecting red line.

"What is that about?" he asked.

"That refers to the training addressing cultural dynamics unique to me and where I work," she explained. "Things like bribery and nepotism, which occur worldwide, are bigger problems in some parts of the world."

"And have implications for us like FCPA," he mused at a low voice showing agreement with the statement.

"Exactly. We made reference to FCPA, the UK Bribery Act, our company policy but we could do more."

"Like what?"

"In China, for example, they have been cracking down on corruption and they have the PRC Criminal Code. Argentina has its own criminal code too. Several countries, like Argentina, encourage self-disclosure and state that compliance programs will mitigate exposure to penalties. Kind of like the US federal sentencing guidelines. We didn't have enough coverage of that in our training."

"What are some of the penalties we are talking about? I can think of fines, but what else?"

"Argentina, for example, states 'suspension of activities, suspension of the use of patents and trademarks'."

"We can't have that happen."

"We'll expand that section in the materials and make sure we provide better coverage of local and cultural dynamics."

"Thanks. What else?" he asked prompting Rachel to proceed with her presentation.

"The highest rating was 5 for several of the questions, and like I said, overall, 4.5," she said as she displayed a slide showing the chart with the results onscreen.

"You mentioned 3.5 for examples I can relate to, what was the score for training duration?" asked Kathleen.

After a moment to locate the corresponding question, she replied, "4.2."

"4.2. If 4.5 is 90 percent then 4.2 is something like what, 85?"

"84," said Rachel.

"Ok, 84. Did they put something in the 'Comments' box explaining why they gave it that score?"

"Yes, let's take a look," said Rachel again as she pulled up another file with comments provided and arranged by question. "Here they are. Ok. So, things like," she said as she read a few examples: "not long enough," "not enough time," "awesome, thanks, but too short," and "too much and too little time," she paused as she moved to the next page while everyone in the room could see the list scrolling before their eyes. "I would give a higher score, but class too short," she read picking another comment off the list.

"I think the reason is clear. They thought it was too short." He said summarizing what everyone concluded about the comments. "The online version was just as long as the instructor-led version, correct?" he asked confirming his understanding.

"Yes, that is correct."

"OK. Make a note to consider making the training a little longer next time. I'm not committing to it just yet because this affects the entire organization and there is a cost involved. I'm leaning towards 'yes' from everything I heard here today, but first let's see what the results are for the next few months. Do this before we run the training again next year."

"We will."

"I need to go. I have another meeting starting right away. Thanks everyone. Good job!, said Ron as he looked and nodded at each team member individually. With that he closed and picked up his padfolio with one hand, grabbed his Starbucks coffee with the other and walked out the room."

---------------------||---------------------

"What happened to you?" asked Rachel.

Tony was wearing an A.C. Milan sweatshirt, but today the logo was not visible because the portion of the sling holding up his arm was covering it. His hand was out of eyesight below the camera frame, but his face showed the markings of something gone terribly wrong. He had several scratches and a bandage on his forehead, right above his right eye.

"I fell off a ladder," he said shrugging his shoulders as he leaned his head to a side in a matter-of-fact way.

"You look like you took quite a fall. Off a ladder? Did you get stiches on your forehead?" asked Carolina.

"No, just a bad bruise. You think I look bad? you should see the rosebush. It won't try attacking me anytime soon!" Tony said making a joke of the situation.

"That doesn't sound good at all. So, how did this happen?"

"Well. It all started with me checking items off my Saturday to-do list. Item three, 'clean the gutters'."

"Oh no. I don't like where this is going."

"Hold on. It was dry when I started the project. Sunny, maybe a few clouds in the sky, a light breeze, warm. Nothing suspicious, right? But the weather turned fast, and before you knew it, it started raining. I wasn't going to quit when I was almost done. I'm not a quitter, don't ever forget that!" he said once again with a big smile creating a stark contrast with his injuries.

"Go on."

"So, I'm up on the ladder, I'm taking the leaves out of the gutter and throwing them down. I'm trying to hurry up because, well, did I tell you it started raining?"

"Yes, you did," responded Rachel dragging out the words in that this-won't-end-well tone.

"OK. So, as I'm scooping out the leaves, I have to stretch to reach some more leaves away from me and for a moment I thought to myself, 'maybe I should move the ladder', but why would I, right? If I only s t r e t c h a little more I can reach those over t h e r e," he explained while acting out his motion, and then he paused as he raised his eyebrows and shook his head from side to side. "Gravity won."

"Is that when you fell?" Rachel asked instinctively expressing concern and curiosity at the same time.

"Not immediately. I grabbed onto the gutter, and it worked for a while, but then it broke, and I pulled a huge section of that with me. We need a new one and the rosebush cushioned the blow when I hit the ground so that was destroyed. Good thing I had not cut back the rosebush yet or I would have fallen onto spikes! Anyway, I remember falling, the gutter making this awful ripping sound, water and leaves coming down with me and branches cracking under my weight. I wish someone was recording it. I would be trending on social media big time!"

"Did you get up on your own?"

"Are you kidding? I couldn't let the neighbors see me down there! I got up right away and walked it off. It hurt like crazy, so my wife told me we had to go check it out."

"Did you?"

"Yes. No broken bones. Just sore from the fall hence the sling."

"Did you finish cleaning the rest of the gutters?" asked Brian jumping into the conversation.

The question made everyone stop talking immediate. "I was joking everyone, but seriously, knowing Tony, I wouldn't be surprised if he finished the job."

"No, I appreciate the vote of confidence, man. I tidied up the scene a little, my wife helped me move the ladder and what was left of the gutter away, then I went to bed. Everything hurt Sunday, so all I did was watch terrible soccer the rest of the weekend."

"Terrible soccer … hm, so Milan lost, eh?"

"Yes, to Juventus. Don't make me relive that."

After letting the conversation run its course, John put an end to it by shifting the focus to work. "Glad you're OK, all things considered. Take it easy and rest when you need to so you heal fully. If you need time off let us know. Are we all here?" he asked to himself since it was easy to tell given the team's size.

"Yes," he said answering his own questions. "Let's begin."

--------------------||--------------------

"Hi Frank."

"John, my good friend! How are you? Happy Holidays."

"Happy Holidays. I'm well. Getting close to year-end. It has been an exciting year, to say the least."

"So, tell me, where are you and what's left to do this year."

"Well, started with a team that needed help focusing on business objectives and risks, working more collaboratively with management, more flexible in their approach, and closing audits faster. We did that. We are now focusing on validating the gains."

"Interesting, how so?"

"A quality assurance program would help us get confirmation from an expert third party that we are on the right track and conforming with the Standards."

"Are you ready for such a review already?"

"No. We'll do it in two steps. First a diagnostic review while we improve our internal review processes, then a full-blown external assessment next year."

"Smart move! Love it! What else?"

"Then institutionalize the changes by cementing the approach, our availability and knowledge with the management team and the board. We're getting there."

"What about the new year. What do you want to do?"

"Work from a flexible audit plan, be agile in the execution, and expand the team so we can do more. I'm introducing a rotation program, encouraging them to get certifications and great training, and that includes strengthening our ability to do data analytics."

"You did well and your plan going forward looks solid too. Write an annual report, John. Summarize your accomplishments and send that to senior management and the audit committee."

"Great idea. I will. Thanks."

"Congratulations!"

"Thanks. I appreciate your help along the way. It was much appreciated."

"My pleasure. Godspeed my friend and may the wind be always at your back."

"Thank you, Frank."

--------------------||--------------------

Summary
Fall

Shortly after the typical pleasantries exchanged at the beginning of every audit committee meeting they reviewed results for the quarter and the aggregate results for the year, Jim asked, "as we finish the year, and the list of items left on the audit plan gets shorter, what are the top five risks that internal audit is not addressing due to a lack of skills or resources?"

John thought quickly about the question and realized the need to educate the audit committee on the difference between having an audit plan and managing the unit to completing it, and adopting a more agile approach where items are added, changed, and removed, as needed. He would address that next year. After thinking about the question and its implications, John replied,"I believe we should look at cybersecurity, supply chain and vendor management, sensitive payments and fraud, business model risk and talent management."

"Can you audit those with the staff and budget you currently have?" asked Sanjay.

"Not all of them and not soon enough. We need to co-source or hire more people, because these topics are either very specialized, like cybersecurity, or will require several people to review it sufficiently and quickly, like supply chain and vendor management. For example, vendor management would be fairly large given our global footprint."

"Could you limit the scope?"

"Yes, we could, but that would limit what I can tell you about them," he paused briefly not wanting to finish his answer sounding negative. "We can look at sensitive payments and fraud with every audit, but I'm still building up the team to be more proficient there." Having added a positive angle to the statement, he concluded with a request: "we could use some help."

"So, we don' have assurance, or comfort, that those topics are in check?" asked Sanjay.

"Not at this point," replied John shaking his head in the negative.

Jennifer asked the next question. "We are hearing quite a bit lately about ESG. What are your thoughts about it?"

"There is a growing worldwide trend to review ESG, which stands for Environment, Social and Governance. We could say that is an extension of GRC, Governance, Risk and Compliance, but far more encompassing because it doesn't only look at what the organization is doing internally, but also its impacts externally."

"What do you mean?" asked Jim.

"GRC was designed to help organizations reliably achieve objectives while addressing uncertainty, or risk, with integrity. With ESG you evaluate how an organization works on behalf of social goals that go beyond the maximization of profits on behalf of stockholders. In fact, the Business Roundtable issued a statement in 2019 where they stated that organizations were not only expected to maximize stock price but should pursue the interests of, I believe five key stakeholders. Let's see if I remember them," he said as he counted with his fingers, "customers, workers, suppliers, and communities. Wait, that's four ..., yes... right, stockholders, that's five."

"I believe there are certain pillars also included in ESG, is that right?" asked Jennifer again,

"Yes, there are four pillars, governance, planet, people, and prosperity. So, with ESG, the social goals include supporting certain social movements, environmental goals, and the organization is governed in a way that supports diversity, equity, and inclusion. With this, governance takes on a broader scope and the entire initiative is concerned not only with the current dynamics but also the sustainability of the organization's actions."

"This sounds like corporate social responsibility," said Sanjay.

"Yes, that is a big part of it. In fact, you could link many of the ESG elements to the original CSR ideas and ideals," replied John.

"If I remember correctly institutional investors are taking a hard look at ESG, is that correct?" asked Sanjay asking a question before Jennifer could speak.

"Yes, this is an expansion of socially responsible investing and now there are trillions of dollars in these funds and growing by billions a year. Many institutional investors are requesting, if not demanding, that ESG matters be addressed, documented, and shared," replied John.

"Did you see the statement from Larry Fink over at BlackRock?" asked Jennifer in what appeared to be some competition between Sanjay and Jennifer for airtime.

"Oh yes, that's right. That was a few years ago, like 2018 or thereabout. Something about society demanding all organizations serve a social purpose and make a positive contribution to society," replied John.

"Yes, benefit all stakeholders," said Sanjay.

"What would an ESG audit include? Roughly, just some preliminary thoughts as we start to think about next year," intervened Jim in the ongoing verbal tennis match.

"Yes. So, on the environment or environmental side of things, we could look at our generation of greenhouse gas emissions and our carbon footprint, waste management, energy management, water use and management, use of renewable sources of energy, our use of rare metals in our electronic components, and so on. We might also look at the risks we are exposed to for example by having manufacturing plants in areas prone to flooding," explained John.

"And social?" asked Sanjay inserting himself in the conversation again.

"In terms of social concerns, a lot of it centers around labor standards. It includes things like wages and benefits. Diversity of the workforce is very big too. It would involve looking at equity and fairness in recruitment, appointment, promotions into management and senior management, the amount of volunteering that our employees are encouraged to perform, how we support local communities and charities like Little League teams, our use of fair trade or similar mechanisms in our supply chain and consumer protection mechanisms as opposed to 'buyer beware', which is what we heard most often in business school when I was getting my degree."

"What about employee relations?" It was now Jennifer's turn.

"Yes, that's there too. An example is the growing number of Top Companies to Work For and the competition for companies to get on one of those lists. Oh, before I forget, and this relates to what I was saying earlier about wages and benefits, is employee compensation. The terms used most often is pay equity and there are audits done and the results may be required by regulators and could be made available to the public, like it is in government."

"Got it. How is governance different now than it was before?" asked Jim.

At that moment Jennifer interrupted by asking, "Excuse me for a moment, before you talk about governance, I understand that this also impacts diversity at the board level, right?" which drew a surprised look from Jim, and as John nodded in agreement without saying anything, Jim spoke, "Hmm. Ok. We need to look at that. We need some new members so this could be a good time to introduce that. I'll talk to Carol so the board's Nominating Committee can look into this." With this, Jim made a mental note that he was possibly going to be tasked with mediating some friction within his committee soon.

"Go on. Governance," Jim instructed John to continue.

"Some things are similar, like looking at ethics, anti-competitive practices, corruption, and transparency. It also includes board diversity, and this one is pretty big because NASDAQ is now requiring that at least one board member be a member of a minority group. Things like executive pay are also mentioned there."

"Does it include separating the CEO and board chairmanship roles?" asked Jennifer. "That is practiced in several European countries."

"There is talk about it. It is not mandatory yet, but there is growing momentum in that direction."

"Who is doing that?" asked Sanjay.

"The UK and Germany, for example," replied Jennifer.

"In general, it is more common in Europe than it is in the US," said John trying to ease what felt like a growing tension in the room. "You could say the G is about governing the E and the S."

"Got it. So, board composition and structure, sustainability as a strategic priority, oversight, and compliance," said Jim summarizing the conversation so far.

But John wanted to add something else. "Yes. Another thing we haven't mentioned is political contributions and lobbying, which also brings up bribery and corruption."

"We look into bribery and corruption through our FCPA work, right?" asked Jim.

"We do. So, we have been doing some of the ESG work, just not calling it that. FCPA, on the other hand, somewhat but maybe we should do more," said John hoping the committee would get the hint.

Instead, Sanjay continued talking about the present topic "When I look at my portfolio, I'm seeing ESG ratings on companies and mutual funds."

Acknowledging Sanjay's comment, John said, "Yes, that is part of how this is making it into our daily lives. Asset managers and institutional investors are increasingly relying on ESG rating agencies to review, measure and benchmark ESG performance."

"Like the most responsible organizations?" said Jim.

"Exactly. Just like for employees in terms of best companies to work for, there are lists of most responsible organizations becoming more common."

"OK then. What would a report look like if you were to review the key parts of this next year?" asked Jim.

"We would review and present financial and non-financial results showing whether we are meeting the expectations of organizations like the Sustainability Accounting Standards Board and the Task Force on Climate-related financial disclosures. I'm watching the SEC for required filings and those are probably coming soon. The other thing is sustainability reports," said John providing some ideas for the committee to consider.

"Green reports?" asked Sanjay.

"Yes, some people call them that, and corporate responsibility reports, so we are looking at both internal and external reporting," John explained.

"John, you're always talking about risk. How do we link risk to ESG, or is that not seen as connected?" asked Jim.

"That's a great question. Yes, they are connected. There is risk and opportunity. For example, I mentioned the risk of flooding to our manufacturing plants. A beverage company would be concerned about clean water to make their beverages and excessive air pollution would be a problem for airliners. But there is also opportunity. By recruiting more broadly and encouraging diversity, we would recruit talent with different backgrounds We need that talent to innovate and if nothing else, understand the customers we try to serve."

"I think there is also reputational risk. Our actions or inaction could feed the media machine and get us on the news cycle," said Jennifer. "The last thing we need is to go viral for being perceived as being out of step with public opinion whether the complaint comes from within the organization or from the outside."

"If we are smart about training and see it as an investment more so than as an expense, we keep workers sharp and productive, maybe even reduce turnover," said Jim.

"Exactly!" said John enthusiastically.

"I don't believe we are ready for a full assessment yet. Make a note to do a readiness assessment first, some kind of investigation to see how far behind we might be, then we can fix the obvious issues and then do the full assessment later. We will need to start making disclosures sooner rather than later, and commitments from investors and other groups won't be far behind, so we need to move on this," said Jim.

"Good idea."

"Let's have Legal involved as we move forward here. With the public statements and forward-looking commitments, we need to make sure those are properly qualified, and we include the appropriate disclaimers," said Jim again.

"There are also financial reporting implications, and Public Relations and maybe even Marketing needs to be in the loop as we go live here because if investors, lenders, and the SEC compare statements, they have to be consistent and accurate. We don't want any problems with our MD&A," said Jennifer.

"Right. John, what other risks or topics come to mind as we start to plan for next year?" asked Jim reverting back to him for his ideas.

"The main ones I'm thinking about are cybersecurity, vendor management, supply chain disruption, privacy, intellectual property, FCPA and corporate culture, and we should also look at the construction projects we have underway due to their large financial and strategic significance to InSports," he replied, repeating topics he had mentioned previously and adding construction, which he had missed the first time around.

"Everything you mentioned sounds good, but do we have to audit FCPA? We're not into banking, so I don't believe our risk is high there," said Sanjay.

"We do a lot of international work. The risk could be high," opined Jennifer. "What do you think, Jim?"

"We don't have to decide right now. We'll see. What do you think John?" said Jim now tossing the hot potato over to John.

"Money laundering is a concern for all organizations, not just financial institutions. For example, Lafarge, a French company specializing in cement, concrete, and construction products, was fined $778 million in the US for paying terrorist groups in Syria, including ISIS. The company was involved in a multi-year arrangement that consisted of issuing monthly payments, and the militants issued papers to the company's drivers guaranteeing safe passage for its shipments."

"How much did you say the fine was?" asked Jim.

"Total of around $778 million imposed by the US Justice Department, but the company still had to face criminal charges in France where charges included complicity with crimes against humanity, financing terrorism and putting the lives of their workers in Syria at risk. Eighth executives were indicted for their role in this plot. They concealed their actions from Holcim, the parent company, and from auditors."

"That's right. They're owned by Holcim. But that happened before they were acquired, right?" commented Sanjay.

"Yes, that's true. But the US Attorney General working on the case also stated that Holcim, did not perform due diligence on the Syria operations. In general, prosecutors stated the company concealed its payments, falsified records, backdated contracts and made approximately $6 million in illegal payments to keep its operations in Syria running," said John.

"Quite a mess, but they were deeply involved in the Middle East, and Syria is way out of our range of operations. Let's park that one. I think we have more pressing things to attend to," wanting to change the subject, Sanjay pivoted to another question.

"What about methodology? You implemented agile auditing, which was a success. What other ideas do you have to improve the way audits are performed?"

"Sanjay. Yes, agile auditing was a success and I'm glad you agree. One thing we would like to do is to leverage data analytics more broadly. The idea is to create some scripts that we can run against data sets and have outliers and otherwise unusual transactions flagged for us. We would then focus on those for review," John replied.

"Only on those?" asked Jennifer.

"Primarily on those. Yes. The idea is to focus on the ones that look suspicious and treat them as risky, rather than sampling transactions and testing to see if the control was applied, we look for risk instead. And we run the script against the entire population," John explained.

"That sounds good. How often would those scripts run?" she asked again.

"It depends on the risk. Some transactions like T&E and Accounts Payable, we could run every six months. We don't want to run these scripts and suggest that we are the control point identifying issues to be fixed. That is management's responsibility. So quarterly or semi-annually would be better."

"Shouldn't management be running scripts and reports like those monthly or even weekly?" she kept probing.

"Yes, that is what management should be doing as part of their regular monitoring work. So, if they are monitoring and correcting issues, then everything should come back clean when we check. That is called continuous auditing. If they don't correct issues, or don't have a report or mechanism to identify issues, then we can develop the algorithm and hand it over to them after a while for them to adopt it," said John hinting at a way to build a more collaborative relationship with management and support their oversight role.

"Good. Teaching them how to monitor their own areas. That's good!" said Jim.

"We need to preserve our independence, so we will be careful how we craft it, communicate and execute it. They should not stand back and wait for us to tell them when there are issues. As the first line, they should do that so yes, teaching them, but they will then finetune it, adapt it as necessary, own it and do it so we don't become part of the day to day control mechanism."

"Can that be done with higher-risk transactions?" asked Jennifer.

"Like journal entries?" John asked for clarification.

"Yes, like journal entries and payments with FCPA compliance risk," she explained.

"Absolutely. We would like to build a series of scripts around risky processes and activities, so some thoughts include journal entries, refunds, change orders in our construction projects, payments to advertising agencies, brokers, freight forwarders, consultants, and one-off international payments to non-recurring beneficiaries," he replied adding a few more examples to the initial list.

"Tell me about the risk assessment. Any thoughts there?" asked Sanjay.

"Yes. We will be updating the process for the enterprise risk assessment, which feeds into our annual plan, but also at the project level. The plan is to include the client more often and substantially," he explained.

"Any other plans for next year?"

"We have MORs, management operational reports. We spoke about them during our last meeting and at that time I referred to them in terms of keeping up to date with new and emerging risks so we could be risk-based. What we have for MORs is good, but a close look shows it focuses disproportionately on KPIs. As you know, KPIs are about performance or production. Sales, number of employees, number of customers, and so on. KRIs are also metrics, but they focus on risk. So, while sales are a good KPI, collections are a good KRI. You can sell, but if you're not collecting, you have a problem. Number of employees is another KPI, but turnover, absenteeism and engagement levels are KRIs. Number and descriptive statistics about our customers. KPI. Customer turnover or churn. KRI. Cost per customer, I mean the cost to get a new customer. KRI. Even vendors. We had a tough year in terms of supply chain management. How much of our incoming supplies come from the top 10 suppliers?" John finished with a question.

With this question John paused to let the new information sink in and for the AC members to react. The reaction was silence, rubbing of chins and hands, but no words for a few, long seconds, until Jim spoke. "I can't believe we haven't separated the two concepts before. This looks like a big miss, or enhancement opportunity."

Without acknowledging or refuting the statement, John continued. "I've already introduced the concept in the department so that with each audit we look at both. As I mentioned previously, we are now much more risk-based than before and that means understanding the objectives of the area under review, the identification and rating of risks that may hinder their ability to achieve those goals, and lastly the controls and other activities that helps them manage those risks. Note I try not to say mitigate the risks, because we have also worked hard to help operating units not try to mitigate every risk. And for the auditors to stop recommending we mitigate all risks."

"You just lost me there for a moment. I thought the purpose of controls was to mitigate risks," asked Sanjay.

"That is just one of the things that controls do," said Jennifer answering before John could speak, then he continued.

"Yes, that's correct. Mitigation is the common default and perhaps the most common action too. However, we should treat risks more carefully. Sometimes you should just avoid doing what is causing the risk. It may not always be an option, but there is no longer petty cash in most of our foreign locations; we got rid of that in the US and Canada a while ago, but we still have petty cash in some locations. Another example, we no longer have P-cards in some locations for the same reasons. Stop doing what can trigger the risk. Sharing is another option."

"Sharing?" said Sanjay in an instinctive reaction.

"Yes, sharing the risk. We are getting better at sharing more with our insurance carriers. We found that our insurance coverage needed some updating so now we stop chasing certain things or overly controlling certain things and just have the insurance company help us manage some predictable, low impact and arguably recurring events," said John finishing his thought and frowning instinctively as he tried to remember how the conversation drifted to control types and where he was before that happened.

"Where were we?" he asked rhetorically more to himself than committee members. "Oh yes, MORs, so recommending some KRIs for better monitoring and management. By the way, one thing I recommended last quarter and has already been put in motion is clear escalation measures. I noticed that many reports covered the KPIs and explanations for deviations, but they were mostly excuses and few if any real explanations and descriptions of corrective actions. Now there is more digging into deviations by screening the comments and adding reverse escalation procedures. What I mean by that is that before the bad news gets on the MOR, the chain of command below should have already filtered the problem and middle management is doing its job correcting deviations. If problems get fixed there, they don't have to be escalated to senior management in quarterly reports. The weeklies and monthlies will already show the drift and the drift will be addressed weekly and monthly. Not after quarter end when everyone is near panic mode at what could be a meaningful quarter over quarter deviation."

John felt he was getting long winded with his explanations, but this was the year-end meeting and wanted to get a few things in. He also noticed all three heads bopping in agreement, so he decided to add another thought to wrap up that part of the conversation.

"Fine-tuning and correcting as conditions warrant. We want to navigate, choose the right waypoints and sail from waypoint to waypoint always trying to stay on our desired line. That's the difference between merely sailing," John said moving his left hand in a dismissive motion like swatting a fly, and navigating, which he punctuated with his right hand and his raised index finger for emphasis. Using different hands further drew the contrast between both approaches.

"Good analogy, John. This might help ease some of the stress off everybody's job," said Jim.

"And everyone can play an enjoyable round of golf every once in a while," said John adding another benefit of the preventive approach he was advocating.

"Appreciate that," said Jennifer smiling.

"John, the internal audit team has come a long way. I believe I speak for all three of us on the committee when I say that this unit is much improved from the department we gave you at the beginning of the year, so thanks and congratulations. Audit reports speak more eloquently about the needs of the organization. With that, what strategies are you putting in motion to make sure that auditors gain a better understanding of the business?

"Thank you for your feedback. I appreciate it. It was a team effort. We're not done yet, and there is more we will do. A very important action is for them to continuously learn how InSports operates. To that end, we will implement a rotation program where we have auditors rotating out so they can learn about the business, and staff from InSports rotate into internal audit. The rotating in portion will begin in January and we already have someone. She comes with construction audit experience. This will also add some capacity to our team. On the rotating out portion, that will be disruptive, I'll admit that right away, but this rotation program can be done successfully. Another key action item is to improve the flow of operational information from InSports to all my staff. I'm thinking of the internal auditors' code of ethics."

"Which is?" interrupted Jennifer because the connection to ethics didn't seem to align with the topic being discussed.

"Yes, there are principles of integrity, objectivity, competency and confidentiality. In terms of the sharing of information with the team, confidentiality would be the primary principle called for, but we're mostly talking about general company information. Anyway, the sharing of information and protection of its contents within the team would help strengthen the third one I mentioned, competency, and gaining a broader and deeper understanding of the organization will help," he explained.

"Based on your coverage this year, connect the dots for us. What is your assessment about InSports' internal controls and risk management?" asked Jim.

"In general, I believe things are moving in the right direction but there are some gaps. There are some areas we should focus a bit more on next year, which I've shared with you. Overall, we've come a long way since January," he stated summarizing his opinion.

"Can we talk about the report from the consultant you hired for the QAIP diagnostic assessment?" asked Jim, and immediately John thought to himself, "'is that a question?' it's not like I can say 'no, let's not talk about the report'."

"Of course," said John. "Did you get to read through it?"

"Yes, the three of us read it and talked about it before this meeting. Good job, John. Very good feedback, some of which you had already alerted us to. In terms of the things that you need to focus on, a larger budget to hire two more auditors and implement an electronic workpaper package, and some more money for training. We already agreed to increase your budget. About the external assessment, when will you begin the search for the reviewer?"

"March or April. I would like to have the review done by the end of Q3, so this will give us enough time to implement some of the recommendations, including having an internal review process, and hire the two additional auditors. So, the review could happen by the end of next fall."

"Sounds good," said Jim. "Now here is another thing the three of us talked about. All this talk about quality assurance review for the internal audit unit, we think as a committee we should take a look at ourselves too and also consider ways to improve the way we work." "I believe our meetings could be streamlined so we make sure to cover the main topics we need to address. John, I like that you provide well-organized, clear, and concise pre-meeting materials. We need to require others to provide better materials about all these compliance things. It would save us some time and reduce redundancy."

"The term auditors use for that is integrated assurance and integrated reporting. I had that in mind as an initiative when internal audit got its mojo back," said John with a smile.

The words took a moment to register in Jim's mind who laughed out loud at the reference. "I hadn't heard that expression in a while, John," he said shaking his head. "Do you think internal audit is getting its mojo back?"

"Yes," said John also smiling.

"You sure look it and the things you're putting in front of us show it too. There's more confidence and energy in the room. It has been building all year long and we appreciate it," said Jim as Jennifer smiled and Sanjay looked on.

"Thank you, said John accepting the compliments. My team is showing renewed enthusiasm too, so it is going all around."

"Good. Internal auditing is a team sport. Well, integrated assurance sounds like something we could use to make our meetings more effective and efficient," Jennifer opined. "Would that also cover EHS, Compliance, QA, Financial Reporting and who am I missing?" she asked everyone and no one in particular.

"ESG," said Jim, dispelling the thought that it was a rhetorical question and answered it instead.

"Yes, ESG," agreed Sanjay. "There are so many reports coming our way, we need to organize, simplify and consolidate all of this."

"Will the external assessment also give us some advice on the audit plan and key risks. How about benchmarking?" asked Jim again.

"Yes, we can ask for all of that. Those are common asks," explained John.

"Well, since there's so much validation we can get from it, let's do it," Jim noted, then said. "We need to wrap up our meeting, but let's summarize things first. What did you accomplish this year, and what are some of your plans for next year?"

"This year we introduced agile auditing, which allows us to perform more audits and report results faster, among other benefits. We enhanced our auditing tools, including group facilitation, root cause analysis, data analytics and better flowcharts. We introduced a road show to raise awareness about internal audit and built stronger relationships with the management team, and we reinvigorated the team so they are now focused on supporting the organization's objectives and looking at risks from that perspective, while working more efficiently. So that's this year."

"Next year we plan to increase staff further, perform more operational audits, conduct a QAIP review, audit corporate culture and ethics companywide, audit cybersecurity, and review IT more. I believe co-sourcing would work best for us, and both vulnerability and penetration testing reviews come to mind as key. Oh, we're also working with HR and training so we expand and strengthen the whistleblowing and ethics training time."

As the meeting adjourned, John left the room pleased with the progress made during the year and energized to do even more the following year. He had succeeded in turning the department around.

As he walked out of the building and onto the street, he stood next to the building listening, watching, and fully sensing the movement, sounds, and smells of a city on the go. This had been a challenging year, and he felt satisfied about the results. The team was doing well, the audit committee trusted him, and people throughout InSports, managers and non-managers alike, respected him. He had been on the go all year and knew the importance of reflection and relaxation. The days were now short as the sun sets earlier, and the holiday season was in full swing; this meant festive lights and decorated windows throughout 5th Avenue and around New York City. He walked for a while around midtown, reflecting on his and his teams' accomplishments this year.

After spending a moment in the thriving Times Square marveling at the lights and its energy, he had dinner in Little Brazil. He took the train back to his hotel and after changing concluded he needed to walk that bridge one last time this year.

As he crossed the Brooklyn Bridge, he soaked in the views in both directions as he reflected on the year that was ending. He had built many bridges this year and accomplished much at InSports, and treated the journey like a challenge; it was worth it.

--------------------||--------------------

The next day the team arrived in New York for the last quarterly meeting of the year. Although it was cold and snowing, the holiday lights were on, and the year-end feeling was everywhere. They got together for dinner in Times Square, where they marveled at the crowds and noise. The lights added to the chaos, and the group absorbed the energy from it all. After taking some pictures and people watching, they traded what was traditionally a nice sit-down dinner for a quick meal because they had previously agreed to buy tickets for a show at a theater nearby.

The next morning, John joined the meeting and found his entire team already seated, talkative but somewhat subdued. It was the last meeting of the year, and he immediately sensed some melancholic looks on their faces. It had been a long year and now the calendar showed late December. The year was almost gone.

"We're getting to the end of the year, folks. Where did it go?" said John broadly to start the conversation.

"I don't know," replied Rachel. "A bit of a blur, I suppose, but you know what, it was an incredible ride."

"It was. We've had these quarterly meetings all year but instead of following our traditional agenda, let's mix this up just a little. How about we borrow from our Thanksgiving tradition and each person provides a quick testimonial of what this year has been like. How about touching on accomplishments, challenges, and your outlook for next year. Sounds good?"

They talked about agile auditing, the shorter reports and reporting cycle, the road show, the different focus during reviews, and how they collaborated more with the clients. They talked about how the Socratic Method, which was a bit uncomfortable at first had helped them develop their critical thinking skills, work collaboratively, and engage in healthy discussions. They also spoke about the increase in consulting work, introducing the rotation program, and reintroducing postaudit surveys. They also reminded each other of their certification achievements as Tony passed Part 1 of the CIA exam and now joined Rachel and Carolina preparing for Part 2. Brian stated the peer pressure was getting to him and he would have to "try and keep up with the Joneses" as he put it; he would join the race and start studying for CISA next year.

"My turn now. I'll speak to what's next. Next year we are going to continue innovating and making the necessary changes to make this a world class internal audit unit. I met with the audit committee yesterday and they have agreed to increase our budget, so we're hiring up. We're also going to start the search for an electronic workpaper package and we're also going to work together to upskill you, so there will be more money in the budget for training. Two additional things I want to encourage you to do is be more active in your local audit, IT audit, or fraud audit chapters, maybe speak at conferences, write articles, and stay on track pursuing your certifications. How does that sound?"

"That's terrific," said Carolina, verbalizing the smiles and nodding heads from team members.

John continued. "As to what I'm grateful for, first and foremost, your support. You welcomed me into your department and supported the vision I put in front of you. I couldn't have done it without you. You, all of you, stepped up, worked hard, dealt with the discomfort of change in a very positive way, and helped me change our processes, and stakeholder relationships. We're raising the unit to the next level. You should be proud of yourselves because I'm proud of you. I shared most of the same things we just talked about with the audit committee, and they are very pleased with the way we've turned things around. We're on a journey making progress and people are noticing it."

That evening the team got together, and they celebrated their accomplishments and shared their enthusiasm for the coming year. As if they needed another reason, this also doubled as a party, because it so happens that this was December and the holiday season.

--------------------||--------------------

Epilogue

John's phone rang while he sat in his car at Lighthouse Beach in Chatham, Massachusetts. The day started, as they say on The Cape, socked in, with so much fog you could hardly see 100 feet ahead. Later that morning, the sun burned off the fog, and a blue sky invited John out of the house and to one of his favorite places.

Down below in front of them, a few people walked on the beach, and a fishing boat sailed between the sand dune and the open ocean on its way to the Fish Pier. He had been watching that sand dune grow over the years and recreate the barrier that would form a buffer, and protected the beach from the constant pounding of the Atlantic Ocean. Going to the Cape in the winter was enjoyable because with fewer people around there were virtually no lines at restaurants and shops; you could stroll down Chatham Center without bumping into too many tourists.

"How are you, John."

"I'm well. Just having coffee and pastries in the car overlooking the beach."

"On Cape Cod? Which beach?"

"Chatham Lighthouse Beach"

"Nice, very nice. How is the weather?"

"Wonderful," replied John, as he thought to himself, why is he calling me out of the blue like this?

He didn't have to wait long.

"Yesterday we had a meeting as we plan for our upcoming Strategy Summit, so I was talking with Ken and he was telling me about some great initiatives they're working on. There are plans to introduce some new features on the equipment that will use biometric information to create personalized exercise programs and we may partner with a clinical firm to prepare medical profiles to tailor exercise regimens even more. Totally new functionality! Also expand the manufacturing capacity by building a new plant in Mexico and automating the facility in Atlanta. We believe Latin America will be a growing market. The Supply Chain group is looking into blockchain to manage our vendors and shipments better. Kathleen told me she would like to do some more work on corporate culture after the work from home or return to the office back-and-forth, and the silent quitting problems that seem to be growing among some of our associates. But those are the easy ones. We'll see what comes out of the Summit, but we're excited about the next twelve months!"

As John thought about it all, and the fact that Ron's voice was unusually energetic, he was also processing the words, "but those are the easy ones" and what that meant. Or better yet, what else was coming.

"So, John, how about you and I talk next week so you tell me what you think about these initiatives. You know that I value your input, but I thought you should know what Ken told me. He said, and I quote, 'Let's ask John now what he thinks about these initiatives so if possible he can speak to them when we get there. We need

DOI: 10.1201/9781003322870-22

that perspective before we go too far down the line and forget something that can push this train off the tracks'."

"John, can you believe him? This is the same guy that last year told me point blank, 'can you get those' and I promised to cut back on my swearing so I'm letting you fill the blank there 'auditors away from me so we can get some real work done?' Looks like you got a new fan."

"Anyway, get on my calendar, let's talk Monday or Tuesday. I have to run, I have a meeting with some bankers to look at some financing options for a possible acquisition next year, then I'm talking with the external auditors about going public in two years."

As John processed some of this information, how this new information fit into what he was already thinking internal audit should review next year and the opportunities and risks that these initiatives represented, Ron asked one more thing.

"You're coming to the Strategy Summit in Boca Raton? Right?"

"Sure, I'll be there."

"Good! Enjoy the beach. Talk to you later!"

As John ended the call, he thought to himself how far the department had come since he joined the organization, and Ken's attitude summed it up nicely. Last January Ken did everything he could to avoid the company's auditors, now he took the initiative to ask for our opinion. He is offering us a seat at the table. Wow, we've come a long way!

At that moment, he saw in his rearview mirror the lighthouse flash twice, like it does every 10 seconds. Predictably and reliably, alerting sailors day or night where the shoreline is. The shoreline is refuge or hazard due to shallow waters, rocks, and shifting currents. As much as the lighthouse tells sailors where hazards are, it also tells sailors someone is out there looking out for them.

John looked up and noticed that the fog was building again, the clouds looked heavier in the horizon, but that lighthouse was always there, standing tall and confident for everyone out at sea, in the air or on land. Clear weather or not.

Internal audit has become InSports' lighthouse.

Preview – The Change Agent: Year 2

The internal audit unit at InSports survived the first year. They successfully implemented Agile Auditing, improved the risk assessment process, increased their use of data analytics, and are performing assurance and advisory projects that have turned skeptics into believers. As the department matures, the expectations from the audit committee and management have also increased. How will they handle the increased cybersecurity, supply chain, project management, ESG, and cultural risks the organization faces globally?

Follow John Taylor and his team of internal auditors as they tackle the organization's strategic and operational challenges in the United States, Mexico, Costa Rica, Nigeria, and the United Arab Emirates.

DOI: 10.1201/9781003322870-23

Excerpt – The Change Agent: Year 2

John's flight from Miami crossed the Costa Rican airspace to the North and he quickly noticed the Pacific Ocean as the plane traversed the country to avoid some of its high mountains. He saw the Golfo de Papagayo in Guanacaste, and Puntarenas to his right as the plane once again turned inland and adjusted its course to fly through the central mountain range in search of San Jose, its destination.

They landed in the middle of a heavy rainstorm, but the flight was otherwise uneventful. He cleared customs and immigration, took the minibus to the car rental agency just off airport property, and drove to the hotel where Carolina, Sandy, and Eduardo had already checked in. The team met poolside for dinner surrounded by tropical plants and flowers, a cacao tree more for display than to harvest cocoa nuts from it to make chocolate, and a domesticated racoon, which was the object of much picture taking and undoubtedly had become one of the hotel's pets.

The next morning, John drove the team to the construction site. It wasn't far from the hotel, but due to the heavy traffic and narrow roads, it took them slightly over an hour. Upon arrival, they noticed the facility sat on a very large plot of land, perhaps larger than might be needed for the type of manufacturing planned.

They parked the SUV close to the front door next to a white Range Rover with tinted windows in a spot with a sign saying "Parking Exclusivo Para El Project Manager." They walked into the office, where they were greeted by a friendly receptionist. As they walked to the conference room, where they would be stationed during their visit, John thought the amount of construction work remaining did not seem to coincide with the percent completion shown in the management reports. The first of Ken's concerns.

Shortly after getting settled and being offered coffee, the receptionist took them to Javier Gonzalez's office. As the project manager, he prepared and sent monthly reports to headquarters showing a project that was meeting all milestones and tracking budget and expenditure projections perfectly. Too perfectly for a project this size. The second of Ken's concerns.

After the customary pleasantries and introductions, the team went for a walk around the administrative offices and the first of two manufacturing areas. The initial impression about the lack of readiness was confirmed as a significant amount of finishing was still required before manufacturing could begin.

They exited the buildings to tour the grounds. Just to the North, in an area cleared for no apparent reason, the team counted several excavators, skid-steer loaders, and bulldozers pushing material, a wheel loader filling up a dump truck, and the rear of a logging truck as it drove away on a dirt road. John turned around to look at the administrative building because he recalled seeing something strange that morning when they arrived. The two agitator trucks were still there. John thought the number

DOI: 10.1201/9781003322870-24

and types of equipment were odd since the amount of work remaining on Phases One and Two of the project did not require heavy equipment anymore, and the construction plan stated that Phase Three would not begin for another six months. Besides, the Phase Three manufacturing building was supposed to be attached to the other two, so why so much land cleared over there?

"¿Ese equipo de trabajo es para la obra que hacemos aquí?" asked Eduardo wondering the same thing as John.

"Yes, it is. That equipment is working on Phase Three," replied Javier.

"¿Y esa carretera a donde va?" asked Carolina inquiring about the dirt road.

"It goes North" was the short answer they received as someone in the work area waved at them and gave them what looked like a thumbs-up. Javier returned the wave and immediately turned telling his visitors, "let me show you where we keep the finishing materials."

Sandy looked at John with a quizzical look and John acknowledged her puzzlement with a head nod.

After the tour, Javier returned to his office and the audit team regrouped in the conference room. As soon as everyone sat down Sandy asked, "do we have a copy of the project plan?"

"Yes, I'm pulling it up," said Carolina. "I heard what Javier said about Phase Three and I thought that wasn't starting for months."

"That's what I thought too," said Sandy confirming their mutual concern with that statement. She added, "I was scanning through the payment information, and I saw charges for heavy equipment usage."

"While the two of you look at that, Eduardo, can you pull up the master contract for me? I sent you a copy two weeks ago while planning for the trip," John said as he sat next to him.

After a moment, Eduardo displayed the contract on his screen, and they scrolled to the charges section. "Rental fees for the use of heavy equipment." According to the contract, rental charges would be paid while equipment was being used during construction. "That land won't be used for Phase Three work. It is too far away!"

Turning to Carolina and Sandy he asked, "did you find the project plan?"

"Yes, six months. Phase Three is supposed to be on hold while they finish the interior for Phase Two and get it ready to begin manufacturing," said Carolina.

"Come on!" said Sandy suddenly in an exasperated voice.

"What's the problem?" John asked surprised by the outburst.

"I'm looking at the charges and they're billing us monthly for all that equipment. According to the plan, Phase Two was done with earth moving months ago but invoices keep coming in. Michael O'Malley sent me the payment information including pending charges and I'm looking at an invoice they submitted two weeks ago. By the way, if anyone wants to drive an agitator truck, we're paying for those two beasts out there too. They are too late for Phase Two, and months too early for Phase Three."

"Carolina and Sandy, while you're looking at the charges, do me a favor and run Benford's Law on the payments. Also look for all payments made to entities in Mexico and Panama, and anything that has the words 'tree', 'arbol', 'forestal' or 'exportacion' in the name or description."

John turned to speak to Eduardo, who was talking with Carolina in Spanish, but before John could say anything, Carolina asked, "do you want us to look at anything mentioning Nicaragua? The Inter American, or Pan American highway is three kilometers away."

John blinked quickly as his thoughts continued to swirl in various directions. "Sí," he replied to Carolina in Spanish before telling Eduardo, "we need to go, let's talk to Javier. I have some questions and I suspect you do too."

"Don't bother," said Sandy looking out the window. "Doesn't he drive a white Range Rover?" as the team saw the project manager's car speeding away past the front gate.

Index

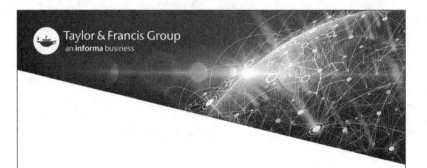

Printed in the United States
by Baker & Taylor Publisher Services